www.wadsworth.com

wadsworth.com is the World Wide Web site for
Wadsworth and is your direct source to dozens of
online resources.

At *wadsworth.com* you can find out about
supplements, demonstration software, and student
resources. You can also send email to many of our
authors and preview new publications and exciting
new technologies.

wadsworth.com
Changing the way the world learns®

POINT–COUNTERPOINT

Readings in American Government

Seventh Edition

Herbert M. Levine

THOMSON

WADSWORTH

Australia · Canada · Mexico · Singapore · Spain · United Kingdom · United States

Publisher: *Clark Baxter*
Executive Editor: *David Tatom*
Development Editor:
   Amy McGaughey
Editorial Assistant: *Dianna Long*
Technology Project Manager:
   Melinda Newfarmer
Marketing Manager: *Janise Fry*
Marketing Assistant: *Mary Ho*
Advertising Project Manager:
   Nathaniel Bergson-Michelson

Project Manager, Editorial Production:
   Paula Berman
Print/Media Buyer: *Rebecca Cross*
Permissions Editor: *Sarah Harkrader*
Production Service:
   Stratford Publishing Services, Inc.
Copy Editor: *Ann Hofstra Grogg*
Cover Designer: *Sue Hart*
Cover Image: *Tedeschi/SIS*
Text and Cover Printer: *Webcom*
Compositor: *Stratford Publishing Services, Inc.*

For more information about our products,
contact us at:

**Thomson Learning
Academic Resource Center
1-800-423-0563**

For permission to use material from
this text, contact us by:

Phone: 1-800-730-2214
Fax: 1-800-730-2215
Web: http://www.thomsonrights.com

Library of Congress Control Number: 2003102300

ISBN 0-534-61416-7

**Wadsworth/Thomson Learning
10 Davis Drive
Belmont, CA 94002-3098
USA**

Thomson Learning
5 Shenton Way #01-01
UIC Building
Singapore 068808

Australia/New Zealand
Thomson Learning
102 Dodds Street
Southbank, Victoria 3006
Australia

Canada
Nelson
1120 Birchmount Road
Toronto, Ontario M1K 5G4
Canada

Europe/Middle East/Africa
Thomson Learning
High Holborn House
50/51 Bedford Row
London WC1R 4LR
United Kingdom

Latin America
Thomson Learning
Seneca, 53
Colonia Polanco
11560 Mexico D.F.
Mexico

Spain/Portugal
Paraninfo
Calle/Magallanes, 25
28015 Madrid, Spain

For Albert, Philippe,
and the late Louise Boudreau

Preface

NEW TO THE SEVENTH EDITION

The seventh edition of *Point-Counterpoint* is heavily revised from the sixth edition. New to the seventh edition are issues dealing with the impact of the war on terrorism to civil liberties (Chapter 3), establishment of a national identification card system (Chapter 4), justification for racial profiling (Chapter 5), separation of church and state (Chapter 7), affirmative action in higher education (Chapter 8), the political power of big corporations (Chapter 9), voting for minor party candidates (Chapter 10), a parliamentary system for the United States (Chapter 14), presidential war powers (Chapter 15), the role of ideology in Senate confirmation of nominees for the U.S. Supreme Court (Chapter 16), the threat of bureaucracy to liberty (Chapter 17), smart growth (Chapter 21), and globalization (Chapter 22). In addition, most of the old debate issues that have been retained from the sixth edition contain newer articles. The Suggested Resources segment has been updated and now also includes Web sites along with book and article references.

THE RATIONALE FOR *POINT–COUNTERPOINT*

The debate tradition in the United States is as old as the Republic itself. Soon after the colonists achieved independence from British rule, they debated issues as fundamental as slavery, tariffs, and the policy of the United States toward the French Revolution. Some debates in U.S. history — Lincoln-Douglas and Kennedy-Nixon — have become part of the national memory, even if misremembered or embellished.

It is with this tradition in mind that *Point-Counterpoint* has been developed. The text is a collection of readings that present contending sides of important issues in U.S. government. It is designed to contribute to a democratic tradition in which vigorous controversy is regarded as both proper and desirable.

The selections deal with the basic structure of the U.S. political system, civil liberties and civil rights, political participation, the power of government policy makers, and the direction of public policy. The format of the book encourages critical thinking. Part and chapter introductions provide important background information and a synopsis of the major points in each selection. For each debate question, one "Yes" response and one "No" response are given. "Questions for Discussion" follow each debate to help students formulate their own answers to the debate question. If both conflicting views on an issue seem convincing, students can then turn to the "Suggested Resources," which provide general background information as well as pro and con arguments.

Three cautionary points are in order. First, issues can rarely be broken down into a neat classification such as liberal or conservative. In this regard, it is often the case that some of the most meaningful controversy goes on among advocates of the same political philosophy.

Second, space limitations and the format of the book dictate that only two views — "Yes" and "No" — are given for each question. More often than not, other answers could be presented, such as "Yes, but . . . ," "No, but . . . ," or even "Maybe." In the process of debate, refinements can be developed. This yes-no approach, however, should provide a start toward understanding problems of U.S. government.

Third, the book does not present a single ideological perspective. As a whole, it does not take a side on the issues but presents, instead, many views. If there is an ideological commitment, it is implicit in the nature of the format: a commitment to vigorous debate as befits the democratic tradition.

ACKNOWLEDGMENTS

I am indebted to numerous people in the academic and publishing communities who helped me at various stages in the writing and production of this edition of *Point–Counterpoint*. The editorial consultants for the book offered excellent suggestions for revising my initial proposal. Specifically, I want to acknowledge the following consultants for Wadsworth: Michael Bailey, Georgetown University; William E. Kelly, Auburn University; James W. Riddlesperger Jr., Texas Christian University; and Suann Shumaker, California State University–Stanislaus.

I am grateful to Ann Hofstra Grogg, who copyedited the manuscript with great care. I also wish to thank Amy McGaughey, the developmental editor of Wadsworth; and Linda DeMasi, director of Publisher's Studio, a division of Stratford Publishing Services, for their magnificent assistance.

Herbert M. Levine

Contents

Part I

Foundations of the United States Political System

I n 1987 the United States celebrated the two hundredth anniversary of the Constitution by drawing attention to the basic institutions and practices of the nation's political system. Political officials, leaders of private associations, and writers assessed anew the fundamental assumptions under which the U.S. political system was established; they examined how a system designed for a largely agrarian society consisting of thirteen eastern seaboard states had evolved over two centuries to meet the needs of a postindustrial society that spans a continent.

These observers often evaluated how well or how poorly the United States was living up to the ideas professed by the Framers of the Constitution. Whether positive or negative in their assessments, they focused on social, economic, and political institutions.

Those who looked favorably at the development of the previous two centuries often drew attention to a number of features: the rise in the nation's standard of living; the integration of groups from diverse ethnic, religious, and racial backgrounds into a "melting pot" in which these groups could live in peace; the resilience of the Constitution in adapting to change; the expansion of democratic practices to include ever larger numbers of people; the competition of political parties for electoral success; the freedoms accorded to U.S. citizens in expressing ideas, protesting peacefully, and responding to accusations in the criminal justice system; and the promotion of the common defense.

Those who were critical of the developments of the previous two centuries pointed to different facts to justify their negative conclusions: the great disparity in assets, in which less than 10 percent of the U.S. population controlled 90 percent of the nation's wealth; the long history of discrimination against African Americans, Hispanics, and Native Americans; the use of the Constitution by the dominant economic groups to prevent or delay social or economic change; the practical means used by government to avoid or slow down the participation of lower-income groups in the political process; the limitation of choice resulting from a two-party rather than a multiparty political system; the use by government of infiltration and disruption tactics to undermine groups holding ideas perceived to be threatening; the failure of the criminal justice system to give all defendants an equal chance regardless of wealth and background; and the use of military force and secret operations in influencing nations abroad, such as in Vietnam in the 1960s and 1970s and in Nicaragua in the 1980s.

The views of contending sides assessing the U.S. political system raise the most fundamental issues underlying that system. This part considers two of these issues: the role of the Framers in creating a "more perfect Union" — and how perfect was and is that Union — and the future of federalism.

Has the Wisdom of the Framers of the Constitution in Promoting a "More Perfect Union" Been Overrated?

The Constitution establishes the ground rules governing the political system of the United States. What the Framers believed and how they acted at the Constitutional Convention at Philadelphia in 1787 raise questions about the effect these rules may have had on political behavior thereafter.

Historians disagree sharply about the Framers of the Constitution. Characterizations of delegates to the Constitutional Convention range from self-serving men of prominence seeking to promote the interests of their own economic class to pragmatic leaders encompassing profound differences of economic interest and political philosophy.

The basic facts about the Constitution, however, are generally accepted. The Articles of Confederation, presented in Congress in 1776 but not finally ratified by all the states until 1781, established a league of friendship among the states rather than a national government. The period under the Articles was marked by widespread debt, Shays's Rebellion (a revolt of poor Massachusetts farmers), economic decay, and an inability to negotiate commercial treaties. In 1786 a Constitutional Convention was called to revise the Articles; it met in Philadelphia from May through September 1787. Most of the delegates were young, politically experienced, financially comfortable, and afraid of the common people, whom they called "the mob." Although they shared some assumptions about government and society, they disagreed profoundly about what should and should not be included in the document they were drafting.

Despite the celebration of the Framers at many civic occasions during the Constitution's bicentennial year, some observers, like the late Supreme Court Justice Thurgood Marshall, think the wisdom of the Framers of the Constitution has been overrated. Marshall was the first African American appointed to the Supreme Court. Earlier in his career, he was an attorney with the National Association for the Advancement of Colored People (NAACP), and he argued major civil rights cases in the courts.

In a speech sparked by commemorations of the bicentennial, Marshall faults the Framers for producing a defective document that allowed for the perpetuation of slavery and denied African Americans and women the right to vote. He contends that developments *after* the writing of the Constitution created a more promising basis for justice and equality than did the accomplishments of the Framers. He emphasizes the adoption of the Fourteenth Amendment ensuring protection of life, liberty, and property of all persons against deprivations without due process and guaranteeing the equal protection of the laws. Credit for change, Marshall says, should go to the people who passed amendments and laws that sought to promote liberty for *all* people of the United States. Marshall celebrates the Constitution as a living document, evolving through amendments and judicial interpretation.

Marshall's speech prompted a direct response by William Bradford Reynolds, at that time the assistant attorney general in the Civil Rights Division of the Justice Department. Reynolds was a controversial figure in the Reagan administration because of his actions on civil rights matters. A number of civil rights leaders criticized him for his opposition to affirmative action and voting rights legislation. Reynolds's supporters defended him as a proponent of real racial equality.

In a speech delivered at Vanderbilt University, Reynolds argues that the Framers deserve the respect accorded to them in the bicentennial celebrations. Accepting Marshall's evaluation that the original Constitution was flawed, Reynolds still asserts that the Constitution marked "the greatest advance for human liberty in the entire history of mankind, then or since." Indeed, Reynolds continues, the constitutional system of divided governmental authority and separated government power eventually allowed African Americans to secure liberty. He notes that much blame for the low status of African Americans in the United States should go not to the Framers but rather to those justices who failed to follow the terms of the Constitution and the laws of the land.

☑ *YES*

Has the Wisdom of the Framers of the Constitution in Promoting a "More Perfect Union" Been Overrated?

THURGOOD MARSHALL
The Constitution: Past and Present

Nineteen eight-seven marks the 200th anniversary of the United States Constitution. A Commission has been established to coordinate the celebration. The official meetings, essay contests, and festivities have begun.

The planned commemoration will span three years, and I am told 1987 is "dedicated to the memory of the Founders and the document they drafted in

Philadelphia." We are to "recall the achievements of our Founders and the knowledge and experience that inspired them, the nature of the government they established, its origins, its character, and its ends, and the rights and privileges of
citizenship, as well as its attendant responsibilities."

Like many anniversary celebrations, the plan for 1987 takes particular events
and holds them up as the source of all the very best that has followed. Patriotic feelings will surely swell, prompting proud proclamations of the wisdom, foresight,
and sense of justice shared by the Framers and reflected in a written document now
yellowed with age. This is unfortunate — not the patriotism itself, but the tendency
for the celebration to oversimplify, and overlook the many other events that have
been instrumental to our achievements as a nation. The focus of this celebration
invites a complacent belief that the vision of those who debated and compromised
in Philadelphia yielded the "more perfect Union" it is said we now enjoy.

I cannot accept this invitation, for I do not believe that the meaning of the Constitution was forever "fixed" at the Philadelphia Convention. Nor do I find the wisdom, foresight, and sense of justice exhibited by the Framers particularly
profound. To the contrary, the government they devised was defective from the
start, requiring several amendments, a civil war, and momentous social transformation to attain the system of constitutional government, and its respect for the
individual freedoms and human rights, we hold as fundamental today. When contemporary Americans cite "The Constitution," they invoke a concept that is vastly
different from what the Framers barely began to construct two centuries ago.

For a sense of the evolving nature of the Constitution we need look no further
than the first three words of the document's preamble: "We the People." When the
Founding Fathers used this phrase in 1787, they did not have in mind the majority
of America's citizens. "We the People" included, in the words of the Framers, "the
whole Number of free Persons." On a matter so basic as the right to vote, for
example, Negro slaves were excluded, although they were counted for representational purposes — at three-fifths each. Women did not gain the right to vote for
over a hundred and thirty years.

These omissions were intentional. The record of the Framers' debates on the
slave question is especially clear: The Southern States acceded to the demands of
the New England States for giving Congress broad power to regulate commerce, in
exchange for the right to continue the slave trade. The economic interests of the
regions coalesced: New Englanders engaged in the "carrying trade" would profit
from transporting slaves from Africa as well as goods produced in America by
slave labor. The perpetuation of slavery ensured the primary source of wealth in
the Southern States.

Despite this clear understanding of the role slavery would play in the new republic, use of the words "slaves" and "slavery" was carefully avoided in the original
document. Political representation in the lower House of Congress was to be based
on the population of "free Persons" in each State, plus three-fifths of all "other Persons." Moral principles against slavery, for those who had them, were compromised, with no explanation of the conflicting principles for which the American
Revolutionary War had ostensibly been fought: the self-evident truths "that all men

are created equal, that they are endowed by their Creator with certain unalienable Rights, that among these are Life, Liberty and the pursuit of Happiness."

It was not the first such compromise. Even these ringing phrases from the Declaration of Independence are filled with irony, for an early draft of what became that Declaration assailed the King of England for suppressing legislative attempts to end the slave trade and for encouraging slave rebellions. The final draft adopted in 1776 did not contain this criticism. And so again at the Constitutional Convention eloquent objections to the institution of slavery went unheeded, and its opponents eventually consented to a document which laid a foundation for the tragic events that were to follow.

Pennsylvania's Gouverneur Morris provides an example. He opposed slavery and the counting of slaves in determining the basis for representation in Congress. At the Convention he objected that

> the inhabitant of Georgia [or] South Carolina who goes to the coast of Africa, and in defiance of the most sacred laws of humanity tears away his fellow creatures from their dearest connections and damns them to the most cruel bondages, shall have more votes in a Government instituted for protection of the rights of mankind, than the Citizen of Pennsylvania or New Jersey who views with a laudable horror, so nefarious a practice.

And yet Gouverneur Morris eventually accepted the three-fifths accommodation. In fact, he wrote the final draft of the Constitution, the very document the bicentennial will commemorate.

As a result of compromise, the right of the Southern States to continue importing slaves was extended, officially, at least until 1808. We know that it actually lasted a good deal longer, as the Framers possessed no monopoly on the ability to trade moral principles for self-interest. But they nevertheless set an unfortunate example. Slaves could be imported, if the commercial interests of the North were protected. To make the compromise even more palatable, customs duties would be imposed at up to ten dollars per slave as a means of raising public revenues.

No doubt it will be said, when the unpleasant truth of the history of slavery in America is mentioned during this bicentennial year, that the Constitution was a product of its times, and embodied a compromise which, under other circumstances, would not have been made. But the effects of the Framers' compromise have remained for generations. They arose from the contradiction between guaranteeing liberty and justice to all, and denying both to Negroes.

The original intent of the phrase, "We the People," was far too clear for any ameliorating construction. Writing for the Supreme Court in 1857, Chief Justice Taney penned the following passage in the *Dred Scott* case, on the issue whether, in the eyes of the Framers, slaves were "constituent members of the sovereignty," and were to be included among "We the People":

> We think they are not, and that they are not included, and were not intended to be included. . . . They had for more than a century before been regarded

as beings of an inferior order, and altogether unfit to associate with the white race . . . ; and so far inferior, that they had no rights which the white man was bound to respect; and that the negro might justly and lawfully be reduced to slavery for his benefit. . . . [A]ccordingly, a negro of the African race was regarded . . . as an article of property, and held, and bought and sold as such. . . . [N]o one seems to have doubted the correctness of the prevailing opinion of the time.

And so, nearly seven decades after the Constitutional Convention, the Supreme Court reaffirmed the prevailing opinion of the Framers regarding the rights of Negroes in America. It took a bloody civil war before the Thirteenth Amendment could be adopted to abolish slavery, though not the consequences slavery would have for future Americans.

While the Union survived the civil war, the Constitution did not. In its place arose a new, more promising basis for justice and equality, the Fourteenth Amendment, ensuring protection of the life, liberty, and property of *all* persons against deprivations without due process, and guaranteeing equal protection of the laws. And yet almost another century would pass before any significant recognition was obtained of the rights of black Americans to share equally even in such basic opportunities as education, housing, and employment, and to have their votes counted, and counted equally. In the meantime, blacks joined America's military to fight its wars and invested untold hours working in its factories and on its farms, contributing to the development of this country's magnificent wealth and waiting to share in its prosperity.

What is striking is the role legal principles have played throughout America's history in determining the condition of Negroes. They were enslaved by law, emancipated by law, disenfranchised and segregated by law; and, finally, they have begun to win equality by law. Along the way, new constitutional principles have emerged to meet the challenges of a changing society. The progress has been dramatic, and it will continue.

The men who gathered in Philadelphia in 1787 could not have envisioned these changes. They could not have imagined, nor would they have accepted, that the document they were drafting would one day be construed by a Supreme Court to which had been appointed a woman and the descendent of an African slave. "We the People" no longer enslave, but the credit does not belong to the Framers. It belongs to those who refused to acquiesce in outdated notions of "liberty," "justice," and "equality," and who strived to better them.

And so we must be careful, when focusing on the events which took place in Philadelphia two centuries ago, that we not overlook the momentous events which followed, and thereby lose our proper sense of perspective. Otherwise, the odds are that for many Americans the bicentennial celebration will be little more than a blind pilgrimage to the shrine of the original document now stored in a vault in the National Archives. If we seek, instead, a sensitive understanding of the Constitution's inherent defects, and its promising evolution through 200 years of history, the celebration of the "Miracle at Philadelphia" will, in my view, be a far more meaningful and humbling experience. We will see that the true miracle was not the birth of the Constitution, but its life, a life nurtured through two turbulent centuries of our own making, and a life embodying much good fortune that was not.

Thus, in this bicentennial year, we may not all participate in the festivities with flag-waving fervor. Some may more quietly commemorate the suffering, struggle, and sacrifice that have triumphed over much of what was wrong with the original document, and observe the anniversary with hopes not realized and promises not fulfilled. I plan to celebrate the bicentennial of the Constitution as a living document, including the Bill of Rights and the other amendments protecting individual freedoms and human rights.

☑ NO

Has the Wisdom of the Framers of the Constitution in Promoting a "More Perfect Union" Been Overrated?

WILLIAM BRADFORD REYNOLDS
The Wisdom of the Framers

Let me start with the observation that I regard myself to be most privileged to be a public servant at a time when we celebrate the 200th Anniversary of the Constitution — a magnificent document that has, in my view, no equal in history and every reason to be feted. It is by now no revelation that the Framers would be aghast at the size and reach of government today; but they would also be enormously proud of how much of their legacy has endured. The vitality of the original Constitution, and its various amendments, is reflected by its ability to withstand spirited debate over its content and meaning, a process that thankfully has been taking place with more and more enthusiasm in town meetings and forums all around the country, involving students, public officials, and citizens of every variety in evaluating how well our Constitution has served us over the past two centuries. I find it remarkable — and an enormous tribute to the Constitution — that in every instance about which I have read, these gatherings have been hard-pressed to think of ways in which to improve it in any meaningful manner.

That is not to say that the original Constitution of 1787 was flawless. And in our celebration of the document, we must not overlook its flaws and our long and painful struggles to correct them.

If there was any tendency to do so, it was no doubt corrected a few weeks ago when Justice Thurgood Marshall spoke in Hawaii on the Constitution's Bicentennial celebration. Whatever degree of disagreement one might have with Justice Marshall's comments, he has invigorated the debate on the meaning and vitality of constitutional principles in a focused way that can only serve to underscore the importance of the document itself and why it is so deserving of this Bicentennial celebration.

In recounting his remarks, I will rely on Justice Marshall's own words. He began by warning against what he called the "tendency for the celebration to oversimplify" the adoption and meaning of the Constitution of 1787 and to "overlook the many other events that have been instrumental to our achievements as a nation" — events that, as he explains, included the Civil War and the amendments added to the Constitution in its wake. Thus, he rejected what he described as a complacent belief that the "vision of those who debated and compromised in Philadelphia yielded the 'more perfect Union' it is said we now enjoy." Justice Marshall remarked further that he does not believe — and I quote — that "the meaning of the Constitution was forever 'fixed' at the Philadelphia Convention"; nor does he find "the wisdom, foresight, and sense of justice exhibited by the Framers particularly profound." The government the Framers of 1787 devised, he declared, "was defective from the start, requiring several amendments, a civil war, and momentous social transformation to attain the system of constitutional government, and its respect for the individual freedoms and human rights, we hold as fundamental today."

More specifically, Justice Marshall faulted the original Framers because, as he put it, the Framers "did not have in mind the majority of America's citizens." The Preamble's "We the People," the Justice said, included only whites. Justice Marshall observes that the Constitution tacitly addressed the slavery issue in two ways: in Article I, section 2, by counting "other Persons" as three-fifths of "free Persons" for purposes of Congressional representation; and in Article I, section 9, by protecting the authority of states to continue importing slaves until 1808. Because the original Constitution was defective in this manner, Justice Marshall holds that "while the Union survived the civil war, the Constitution did not." Taking its place, he said, was "a new, more promising basis for justice and equality, the Fourteenth Amendment, ensuring protection of the life, liberty, and property of *all* persons against deprivations without due process, and guaranteeing equal protection of the laws." For Justice Marshall, it is this new Constitution that we should celebrate; not the old one, which contains "outdated notions of 'liberty,' 'justice,' and 'equality.'" Thus, Justice Marshall declines to participate in the festivities with "flag-waving fervor," but rather plans to celebrate the Bicentennial of the Constitution as a "living document, including the Bill of Rights and the other amendments protecting individual freedoms and human rights."

Justice Marshall chose to focus almost exclusively on the most tragic aspects of the American experience, but he is absolutely right to remind us of them. For the Constitution was intended to be the culmination of a great struggle for the natural rights of men — a philosophy whose cornerstone is the absolute guarantee of equality under the law. When the Framers sought to protect in the Constitution the fundamental rights of man but failed to guarantee explicitly those rights to every individual, they introduced a self-contradiction that preordained struggles and conflicts we continue to confront today.

I am concerned, however, that what Justice Marshall has encouraged is far more than a simple mid-course correction in our celebration of the Constitution. It is one thing to be reminded of the compromise on slavery during the making of the Constitution. It is quite another, however, to encourage the view that there are two constitutions, the one of 1787, the other consisting of the Bill of Rights and the Fourteenth Amendment; that the old one is so thoroughly defective that it did not survive the Civil War, and that the new one alone is worthy of celebration. Certainly, we ought to understand and appreciate the original Constitution in light of its weaknesses as well as its considerable strengths. But in the process, we ought to respectfully decline the invitation to consign it to the dust-bin of history. That is a judgment as wrong as any on the other side of the ledger that uncritically praises the document of 1787. We indeed need what Justice Marshall called for — a "proper sense of perspective."

Notwithstanding its very serious flaws, the Constitution in its original form constituted the greatest advance for human liberty in the entire history of mankind, then or since. Indeed, it was only by preserving our underlying *constitutional system* — one of divided governmental authority and separated government powers — that blacks could enjoy the fruits of liberty once that self-contradiction I alluded to was corrected.

Fresh from the experience of subjugation under the British crown on one hand, and the failure of the Articles of Confederation on the other, the Framers understood that there is an interdependent relationship between fundamental rights and the structure and powers of government. Thus, they crafted a government of limited powers, grounded in natural law principles and deriving its authority from the consent of the governed. They designed a system to protect individual rights through a balance and separation of governmental powers, which would forever ensure that the new national government would not exceed its enumerated powers. Not the least of these checks against governmental invasion of individual rights was the creation in Article III of an independent judiciary as a guardian of constitutional values.

Many of the Framers were not satisfied to protect individual rights merely by limiting the power of national government; they insisted upon a Bill of Rights to safeguard explicitly those rights they deemed most fundamental. Although the Bill of Rights was separately adopted, it would be error to view the original Constitution apart from the first ten amendments, for the Framers agreed from the outset that the rights enumerated in the Bill of Rights were the object of government to protect. Beyond setting forth specific rights essential to a free people, the Framers established in the Ninth and Tenth Amendments a decentralized federal structure to more fully secure the free exercise of individual rights and self-government.

This was the basic structure of government the Framers deemed necessary to vindicate the principles of the American Revolution as set forth in the Declaration of Independence; and that, in my view, is the unique and remarkable achievement we celebrate today. But in celebrating the triumph of the Constitution, I am in full agreement that we must not overlook those parts of the constitutional experiment that were not noble and which, fortunately, have long since been corrected.

Indeed, the experience of the Framers' compromise on the issue of "equality under law" provides us with important lessons even today.

From our historical vantage point, there is certainly no excuse for the original Constitution's failure to repudiate slavery. In making this deal with the devil — and departing from the absolute principle of "equality under law" — the Framers undermined the moral legitimacy of the Constitution.

But we ought to recognize that on this issue the Framers were faced with a Hobson's choice. The Constitution required unanimous ratification by the states, and at least two of the states refused to consent unless the slave trade was protected. James Wilson explained the dilemma: "Under the present Confederation, the states may admit the importation of slaves as long as they please; but by this article, after the year 1808, the Congress will have power to prohibit such importation. . . . I consider this as laying the foundation for banishing slavery out of this country." We know now that this hope was far too optimistic; and indeed, it would take the Civil War to rid the nation of that evil institution.

But even as the Framers were acceding to this compromise, they were sowing the seeds for the expansion of freedom to all individuals when circumstances would permit. James Wilson, for example, emphasized that "the term *slave* was not *admitted* in this *Constitution*." Instead, the term "Person" was used, suggesting that when the slaves became "free Persons," they would be entitled to all the rights appertaining to free individuals.

Indeed, many abolitionist leaders argued that the Constitution, by its omission of any mention of slavery, did not tolerate slavery. Noting that the Constitution nowhere mentions the word "slave," Frederick Douglass declared that "[i]n that instrument, I hold there is neither warrant, license, nor sanction of the hateful thing." Yet such arguments were tragically unheeded by the United States Supreme Court in the *Dred Scott* decision, which provided succor to the notion that there are justifications for exceptions to the principle of "equality under law" — a notion that despite its sordid origins has not been totally erased to this day.

Indeed, the *Dred Scott* decision illustrates that a significant part of the responsibility for our failure to make good on the principle of "equality under law" can and should be assigned less to shortcomings in the original Constitution — as Justice Marshall would have us believe — but to those who sat where Justice Marshall now sits, charged with interpreting that document.

Justice Marshall apparently believes that the original flaws in the Constitution dictated the result in *Dred Scott*. I am more inclined toward the view of my colleagues at the Department of Justice, Charles J. Cooper and Nelson Lund, who argue that Chief Justice Taney's constitutional interpretation was "loose, disingenuous, and result-oriented." Justice Curtis' dissent sounded a warning over this type of judicial interpretation unattached to constitutional moorings that is as compelling now as it was 125 years ago:

Political reasons have not the requisite certainty to afford rules of interpretation. They are different in different men. They are different in the same men at different times. And when a strict interpretation of the Constitution,

according to the fixed rules which govern the interpretation of laws, is abandoned, and the theoretical opinions of individuals are allowed to control its
meaning, we no longer have a Constitution; we are under the government of
individual men, who for the time being have power to declare what the Constitution is, according to their own views of what it ought to mean.

The judiciary's tragic failure to follow the terms of the Constitution did not occur
in this one instance only. Indeed, the Civil War amendments and civil rights legislation passed in that era were in the next several decades emptied of meaning by the
Supreme Court in decision after decision. In *Plessy v. Ferguson,* to cite but one
example, the Court once again stepped in and, over the lone, brilliant dissent of the
elder Justice Harlan, shamefully sacrificed the principle of "equality under law."

I daresay that had the Court fully honored its mandate under the original Constitution in *Dred Scott,* or under the Fourteenth Amendment in *Plessy v. Ferguson,*
we could well have escaped much of the racial strife and social divisiveness that
Justice Marshall lays at the doorstep of the Constitution itself. Indeed, the tragic
legacy of those decisions — the deadening consequences that so regularly flow
from a compromise (no matter how well intended) of the principle of "equality
under law" — provides a sobering lesson for the present Court as it struggles with
similar issues involving race and gender discrimination. These are issues that no
less so than in an earlier era leave hanging in the balance the overarching question
of whether the liberating promise of the Constitution, as originally understood and
subsequently articulated in explicit terms by ratification of the Civil War amendments, will or will not be fulfilled for all Americans.

Justice Marshall, I would respectfully submit, too casually brushes so weighty a
concern to one side in contending that the Constitution did not survive the Civil
War. One would think that this assertion would at least invite from some quarter
the obvious questions: Did separation of powers survive the Civil War? Did the
executive branch and the Congress? Did, indeed, the institution of judicial review?

I must admit to quite a different reading of history, one that has an abiding appreciation of the fact that our Constitution did survive so cataclysmic an upheaval as
the Civil War. In all too many instances of internal strife among a People, one form
of subjugation is ultimately replaced by another. But the Civil War produced a far
different (indeed unique) result: its consequence was to more perfectly secure and
extend to all Americans — through the Thirteenth, Fourteenth, and Fifteenth
Amendments — the blessings of liberty as set forth in the Declaration of Independence, blessings of liberty that had already been secured for other Americans in the
original Constitution and Bill of Rights. It is revisionist history of the worst sort to
suggest that the Fourteenth Amendment created a blank constitutional slate on
which judges could write their own personalized definition of equality or fundamental rights. The Civil War Amendments were a logical extension of what had
come before: they represented *evolutionary,* not *revolutionary* change.

To be sure, the Fourteenth Amendment does offer support for Justice Marshall's
claim that the Constitution is "a living document," but only in the sense that the
Constitution itself provides a mechanism — namely, the amendment process — to

reflect changing social realities. Indeed, this orderly process for constitutional "evolution" is a part of the original Constitution's genius, for it provides a mechanism to correct flaws while safeguarding the essential integrity of our constitutional structure. But the existence of this mechanism — coupled with the system of checks and balances among the three branches of the federal government and the strong endorsement of federalism principles embodied in the Tenth Amendment — makes it abundantly clear that the Framers gave no license to judges (members of the Branch regarded, to borrow from Alexander Hamilton, as the "least dangerous" of the three) to construe constitutional provisions as they see fit.

There is good reason for all this confluence of restraints on judicial activism. The Constitution is not a mass of fungible, abstract principles whose meaning varies with time; rather, it comprises a broad societal consensus on certain fundamental, absolute principles necessary for the protection of individual liberty. The Framers believed that these constitutional values should not be lightly disturbed or set aside. Accordingly, the Constitution was structured so as to require that any change reflect the broadest expression of societal consensus.

This does not leave the Supreme Court or lower federal courts unable to apply the Constitution to circumstances never contemplated by the Framers. But the Judges are not free to disengage from our constitutional moorings in furtherance of their own social agendas; they are not free to determine that the constitutional principles themselves are unwise or obsolete.

Indeed, the very premise on which rests the notion that the Constitution as originally framed has no relevance today is fatally flawed. For the fact remains that the core structure upon which the Constitution was based — a government of limited powers, federalism, separation of powers, protection of fundamental individual rights — has proven in the past two centuries far superior to any other governmental system in protecting human freedoms. And where proponents of change have successfully secured the broad consensus necessary to amend the Constitution, they have expanded and perfected those protections. But judicial activism as an illegitimate substitute for the amendment process can only jeopardize our fundamental freedoms by denigrating the structural underpinnings vital to their survival.

Justice Marshall's contrary thesis is gerry-built on a regrettable overstatement of perceived flaws in the Constitution without so much as a passing reference to the qualities that have endured for the past two hundred years: a governmental structure that has withstood the test of time, weathered turbulent conflicts, and proven itself to be the greatest engine for individual freedom in the history of mankind. That remarkable accomplishment is certainly worth the celebration it is receiving, and much, much more.

Let us not be content with less than a complete appreciation for this document on which our Republic stands. Let us accept Justice Marshall's invitation to explore fully the lessons of the past two centuries. But let us decline his invitation to break the Constitution into two, and to reject the document of 1787 and accept only that which followed the Civil War. We are under a Constitution; it is the original Constitution together with its twenty-six amendments that we must seek to understand and uphold. Let us never forget that the Constitution is in its entirety the Supreme Law of the Land, and all of the branches — the executive, legislative, and judicial — are subordinate to it. We must embrace the Constitution as a whole: not uncritically, but not unlovingly either. Our task, in this Bicentennial year, should be that of loving critics. For our Constitution has provided this great nation of ours with a charter for liberty and government that has enabled us to move ever closer to that "more perfect Union" the Framers envisioned.

In conclusion, it is fitting that I call on the words of former Chief Justice Warren Burger, the Chairman of the Bicentennial Commission. He said it best when he remarked that the Constitution "isn't perfect, but it's the best thing in the world." Our Constitution embodies the American spirit, the American Dream, and America's doctrinal commitment to civil rights — those fundamental rights we all hold equally as American citizens. For this reason, I respectfully part company with Justice Marshall in my view that it is indeed our Constitution as framed two centuries ago, and amended thereafter from time to time, that stands tall today as "the source of all the very best that has followed." Let us not hesitate to celebrate.

Questions for Discussion

1. How did the political system adopted by the United States in the late eighteenth century compare to the political systems in other countries during the same period in terms of ensuring individual freedom?
2. What would have been the consequences to the political development of the United States had the Framers included provisions outlawing slavery and granting political equality for African Americans?
3. What were the assumptions of the Framers about the relationship between individuals and the government?
4. What effect did the constitutional prescription to divide power between a central government and the states and among the different branches of the central government have on the condition of African Americans?
5. What evidence can you supply to accept or reject the proposition that the Constitution did not survive the Civil War?
6. What impact should the intent of the Framers have on Supreme Court justices in deciding cases today? What are the reasons for your answer?

Suggested Resources

Web Sites

Avalon Project at Yale Law School: Constitution of the United States
    http://www.yale.edu/lawweb/avalon/usconst.htm

Constitution Society
    http//www.constitution.org

National Constitution Center
  http://www.constitutioncenter.org

University of Oklahoma College of Law: A Chronology of U.S. Historical
Documents
  http//www.law.ou.edu/hist

Publications

Bailyn, Bernard. *The Ideological Origins of the American Revolution*, enl. ed. Cambridge, Mass.: Belknap Press of Harvard University Press, 1992.

Beard, Charles A. *An Economic Interpretation of the Constitution of the United
  States*. New Brunswick, N.J.: Transaction Publishers, 1998. (Originally published New York: Macmillan, 1913.)

Dahl, Robert A. *How Democratic Is the American Constitution?* New Haven, Conn.:
  Yale University Press, 2001.

Ellis, Joseph A. *Founding Brothers: The Revolutionary Generation*. New York: Alfred
  A. Knopf, 2000.

Farrand, Max, ed. *The Records of the Federal Convention of 1797*, rev. ed. 4 vols. New
  Haven, Conn.: Yale University Press, 1966.

Goldwin, Robert A. *Why Blacks, Women, and Jews Are Not Mentioned in the Constitution and Other Unorthodox Views*. Washington, D.C.: American Enterprise
  Institute for Public Policy Research, 1990.

Hamilton, Alexander, John Jay, and James Madison. *The Federalist: A Commentary
  on the Constitution of the United States*, ed. Robert Scigliano. New York: Modern Library, 2001.

Ketcham, Ralph, ed. *The Anti-Federalist Papers; and, The Constitutional Convention Debates*. New York: New American Library, 1986.

————. *Framed for Posterity: The Enduring Philosophy of the Constitution*.
  Lawrence: University Press of Kansas, 1993.

McDonald, Forrest. *We the People: Economic Origins of the Constitution*. New
  Brunswick, N.J.: Transaction Publishers, 1992. (Originally published University
  of Chicago Press, 1958.)

Mee, Charles L., Jr. *The Genius of the People*. New York: Harper & Row, 1987.

Morris, Richard B. *Witnesses at the Creation: Hamilton, Madison, Jay and the Constitution*. New York: New American Library, 1986.

Ollman, Bertell, and Jonathan Birnbaum, eds. *The United States Constitution: 200
  Years of Anti-Federalist, Abolitionist, Feminist, Muckraking, Progressive, and
  Especially Socialist Criticism*. New York: New York University Press, 1990.

Rakove, Jack M. *Original Meanings: Politics and Ideas in the Making of the Constitution*. New York: Knopf, 1996.

2

Should Power Be Transferred from the Federal Government to the States?

An understanding of the federal system today requires an examination of what federalism is, why it was established, and how it has evolved. Federalism is a system of government under which power is distributed between central and regional authorities in a way that provides each with important power and functions. The United States is but one of many federal systems around the world. Canada, India, and Germany are examples of nations that have federal systems. In the United States the central authority is known as the federal government, and the regional authorities are the state governments.

Federalism is a structural feature not necessarily coterminous with democracy. A federal system divides power. A unitary system, in contrast, concentrates power. In a unitary system power is controlled by the central authorities, as it is, for example, in Great Britain and France. In Great Britain, regional governing authorities are created, abolished, or rearranged by the central government at Westminster. In the federal system of the United States, however, state governments cannot be so restructured. No state boundary can be changed by the government in Washington, D.C., acting on its own authority. (An exception occurred during the Civil War when the state of West Virginia was created out of Virginia.)

A federal system was adopted in 1787 because a unitary structure would have been unacceptable to the people of the United States, who had strong loyalties to their states. In addition, the Framers of the Constitution wanted a government that would be stronger than the one existing under the Articles of Confederation, but they feared a central government that was too powerful. The federal system allowed for a compromise between those who favored a strong central government and those who supported a weak central government.

The central government was given some exclusive powers (e.g., to coin money and to establish tariffs). The states and federal government shared some powers (e.g., to tax and to spend money). The Tenth Amendment to the Constitution provides that "the powers not delegated to the United States by the Constitution, nor prohibited by it to the States, are reserved to the States respectively, or to the people."

The Constitution is not so clear about where the powers of the central government end. Two centuries of conflict over states' rights followed its ratification. In general, the trend was away from states' rights and toward national supremacy, until the past few decades. Since the administration of President Richard Nixon, state power has received new emphasis. The Nixon administration launched a program of New Federalism in which revenue sharing was the central feature. Revenue sharing provided a general grant to states and localities to be used as they saw fit, but with certain restrictions. The Nixon administration also devised block grants, in which the federal government provided funds to state and local governments for use in general policy areas rather than targeted to specific purposes. These grants gave states increased flexibility. President Ronald Reagan's New Federalism slowed down the rate of increase in funding grants and promoted grants to state governments rather than local governments.

The Republican victory in midterm elections of 1994 reinvigorated the policy of transferring power from the federal government to the states. Republicans also held thirty governorships, including nine out of the ten largest states, a dominance that made it additionally desirable for the Republican Congress to transfer power to the states.

The key elements of the Republican program were devolution of power from the federal government to the states, block grants, and an end to unfunded mandates — federal laws requiring the states and localities to perform certain tasks or meet certain standards but not supplying funds for doing so. Supporters argued that devolution would return power to the people, make government more efficient, and increase the flexibility of state and local authorities. In 1995, Congress passed, and President Bill Clinton signed, the Unfunded Mandates Reform Act requiring a point of order vote on bills imposing more than $50 million in implementation costs to states or localities not reimbursed by the federal government. While the law may slow down the pace of unfunded mandates, it does not repeal existing mandates, nor does it furnish funds for existing underfunded mandates. Clinton also encouraged the trend toward transferring power to the states by granting waivers from federal regulations that allowed states to experiment in welfare reform. And in 1996 he signed a bill that transferred power over many welfare programs from the federal government to the states and gave the states vast discretion in the use of block grant funds.

Supreme Court decisions also returned power to the states. In 1995, in *United States v. Lopez*, the Supreme Court reversed sixty years of increasing federal power under the Constitution's Commerce Clause, which grants Congress the power to regulate interstate and foreign commerce. In its 5–4 decision, the Court declared unconstitutional the Gun-Free School Zone Act, which prohibited firearms near schools, on the grounds that Congress had not shown that the possession of a firearm near an education building would disrupt interstate commerce. Regulating guns in and around schools, said the Court, was the responsibility of the states, not the federal government.[1]

Sorting out the division of power between the federal government and the states is a continuing issue. In a prepared statement before the House Budget Committee, Kirk Cox, a member of the Virginia House of Delegates, argues that many federal programs are not necessary, justified, or efficient. He calls for additional block grants and an end to federal mandates. He justifies his position by making these points:

1. State governments have proven they can deliver more service for less money.
2. State governments are leading the way in innovating programs, such as privatization and collections from "deadbeat dads."
3. Unlike state governments, the federal government spends unnecessary funds for pork-barrel projects — local programs that have no national significance.
4. The states are laboratories of democracy. By experimenting with different approaches, states can adopt the most effective ways of doing things.
5. States are ready to accept the challenge of taking over responsibilities from the federal government.
6. State governments are closer to the people than is the federal government.

Washington attorney John G. Kester argues that a system in which state governments wield great power is a pipe dream. He contends:

1. States want only rights — not responsibilities.
2. States will not play a central role in domestic affairs so long as Washington has confiscated the tax base.
3. The United States has a national economy.
4. States have allowed the federal government to deal with social problems.
5. The United States is a homogenized country. It is not as diverse as it was before World War II.
6. The United States is a mobile society.
7. People are not as loyal to their states as they were in the nineteenth century.
8. New immigrants to the United States have little reason for developing a sense of attachment to a particular state.
9. Americans are modernists; few look to the past for guidance.
10. State bureaucracies are not noticeably more efficient than federal bureaucracies.

NOTE

1. *United States v. Lopez*, 115 S. Ct. 1624 (1995).

☑ *YES*

Should Power Be Transferred from the Federal Government to the States?

KIRK COX
Power to the States

In the broadest possible sense, block grants should be used to restore State powers that have been inappropriately assumed by the Federal Government. This should be accomplished as part of a conscious strategy to balance the Federal budget by 2002. Let me suggest an outline of such a process. There are three fundamental steps.

First, there should be a comprehensive review of Federal programs in relation to State and local governments. Each program should be examined to determine whether or not the Federal Government has the authority under the Constitution, and whether the Federal Government is best suited to accomplish our goals and objectives. In most cases, I believe that an objective analysis will find that a Federal role is not necessary, justified, or efficient. These programs should be devolved.

Second, with respect to programs that should be devolved, Congress should establish block grant programs immediately. These block grants should be as functionally broad as feasible. At a minimum, block grants should encompass broad program functions, such as education, transportation, health and human services, and so on.

And, perhaps most importantly, virtually all Federal mandates should be removed as an element of the block grant program. These mandates dramatically increase costs while substantially reducing services.

Let me also emphasize the importance of providing block grants directly to State governments, to be administered consistently with the existing mechanisms of State laws and constitutions. All local governments are creations of the State. It is not appropriate for the Federal Government to skip over the States to establish relationships with local governments. We have already paid substantially for such inappropriate arrangements, through overlapping programs, duplication, and even lobbying before Congress that pits the interests of State governments against those of local governments.

State governments have proven they can deliver more service for less money. Federal programs have been particularly costly. Centralization of power at the Federal level has resulted in waste, duplication, and contradiction as the Federal Government has intruded into functions that are also handled by State and local governments.

Yet State and local governments have been forced to spend more than they would have if they had spent taxes raised directly from their own citizens. States and localities, like people, are more careful with their own money than with other people's money.

For example, the Congressional Budget Office has confirmed that local governments routinely spend more to construct federally funded wastewater treatment plants than they spend to construct the same locally funded wastewater treatment plants. In the final analysis, we should all remember that Federal money is not other people's money, it is *the* people's money.

There is considerable potential for improving the cost effectiveness of federally funded programs. State and local governments have taken the lead in implementing strategies that improve government efficiency.

From privatization to right-sizing, State governments are leading the way. Take my home State for instance. In Virginia we are actively pursuing privatization in a whole host of areas from transportation to corrections to child support collections.

Let's look at just one example: Deadbeat dads are a serious problem. To increase collections we are experimenting with privatizing collections. Private collection companies were allowed to compete with their public counterparts. The results are dramatic.

A private company collects over 11 percent more a month from deadbeat dads than their government counterparts, and at substantially less cost. The direct cost for government collections was $7.03 per case. The direct cost for the private company was $5.77 per case.

And best of all, customer service increased. The private company offered 24 phone lines — the State office had 5 phone lines. Further, the private office was open 11 hours more a week than the government offices. The private offices were open on Saturday and provided child care. All this for less money.

And then there's pork. The Federal Government grants billions of dollars annually to State and local governments for pork-barrel projects. By definition, pork-barrel projects have no national significance. Moreover, State and local taxpayers are generally unlikely to consider such programs important enough to finance themselves.

Further, the States are laboratories of democracy. By experimenting with different approaches, the most effective public policy approaches can be identified, and copied by other States.

Just last week [1995], Virginia's Gov. George Allen signed into law the most revolutionary welfare reform program in the Nation. It features a real work requirement, a two-year benefit limit, and a cutoff of aid for additional children.

I can't help but note that the welfare reform movement currently sweeping the Nation began in the States and is still being led by the States. Virginia was able to build on the efforts of Wisconsin and Illinois, and now other States will be able to build on Virginia's example. That is why we call the States laboratories of democracy.

Federal policies that hamstring our efforts and unnecessarily increase public costs are unwise. Indeed they are unconscionable.

Government at all levels must become more efficient. America's private sector has been restructuring and reengineering for some time. This has not occurred simply because of a desire to become more efficient; it has rather occurred because restructuring was required to survive in an increasingly competitive market. Government, too, must be restructured — it must be restructured because our present method of operation threatens the living standards of future generations. Devolution of programs to the States, through block grants, is an important component of this long overdue restructuring.

I am happy to report that the States, and their local units of government, are up to the challenge — we are prepared to do our part — but we must be freed to perform. Immediate and comprehensive relief from Federal mandates is an absolute necessity.

I want to make sure that we have not been misunderstood. We are not here today to suggest to you that State and local governments are more virtuous than the Federal Government. They are not. Nor are the State and local governments necessarily more competent than the Federal Government.

But they are closer to the people, and that makes all the difference in the world. Their closeness simply permits them to be more reflective of the public will, and provides incentives for them to spend the tax money they collect from their citizens more effectively. Moreover, it is easier for the people to effect changes through the electoral process where government is closer to the people. Greater accountability is naturally and necessarily associated with government that is closer to the people.

So, in summary, here is what I am proposing:

Congress should devolve substantial powers to the States that are not appropriately the responsibility of the Federal Government; and Congress should use a broad block grant mechanism to return funding responsibility to the States over a seven-year period. At the same time, Federal tax rates should be reduced.

We as a nation have strayed from our democratic ideals. Government has become too remote, too wasteful, and too expensive. It is time to reverse course and return government to the people. All of us hope that Congress will take effective action to return power to the States, to restore the balance envisioned in the Tenth Amendment of the Constitution of the United States.

 NO

---

*Should Power Be Transferred from the Federal Government
to the States?*

JOHN G. KESTER
Forever Federal

There is a loud buzz about reallocating power away from Washington and back to the states — something most Republicans claim to favor. Gurus sell books on the virtues of decentralization, local decision-making, and neighborliness. Judgment day for Washington is forecast.

Not so fast. Meaningful federalism — the classical concept of states that actually behave like sovereign governments with real power — is an idea with a past brighter than its future.

Some of the anti-Washington talk stems from the successful conclusion of the Cold War. It ended big central government's most tolerable excuse for being: defense from foreign military force. A federal government busy guarding you from missiles can't be all bad. One focused on taking your money to give to someone else seems less legitimate.

Some decentralization is possible, and perhaps along with it some shrinking of hyperactive government. But restoring the states to anything like real sovereigns, with noticeably different laws and unique customs, is a notion that crested at Gettysburg on July 3, 1863. And although many Americans hope for curbs on federal spending, few want simply to substitute state bureaucracies for federal in running their lives.

Always the federal government has held two unbeatable ways to expand — provided that the voters who select the Congress wanted it to do so.

First, the Constitution makes federal laws supreme over any state laws to the contrary. Until 1913, that power was restrained by having U.S. senators chosen by state legislatures.

Starting in the 1930s, the federal government decided it could regulate practically everything to make life better. The Supreme Court by 1937 decided to give up and let it try. The court turned its own energy to interpreting general clauses in the Constitution as tight limits on state laws. All Congress needs is some constitutional handle to legislate, and state laws must give way.

Second, that stick of federal supremacy is backed up by the carrot of federal grants. Grants can have conditions that Washington otherwise would lack power to order. Let us feds pay for part of that new school — as long as its curriculum adds the programs the national government wants. The Supreme Court doesn't worry; in 1987 it held that Congress could use the highway pork barrel to dictate the minimum age a state set for beer drinking.

So with legal restrictions on federal power gone except for occasional extreme cases, any real restoration of state power would have to come from the voters themselves, with an assist if the Supreme Court ever decided to loosen its supervision of state laws, including touchy issues like abortion and school prayer.

Real federalism in the United States — a twenty-first century in which state governments wield great power — is a pipe dream. Here is why.

STATES ARE GREEDY

The dirty little secret of states' rights is that the states want only rights — not responsibilities. Justice Sandra Day O'Connor wrote in 1992 that the Constitution did not convert the states into "regional offices nor administrative agencies of the Federal Government." But the states themselves don't seem to agree. Often they look like caricatures of welfare mothers: They look for regular handouts from federal officials, they don't say thank you, they expect to be bailed out of their problems — in short, they exhibit all the passive cunning of classic dependent behavior.

The states have not been turning away those federally funded grants, which add up to a quarter-trillion dollars a year. Even let's-run-against-Washington governors like California's Pete Wilson or Virginia's George Allen do not hesitate to ask the nation's taxpayers to pick up their earthquake and hurricane bills. Many state officials complain about the strings attached to federal education grants, but only a handful decline the money.

State irritation about distasteful conditions has brought the current block-grant frenzy. This old Republican favorite — bundles of federal money given to the states without strings — began as Richard Nixon's "revenue sharing" and was revived in Reagan's "new federalism." The 1970s notion was that the federal government was so rolling in tax revenue that it would send extra dollars back to the states (but not to the taxpayers, except when Congress under Reagan actually cut taxes).

Unclear then and unclear now is why federal money should be handed out to state governments, or anyone else, without careful regulation of how it is to be spent. The best answer may be that the regulatory red tape and bureaucracy that Democrats persistently write into federal aid is an even worse alternative.

Still, why should the federal government tax people to give money to the states at all? If the states need funds, they have their own power to tax. And if for its own activities the federal government does not need all the revenues it takes in, why are the taxes it collects so high?

Do not, however, count on Congress to forgo the pleasure of giving away money. No one said it better than FDR [Franklin D. Roosevelt] crony Harry Hopkins: "We will spend and spend, and tax and tax, and elect and elect." And state politicians are not competing to raise state taxes to pay for what the states want to spend.

FEDERAL TAXES ARE VERY HIGH

In a federal system in which the states really mattered, the significant taxes that people pay would be levied by the states. The big checks in April would be addressed to Annapolis or Richmond, not the IRS [Internal Revenue Service].

For a century and a half, that was so; for the first hundred years, except during the Civil War, the federal government was financed entirely by the tariff and a few excises, and until the Sixteenth Amendment in 1913, it could not tax incomes. The federal income tax affected scarcely anyone until the New Deal, and did not bite ordinary people until money was needed to fight World War II.

Since then, there have been no peace dividends, just federal programs that expand to meet and exceed revenue. Congress and lobbyists have never failed to discover reasons why federal taxes must stay stratospheric.

So for two generations now, the tax structure has been inverted. Federal taxes, which now go principally to pay off interest groups (agribusinesses, shipbuilders, retired people, government employees), are the big portion of the tax burden. State income taxes, though no longer trivial, are puny in comparison — not what one would expect if the principal functions of government were carried out by states. Local functions like schools and police rely on local property taxes, plus some conditional federal handouts.

As long as the federal government's voracious income tax vacuums up most of the country's tax revenue, there is little left for the states. States will not play a central role in domestic affairs as long as Washington has confiscated the tax base.

WE HAVE A NATIONAL ECONOMY

States have trouble maintaining autonomy when each is part of a larger economic unit, where goods and capital and workers move freely about. More economic integration means reduced sovereignty. (That is NAFTA's [North American Free Trade Agreement] downside, as Ross Perot and Pat Buchanan with purple prose tried to point out, while ignoring its advantages.)

The United States is a free-trade zone without state border guards. If a state cuts taxes and welfare benefits, it will wind up with businesses and taxpayers. If it adopts generous welfare or medical programs, eager recipients will be moving in.

Perhaps up to some point states should not have to bear the competitive cost of their social policies. Their helplessness to control who lives there is a reason to keep the federal government involved, at least by setting some minimum national standards. Otherwise, few states would dare provide social benefits much above the average, lest they attract too many takers.

STATES ARE LETHARGIC

A Herblock cartoon not long ago pictured a leering figure of "Congress" handing a horse collar and harness to a naïf labeled "States and Cities," asking him to pull a huge cartload of baggage. The burdens being handed over were called:

- "Welfare Costs"
- "Crime Prevention"
- "Emergency Relief"
- "Health Costs"
- "Increased Local Spending Responsibilities"

Anyone who looked at that cartoon when the Constitution was drafted, or even 30 or 40 years ago, would not have understood it. Each item on the list, assuming such matters concerned government at all, was almost entirely a concern of local mayors and city councils. Only in extraordinary emergencies would even state governors and legislatures get involved, much less the federal government, whose main tasks were national defense, foreign affairs, the tariff, coinage, and keeping out of the way of business. Who else but "states and cities," grandfather would have asked, would Herblock expect to handle such responsibilities — assuming that these were governmental responsibilities at all?

As late as [John] Kennedy's administration, it was still possible for Congress to debate whether a particular issue was appropriate for the federal government to address. By the end of [Lyndon] Johnson's, the only issue was how much government money was needed. That social problems are federal problems had become assumed.

State governments display the Patty Hearst syndrome. They have been subjected to federal coercion for so long that now they depend on it, and forget what self-government means. For a pathetic exhibit, look at your state income-tax form. Little effort is made by Maryland, Virginia, or other supposed sovereigns to decide what is income, how incomes should be taxed, or to build a tax structure reflecting local judgments. Instead, state legislatures simply adopt whatever rules Congress decides for the current year, make a handful of adjustments, and apply a percentage rate. Basic decisions of social policy, which any tax code is full of, are decided not in Richmond or Annapolis, but on Capitol Hill.

The taxpayer's form-filling is made simpler. But if something as basic as tax structure is to be designed elsewhere, what are state legislatures for?

WE HAVE A HOMOGENIZED COUNTRY

A real federalist system presupposes diversity. There may be a national interest in drivers staying on the right side of the highway from coast to coast, but the speed limit in Wyoming is quite a different call. States with real power would have different definitions of crimes, and even different choices as to whether particular behavior is criminal. Some would enact local preferences on many subjects into law, while others would remain permissive. Differing legal codes and customs would reflect the differences in the attitudes of their citizens.

Before World War II, and even into the 1960s before the civil-rights acts, there were distinct local cultures in this country, which a simple automobile trip could reveal. Now they are blotted out — first by radio and then television, by national control of schools, by cheap air travel. That is not all bad. The career of federalism — more aggressively described as states' rights — suffered for two centuries from becoming entangled with, first, the cause of southern slavery, and then its follow-up of racial segregation. Baggage like that could make any political theory look disreputable.

WE HAVE A MOBILE SOCIETY

Scarcely anyone born in this country has chosen to become a citizen of some other country, and then another, and then another. Yet Americans change their state citizenship almost without thinking. To them the issues in moving are jobs or real estate, not emigration to a strange land. If they feel pangs about moving, these usually relate to what a particular community is like, not the nature of its state government.

The willingness to pull up stakes is nothing new; it is how the West was won. This is a country with cheap transportation and an economy that moves workers around, so that it is not unusual for a person to live in four or five states in a lifetime. And most Americans are not looking for surprises when they travel from one state to another. Ask the people at McDonald's and every hotel chain from Super Eight to Four Seasons.

LOYALTY

When secession came, Robert E. Lee followed his first allegiance: to Virginia. The regiments that fought the Civil War, on both sides, were enlisted under state banners. Now, even the national guards of each state, successors of the state militias, have long been federally funded and supervised.

Except in some corners of the South and on a few football weekends, states no longer mean much emotionally to most of their citizens. Such people do not feel great pain when states' rights are slighted by the feds.

NEW AMERICANS

The flood of immigrants to the United States over the past two decades makes federalism an even less likely bet. These new faces, who quickly become voters, have little reason for attachment to a particular state. Consider Quebec, whose citizens of French descent would have seceded from Canada in October [1995] but for the decisive votes of national-minded newcomers.

To expect more than a few immigrants to become attached to what surely seems a mere political subdivision of the country they joined is unrealistic, particularly when dysfunctional public schools will not teach history to their children. It is not likely that new inhabitants will go to great pains for states that are abstractions — particularly states that may be theirs only for the moment.

MODERNISM

Federalism is not going to prevail based on nostalgia. Reverence for the past has never been this country's strong suit, and the current generation is a little vague about events before, say, 1992. Our commander-in-chief, indeed, on this summer's [1995] V-J Day anniversary, recalled that Japan had surrendered on "the aircraft carrier *Missouri*." People like that don't ponder in awe political arrangements designed in the good old days.

STATE GOVERNMENTS AREN'T SO GREAT

Republicans are correct that many citizens are tired of the things the federal government does. But one cannot assume that the states are the level of government that people miss. Where people want more decision-making power, and less outside interference, is in their cities and communities. The local level is where hope lies for doing something constructive about education and public safety, and it is locally that individuals can make their view felt.

State governments, by federal pressure and funds, often now are simply clones of the federal bureaucracy, though sometimes staffed with less talent. Federal domestic programs always have demanded paperwork and compliance with regulations. So state governments have grown departments to do so, and even added a few forms and regulations of their own — for which, in turn, local school districts and police departments have to hire employees who can speak and write bureaucratese. State bureaucracies are not noticeably more efficient than federal. If you think the U.S. Postal Service is bad, spend an hour or two (you seldom can spend less) at the Virginia Department of Motor Vehicles.

There is a widespread concern that the federal government has overreached, and now intrudes too far into local affairs. By setting up programs and issuing mandates, it can displace the lower levels of government from their own responsibilities.

To political scientists, decentralization may be an attractive way of channeling political participation, and to economists an efficient prod for governmental responsiveness to regional needs. But the need to decentralize does not mean that Americans are ready for states that are really governments.

There are many cleavages in today's society, but regionalism is not a big one. Emotionally, this is a country of Americans. The political theory of federalism is not going to sell to people whose hearts do not feel state allegiance.

Nor is there any reason to encourage regional differences, which states' rights promote, as if they were good. Countries get torn up by such things. The United States already has racial and ethnic frictions that need to be healed.

It is unwise for a country to try to govern local matters from Washington. But it would be folly for a country to encourage significant divisions. Ask the prime minister of Canada, or the former president of the former Yugoslavia.

Much can be done to detach federal tentacles from local affairs. But the states aren't going to handle the biggest domestic decisions, because the people don't expect them to.

Questions for Discussion

1. Which is closer to the people: the state or the federal government? Why?
2. What criteria can be used in evaluating whether a policy area properly belongs to the states or to the federal government?
3. What can the federal government do today to strengthen state governments?

4. Should the federal government strengthen state governments? What are the reasons for your answer?
5. What are the advantages and disadvantages of the United States becoming a unitary system?
6. Which groups would benefit and which would be hurt if the federal government gave more power to the states? What are the reasons for your answer?

Suggested Resources

Web Sites

American Enterprise Institute
    http://www.federalismproject.org/

Council of State Governments
    http://www.csg.org/

National Conference of State Legislatures
    http://www.ncsl.org

National Governors' Association
    http://www.nga.org

Stateline.org
    http://www.stateline.org

Publications

Andrisani, Paul, Simon Hakim, and Eva Leeds, eds. *Making Government Work: Lessons from America's Governors and Mayors.* Lanham, Md.: Rowman & Littlefield, 2000.

Derthick, Martha. "American Federalism: Half-Full or Half-Empty?" *Brookings Review* 18, no. 1 (Winter 2000): 24–27.

————. *Keeping the Compound Republic: Essays on American Federalism.* Washington, D.C.: Brookings Institution Press, 2001.

Dye, Thomas R., and Susan A. MacManus. *Politics in States and Communities,* 11th ed. Upper Saddle River, N.J.: Prentice Hall, 2003.

Greve, Michael S. *Real Federalism: Why It Matters, How It Could Happen.* Washington, D.C.: American Enterprise Institute, 1999.

McDonald, Forrest. *States' Rights and the Union: Imperium in Imperio, 1776–1876.* Lawrence: University Press of Kansas, 2000.

Nagel, Robert F. *The Implosion of American Federalism.* New York: Oxford University Press, 2001.

Nathan, Richard P., and Thomas K. Gais. "Is Devolution Working?" *Brookings Review* 19, no. 3 (Summer 2001): 30–33.

Nivola, Pietro S. "Does Federalism Have a Future?" *Public Interest* no. 142 (Winter 2001): 44–60.

O'Toole, Laurence J., ed. *American Intergovernmental Relations: Foundations, Perspectives, and Issues,* 3d ed. Washington, D.C.: Congressional Quarterly, 1999.

Thierer, Adam D. *The Delicate Balance: Federalism, Interstate Commerce, and Economic Freedom in the Technological Age.* Washington, D.C.: Heritage Foundation, 1999.

U.S. Cong., Senate. *Federalism.* Hearings before the Committee on Governmental Affairs, 106th Cong., 1st Sess., 1999.

Walker, David B. *The Rebirth of Federalism: Slouching toward Washington,* 2d ed. Chappaqua, N.Y.: Chatham House, 2000.

Walters, Jonathan. "Save Us from the States!" *Governing* 14, no. 9 (June 2001): 20–21, 23–24, 26–27.

Part II

Civil Liberties
and Civil Rights

Political systems make rules that are binding upon their members. But political systems differ in the amount of freedom permitted to citizens. In twentieth-century totalitarian dictatorships, the state imposed severe restrictions on individual liberty. Not only was it concerned with what people did, but it sought to mold people's minds to a government-approved way of thinking.

Modern democracies permit a large amount of individual freedom. As a modern democracy, the U.S. government accepts the principle of civil liberties, recognizing that individuals have freedoms the government cannot take away. Among these are freedom of speech, freedom of the press, freedom of assembly, and freedom of religion. The Constitution as originally written in 1787 contains some protections for the individual against the encroachment of government, but the most important are set forth in the first ten amendments to the Constitution, known as the Bill of Rights and adopted in 1791. They are also found in federal government laws and court decisions, as well as in state constitutions and laws.

As the arbiter in constitutional disputes between the government and the individual, the Supreme Court is often at the center of the storm when it tries to determine whether government has overstepped the bounds and illegally violated the liberties sanctioned by the Constitution. The Court has decided issues such as whether the government can force a person whose religion forbids worship of graven images to salute the flag (it cannot) and whether the government can ban obscene books, magazines, motion pictures, or television programs (it can).

The Court's decisions on privacy have been particularly controversial. Privacy is the right to determine one's personal affairs without government interference and without required disclosure of information about oneself. The Constitution does not specifically mention a right of privacy. The Court, however, decided that such a right can be inferred from the First, Fourth, Fifth, Ninth, and Fourteenth Amendments to the Constitution. The right of privacy has been a consideration in the Court's decisions allowing for the right of a woman to have an abortion under certain conditions. And it is now central to cases involving fetal rights.

Court decisions on freedom of speech issues have also been very controversial. The Court has often supported the rights of unpopular groups, such as Nazis and communists, to make speeches advocating their political ideas. It has at times also set limits on speech.

As a nation of immigrants, the United States has a more diverse population than many modern democracies. Its citizens have a variety of religious, racial, and ethnic backgrounds. In addition to promoting civil liberties, the U.S. government is committed to protecting civil rights — those rights that assure minority group equality before the law.

As the speech by Thurgood Marshall in Chapter 1 indicates, the record of civil rights protection for African Americans has been a sorry one. Brought to the New World as slaves, African Americans were not granted U.S. citizenship until after the Civil War. And even after the adoption of the Thirteenth, Fourteenth, and Fifteenth Amendments, which eliminated slavery and gave legal and political rights to former enslaved people, those rights were often denied in practice until the 1960s.

Although the formal barriers to civil rights have largely fallen, many African Americans believe that the nation still does not adequately promote genuine equality. They point to discrimination in employment, housing, and professional advancement as examples of unfinished business.

Part II deals with six issues of civil liberties and civil rights: the impact of the war on terrorism on civil liberties, the establishment of a national identification system, racial profiling, the death penalty, separation of church and state, and affirmative action in higher education.

In Fighting a War on Terrorism, Is the United States Acting within Reasonable Limits to Maintain Its Civil Liberties?

On September 11, 2001, hijackers on a suicide mission who had seized control of two commercial aircraft in flight crashed their planes into the two buildings that make up the World Trade Center in Manhattan. In so doing, they killed themselves and more than 2,800 people, including the passengers, and they injured many other people. Both buildings collapsed as a result of this attack. A third plane, which had also been hijacked, smashed into the Pentagon, just outside of Washington, D.C., and also killed everyone aboard the plane as well as 125 people in the building. And a fourth illegally commandeered commercial aircraft plunged into a field in Pennsylvania, probably as a result of passenger efforts to overcome the hijackers. Still, everyone on board was killed, but no one on the ground.

President George W. Bush called these events, which had taken a heavier toll in life than the Japanese attack on Pearl Harbor on December 7, 1941, "an act of war" and declared a "war on terrorism." As in 1941, a horrified nation mourned the loss of its victims and sought action against the people who conspired to commit such deeds.

It was quickly learned that the mastermind of the attack was Islamic militant Osama bin Laden, a Saudi Arabian exile and the leader of an organization known as al Qaeda (The Base). For bin Laden, the United States was an enemy that had to be destroyed. Al Qaeda recruited supporters in many countries, mostly in the Middle East, who shared his views. He established bases to train his supporters in military action. And the United States government viewed his organization as a terrorist group.

Bin Laden had been living in Afghanistan as a "guest" of that country's government. According to American authorities, he had training camps in Afghanistan. As early as 1998, the United States launched cruise missiles at these suspected sites.

In response to the September 11 incident, President Bush sent troops and gave support to forces in Afghanistan that were opposed to the Afghan government then in power. Public opinion polls in the United States showed great popular support for the president for taking such action against the enemy. The attack on Afghanistan was successful, and a new

Afghan government, friendly to the United States, came to power. Since the war in Afghanistan, bin Laden was reported to have been killed. As of March 2003, some U.S. intelligence officials believed that he was alive and in hiding, possibly in Pakistan.

Although the extent of the September 11 assault was extraordinary, the United States had been attacked by terrorists before — both overseas and at home. Overseas, for example, two American embassies were attacked in East Africa in 1998. (Bin Laden had been indicted in a U.S. court for these attacks. He was also a suspect in the bombing attack on the *USS Cole*, a navy destroyer, in Yemen in 2000.) Within the United States, moreover, a militant Islamic group bombed the World Trade Center in 1993, killing six people and injuring more than one thousand. And in 1995, a domestic American terrorist with strong antifederal government beliefs detonated a truck bomb outside a federal government office building in Oklahoma City, killing 168 people and injuring hundreds.

Although even before the attacks of September 11 the United States government and private organizations, as well, took measures at home and abroad to minimize the risks of further terrorist violence, the scale of September 11 produced a greater antiterrorist effort. The president and Congress agreed to add additional funds to the Department of Defense and to increase budgets for intelligence and law enforcement agencies. The president established an Office of Homeland Security and sought legislation to reorganize federal government agencies into a centralized Department of Homeland Security.

In addition, the Bush administration proposed laws, issued executive orders, and engaged in matters involving law enforcement and individual liberty that it said were necessary to promote national security. Most of these actions had popular support. Advocates of civil liberties, however, regarded many of these acts as dangerous to the tradition of civil liberties based on the Bill of Rights and laws and judicial precedents protecting people accused of crimes from certain acts of government.

The idea of rights is based on the notion that a government has limits on what it can do to people who live within its authority. These limitations exist even if the overwhelming majority of the people want to ignore them. Over more than two centuries since the adoption of the Constitution, the courts have extended individual rights through interpretation of the Constitution and the laws. For example, courts have said that police must inform a criminal suspect of his or her rights, including the right to be silent when interrogated by the police. But the courts have often allowed certain otherwise limited practices by the government to be followed when the nation is at war or threatened by war. And on occasions, presidents have taken actions in wartime that violated individual liberties even when they knew such acts were unconstitutional.

On April 27, 1861, two weeks after commencement of the Civil War, President Abraham Lincoln suspended the right of habeas corpus, so that the government could then hold a suspect indefinitely without explaining reasons for such action to the courts. He ordered the military to arrest some northern citizens just for opposing his administration. In a famous statement, he asked: "Are all the laws, but one, to go unexecuted and the government itself go to pieces, lest that one be violated?"

World War I brought new threats to liberty. In 1918, the Sedition Act made criticism of U.S. involvement in the war a criminal offense. And in 1919 and 1920, the United States arrested individuals and harassed organizations thought to be communist sympathizers.

The trend to sacrifice liberty for national security continued in World War II. In February 1942, President Franklin D. Roosevelt ordered that people of Japanese heritage — in some cases Japanese American citizens — on the West Coast be removed to the interior. In all, 110,000 people were interned in what became known as "relocation camps." During the Cold War — the period for four and a half decades following World War II in which the United States and the Soviet Union were bitter enemies — the United States took a number of measures, such as spying on and disrupting anti–Vietnam War political protest groups that were engaged in peaceful advocacy.

The actions taken in the post–September 11 period expanded federal government authority in civil liberties matters, too. Among the measures taken by the federal government were the following:

- Without providing reasons in many cases, the federal government detained more than a thousand men, mostly male foreigners from Muslim countries, who were in the United States. Some of these people were held for weeks, and others for months. In hundreds of these cases, people were being held for some violation of their immigration status.
- It permitted federal agents to eavesdrop on conversations between foreign inmates and attorneys in terrorism-related cases.
- It announced it would use military tribunals, rather than civilian courts, to try foreign terrorism suspects. Military tribunals have fewer protections for the accused than do civilian courts.
- It enacted the USA PATRIOT [Uniting and Strengthening America by Providing Appropriate Tools Required to Intercept and Obstruct Terrorism] Act on October 25, 2001, which had such provisions as (1) allowing the government to detain indefinitely any noncitizen so long as the attorney general feels that the individual is a threat to national security; (2) expanding the government's authority to wiretap suspects; (3) giving power to law enforcement authorities to enter homes, offices, and other private places to search and download computer files without notifying the individuals involved until after government authorities had performed this activity; and (4) giving a domestic role to the Central Intelligence Agency (CIA) in managing intelligence even when the subject of investigation is a U.S. citizen.

(In establishing the CIA in 1947, Congress had written into the CIA's charter that the agency was prohibited from exercising "police, subpoena, or law-enforcement powers or internal security functions.")

- It created the Department of Homeland Security, combining twenty-two separate federal agencies for the purpose of protecting the United States from terrorism. Among the agencies brought into the department are the Immigration and Naturalization Service, Secret Service, Customs Service, Federal Emergency Management Agency, Transportation Security Administration, and Border Patrol.

Were such measures necessary for the sake of national security? In testimony before the Senate Judiciary Committee, Attorney General John Ashcroft argues that the policies of the United States were necessary and showed respect for civil liberties. Specifically, he contends:

1. In the period of three months since September 11, the United States strengthened its efforts to fight terrorist dangers through vigorous law enforcement measures, and, consequently, the nation is more secure than before the attacks.
2. These efforts include the arrest and detention of suspected terrorists, more collaboration among law enforcement and intelligence agencies to fight terrorism, and tightening up of border controls.
3. Terrorism is a serious danger to the American people.
4. Terrorists know how to use the benefits of a free society as a weapon.
5. The target of law-enforcement efforts is terrorists and not civil liberties.
6. People who scare peace-loving Americans with phantoms of lost liberty engage in fear-mongering, and they "give ammunition to America's enemies, and pause to America's friends."
7. The government is avoiding the infringement of constitutional rights while saving American lives.
8. The executive branch of government is acting according to authority given to it under the Constitution.

Michael Ratner, the president of the Center for Constitutional Rights, argues that the war on terrorism includes measures that are a threat to freedom and constitutional rights. He contends:

1. The United States is moving toward becoming a police state.
2. The domestic consequences of the war on terrorism that are so threatening to liberty are massive arrests and interrogation of immigrants, possible use of torture to obtain information, the creation of an Office of Homeland Security, increased government authority to invade individual privacy, and expanded wiretapping authority.

☑ *YES*

In Fighting a War on Terrorism, Is the United States Acting within Reasonable Limits to Maintain Its Civil Liberties?

JOHN ASHCROFT
Civil Liberties, the War on Terrorism, and National Security

On the morning of September 11, as the United States came under attack, I was in an airplane with several members of the Justice Department en route to Milwaukee, in the skies over the Great Lakes. By the time we could return to Washington, thousands of people had been murdered at the World Trade Center, 189 were dead at the Pentagon. Forty-four had crashed to the ground in Pennsylvania. From that moment, at the command of the President of the United States, I began to mobilize the resources of the Department of Justice toward one single, overarching and overriding objective: to save innocent lives from further acts of terrorism.

America's campaign to save innocent lives from terrorists is now 87 days old. It has brought me back to this committee to report to you in accordance with Congress's oversight role. I welcome this opportunity to clarify for you and the American people how the Justice Department is working to protect American lives while preserving American liberties.

Since those first terrible hours of September 11, America has faced a choice that is as stark as the images that linger of that morning. One option is to call September 11 a fluke, to believe it could never happen again, and to live in a dream world that requires us to do nothing differently. The other option is to fight back, to summon all our strength and all our resources and devote ourselves to better ways to identify, disrupt and dismantle terrorist networks.

Under the leadership of President Bush, America has made the choice to fight terrorism — not just for ourselves but for all civilized people. Since September 11, through dozens of warnings to law enforcement, a deliberate campaign of terrorist disruption, tighter security around potential targets, and a preventative campaign of arrest and detention of lawbreakers, America has grown stronger — and safer — in the face of terrorism.

Thanks to the vigilance of law enforcement and the patience of the American people, we have not suffered another major terrorist attack. Still, we cannot — we must not — allow ourselves to grow complacent. The reasons are apparent to me each morning. My day begins with a review of the threats to Americans and American interests that were received in the previous 24 hours. If ever there were proof of the existence of evil in the world, it is in the pages of these reports. They are a chilling daily chronicle of hatred of America by fanatics who seek to extinguish freedom, enslave women, corrupt education and to kill Americans wherever and whenever they can.

The terrorist enemy that threatens civilization today is unlike any we have ever known. It slaughters thousands of innocents — a crime of war and a crime against humanity. It seeks weapons of mass destruction and threatens their use against America. No one should doubt the intent, nor the depth, of its consuming, destructive hatred.

Terrorist operatives infiltrate our communities — plotting, planning and waiting to kill again. They enjoy the benefits of our free society even as they commit themselves to our destruction. They exploit our openness — not randomly or haphazardly — but by deliberate, premeditated design.

This is a seized al Qaeda training manual — a "how-to" guide for terrorists — that instructs enemy operatives in the art of killing in a free society. Prosecutors first made this manual public in the trial of the al Qaeda terrorists who bombed U.S. embassies in Africa. We are posting several al Qaeda lessons from this manual on our website today so Americans can know our enemy.

In this manual, al Qaeda terrorists are told how to use America's freedom as a weapon against us. They are instructed to use the benefits of a free press — newspapers, magazines and broadcasts — to stalk and kill their victims. They are instructed to exploit our judicial process for the success of their operations. Captured terrorists are taught to anticipate a series of questions from authorities and, in each response, to lie — to lie about who they are, to lie about what they are doing and to lie about who they know in order for the operation to achieve its objective. Imprisoned terrorists are instructed to concoct stories of torture and mistreatment at the hands of our officials. They are directed to take advantage of any contact with the outside world to, quote, "communicate with brothers outside prison and exchange information that may be helpful to them in their work. The importance of mastering the art of hiding messages is self-evident here."

Mr. Chairman and members of the committee, we are at war with an enemy who abuses individual rights as it abuses jet airliners: as weapons with which to kill Americans. We have responded by redefining the mission of the Department of Justice. Defending our nation and its citizens against terrorist attacks is now our first and overriding priority.

We have launched the largest, most comprehensive criminal investigation in world history to identify the killers of September 11 and to prevent further terrorist attacks. Four thousand FBI [Federal Bureau of Investigation] agents are engaged with their international counterparts in an unprecedented worldwide effort to detect, disrupt and dismantle terrorist organizations.

We have created a national task force at the FBI to centralize control and information sharing in our investigation. This task force has investigated hundreds of thousands of leads, conducted over 500 searches, interviewed thousands of witnesses and obtained numerous court-authorized surveillance orders. Our prosecutors and agents have collected information and evidence from countries throughout Europe and the Middle East.

Immediately following the September 11 attacks, the Bureau of Prisons acted swiftly to intensify security precautions in connection with all al Qaeda and other terrorist inmates, increasing perimeter security at a number of key facilities.

We have sought and received additional tools from Congress. Already, we have begun to utilize many of these tools. Within hours of passage of the USA PATRIOT [Uniting and Strengthening America by Providing Appropriate Tools Required to

Intercept and Obstruct Terrorism] Act, we made use of its provisions to begin enhanced information sharing between the law-enforcement and intelligence communities. We have used the provisions allowing nationwide search warrants for e-mail and sub-poenas for payment information. And we have used the Act to place those who access the Internet through cable companies on the same footing as everyone else.

Just yesterday, at my request, the State Department designated 39 entities as terrorist organizations pursuant to the USA PATRIOT Act.

We have waged a deliberate campaign of arrest and detention to remove sus-pected terrorists who violate the law from our streets. Currently, we have brought criminal charges against 110 individuals, of whom 60 are in federal custody. The INS [Immigration and Naturalization Service] has detained 563 individuals on immigration violations.

We have investigated more than 250 incidents of retaliatory violence and threats against Arab Americans, Muslim Americans, Sikh Americans and South Asian Americans.

Since September 11, the Customs Service and Border Patrol have been at their highest state of alert. All vehicles and persons entering the country are subjected to the highest level of scrutiny. Working with the State Department, we have imposed new screening requirements on certain applicants for non-immigrant visas. At the direction of the President, we have created a Foreign Terrorist Tracking Task Force to ensure that we do everything we can to prevent terrorists from enter-ing the country, and to locate and remove those who already have.

We have prosecuted to the fullest extent of the law individuals who waste precious law enforcement resources through anthrax hoaxes.

We have offered non-citizens willing to come forward with valuable information a chance to live in this country and one day become citizens.

We have forged new cooperative agreements with Canada to protect our com-mon borders and the economic prosperity they sustain.

We have embarked on a wartime reorganization of the Department of Justice. We are transferring resources and personnel to the field offices where citizens are served and protected. The INS is being restructured to better perform its service and border security responsibilities. Under Director Bob Mueller, the FBI is under-going an historic reorganization to put the prevention of terrorism at the center of its law enforcement and national security efforts.

Outside Washington, we are forging new relationships of cooperation with state and local law enforcement.

We have created 93 Anti-Terrorism Task Forces — one in each U.S. Attorney's district — to integrate the communications and activities of local, state and federal law enforcement.

In all these ways and more, the Department of Justice has sought to prevent ter-rorism with reason, careful balance and excruciating attention to detail. Some of our critics, I regret to say, have shown less affection for detail. Their bold declara-tions of so-called fact have quickly dissolved, upon inspection, into vague conjec-ture. Charges of "kangaroo courts" and "shredding the Constitution" give new meaning to the term, "the fog of war."

Since lives and liberties depend upon clarity, not obfuscation, and reason, not hyperbole, let me take this opportunity today to be clear: Each action taken by the Department of Justice, as well as the war crimes commissions considered by the President and the Department of Defense, is carefully drawn to target a narrow class of individuals — terrorists. Our legal powers are targeted at terrorists. Our investigation is focused on terrorists. Our prevention strategy targets the terrorist threat.

Since 1983, the United States government has defined terrorists as those who perpetrate premeditated, politically motivated violence against noncombatant targets. My message to America this morning, then, is this: If you fit this definition of a terrorist, fear the United States, for you will lose your liberty.

We need honest, reasoned debate; not fear-mongering. To those who pit Americans against immigrants, and citizens against non-citizens; to those who scare peace-loving people with phantoms of lost liberty; my message is this: Your tactics only aid terrorists — for they erode our national unity and diminish our resolve. They give ammunition to America's enemies, and pause to America's friends. They encourage people of good will to remain silent in the face of evil.

Our efforts have been carefully crafted to avoid infringing on constitutional rights while saving American lives. We have engaged in a deliberate campaign of arrest and detention of lawbreakers. All persons being detained have the right to contact their lawyers and their families. Out of respect for their privacy, and concern for saving lives, we will not publicize the names of those detained.

We have the authority to monitor the conversations of 16 of the 158,000 federal inmates and their attorneys because we suspect that these communications are facilitating acts of terrorism. Each prisoner has been told in advance his conversations will be monitored. None of the information that is protected by attorney-client privilege may be used for prosecution. Information will only be used to stop impending terrorist acts and save American lives.

We have asked a very limited number of individuals — visitors to our country holding passports from countries with active al Qaeda operations — to speak voluntarily to law enforcement. We are forcing them to do nothing. We are merely asking them to do the right thing: to willingly disclose information they may have of terrorist threats to the lives and safety of all people in the United States.

Throughout all our activities since September 11, we have kept Congress informed of our continuing efforts to protect the American people. Beginning with a classified briefing by Director Mueller and me on the very evening of September 11, the Justice Department has briefed members of the House, the Senate and their staffs on more than 100 occasions.

We have worked with Congress in the belief and recognition that no single branch of government alone can stop terrorism. We have consulted with members out of respect for the separation of powers that is the basis of our system of government. However, Congress's power of oversight is not without limits. The Constitution specifically delegates to the President the authority to "take care that the laws are faithfully executed." And perhaps most importantly, the Constitution vests the President with the extraordinary and sole authority as Commander in Chief to lead our nation in times of war.

Mr. Chairman and members of the committee, not long ago I had the privilege of sitting where you now sit. I have the greatest reverence and respect for the constitutional responsibilities you shoulder. I will continue to consult with Congress so that you may fulfill your constitutional responsibilities. In some areas, however, I cannot and will not consult you.

The advice I give to the President, whether in his role as Commander in Chief or in any other capacity, is privileged and confidential. I cannot and will not divulge the contents, the context, or even the existence of such advice to anyone — including Congress — unless the President instructs me to do so. I cannot and will not divulge information, nor do I believe that anyone here would wish me to divulge information, that will damage the national security of the United States, the safety of its citizens or our efforts to ensure the same in an ongoing investigation.

As Attorney General, it is my responsibility — at the direction of the President — to exercise those core executive powers the Constitution so designates. The law enforcement initiatives undertaken by the Department of Justice, those individuals we arrest, detain or seek to interview, fall under these core executive powers. In addition, the President's authority to establish war-crimes commissions arises out of his power as Commander in Chief. For centuries, Congress has recognized this authority and the Supreme Court has never held that any Congress may limit it.

In accordance with over two hundred years of historical and legal precedent, the executive branch is now exercising its core Constitutional powers in the interest of saving the lives of Americans. I trust that Congress will respect the proper limits of Executive Branch consultation that I am duty-bound to uphold. I trust, as well, that Congress will respect this President's authority to wage war on terrorism and defend our nation and its citizens with all the power vested in him by the Constitution and entrusted to him by the American people.

 NO

In Fighting a War on Terrorism, Is the United States Acting within Reasonable Limits to Maintain Its Civil Liberties?

MICHAEL RATNER

Moving Toward a Police State or Have We Arrived?
Secret Military Tribunals, Mass Arrests and Disappearances,
Wiretapping and Torture

I live a few blocks from the World Trade Center. In New York, we are still mourning the loss of so many after the attacks on our city. We want to arrest and punish the terrorists, eliminate the terrorist network and prevent future attacks. But the government's declared war on terrorism, and many of the anti-terrorism measures include a curtailment of freedom and constitutional rights that have many of us very worried.

I wrote the above paragraph and much of the article that follows toward the end of October [2001]. At that time, the repressive machinery then being put into effect was already terrifying. Since that time the situation has gotten unimaginably worse; rights that we thought embedded in the Constitution and protected by international law are in serious jeopardy or have already been eliminated. It is no exaggeration to say we are moving toward a police state. In this atmosphere, we should take nothing for granted. We will not be protected, nor will the courts, the congress, or the many liberals who are gleefully jumping on the bandwagon of repression guarantee our rights. We have no choice but to make our voices be heard; it is time to stand and be counted on the side of justice and against the ante-diluvian forces that have much of our country in a stranglehold.

The domestic consequences of the war on terrorism include massive arrests and interrogation of immigrants, the possible use of torture to obtain information, the creation of a special new cabinet office of Homeland Security and the passage of legislation granting intelligence and law enforcement agencies much broader powers to intrude into the private lives of Americans. Recent new initiatives — the wiretapping of attorney-client conversations and military commissions to try suspected terrorists — undermine core constitutional protections and are reminiscent of inquisitorial practices.

Although it is not discussed in this article, the war on terrorism also means pervasive government and media censorship of information, the silencing of dissent, and widespread ethnic and religious profiling of Muslims, Arabs and Asian people. It means creating a climate of fear where one suspects one's neighbors and people are afraid to speak out.

The claimed necessity for this war at home is problematic. The legislation and other governmental actions are premised on the belief that the intelligence agencies failed to stop the September 11th attack because they lacked the spying capability to find and arrest the conspirators. Yet, neither the government nor the agencies have demonstrated that this is the reason.

This war at home gives Americans a false sense of security, allowing us to believe that tighter borders, vastly empowered intelligence agencies, and increased surveillance will stop terrorism. The United States is not yet a police state. However, even a police state could not stop terrorists intent on doing us harm. In addition, the fantasy of Fortress America keeps us from examining the root causes of terrorism, and the consequences of decades of American foreign policy in the Middle East, Afghanistan and elsewhere. Unless some of the grievances against the United States are studied and addressed, terrorism will continue.

MILITARY COMMISSIONS: THE PERUVIAN OPTION

On November 13 President Bush signed an executive order establishing military commissions or tribunals to try suspected terrorists. Under this order non-citizens, whether from the United States or elsewhere, accused of aiding international terrorism, at the discretion of the President, can be tried before one of these commissions. These are not court-martials, which provide far more protections. The divergence from constitutional protections the executive order allows are breathtaking. Attorney General Ashcroft has explicitly stated that terrorists do not deserve constitutional protections. These are "courts" of conviction and not of justice.

The Secretary of Defense will appoint the judges, most likely military officers, who will decide both questions of law and fact. Unlike federal judges who are appointed for life, these officers will have little independence and every reason to decide in favor of the prosecution. Normal rules of evidence, which provide some assurance of reliability, will not apply. Hearsay and even evidence obtained from torture will apparently be admissible. This is particularly frightening in light of the intimations from U.S. officials that torture of suspects may be an option. Rules of evidence help insure the innocent are spared, but also that law enforcement authorities adhere to what we thought were evolving standards of a civilized society.

Unanimity among the judges is not required even to impose the death penalty. Suspects will not have free choice of attorneys. The only appeal from a conviction will be to the President or the Secretary of Defense. Incredibly, the entire process, including execution, can be in secret and the trials can be anywhere the Secretary of Defense decides. A trial might occur on an aircraft carrier and the body of the executed "buried" at sea. The President is literally getting away with murder.

Surprisingly, a number of prestigious law professors (e.g. Laurence Tribe and Ruth Wedgwood) have accepted and even argued in favor of these tribunals. The primary claim is that it might be necessary to disclose classified information in order to obtain convictions. This is a pretext. There are procedures for handling classified information in federal courts as was done in the trial of those convicted in the 1993 bombing of the World Trade Center. It certainly does not provide a reason for sending suspects into the equivalent of a "justice" system akin to that the U.S. condemned in Peru. The 1993 trials also demonstrate that these trials can be held in federal courts.

Trials before military commissions will not be trusted in either the Muslim world or elsewhere. Nor should they. They will be viewed as what they are — "kangaroo courts." How much better to demonstrate to the world that the guilty have been apprehended and fairly convicted. A better solution would be for the U.S. to go to the U.N. [United Nations] and have the U.N. establish a special court for the trials. Judges from different legal systems including that of the U.S., Muslim and civil law countries could constitute such a court.

WIRETAPPING ATTORNEY-CLIENT COMMUNICATIONS

At the heart of the effective assistance of counsel is the right of a criminal defendant to a lawyer with whom he or she can communicate candidly and freely without fear that the government is overhearing confidential communications. This right is fundamental to the adversary system of justice in the United States. When the government overhears these conversations, a defendant's right to a defense is compromised.

Now, with the stroke of pen, Attorney General Ashcroft has eliminated the attorney-client privilege and will wiretap privileged communications when he thinks there is "reasonable suspicion to believe" that an "inmate may use communications with attorneys or their agents to further facilitate an act of violence or terrorism." He says that approximately one hundred such suspects and their attorneys may be subject to the order. He claims the legal authority to do so without court order, in other words without the approval and finding by a neutral magistrate that attorney-client communications are facilitating criminal conduct. This is utter lawlessness by our country's top law enforcement officer and is flatly unconstitutional. This wiretapping of attorney-client communications has already begun.

THE NEW LEGAL REGIME

The government has established a tripartite plan in its efforts to eradicate terrorism in the United States. President Bush has created a new cabinet-level Homeland Security Office; the Federal Bureau of Investigation is investigating thousands of individuals and groups and making hundreds of arrests; and Congress is enacting new laws that will grant the FBI and other intelligence agencies vast new powers to wiretap and spy on people in the United States.

THE OFFICE OF HOMELAND SECURITY

On September 20th President Bush announced the creation of the Home-land Security Office, charged with gathering intelligence, coordinating anti-terrorism efforts and taking precautions to prevent and respond to terrorism. It is not yet known how this office will function, but it will most likely try to centralize the powers of the intelligence and law enforcement agencies — a difficult, if not impossible, job — among some 40 bickering agencies. Those concerned with its establishment are worried that it will become a super spy agency and, as its very name implies, that the military will play a role in domestic law enforcement.

FBI INVESTIGATIONS AND ARRESTS

The FBI has always done more than chase criminals; like the Central Intelligence Agency [CIA] it has long considered itself the protector of U.S. ideology. Those who opposed government policies — whether civil rights workers, anti–Vietnam war protestors, opponents of the covert Reagan-era wars or cultural dissidents — have repeatedly been surveyed and had their activities disrupted by the FBI.

In the immediate aftermath of the September 11 attack, Attorney General John Ashcroft focused on non-citizens, whether permanent residents, students, temporary workers or tourists. Normally, an alien can only be held for 48 hours prior to the filing of charges. Ashcroft's new regulation allowed arrested aliens to be held without any charges for a "reasonable time," presumably months or longer. (See below for new legislation regarding detention of immigrants.)

The FBI began massive detentions and investigations of individuals suspected of terrorist connections, almost all of them non-citizens of Middle Eastern descent; over 1,100 have been arrested. Many were held for days without access to lawyers or knowledge of the charges against them; many are still in detention. Few, if any, have been proven to have a connection with the September 11 attacks and remain in jail despite having been cleared. In some cases, people were arrested merely for being from a country like Pakistan and having expired student visas. Stories of mistreatment of such detainees are not uncommon.

Apparently, some of those arrested are not willing to talk to the FBI, although they have been offered shorter jail sentences, jobs, money and new identities. Astonishingly, the FBI and the Department of Justice are discussing methods to force them to talk, which include "using drugs or pressure tactics such as those employed by the Israeli interrogators." The accurate term to describe these tactics is torture. Our government wants to torture people to make them talk. There is resistance to this even from law enforcement officials. One former FBI Chief of Counter Terrorism said in an October New York *Newsday* article, "Torture goes against every grain in my body. Chances are you are going to get the wrong person and risk damage or killing them."

As torture is illegal in the United States and under international law, U.S. officials risk lawsuits by such practices. For this reason, they have suggested having another country do their dirty work; they want to extradite the suspects to allied countries where security services threaten family members and use torture. It would be difficult to imagine a more ominous signal of the repressive period we are facing.

The FBI is also currently investigating groups it claims are linked to terrorism — among them pacifist groups such as the U.S. chapter of Women in Black, which holds vigils to protest violence in Israel and the Palestinian Territories. The FBI has threatened to force members of Women in Black to either talk about their group or go to jail. As one of the group's members said, "If the FBI cannot or will not distinguish between groups who collude in hatred and terrorism, and peace activists who struggle in the full light of day against all forms of terrorism, we are in serious trouble."

Unfortunately, the FBI does not make that distinction. We are facing not only the roundup of thousands on flimsy suspicions, but also an all-out investigation of dissent in the United States.

THE NEW ANTI-TERRORIST LEGISLATION

Congress has passed and President Bush has signed sweeping new anti-terrorist legislation, the USA PATRIOT Act (Uniting and Strengthening America by Providing Appropriate Tools Required to Intercept and Obstruct Terrorism), aimed at both aliens and citizens. The legislation met more opposition than one might expect in these difficult times. A National Coalition to Protect Political Freedom of over 120 groups ranging from the right to the left opposed the worst aspects of the proposed new law. They succeeded in making minor modifications, but the most troubling provisions remain, and are described below:

RIGHTS OF ALIENS

Prior to the legislation, anti-terrorist laws passed in the wake of the 1996 bombing of the federal building in Oklahoma had already given the government wide powers to arrest, detain and deport aliens based upon secret evidence — evidence that neither the alien nor his attorney could view or refute. The current proposed legislation makes it even worse for aliens.

First, the law would permit "mandatory detention" of aliens certified by the attorney general as "suspected terrorists." These could include aliens involved in barroom brawls or those who have provided only humanitarian assistance to organizations disfavored by the United States. Once certified in this way, an alien could be imprisoned indefinitely with no real opportunity for court challenge. Until now, such "preventive detention" was believed to be flatly unconstitutional.

Second, current law permits deportation of aliens who support terrorist activity; the proposed law would make aliens deportable for almost any association with a "terrorist organization." Although this change seems to have a certain surface plausibility, it represents a dangerous erosion of Americans' constitutionally protected rights of association. "Terrorist organization" is a broad and open-ended term that could include liberation groups such as the Irish Republican Army, the African National Congress, or civic groups that have never engaged in any violent activity, such as Greenpeace. An alien who gives only medical or humanitarian aid to similar groups, or simply supports their political message in a material way could be jailed indefinitely.

MORE POWERS TO THE FBI AND CIA

A key element in the new law is the wide expansion of wiretapping. In the United States wiretapping is permitted, but generally only when there is probable cause to believe a crime has been committed and a judge signs a special wiretapping order that contains limited time periods, the numbers of the telephones wire-tapped and the type of conversations that can be overheard.

In 1978, an exception was made to these strict requirements, permitting wiretapping to be carried out to gather intelligence information about foreign governments and foreign terrorist organizations. A secret court, the Foreign Intelligence Surveillance Court, was established that could approve such wiretaps without requiring the government to show evidence of criminal conduct. In doing so, the constitutional protections necessary when investigating crimes could be bypassed. The secret court is little more than a rubber stamp for wiretapping requests by the spy agencies. It has authorized over 13,000 wiretaps in its 22-year existence, approximately a thousand last year, and has apparently never denied a request.

Under the new law, the same secret court will have the power to authorize wiretaps and secret searches of homes in criminal cases — not just to gather foreign intelligence. The FBI will be able to wiretap individuals and organizations without meeting the stringent requirements of the Constitution. The law will authorize the secret court to permit roving wiretaps of any phones, computers or cell phones that might possibly be used by a suspect. Widespread reading of e-mail will be allowed, even before the recipient opens it. Thousands of conversations will be listened to or read that have nothing to do with the suspect or any crime.

The new legislation is filled with many other expansions of investigative and prosecutorial power, including wider use of undercover agents to infiltrate organizations, longer jail sentences and lifetime supervision for some who have served their sentences, more crimes that can receive the death penalty and longer statutes of limitations for prosecuting crimes. Another provision of the new bill makes it a crime for a person to fail to notify the FBI if he or she has "reasonable grounds to believe" that someone is about to commit a terrorist offense. The language of this provision is so vague that anyone, however innocent, with any connection to anyone suspected of being a terrorist can be prosecuted. We will all need to become spies to protect ourselves and the subjects of our spying, at least for now, will be those from the Mid East.

THE NEW CRIME OF DOMESTIC TERRORISM

The act creates a number of new crimes. One of the most threatening to dissent and those who oppose government policies is the crime of "domestic terrorism." It is loosely defined as acts that are dangerous to human life, violate criminal law and "appear to be intended to intimidate or coerce a civilian population" or "influence the policy of a government by intimidation or coercion." Under this definition, a protest demonstration that blocked a street and prevented an ambulance from getting by could be deemed domestic terrorism. Likewise, the demonstrations in Seattle against the WTO [World Trade Organization] could fit within the definition. This was an unnecessary addition to the criminal code; there are already plenty of laws making such civil disobedience criminal without labeling such time honored protest as terrorist and imposing severe prison sentences.

Overall, the new legislation represents one of the most sweeping assaults on liberties in the last 50 years. It is unlikely to make us more secure; it is certain to make us less free.

It is common for governments to reach for draconian law enforcement solutions in times of war or national crisis. It has happened often in the United States and elsewhere. We should learn from historical example: times of hysteria, of war, and of instability are not the times to rush to enact new laws that curtail our freedoms and grant more authority to the government and its intelligence and law enforcement agencies.

The U.S. government has conceptualized the war against terrorism as a permanent war, a war without boundaries. Terrorism is frightening to all of us, but it's equally chilling to think that in the name of anti-terrorism our government is willing to suspend constitutional freedoms permanently as well.

Questions for Discussion

1. In times of war, what restrictions on civil liberties are justified? What are the reasons for your answer?
2. To what extent is the war on terrorism similar to and/or different from the wars that the United States has fought since the Constitution was adopted? What relevance does your answer have to matters dealing with restrictions on civil liberties in wartime?
3. If some Americans protest U.S. government restrictions on civil liberties when the United States is at war, are those people actually giving "aid and comfort" to the nation's enemies? What are the reasons for your answer?
4. What impact do restrictions on civil liberties have on winning a war?
5. Do you think that the war on terrorism since the events of September 11, 2001, is going to turn the United States into a police state? What are the reasons for your answer?

Suggested Resources

Web Sites

American Civil Liberties Union
   http://www.aclu.org

Center for Constitutional Rights
   http://www.ccr-ny.org/

Heritage Foundation
  http://www.heritage.org

National Center for Policy Analysis: Civil Liberties
  http://www.ncpa.org/iss/ter/civil.html

Publications

Cole, David. "National Security State." *Nation* 273, no. 20 (December 17, 2001): 4–5.

Cole, David, and James X. Dempsey. *Terrorism and the Constitution: Civil Liberties in the Name of National Security*, 2d ed. Washington, D.C.: First Amendment Foundation, 2002.

Dworkin, Ronald. "The Threat to Patriotism." *New York Review of Books* 49, no. 3 (February 28, 2002): 44–49.

Etzioni, Amitai, and Joseph H. Marsh. *Rights vs. Public Safety after 9/11*. Lanham, Md.: Rowman & Littlefield, 2003.

Fletcher, George P. "War and the Constitution." *American Prospect* 13, no. 1 (January 1–14, 2002): 26–29.

France, Mike, et al., "Privacy in an Age of Terror," *Business Week*, November 5, 2001, pp. 83–87.

Godwin, Mike. "Fear of the Unknown: Should Strong Encryption Be a Casualty of War?" *Legal Times*, November 26, 2001, p. 36.

Kelly, Michael. "It Is a War, After All." *Washington Post*, June 12, 2002, p. A31.

Krauthammer, Charles. "In Defense of Secret Tribunals — Why Bush Is Right: At a Time of Critical Danger, We Can't Afford a Legal Circus," *Time* 158, no. 23 (November 26, 2001): 104.

Linfield, Michael. *Freedom under Fire: U.S. Civil Liberties in Times of War*. Boston: South End Press, 1990.

Lynch, Timothy. "Breaking the Vicious Cycle: Preserving Our Liberties while Fighting Terrorism." *Policy Analysis*, no. 443. Washington, D.C.: Cato Institute, June 26, 2002.

Masci, David, and Patrick Marshall. "Civil Liberties in Wartime." *CQ Researcher* 11, no. 43 (December 14, 2001): 1017–40.

Posner, Richard A. "Security Versus Civil Liberties." *Atlantic* 288, no. 5 (December 2001): 46–48.

Rehnquist, William. *All the Laws but One: Civil Liberties in Wartime*. New York: Knopf, 1998.

Romero, Anthony D. "In Defense of Liberty at a Time of National Emergency." *Human Rights* 29, no. 1 (Winter 2002): 16–17, 24–25.

Taylor, Stuart, Jr. "War on Detainees?" *Legal Times*, December 10, 2001, pp. 35, 37.

Tribe, Laurence H. "We Can Strike a Balance on Civil Liberties." *Responsive Community* 12, no. 1 (Winter 2001/2002): 28–31.

U.S. Cong., Senate. *DOJ Oversight: Preserving Our Freedoms while Defending against Terrorism*. Hearing before the Committee on the Judiciary, 107th Cong, 1st Sess., 2001.

Should a National Identification Card System Be Established?

Furnishing identification (ID) to prove that you are the person you say you are is no doubt a frequent occurrence in your life. When you withdraw money at a bank teller's window, you are asked to present some identification. You have to furnish ID when you are hired for a job, apply for a passport, cash a check, or stop your car if a police officer thinks that you have committed some driving offense. If you are youngish looking, you may have had the uncomfortable experience of ordering alcohol at a bar or restaurant and being asked to show proof that you are at the legal age for drinking alcohol. If you are older but still look young for your years, you may be asked to show identification that you are really a senior citizen and are entitled to a discount.

The identification that you must present for many of these requests is a driver's license and/or a Social Security card. The driver's license, unlike the Social Security card, has a photograph image of you — a feature that allows for presumed instant recognition that you are who you say you are. And you are not alone, as millions of people in the United States carry their own identification information for their many needs. In particular, the driver's license has become the most widely used personal ID in the United States.

Two major problems with the prevailing identification system are fraud and lack of uniformity. Criminal organizations can provide phony Social Security cards and driver's licenses for a small fee. Illegal immigrants have sometimes used such illegal IDs to get jobs in the United States. To be sure, electronic means are able to link law enforcement authorities with a centralized database to determine ID authenticity in many cases. But in day-to-day life experiences, some people can get by with false identity documentation.

A second problem is that no uniform system of national identification of driver's licenses exists. Each state makes its own rules as to the information that must be included on its driver's license. Each state also makes its own rules about eligibility to obtain a driver's license.

Since the 1990s, proposals have been put forward to establish a national ID in the United States. Some law enforcement officials believe that such a system would be a good way to prevent many crimes. They note that new technology makes it possible to provide much valuable information on a national identification card, such as fingerprints, a record of prior crimes, and current and criminal status, that would be helpful to law enforcement authorities.

In the 1990s, moreover, one form of crime — illegal immigration — was a motivating factor in the call for a national ID. But since the events of September 11, 2001, in which terrorists crashed hijacked aircraft into the World Trade Center and the Pentagon, killing thousands of people, the movement for a national ID gained strength as a means of counterterrorism since some of the terrorists involved in these hijackings had obtained fraudulent ID papers. Also as a result of September 11, much discussion about a national ID centered on the ability of foreign visitors — whether students, vacationers, or temporary employees — to overextend the amount of time granted to them on their visas and to use that time for terrorist purposes.

In response to the events of September 11, to travel on airplanes, long-distance buses, and Amtrak trains, a person must show acceptable personal identification — an inconvenience that most travelers willingly accept as a necessity in our dangerous times. Moreover, public opinion polls reveal immense popular support for a national ID. Some vocal individuals and organizations have shown enthusiasm for the idea, too. For example, Oracle chief executive officer Larry Ellison called for the establishment of a national ID card and offered to donate software to establish a government national ID system.

If the United States adopts a national ID, it will not be the only country to do so. About 100 countries have official national identity cards that citizens of those countries are required to possess. Among the economically developed countries that have them are Belgium, France, Germany, Greece, Portugal, and Spain. But many developing countries have either a national card system or a document system, often based on regional rather than national authorization.

The use and nature of the existing national cards vary. Some ID cards are for many purposes, and others are for specific purposes, such as health care. There is certainly no one universal national ID card used by all the countries that require an ID card. Among the kinds of information called for on a card are name, birth date, gender, signature, permanent address, current address, photograph, fingerprints, national identification number, religion, ethnicity, military record, profession, and marital status.

Although a national ID has much popular support in the United States, some Americans are wary of them. They associate a national ID with a dictatorship in which the government seeks to amass all kinds of personal information about its citizens that it can use to maintain its power. Today, as in the past, many civil liberties advocates in particular are concerned that such cards could facilitate the invasion of personal privacy.

Any consideration of a national ID will have to address a number of policy questions, such as the kind of data that would be included, the scope of the population required to possess the national ID, the private organizations and government agencies that would be allowed use of the information contained in the national ID database, and privacy protections. No doubt, such matters would be debated within and outside of government.

Amitai Etzioni, a professor at George Washington University, argues that Americans are often required to produce identification for all kinds of purposes, from cashing a check to going overseas. But currently, fraudulent means are easily available to acquire identification. According to Etzioni:

1. A national ID based on biometrics — the measurement and analysis of unique physiological and behavioral characteristics of individuals — might make it difficult for terrorists and other criminals to produce documents with false identities.
2. The ID card could be used to track foreign citizens in the United States who claim to be here for study but who do not show up for classes or who overextend their visas.
3. It will greatly curtail the hiring of child abusers or sex offenders as workers in child-care centers, schools, and elder-care facilities and will limit the amount of identity theft that is so costly for its victims.
4. A national ID requirement will diminish fraud in taxes and welfare.
5. Given the nature of our times, a national ID is a reasonable measure for the nation to take.

Katie Corrigan, the legislative counsel on privacy at the American Civil Liberties Union, criticizes a potential national ID card or system as ineffective and hostile to liberty. Specifically, she argues:

1. National ID cards would create a false sense of security and divert valuable resources from other, more effective counterterrorism efforts.
2. National ID cards would provide a new tool for racial and ethnic profiling and lead to more illegal discrimination, not less.
3. Massive databases of information are a direct threat to the privacy of average Americans and the basic freedom to move freely around our neighborhoods and towns.
4. National ID proposals ask Americans to trust that a massive identification bureaucracy would facilitate our way of life rather than undermine the freedoms we take for granted.
5. Once government establishes an infrastructure to track its citizens, even if it claims privacy protections, it will expand its goals into a broad-based assault on privacy, as the history of Social Security cards shows.

☑ *YES*

Should a National Identification Card System Be Established?

AMITAI ETZIONI
You'll Love Those National ID Cards

Today, we learn the conclusions of a special task force examining the merits of a national, tamper-proof ID card. The task force, set up by the American Association of Motor Vehicle Administrators, is working closely with various federal agencies and Congress. I hope it won't dance around the issue, fearing public reaction, and will recommend outright that everyone within this great country be required to be able to prove their identity.

As a sociologist, I realize that many Americans have long had a visceral reaction against mandatory ID cards, which they associate with the "domestic passports" used in the old Soviet Union. The right to be left alone is widely linked to the notion that a person has a right to remain anonymous unless authorities can show cause to suspect the person committed a crime.

But Americans increasingly recognize that one cannot fly, drive, go overseas, enter many public buildings, or, often, even cash a check without identification. To say that these are voluntary ID cards is a joke to anyone who must drive to work or fly to conduct business. IDs are so widely required that motor vehicle departments issue nondriver's licenses.

Terrorists and criminals are also covered by the de facto requirement to have an ID. The problem is that they have many, one for each alias. While most Americans have no reason to purchase false IDs (unless they are college kids trying to sneak into a bar), they are easily obtainable by terrorists and other criminals.

Social Security and green cards are sold in border towns for about $50. Local authorities readily issue birth certificates with any name — the favorite avenue to a false passport. Before Sept. 11, several states — including Virginia and Florida — were notorious for providing cheap driver's licenses for people out of state. So issuing fraud-resistant ID cards will take nothing from law-abiding Americans, while hindering lawbreakers.

First among those to be greatly inconvenienced, thanks be given, will be terrorists. Most of the 19 hijackers had multiple IDs, which they used to open bank accounts, get pilot licenses, and buy airline tickets, all without revealing their true identity. Public authorities now call for tracking systems that will allow us to find out if a person who came to study in the U.S. is really taking classes on some campus, or if people who came on a tourist visa left after its term expired.

But all this is impossible unless we can establish the identity of the person we are tracing. If a person can enter the U.S. as Mohammed Laden and live here as Murphy Liden, we will have a hard time finding terrorists.

Beyond making it much harder for terrorists to abuse our free society, tamper-proof, national ID cards should be embraced for all the other good service they will do. Currently, there are some 300,000 criminals on the lam in the U.S. These are not mere suspects, but convicts who somehow escape the jurisdiction of the courts, say, by fleeing prison. Many of them commit additional crimes, because they know they're heading for a stiff jail sentence anyhow. One of the best ways to get them off the streets is to introduce foolproof ID cards.

Such cards will also help ensure that people who work in child-care centers and schools are not child abusers or sex offenders. This is not an idle threat. When six states did screen such employees, more than 6,200 individuals convicted of serious crimes were found among those seeking child-care jobs. Elder-care facilities face a similar challenge when they try to screen out people with a record of violence. No ID — no valid screening.

Also, validated IDs would greatly curtail the price of identity theft, which costs the public at least $750 million in 1997. They would also shave income tax fraud committed by those who file multiple tax returns at an estimated cost of more than $1 billion per year, and welfare fraud amounting to $10 billion annually in entitlement programs alone.

Indeed, the public is wising up. While in 1993 a minority (39 percent) favored ID cards and a majority (53 percent) objected to them, a post–9/11 poll finds a sea change. Now 70 percent favor a national identity card to show to police upon request and only 1 out of 4 (26 percent) oppose it. You may say all this makes sense if one could really have a foolproof ID card. The good news is that new ways of identifying people do not involve old-fashioned pieces of paper with ugly mug shots. Now they're based on biometrics. Luckily, no two people — even identical twins — have identical faces or irises. Computers can now recognize these.

We live in a new world, and now must make some careful adjustments to our way of life. To require everyone within our borders to identify themselves in a reliable manner is a reasonable step in the right direction.

Should a National Identification Card System Be Established?

KATIE CORRIGAN
The Case against National ID Cards

The American Civil Liberties Union (ACLU) is a nationwide, non-partisan organization with nearly 300,000 members dedicated to protecting the individual liberties and freedoms guaranteed in the Constitution and laws of the United States. . . . Like all Americans, the ACLU supports efforts to ensure our security from terrorist threat; but we remain convinced that we need not sacrifice our civil liberties to protect safety. We believe our country can be both safe and free.

We ask Congress to use a three-prong analysis to promote safety and to reduce the likelihood that new security measures would violate civil liberties.

First, any new security proposals must be genuinely effective, rather than creating a false sense of security. Second, security measures should be implemented in a non-discriminatory manner. Individuals should not be subjected to intrusive searches or questioning based on race, ethnic origin or religion. Finally, if a security measure is determined to be genuinely effective, the government should work to ensure that its implementation minimizes its cost to our fundamental freedoms, including the rights to due process, privacy and equality.

A national identification card does not pass these basic tests. A national ID card would substantially infringe on the rights of privacy and equality of many Americans, yet would not prevent terrorist attacks. The ACLU strongly opposes the creation of a national ID card, whether the card is embodied in plastic, or whether the "card" is intangible — a sort of "virtual reality" card consisting instead of a government-mandated computerized database containing information about most people in the United States linked by a government-issued identifier.

Over the past few decades, proposals for a national identification system have appeared as a "quick fix" to a national problem of tracking one segment of the population or another, including immigrants and deadbeat dads. Since September 11, national ID proposals have been discussed in the media and in the Congress as possible counterterrorism measures. . . .

NATIONAL ID CARD OR SYSTEM WOULD BE AN INEFFECTIVE COUNTERTERRORISM MEASURE AND WOULD SERIOUSLY UNDERMINE BASIC LIBERTIES

A national ID card or system would not be an effective counterterrorism measure. Instead, such a system could divert resources away from other counterterrorism activities and create a government bureaucracy that would undermine basic rights to privacy and equality.

First, National ID Cards Would Create a False Sense of Security and Divert Valuable Resources from Other More Effective Counterterrorism Efforts

The rationale for creating a national ID system post–September 11 is to create a clear line between "us" (innocent people) and "them" (dangerous terrorists). Everyone would like an ID card that would put them squarely on the right side of the line and exempt them from suspicion and heightened security scrutiny when they board a plane or go to work.

Unfortunately, none of the proposed identification systems would effectively sort out the "good" from the "bad." First, an identification card simply confirms that you are who you say you are. It does not establish motive or intent to attack a plane. All 19 of the September 11 hijackers had Social Security numbers (SSNs), although not all of them were legitimate. One of the hijackers was listed in the San Diego phone book — both name and address. And still others rented automobiles with their debit cards and lived in suburban Florida neighborhoods. But only a few of the hijackers were on FBI [Federal Bureau of Investigation] watch lists. An ID card would simply have reaffirmed the hijackers' real or assumed identities. It would have done nothing to establish their criminal motives for renting cars and going to flight school.

Second, an identity card is only as good as the information that establishes an individual's identity in the first place. It does not make sense to build a national identification system on a faulty foundation, particularly when possession of an ID card would give you a free pass to avoid heightened security measures.

No form of documentation is completely foolproof. There are always ways to beat the system. Presumably, an individual would obtain an identity card using documents such as a birth certificate or driver's license. Anyone, including terrorists, could falsify or forge such documents. The Inspector General of the Social Security Administration [SSA] testified last week that six of the hijackers obtained SSNs through fraudulent means.[1] And, at least one person who is a suspected associate in the September 11 attack has been indicted for using false information to obtain a SSN. In addition, a national ID card would do nothing to sort out domestic terrorists. As a U.S. citizen, Timothy McVeigh would have certainly qualified for a national ID.

A national ID system would inevitably foster the black market in fake identification. For instance, in 1990, several DMV [Department of Motor Vehicles] employees in Virginia were indicted for selling possibly thousands of driver's licenses to illegal immigrants in violation of the law.[2] The creation of these cards and supporting infrastructures create new risks of insiders issuing phony IDs and outsiders gaining access. There is always the potential for misuse by individuals in any large organization.

At best, a national ID would serve as a placebo to make us all feel better when we show the card at the airport, a turnpike tollbooth, or at our workplaces. At worst, the ID card would create a false sense of security and divert resources from other more productive counterterrorism activities. In 1998, General Accounting Office (GAO) reported that mass issuance of counterfeit-resistant Social Security cards would be very expensive.[3] The Social Security Administration estimated that no matter what material the card was made from or what type of technology was used for security purposes, such as biometric identifiers, "issuing an enhanced card to all number holders using current procedures would cost a minimum of about $4 billion or more." And, even with the offer from Larry Ellison (Chairman and CEO of Oracle) of free database software, the processing costs alone of issuing new ID cards are estimated to be 90 percent of the $4 billion expense.

Second, National ID Cards Would Provide a New Tool for Racial and Ethnic Profiling and Lead to More Illegal Discrimination, Not Less

The cards would provide new opportunities for discrimination and harassment of people who are perceived as looking or sounding "foreign." Some people have argued that ID cards would end racial profiling and other discriminatory practices. We need only look to history to see how "identification" requirements can impact the daily lives of Americans. The Immigration Reform and Control Act of 1986 required employers to verify the identity of potential employees and their eligibility to work in the U.S. The Act also imposed sanctions for failing to comply with the verification requirements. As a result, there has been widespread discrimination based on citizenship status and against foreign-looking American workers, especially Asians and Hispanics. A 1990 General Accounting Office (GAO) study found almost 20 percent of employers engaged in such practices.[4]

A national ID card would have the same effect on a broader scale. Latinos, Asians, African-Americans and other minorities would become subject to more and more status and identity checks — not just from their employers, but also from police, banks, merchants and others. The failure to carry a national ID card would likely come to be viewed as a reason for search, detention or arrest of minorities. This would mean certain individuals, including immigrants, would be increasingly vulnerable to a system that subjected them to the stigma and humiliation of constantly having to prove their citizenship or legal immigrant status.

Third, Massive Databases of Information Are a Direct Threat to the Privacy of Average Americans and the Basic Freedom to Move Freely Around Our Neighborhoods and Towns

A national ID system would violate the freedom Americans take the most for granted and the one that most defines our liberty: the right to be left alone. Unlike workers in Nazi Germany, Soviet Russia, apartheid South Africa, and Castro's Cuba, no American need fear the demand, "Papers, please." As a free society, we cherish the right to be individuals, to be left alone, and to start over, free from the prying eyes of the government.

As former California Representative Tom Campbell recently argued, "If you have an ID card, it is solely for the purpose of allowing the government to compel you to produce it. This would essentially give the government the power to demand that we show our papers. It is a very dangerous thing."[5]

Internal Passports Required

A national ID card would set up the infrastructure for a surveillance society. Day to day, individuals could be asked for ID when they are walking down the street, applying for a job or health insurance, or entering a building. This type of daily intrusiveness would be joined with the full power of modern computer and database technology. If a police officer or security guard scans your ID card with a pocket bar-code reader, for example, will a permanent record be created of that check, including the time and location? How long before office buildings, doctors' offices, gas stations, highway tolls, subways and buses incorporate the ID card into their security or payment systems for greater efficiency? The result could be a nation where citizens' movements inside their own country are monitored and recorded through these "internal passports."

Misuse of Highly Personal Information

Once all of this information is in the government databases, there is no guarantee its use would be limited to protecting security. There are clear examples of how government-collected information has been used for purposes other than that which it was originally intended. For instance, the confidentiality of Census Bureau information was violated during World War II to help the War Department locate Japanese-Americans so they could forcibly be removed to internment camps. During the Vietnam War, the FBI secretly operated the "Stop Index" by using its computerized National Crime Information Center (NCIC) to track and monitor the activities of people opposed to the United States' involvement in the war.

Every day privacy violations victimize average Americans and undermine public confidence in the government. Thousands and thousands of government officials and perhaps even private industry would have access to a massive database of personal information required to support a national ID system. Even now internal breaches of database information happen all the time at the federal and state levels. In 1997, the General Accounting Office found serious weaknesses in the IRS's computer security and privacy protections and a year later many of the problems remained.[6] Just last week, a former top Chicago detective admitted to running a jewel-theft ring across several states for more than a decade. Prosecutors said the detective had used law enforcement and other databases to get information about the travel schedules of traveling jewelry salesmen.[7] And, an investigation by the *Detroit Free Press* shows other types of abuses that can happen. Looking at how a database available to Michigan law enforcement was used, the newspaper found that officers had used it to help their friends or themselves stalk women, threaten motorists, track estranged spouses — even to intimidate political opponents.

Even an innocent mistake by a single government employee can have a huge impact on an individual's life. In the past month, the University of Montana accidentally posted the psychological records of 62 children on the Internet. Names, addresses, and psychological tests were posted along with intimate details such as the boy prone to "anger outbursts, gender identity issues" and bedwetting. The immediate impact of such disclosures includes embarrassment and humiliation or further psychological trauma. The long-term impact could be depression, poor performance in school and, depending on which databases the psychological information ended up, it could come back to haunt children later in life when they are trying to find a job or get a security clearance.

Any one of these privacy violations would be magnified in the context of a national ID system. A national ID system would allow government officials to access information contained in numerous and unrelated databases through one centralized system. Fraud or mistake would no longer be limited to one state law enforcement database or one university's research files. Government employees could tap into a database that included all kinds of information about an individual — from tax returns to health care data to student loan information. One employee or one wrong keyboard stroke could send a person's entire file into public distribution.

Finally, National ID Proposals Ask Americans to Trust That a Massive Identification Bureaucracy Would Facilitate Our Way of Life Rather Than Undermine the Freedoms We Take for Granted

The scale of the bureaucracy required to implement a national ID system cannot be underestimated. Thousands of government employees would be required to develop, implement, and maintain the supporting computer infrastructure and technology standards and process the cards for every American. The SSA estimated the cost of issuing counterfeit-resistant Social Security cards at $4 billion. The Administration did not even consider, however, the cost of updating the picture or other identifier on the card over a person's lifetime, periodically replacing the magnetic or electronic storage technology to ensure reliability, or the simple costs of having to replace lost cards.[8] In addition, this report did not consider the information database that would also have to be developed, implemented, and maintained.

What would happen if an ID card is stolen? What proof of identity would be used to decide who gets a card? What would happen if you lose your ID? An overnight business trip might have to be cancelled because you don't have the time to go through heightened security at the airport. You might not be able to drive across a bridge to work without ID that says you are who you say you are. Even worse, you might not be employable without proof of ID. And, what if you run out of your house to buy a quart of milk and forget your ID? If a police officer stops you, you would automatically be considered suspect.

Anyone who has had to correct an inaccurate credit history will understand how hard it could be to correct an error that has found its way into your national ID file. Error rates in government databases tend to be high. Internal Revenue Service data and programs have been found to have error rates in the range of 10 to 20 percent.[9] And, according to the GAO, there has been a significant increase in identity theft over the years.[10] It is estimated that 40,000 victims of identity theft must struggle each year to clear their names and fix their credit histories.

Even with biometric identifiers on each and every ID, experts say there is no guarantee that individuals won't be identified — or misidentified — in error. Professor David J. Farber, a technology expert at the University of Pennsylvania, recently said, "Biometrics are fallible."[11] Fingerprints and retinal scans are reasonably reliable when used with an expensive reader. Other forms of biometrics such as hand readers and facial recognition, however, have high error rates. (See ACLU's Feature on Facial Recognition Technology at http://www.aclu.org/features/f110101a.html.)

Under a national ID system, employee mistake, database error rates, and common fraud would not simply affect individuals in one area of life. Instead, problems with the ID system or card could take away an individual's ability to move freely from place to place or even make someone unemployable until the file got straightened out.

The proponents of a national identification system argue that our circumstances have changed since September 11, and now Americans must accept "a little less anonymity for a lot more security." Unfortunately, this trade-off is rooted in the false assumption that a national ID card would make us more secure and fails to account for the full range of civil liberties at stake in this debate.

HISTORY OF THE SSN POINTS TO PROBLEMS WITH NATIONAL ID SYSTEM

A "Golden Rule" of informational privacy is that information collected by the government for one purpose should not be used for another purpose without the consent of the person to whom such information pertains. The history of the Social Security number (SSN) shows just how difficult it is for the government and private industry to abide by this simple rule. It also documents Congress' longtime resistance to national ID systems.

In 1935, the Social Security number (SSN) was created solely for the purpose of tracking contributions to the Social Security fund. But as soon as 1943, President Roosevelt issued an Executive Order encouraging other federal agencies to use the SSN when establishing a "one system of permanent account numbers pertaining to an individual's person." In 1961, the Civil Service Commission began using the number to identify all federal employees. The next year the IRS [Internal Revenue Service] required the number on all individual tax returns. And, by the mid-1960s, the use of the SSN exploded in both the public and private sector as the introduction of the computer coincided with the expansion of government assistance programs.

Based on reports from the Administration and congressional hearings, Congress realized the SSN posed grave privacy concerns for the American public. In response, Congress enacted the Privacy Act in 1974 based on a finding that the right to privacy was "directly affected by the collection, maintenance, use and dissemination of personal information by federal agencies," and that the increasing use of computers and sophisticated information technology "greatly magnifies the harm to individual privacy that can occur from any collection, maintenance, use or dissemination of personal information."

Of course, Congress has considered numerous proposals to institutionalize the SSN as a national ID and consistently rejected them. Most memorably, President Clinton proposed a health security card as part of his nationalized health care plan. Both proposals met strong opposition and became a symbol of big government.

Most dramatically, in 1996 the House of Representatives rejected national ID cards during the consideration of the Illegal Immigration Reform and Immigrant Responsibility Act (HR 2202, 104th Congress). Rep. [Bill] McCollum (R-FL) offered an amendment "to make a Social Security card as counterfeit-proof as the $100 bill . . . and as free and protected from fraudulent use as a passport."[12] The Commissioner of Social Security opposed the amendment because the Administration was opposed "to the establishment, both de jure and de facto, of the Social Security card as a 'National Identification document.'"[13] The Commissioner also pointed out that SSA already included most of the anti-fraud features of the $100 bill.

Most recently, in 1999, a left-right coalition worked with Members on both sides of the aisle to repeal a provision in the 1996 Illegal Immigration and Immigrant Responsibility Reform Act that effectively coerced every state to place SSNs on every driver's license.

The lesson of the SSN is that once Congress establishes an infrastructure for tracking citizens, even if privacy protections are included, efficiency-driven "mission creep" turns a limited tool into a broad-based assault on privacy.

CONCLUSION

Congress should not set us on a track that would undermine our privacy, threaten equality, and challenge our very understanding of freedom. The ACLU strongly believes that our country must be safe, but security measures must be effective and need not come at the cost of our fundamental liberties. Congress should reject national identification systems in any form.

NOTES

1. *Hearing on Social Security Administration's Response to the September 11, 2001, Terrorist Attacks before the Subcommittee on Social Security of the House Committee on Ways and Means*, 107th Cong. (Nov. 1, 2001) (statements of Hon. James G. Huse Jr., Inspector General, Office of Inspector General, Social Security Administration).

2. Frank Wolfe, *Drivers License Scam Busted, Washington Times*, Dec. 7, 1990.

3. 1998, GEN. ACCT. OFF. REP. NO. GAO/HEHS-98-170, SOCIAL SECURITY: MASS ISSUANCE OF COUNTERFEIT-RESISTANT CARDS EXPENSIVE, BUT ALTERNATIVES EXIST.

4. 1990 GEN. ACCT. OFF. REP. NO. GAO/GGD-90-62, IMMIGRATION REFORM: EMPLOYER SANCTIONS AND THE QUESTION OF DISCRIMINATION.

5. Paul Rogers and Elise Ackerman, "National ID Prompts Feasibility Doubts in Technology Industry," *San Jose Mercury News*, Sept. 25, 2001.

6. 1998 GEN. ACCT. OFF. REP. NO GAO/IMD-99-38, IRS SYSTEMS SECURITY: ALTHOUGH SIGNIFICANT IMPROVEMENTS MADE, TAX PROCESSING OPERATIONS AND DATA STILL AT SERIOUS RISK.

7. John W. Fountain, "Former Top Chicago Detective Admits to Leading Theft Ring," *New York Times*, Oct. 26, 2001.

8. *See* note 3.

9. John J. Miller and Stephen Moore, *A National ID System: Big Brother's Solution to Illegal Immigration*, Cato Policy Analysis No. 237, Sept. 7, 1995.

10. 1998 GEN. ACCT. OFF. REP. NO GAO/GGD-98-100BR, IDENTITY FRAUD.

11. Lorraine Woellert, "Commentary: National IDs Won't Work," *Business Week*, Nov. 5, 2001.

12. 142 CONG. REC. H2452, (daily ed. March 19, 1996).

13. Letter from Shirley S. Chater, Commissioner, Social Security Administration, to the Honorable Jim Bunning, (March 19, 1996) (published in 142 CONG. REC. H2452, (daily ed. March 19, 1996)).

Questions for Discussion

1. If a national ID system is established, what kind of information should it contain?
2. What are the privacy implications of an ID card?
3. Who would favor a system of national ID and who would be opposed? What are the reasons for your answer?
4. To what do you attribute popular support of a national ID?
5. What impact would a national ID system have on (a) terrorism and (b) other crimes?
6. If a national ID system is established, who *should* be its users? And who *would* be its users?

Suggested Resources

Web Sites

Center for Democracy and Technology
   http://www.cdt.org

Computer Professionals for Social Responsibility: National Identification Schemes
   http://www.cpsr.org/program/natlID/natlIDfaq.html

Electronic Privacy Information Center: National ID Cards
   http://www.epic.org/privacy

Privacy.org
   http://www.privacy.org

Publications

Dershowitz, Alan M. "Why Fear National ID Cards?" *New York Times,* October 13, 2001, p. A23.
Eaton, Joseph W. *The Privacy Card: A Low Cost Strategy to Combat Terrorism.* Lanham, Md.: Rowman & Littlefield, 2002.
Eaton, Joseph W., and Amitai Etzioni. *The Limits of Privacy.* New York: Basic Books, 1999.
Garfinkel, Simson. *Database Nation: The Death of Privacy in the 21st Century.* Cambridge, Mass.: O'Reilly, 2001.
Kent, Stephen T., and Lynette I. Millett, eds. *IDs — Not That Easy: Questions about Nationwide Identity Systems.* Committee on Authentication Technologies and Their Privacy Implications, Computer Science and Telecommunications Board, Division on Engineering and Physical Sciences, National Research Council. Washington, D.C.: National Academy Press, 2002.

Kim, Walter. "The Matter of Reinvention." *Atlantic* 289, no. 5 (May 2002): 28–29.

Magnusson, Paul. "Yes, They Certainly Will." *Business Week,* November 5, 2001, pp. 90–91.

Miller, John J., and Stephen Moore. "A National ID System: Big Brother's Solution to Illegal Immigration." *Policy Analysis* no. 237. Washington, D.C.: Cato Institute, September 7, 1995.

Sykes, Charles J. *The End of Privacy.* New York: St. Martin's Press, 1999.

U.S. Cong., House. *Does America Need a National Identifier?* Hearing before the Subcommittee on Government Efficiency, Financial Management and Intergovernmental Relations of the Committee on Government Reform, 107th Cong., 1st Sess., 2001.

U.S. Cong., Senate. *A License to Break the Law? Protecting the Integrity of Driver's Licenses.* Hearing before the Senate Subcommittee on Oversight of Government Management, Restructuring, and the District of Columbia of the Committee on Government Affairs, 107th Cong., 2d Sess., 2002.

———. *Verification of Applicant Identity for Purposes of Employment and Public Assistance.* Hearing before the Subcommittee on Immigration of the Committee on the Judiciary, 104th Cong., 1st Sess., 1995.

Whitaker, Reg. *The End of Privacy: How Total Surveillance Is Becoming a Reality.* New York: New Press, 1999.

Woellert, Lorraine. "National IDs Won't Work." *Business Week,* November 5, 2001, pp. 90–91.

Is Racial Profiling
Ever Justified?

In 1992, the Maryland State Police stopped a car in which Robert Wilkins, an African American attorney, and his family were riding as they were returning from the funeral of Wilkins's grandfather in Chicago. Suspecting that the automobile carried drugs, a police officer asked the family to sign a consent order that would have permitted a police search of the contents of the vehicle. Wilkins refused, arguing that there was no basis for the police to conduct such a search.

The officer called in a drug-sniffing dog and other police officers while the Wilkins family waited in the rain outside of the car. The dog sniffed but the police found no drugs. Wilkins felt that the police had violated the constitutional rights of his family. With the help of the American Civil Liberties Union and two local law firms, Wilkins filed a federal civil rights damage suit against the Maryland State Police. He contended that he was a victim of racial discrimination, and that his constitutional rights had, consequently, been violated.

The particular kind of discrimination to which Wilkins was referring was racial profiling. Although there is no universally accepted agreement about the definition of the term, it can mean "the use of race, color, ethnicity or national origin as the determinative factor for initiating police action." Such was the definition used by New York City Police Commissioner Raymond Kelly in a directive to that city's police in March 2002 in which he stated that the New York Police Department could not use this procedure.

The State of Maryland settled the lawsuit by awarding Wilkins $96,000. It also agreed to end its official police policy of racial profiling. As a result of the investigation in this matter, it was learned that in 1995 for every 100 white people the Maryland police searched for drugs on highways, it searched 400 or 500 black people. It was also determined that the percentage of police success in finding drugs in this effort was about the same for white people as for black people.

The Maryland experience was not unique in the United States. Data for some other areas of the country show that members of minorities are stopped and searched more often than are white people. In 2000, for example, New Jersey State documents indicated that at least eight out of every ten automobile searches conducted by state troopers on the New Jersey Turnpike during most of the 1990s were carried out on vehicles driven by African Americans and Hispanics. Many other areas of the country showed somewhat similar disparities based on ethnic or racial grounds.

"Driving while black" is the expression used by some to describe the alleged offense of African Americans who are targets of police searches of their automobiles. Some African Americans driving expensive cars have been stopped by police, presumably on suspicion that the cars might be stolen. And a black man just sitting in a car in a white neighborhood could be interrogated by police, who suspected that he was there to commit a crime. African Americans have also been stopped while walking, or just sitting down while minding their own business. Polls show that many blacks and Hispanics — whether rich or poor, famous or relatively unknown — say that they personally have experienced racial profiling — targeted solely because of the color of their skin.

For their part, police often say that they do not engage in profiling; they are just doing their job. They do what is necessary to fight crime, they claim.

Critics of racial profiling point out that racial or ethnic identity alone is not by itself reasonable justification for conducting a search. They say that the Fourth Amendment of the Constitution grants citizens protection against unreasonable searches and seizures. And police behavior based on racial profiling is, consequently, a violation of a fundamental constitutional right.

Opposition to racial profiling is overwhelming both in and outside of government. A nationwide Gallup poll in 1999 revealed that 80 percent or more of whites and blacks disapproved of racial profiling. As president, Bill Clinton condemned the practice. In 2000, Vice President Al Gore and former senator Bill Bradley, opponents for the Democratic Party nomination for president that year, both promised to ban racial profiling by federal authorities. Republican presidential candidate George W. Bush came out against it in the presidential campaign, too.

In his first speech to Congress in February 2001, moreover, President Bush said of racial profiling: "It is wrong, and we will end it in America." He instructed Attorney General John Ashcroft to develop specific recommendations to terminate it. For his part, Ashcroft said that he thinks that racial profiling is unconstitutional. In the same year members of Congress of both major political parties proposed legislation to end racial profiling.

The problem of ending racial profiling is in the details. As indicated above, no universally accepted definition of racial profiling exists, so that the same act can be viewed as racism by one person and legitimate law enforcement by another. If a male member of a racial or ethnic minority group is playing his car's radio music so loud that the noise bothers people in the neighborhood in which he is driving, would a police officer who stops that individual be engaging in racial profiling? Some observers would say yes, on the grounds that the police were finding excuses to harass minority group members. Other observers would say no, because the police were just upholding the laws dealing with unwanted noise.

The issue of profiling took a new turn after the events of September 11, 2001. It became a matter involving people of Middle Eastern or South Asian heritage. The nineteen men who hijacked the four U.S. aircraft all had that background. A similar background, consequently, became the basis for questioning and sometimes searching and detaining airline travelers. Some people argued that the dangers of terrorism made profiling a necessity.

Is racial profiling ever justified? Economist Walter E. Williams argues that racial profiling is justified:

1. Race and other characteristics are correlated with many types of behavior, including criminal behavior.
2. Making assumptions about the behavior of an individual from a particular racial group, consequently, does not make the person who holds these assumptions a racist.
3. Ending racial profiling by police would put more black people at risk of being harmed than would be the case if there were no racial profiling because black people are the major victims of black criminals.

Law professor David A. Harris takes a critical view of racial profiling by offering these arguments:

1. Racial profiling is poor policing because it results unfairly in a disproportionate number of arrests of members of racial minorities who commit crimes rather than members of the white community who commit crimes even when the rate of criminal activity is actually the same for both groups.
2. Racially targeted traffic stops cause deep cynicism among black people about the fairness and legitimacy of law enforcement and courts.
3. The police can reduce crime without racial profiling, as the record of crime reduction shows in many cities in which the police have worked well with members of the minority community.
4. Community policing in which police have been involved with residents from minority areas and have become interested in their problems results in mutual trust among them. Racial profiling undermines that kind of trust.
5. Removing racial profiling can promote good policing and in so doing avoids federal government intervention in state and local law-enforcement matters.
6. The experience of London police in reforming its "stop and searches" policies is an example of how better police-community relations can be established.

☑ *YES*

Is Racial Profiling Ever Justified?

WALTER E. WILLIAMS
Racial Profiling

Former President Clinton called for a national crackdown on racial profiling and ordered federal law-enforcement authorities to begin an investigation. While running for president Al Gore promised the NAACP that if elected, eliminating racial profiling by the nation's police departments would be a top priority. New Jersey Governor Christie Todd Whitman fired Police Superintendent Carl Williams after the 35-year veteran trooper said in an interview that minorities are more likely to be involved in drug trafficking.

In 1996 New Jersey Superior Court Judge Robert E. Francis suppressed evidence and dismissed criminal charges against 19 black defendants because he found a "de facto policy of targeting blacks for investigation and arrest . . . violating the equal protection and due process clauses."

What is racial profiling? Does it serve any purpose? In the most general terms, racial profiling is a process whereby people employ a cheap-to-observe physical characteristic, such as race, as a proxy for a more costly-to-observe characteristic. It is prejudice, in the sense of the word's Latin root — the act of pre-judging, or the practice of making decisions on the basis of incomplete information.

Since the acquisition of information is not costless and requires the sacrifices of time and/or money, we all seek methods to economize on its acquisition. Prior to making a decision, people never obtain all of the information available or possible to obtain. For example, people prefer low prices to higher prices for a given purchase, but they never canvass *all* prices. In choosing a mate, we never obtain all possible information about our prospective spouse. In these and other decisions, we decide that a certain amount of information is "enough" and we search no more.

Consider the following example of pre-judging. Suppose on entering a room a person is unexpectedly confronted with the sight of a fully grown tiger. A fairly reliable prediction is that one would endeavor to leave the area in great dispatch or otherwise seek safety. All by itself that prediction is uninteresting. More interesting is the explanation for the behavior. Would the person's decision to run be based on any detailed information held about that *particular* tiger? Or would the decision be based on the person's stock of information about tigers in general, what his parents have told him about tigers, and tiger folklore? Most likely the individual's decision would be based on the latter. He simply pre-judges, or stereotypes, the tiger. The fact that it is a tiger is deemed sufficient information for action.

If a person did not pre-judge, or employ tiger stereotypes, his behavior would be different. He would endeavor to acquire additional information about the tiger before taking any action. Only if the tiger became menacing or lunged at him would he seek safety.

Most people so confronted by a tiger would not seek additional information. They would quickly calculate that the expected cost of an additional unit of information about the tiger is greater than the expected benefit.

PRE-JUDGING PEOPLE

What is popularly termed racial profiling represents pre-judging, where policemen disproportionately stop black motorists or pedestrians for identification, questioning, and contraband searches. We might ask: can one's racial characteristics serve as a proxy for some other characteristic not as readily observed? The answer is unambiguously in the affirmative. Knowing a person's race allows one to make some fairly reliable generalizations because race is correlated with a number of social and physical characteristics. Knowing that a man is black, one can assign a higher likelihood of his having diseases such as prostate cancer, sickle cell anemia, and hypertension. Knowing a person's race allows one to assign a probability to a host of socioeconomic characteristics such as scores on achievement tests, wealth status, criminal record, or basketball proficiency. Given this reality, we can no more reliably say that a policeman is a racist when he assigns a higher probability to a black's being a criminal, and stops him for questioning or search, than we can reliably say that a physician is a racist when he assigns a higher probability of prostate cancer to his black patients and screens them more carefully.

Jesse Jackson once commented, "There is nothing more painful for me at this stage in my life than to walk down the street and hear footsteps and start thinking about robbery — then look around and see somebody white and feel relieved." Jesse Jackson asserted a relationship between race and crime. Does that make him a racist?

There are certain high-crime areas of a city — maybe it is New York's Harlem or Washington, D.C.'s Anacostia — where taxicab drivers have been assaulted, robbed, and murdered. Out of safety concerns, white and black taxi drivers seek to identify and hence avoid passengers they suspect might ask to be driven to those areas. This is racial profiling, but it does not necessarily indicate racial preferences.

I've experienced racial profiling. One instance was when I resided in Chevy Chase, Maryland, an exclusive Washington suburb. A Saturday chore, resulting from owning a corner house, was to pick up trash discarded by motorists. Once while doing this, a white gentleman offered me a job cleaning up his property. When I thanked him and told him that I would be busy the rest of the day working on my dissertation, he apologized profusely.

The reality is that race and other characteristics are correlated, including criminal behavior.[1] That does not dispel the insult, embarrassment, anger, and hurt a law-abiding black person might feel when being stopped by police, watched in stores, being passed up by taxi drivers, standing at traffic lights and hearing car door locks activated, or being refused delivery by merchants who fear for their safety in his neighborhood. It is easy to direct one's anger at the taxi driver or the merchant. However, the behavior of taxi drivers and owners of pizza restaurants cannot be explained by a dislike of dollars from black hands. A better explanation is they might fear for their lives. The true villains are the tiny percentage of the black community who prey on both blacks and whites and have made black synonymous with crime.

One cannot unambiguously say that police racial profiling represents racist preferences. Racial profiling is practiced by both black and white policemen. Ending racial profiling by police would put more black people at risk. To the extent that black people commit more crimes than white people, to the extent that black people are the major victims of black criminals, to the extent that police stops catch criminals — to that extent, eliminating racial profiling would deprive law-abiding blacks protection from criminals.

NOTE

1. Percentage of black arrests for selected crimes, 1995: murder and non-negligent manslaughter, 54.4; forcible rape, 42.4; robbery, 59.5; aggravated assault, 38.4; burglary, 31; vehicle theft, 38.3; fraud, 34.7; receiving stolen property, 39.4; weapons violations, 38.8; drug violations, 36.9. *Crime in the United States, 1995 Uniform Crime Reports: Uniform Crime Reports* (Washington, D.C.: U.S. Government Printing Office, 1995), p. 226.

Is Racial Profiling Ever Justified?

DAVID A. HARRIS
Racial Profiling Is Not Justified

My subject this morning could not be more timely or — unfortunately — more familiar. I am here today to talk about racial profiling: the use of traffic offenses as an excuse — a pretext — to stop, question and search African-American and other minority drivers in numbers far out of proportion to their presence on the road. Police use this practice because there are officers who believe that having black or brown skin is an indication of a greater risk of criminality, and they therefore view all minorities as potential criminals. Skin color becomes evidence; the upshot is that all African-Americans and Hispanics become suspects every time they engage in the most common and prototypically American act: driving. Law enforcement officials try to explain profiling away as a rational response to crime, or as an efficient approach to policing. But the down and dirty of profiling is this: skin color used as evidence against thousands of innocent people every day.

African-Americans, Hispanics, and other minorities have complained about this police practice for years. Yet some still deny that it happens, in the face of strong statistical evidence to the contrary. In New Jersey, a rigorous statistical study showed that race was the only variable that could explain which drivers were stopped by the New Jersey State Police. The statistician who performed the analysis described these numbers as "literally off the charts" in terms of their statistical significance. In April of 1999, after five years of bitter struggle, New Jersey officials from Governor Whitman on down finally admitted what had long been obvious to people of color: troopers were engaged in profiling on the Turnpike. In Maryland, statistics turned over to a federal court by the Maryland State Police after the settlement of a major public civil rights lawsuit challenging profiling showed that on Interstate 95, where 17 percent of the drivers were black, more than 75 percent of those stopped and searched were black. In my own study of four cities in Ohio, completed just last year, police were roughly twice as likely to ticket black drivers as they were to ticket nonblack drivers. When lower vehicle ownership by blacks was factored in, the ratio rose to two and a half to three times as likely. The Ohio results dovetail with the results of ticketing studies in Texas, North Carolina, and other states.

The Traffic Stops Statistics Study Act, S.B. 821, can be the beginning of a serious discussion, and perhaps a resolution, of these issues. That bill, the first of its kind, proposes a study that would include the collection of statistics on all routine traffic stops in a national sample of jurisdictions. It would give us the first chance to get a firm and comprehensive grip on the scope and scale of the problem known to many as "driving while black." The idea behind the bill is to take a first step on the road toward addressing these practices by gathering the necessary evidence to lay the denials to rest once and for all. With data collection of all kinds becoming a standard practice in many aspects of law enforcement (New York's "COMPSTAT" program for mapping crime comes to mind), it seems odd that as of the beginning of last year, no state or major city had any mechanism in place for systematic collection of data on all traffic stops, a key law enforcement tactic that had been used for years. There were no numbers collected anywhere that would allow one to see the patterns of which drivers were stopped, how often, and for what. I argued in an article I published in 1997 that I had the privilege of presenting to the Congressional Black Caucus that legislation should require the collection of such statistics. S.B. 821, the bill we are here to discuss today, does just that. S.B. 821 requires participating police departments to collect comprehensive statistics for each and every routine traffic stop. Police would collect crucial data for analysis — age, race, and ethnicity of the driver, the reason for the stop, whether or not a search was conducted, the legal rationale for the search, whether any contraband was found, and what it was. The Justice Department would perform an initial analysis on currently available data within 120 days of the bill's passage; after two years of data collection, the Department would issue a comprehensive report containing a study of all the information collected.

STATE AND LOCAL DATA COLLECTION
LEGISLATIVE PROPOSALS AND INITIATIVES

The Traffic Stops Statistics Study Act has already had an important, perhaps unforeseen impact, beyond the Congress. The bill has inspired a host of similar measures at the state level. It has also become the catalyst and the template for data collection by local law enforcement agencies all across the country. These include police departments in Houston, San Diego, San Jose, Salt Lake City, San Francisco, and more than a hundred other municipalities, as well as state police departments in Florida, Washington State, Michigan, and other states. This past April, North Carolina became the first state to pass a bill requiring data collection. The head of the North Carolina Highway Patrol, Colonel Richard Holden, has said that he was glad to support this effort because, quite simply, "it was the right thing to do." In June, Connecticut became the second state to pass such a law. It is even more comprehensive than North Carolina's, since it covers every police agency in the state. (North Carolina's legislation applies only to stops by the Highway Patrol.) In just the last twelve months, the number of state legislative proposals to begin data collection on traffic stops grew from just a few to twenty, with new efforts sprouting all the time. There are now or have been bills pending in, among other states, California, Pennsylvania, Washington State, Utah, Missouri, Massachusetts, South Carolina, Illinois, Florida, Ohio, Maryland, New Jersey, Virginia, Rhode Island, and Oklahoma. Almost all of these bills are variations on the theme of comprehensive data collection first put forth in the Conyers bill. Most are customized, in some sense, to their individual states.

These actions and initiative manifest a real desire to begin correcting what people of color everywhere know to be a long-standing problem in their relationship with police and the entire criminal justice system. Bills requiring data collection (and, in the case of Connecticut, requiring anti-profiling policies) have become the way to focus this energy and begin the long journey toward addressing this civil rights issue on the state level.

SIX REASONS THAT COMING TO GRIPS WITH RACIAL PROFILING IS IN THE INTEREST OF LAW ENFORCEMENT

It is easy to understand why those immediately affected by profiling would want the country to confront the problem and root it out. It is an experience that produces fear, anger, humiliation, and can at times be physically dangerous. Perhaps less well understood is the fact that law enforcement itself has a huge stake in coming to grips with the problem. Simply put, police officers and law enforcement agencies have a tremendous amount to lose if profiling continues. Conversely, they have much to gain by addressing the problem forthrightly and directly.

1. Profiling as Poor Policing:
The Rational Discrimination Argument

When one hears the most common justification offered for the making of disproportionate numbers of traffic stops of African-Americans, it usually takes the form not of racism, but of rationality. Blacks commit a disproportionate share of certain crimes, the argument goes. Therefore, it only makes sense for police to focus their efforts on African-Americans. As a spokesman for the Maryland State Police said, this isn't racism — it is "the unfortunate byproduct of sound police policies." It only makes sense to focus law enforcement efforts and resources where they will make the most difference. In other words, targeting blacks is the rational, sound policy choice; it is the efficient approach as well.

This argument may sound appealing, but it ultimately fails. First, its underlying premise is wrong. Government statistics on arrests for drug crime (and drug crimes, not other offenses, are what the great majority of pretext traffic stops are about) tell us virtually nothing about the racial breakdown of those involved in drug crime. Think for a moment about arrest data in general. These statistics show that blacks are indeed overrepresented among those arrested for homicide, rape, robbery, aggravated assault, larceny/theft, and simple assault crimes. Note that all of these crimes are at least somewhat likely (much more likely in the case of homicide, less likely in the case of rape) to be reported to police and may then result in arrest; these crimes have victims, people directly affected by the crimes, who may do the reporting. By contrast, drug offenses are much less likely to be reported, since possessors, buyers, and sellers of narcotics are all willing participants in these crimes. This makes arrest data for drug crimes highly suspect. These data do not measure the extent of drug crimes. Rather, they measure law enforcement activity and the policy choices of many of the institutions and actors involved in the criminal justice system. Similarly, looking at the racial composition of prison and jail populations or the racial breakdown of sentences for these crimes only measures the actions of those who run our penal institutions and the officials who put together our criminal law and sentencing systems.

In point of fact, statistics on both drug use and drug crime belie the usual stereotypes: blacks may not, in fact, be more likely than whites to be involved with drugs. John Lamberth's study of traffic stops and searches in Maryland showed that among vehicles stopped and searched, the "hit rates" — the percentage of vehicles searched in which drugs were found — were statistically indistinguishable for blacks and whites. In a related situation, the U.S. Customs Service, which is engaged in drug interdiction efforts at the nation's airports, has used various types of invasive searches from pat downs to body cavity searches against travelers suspected of drug smuggling. The Custom Service's own nationwide figures show that while over 43 percent of those subjected to these searches were either black or Hispanic, "hit rates" for these searches were actually lower for both blacks and Hispanics than for whites — 6.7 percent for whites, 6.3 percent for blacks, and 2.8 percent for Hispanics. Similarly, it has long been established that most drug users are white, and that most users buy their drugs from people of their own race. This throws even more doubt on the usual stereotype of the drug dealer as a black or Latino.

We find the same counter stereotypical information when we look at data on drug use. The percentage of drug users among blacks and whites is roughly the same as the presence of those groups in the population as a whole. For example, blacks are roughly 12 percent of the population of the country; in 1997, the most recent year for which statistics are available, 13 percent of all drug users were black. In fact, among black youths — a demographic group often portrayed as most likely to be involved with drugs — there is evidence that use of all illicit substances has actually been consistently lower than among white youths for twenty years running.

Nevertheless, many continue to believe that African-Americans and members of other minority groups are responsible for most drug use and drug trafficking. Carl Williams, the head of the New Jersey State Police dismissed by the Governor in March of 1999, stated that "mostly minorities" trafficked in marijuana and cocaine, and pointed out that when senior American officials went overseas to discuss the drug problem, they went to Mexico, not Ireland. Even if he is wrong, if Williams and the many troopers who worked for him share these opinions, they will likely act accordingly. And they will do so by looking for drug criminals among black drivers. Blackness will become an indicator of suspicion of drug crime involvement. This, in turn, means that the belief that blacks are disproportionately involved in drug crimes will become a self-fulfilling prophecy. Because police will look for drug crime among black drivers, they will find it disproportionately among black drivers. This will mean more blacks arrested, prosecuted, convicted, and jailed, which of course will reinforce the idea that blacks are disproportionately involved in drug crimes, resulting in a continuing motive and justification for stopping more black drivers as a rational way of using resources to catch the most criminals. At the same time, of course — and this may be the worst part of rational discrimination from a pure law enforcement point of view — because police focus on black drivers, white drivers will receive less attention than they otherwise might, and the drug dealers and possessors among them will be apprehended in proportionately smaller numbers than their presence in the population would predict. In other words, rational discrimination will result in white drug dealers and possessors escaping prosecution in huge numbers, even as disproportionately high numbers of blacks are stopped and searched.

The upshot of this thinking is visible in the stark numbers that show what our criminal justice system does when it uses law enforcement practices like the racially-biased traffic stops to enforce drug laws. African-Americans are just 12 percent of the population and 13 percent of the drug users, but they are about 38 percent of all those arrested for drug offenses, 59 percent of all those convicted of drug offenses, and 63 percent of all those convicted for drug trafficking. Only 33 percent of whites but 50 percent of blacks convicted of drug crimes have been sent to prison, and incarcerated blacks get longer sentences than whites for the same crimes: for state drug defendants, the average maximum sentence length was fifty-one months for whites and sixty months for blacks.

2. The Creation of Corrosive Cynicism

Without doubt, racially-targeted stops cause deep cynicism among blacks about the fairness and legitimacy of law enforcement and courts. Thus it is no wonder that blacks view the criminal justice system in totally different terms than whites do; they have completely different experiences within the system than whites have, so they do not hold the same beliefs about it. Since traffic stops are among the most common encounters regular citizens have with police, it is hardly surprising that pretextual traffic stops might lead blacks to view the whole system differently. One need only think of the split screen television images that followed the acquittal in the O.J. Simpson case — stunned, disbelieving whites, juxtaposed with jubilant blacks literally jumping for joy — to understand how deep these divisions are.

But this cynicism is now beginning to creep into the general population's perception of the system. Polling data have long shown that blacks believe that the justice system is biased against them. For example, in a Justice Department survey released in 1999, blacks were more than twice as likely as whites to say they are dissatisfied with their police. More recent data show that a majority of whites believe that police racism toward blacks is common; specifically, a majority of both blacks and whites believe that racial profiling is a widespread problem that must be rooted out. Thus the damage done to the legitimacy of the system has spread across racial groups, from those most immediately affected to others.

Perhaps the most direct result of this cynicism is that there is considerably more skepticism about the testimony of police officers than there used to be. Predictably, this is especially true in minority communities, and pretextual traffic stops hammer this point home for these citizens. When a black driver asks a police officer why he has been stopped, the officer will probably explain that the driver committed a traffic violation. This may be literally true — a traffic offense probably has been committed, since virtually no driver can avoid committing one. But when the officer asks the driver whether he or she is carrying drugs or guns, and for consent to search the car, it becomes more than obvious that the traffic offense is not, in fact, the real reason that the officer stopped the driver. If the stop was really about enforcement of the traffic laws, there would be no need for these questions or any search. Of course, both the officer and the driver know this. It should surprise no one, then, that those subjected to this treatment regard the testimony and statements of police with suspicion. The result will likely be increasing difficulty for prosecutors when they go into court to try to convict the guilty in any case that depends upon police testimony, as so many cases do. The result may be more cases that end in acquittals or hung juries, even factually and legally strong ones.

3. Plunging Crime Rates:
There's More Than One Way to Skin a Cat

Over the last seven years, many cities in the United States have experienced steep and sustained drops in their crime rates, including homicide and other violent offenses. This is a national trend; it has happened in cities from one corner of the country to the other. Though experts are divided over what accounts for the drop — many say, candidly, that no one really knows what has caused it — one oft-mentioned possibility is the role that policing and crime-fighting tactics may have played in bringing this about.

No city has been more at the forefront of this debate than New York. Often thought of in the 1980's and early 1990's as a cesspool of crime, vice, and decay, New York has enjoyed rapid declines in all major categories of crimes. And New York's mayor, Rudolph Giuliani, has not been shy about taking credit for these developments and attributing them to his tough approach to policing: aggressive enforcement of laws against quality of life offenses like turnstile jumping, zero tolerance policies on offenses like putting graffiti on structures, and the use of hyper-aggressive squads like the Street Crimes Unit focused on stopping and frisking large numbers of people to look for guns and drugs. These measures may have been tough, but sometimes toughness is necessary, the mayor and his allies have argued. Judge us by our results. And by any measure, the results are impressive. Between 1991 and 1998, the number of homicides in New York City went from 29.31 to 8.60 per 100,000 citizens, a drop of 70.6 percent. In the same period, robberies dropped from 1,340 to 535 per 100,000 citizens, a 60.1 percent decline.

But this progress has come at a steep price. Even as crime has come down, the perception has grown that the New York City Police Department is especially hard on minorities, especially blacks and Latinos, and that these groups are being sacrificed — in the form of frequent stops, frisks, traffic stops, arrests, and general tough treatment accorded suspects — for the greater good. Indeed, crime rates are down, but minorities in New York — precisely those people most in need of the help of the police, since they are disproportionately the victims of crime — are more than twice as likely to express distrust of police than whites. Many express fear of the police. William J. Bratton, the Commissioner of Police during the first two years of the Giuliani administration, says that while the tough policing strategies may have been necessary at first, the next phase should have included reaching out and working with the black community and its leaders to build a solid foundation of cooperation. Failure to do so, he said, represents a lost chance to make progress not only on law and order in the city, but on race relations. And now, in the wake of the trial and acquittal of the four Street Crimes Unit officers who shot Amadou Diallo, the hidden costs of Giuliani's aggressive strategy have become apparent ever greater distrust and poisoned relations between police and minority citizens that will take years to overcome. New York City will be living with the consequences of these policies for a long time after its current leadership has left the scene.

But, as the old saying goes, there is more than one way to skin a cat. Contrast what has been happening in New York to events in the same time frame in two other cities: San Diego and Boston. Both have seen their crime rates plummet, but these cities have used very different approaches to policing from New York's. And in neither city will there be five, ten, or twenty years of poor relationships between police and citizens that will linger in the air like a noxious mist, as is likely to be the case in New York.

San Diego took an almost polar opposite position to New York. In the early 1990's, having already taken steps to improve training and statistical analysis of crime trends, San Diego looked for other promising approaches that might lead to further reductions in crime. Jerome Sanders, San Diego's police chief at the time, said that staffing realities — while New York has 5 officers per thousand citizens, San Diego had only 1.7 per thousand — dictated a different tack. New York's aggressive approach was simply out of the question. "Our basic premise was, we didn't have enough police officers to do it all, so we needed participation by the community," Sanders said. So San Diego's police force wholeheartedly adopted community policing, under which police and citizens become partners in the effort to make cities safer. The police divided the city into 99 neighborhoods, and assigned teams of officers to each. This allowed citizens to get to know their "own" officers; eventually, they began to give them information, cooperate with them, and help them solve problems in the neighborhood. San Diego also recruited and trained a force of 1,200 volunteer citizens to patrol neighborhoods, serving as the Department's eyes and ears.

Boston's approach has been different from those used in both San Diego and New York. But like San Diego's initiative, Boston did not rely on New York–style hardball tactics. It began with careful study, in an effort to figure out what the key sources of crime, especially violent crime, were, and how to reduce it with the least possible racial consequences. The racial impact of any effort was an important ingredient in the plan, since Boston had seen a number of high-profile crimes grow into community confrontations with significant racial overtones in recent years. The results of this examination pointed toward a focus not on drugs or gangs, but on gun violence, and on a small cluster of ringleaders who were responsible for the presence of guns on the street. Then, instead of taking it upon themselves to handle the enforcement effort alone, the police appealed to a coalition of black ministers and leaders for help and cooperation in going after the real bad guys. They then held "call-ins" — meetings among the ministers, the police and the individuals targeted for enforcement. These individuals were warned that if violence and the use of guns on the streets did not stop, they would be arrested and prosecuted in federal court, where they would face long sentences. Most heeded these warnings; those that did not were dealt with as promised. The focused nature of the program — both as to what problem to attack (guns and associated violence) and which people to target (the truly bad folks who refused to change their ways) alleviated the need to make widespread use of targeted traffic or pedestrian stops as New York did, with the racial antagonism that this brings. In the bargain, the Boston police built long-term cooperative relationships with the community that will allow them to approach other problems in the same way in the future, and at the very least to lessen the damaging "us vs. them" mentality so common in New York.

The result in San Diego and Boston has been progress against serious crime as good or even better than police in New York City have achieved with their zero tolerance, sweep-the-streets tactics. While homicide in New York fell 70.6 percent between 1991 and 1998, it declined almost as much — 69.3 percent — in Boston. And San Diego's results were even more impressive than New York's: a fall of 76.4 percent, the best in the country. The pattern was the same for robbery: a 62.6 percent decline in San Diego (again, the nation's best), followed by New York at 60.1

percent. Boston's robbery rate declined 50.2 percent. The lesson is obvious. There is no hard and fast trade-off required between making headway on crime and the relationship between police and the communities they serve. Making the streets safer does not require the sacrifice of the civil liberties of those in areas with crime problems, generating a significant backlash against the police. Simply put, there are other ways.

4. The Undermining of Community Policing

Another reason that it is in the interest of the police to come to grips with racial profiling follows directly from the discussion above of the successful efforts of the police in San Diego. Until recently, police departments have concentrated on answering distress calls. The idea was to have police respond to reports of crime relayed to them from a central dispatcher. In essence, these practices were reactive; the idea was to receive reports of crimes committed and respond to them.

But over the past few years, modern policing has moved away from the response model, which was thought to be too slow and too likely to isolate officers from the places in which they worked and the people there. In community policing, used so successfully in San Diego, the idea is for the police to serve the community and become part of it, not to dominate it or occupy it. This is done by becoming known to and involved with residents, understanding their problems, and attacking crime in ways that help address those difficulties. The reasoning is that if the police become part of the community, members of the public will feel comfortable enough to talk freely to officers and tell them what the troubled spots — and who the troublemakers — are. This will make for better, more proactive policing, aimed at problems residents really care about, and will make for a greater degree of appreciation of police efforts by residents and more concern for neighborhood problems and concerns by the police.

In many minority communities, the history of police community relations has been characterized not by trust, but by mutual distrust. In *Terry v. Ohio,* the 1968 case that is the fountainhead of modern street-level law enforcement, the Supreme Court candidly acknowledged this, saying that police had often used stop and frisk tactics to control and harass black communities. As one veteran African-American police officer put it, "Black people used to call the police 'the law.' They were the law. . . . The Fourth Amendment didn't apply to black folks; it only applied to white folks." For blacks, trusting the police is difficult; it goes against the grain of years of accumulated distrust and wariness, and countless experiences in which blacks have learned that police aren't necessarily there to protect and serve them.

Yet it is obvious that all of community policing — both its methods and its goals — depends on mutual trust. As difficult as it will be to build, given the many years of disrespect blacks have suffered at the hands of the police, the community must feel that it can trust the police to treat them as law-abiding citizens if community policing is to succeed. Using traffic stops in racially disproportionate ways works directly at cross purposes with this effort. Why should residents of these communities trust the police if, every time they go out for a drive, they are treated like criminals, even if this is done in an effort to catch wrongdoers? If the "driving while black" problem is not addressed, community policing will be made much more difficult or even fail. Thus, aside from the damage profiling inflicts on African-Americans, there is another powerful reason to change this police behavior: It is in the interest of police departments themselves to correct it.

5. Keeping the Feds Out

Several months ago, I testified at a legislative hearing in Pennsylvania concerning a bill aimed at tackling racial profiling. Among the witnesses was John Timoney, the Commissioner of the Philadelphia Police Department. Commissioner Timoney is a former New York City police officer and administrator, and by all accounts a cop's cop. In his approximately two years at the helm of Philadelphia's department, he has made substantial changes and improvement, and enjoys widespread support among both the public and his own officers. I found him a personally engaging and well-informed man — tough, no nonsense, but knowledgeable and ready with a joke, too. He advocated very effectively that day for law enforcement interests.

Two things Commissioner Timoney said that day have stayed with me. Asked at one point about the issues of race and policing generally, Timoney gave an answer startling for its candor. "You'd have to be brain dead," he said, to fail to recognize that police departments were going to have to deal with issues of race and law enforcement. Attempting to ignore the issue represented ostrich-like thinking, and it was clearly in the interest of law enforcement to meet these challenges head on, on its own terms. He also said something that pointed very strongly to the current headlines on racial profiling. He had, he said, a selfish reason of his own for wanting to deal with racial profiling and associated issues in his department: he wanted to keep the federal government away. Timoney reiterated this thought the next month in an interview with the New York Times. With an eye to federal consent decrees in New Jersey, Pittsburgh, Maryland, and elsewhere, as well as on a number of federal court orders governing the Philadelphia department when he began his stint as Commissioner, Timoney said "right now, my selfish ancillary goal is to keep the feds out of Philadelphia."

I certainly intend no disrespect here toward the federal government's efforts to rein in troubled police departments. Indeed, the use of "pattern and practice" jurisdiction by the U.S. Department's Civil Rights Division represents one of the most promising developments in the battle to force change upon law enforcement agencies with records of violating the civil rights of their citizens and failing to address these problems. Cases brought by the Department of Justice under these statutes have resulted in substantial reforms in a number of police departments at both the state and local level; the threat of litigation in these situations has acted as a stick to prod troubled police departments toward changes in situations in which a carrot alone would have been ineffective. In the first six years after the statute was passed, there have been four consent decrees entered, and there is one active contested piece of litigation going on now in Columbus, Ohio. Timoney's comment shows just how effective a tool these actions and the possibility of federal court intervention can be.

Timoney is right to want to avoid having federal officials or judges dictate the terms under which he runs his department. Presumably, he is the person responsible to Philadelphians and their elected officials for the quality of the police force and its work. And accountability requires authority. It is almost inconceivable that anyone would want such a demanding job — leader of a large police agency — without the ultimate authority to run the operation. Additionally, rules and directives imposed from the outside of a police department are less likely to be complied with by the rank and file than policies and orders generated from within. Timoney calls his desire to avoid federal intervention "selfish," but one could just as easily view it as a desire to lead his department himself, without unaccountable outsiders who are less knowledgeable than he is telling him what to do. If he is influenced in making his choices by the possibility that the federal government will intervene, so be it. The central concern is what Timoney does, not his reasons for doing it. For example, Timoney has taken some modest actions on racial profiling. These actions include focusing officers who stop cars on arrests of criminals, not just the making of traffic stops for their own sake. "When I came here cops were getting credit for the number of people they simply stopped every month. Can you believe that nonsense? We've reduced our stops by 50 percent. You get credit when you lock them up." Reducing abusive practices such as these is good policing — even if the reason for them is simply avoiding federal intervention.

6. The Experience of Great Britain: Better Policing

Some of you may know the name of Stephen Lawrence. Mr. Lawrence was a black citizen of Great Britain, living in the London area. Several years ago, he was murdered, a victim of racially motivated killing. By all accounts, London police, a force that has usually been seen as among the most professional and well trained in the world, not only bungled the investigation but did things that showed a truly startling degree of racial prejudice and insensitivity during the investigation. In the aftermath of the case, an official inquiry exposed this incompetence and outright racism, and this led to an examination of the relations between London police and racial minorities and to some concrete reforms. Among those reforms were stricter regulations on when and how police could perform "stops and searches" including — in a parallel to our own current debate — collection of data and statistical analysis of the data to see any racial patterns. Police decried the data collection requirement almost uniformly, saying it would waste their time and divert them from the real task of crime fighting.

Now, several years later, preliminary results are in, and they are striking. According to police officials, data collection and other reforms have had the effect of decreasing the number of pedestrian and traffic stops made by police. This was especially true initially; the effect is less dramatic now, but it still persists. But the upshot has been a much more effective use of these tactics than was previously the case. Police are using stops more judiciously and cautiously, focusing on those most worthy of police attention instead of using stops in a wholesale, dragnet fashion.

The result has been better policing — more focused, better crime fighting, better use of resources, and interactions with the public that are much less likely to produce cynicism and long-term damage to police community relations.

CONCLUSION

There is still some denial that racial profiling exists. But S.B. 821, the Traffic Stops Statistics Study Act, has begun a transformation in both the public's thinking and the public discourse about this problem. That change has now percolated down to the state and local level, as evidenced by the many state legislative proposals and local initiatives that have now begun. There is movement on this problem; there is momentum. And what we must realize is that while S.B. 821 shows us the right direction, it is up to every one of us to begin to do the heavy lifting that is ahead. Data collection on all traffic stops is surely the first step on this long road.

Questions for Discussion

1. Are there any circumstances in which police are justified in profiling members of a particular racial or ethnic group for law enforcement purposes? If so, what are those circumstances? If not, why not?
2. What criteria should be used by police in dealing with potential or actual criminal behavior in an area predominantly populated by a particular racial or ethnic group?
3. What impact does racial profiling have on crime?
4. What effect does racial profiling have on crime statistics?
5. What factors play a role in increasing trust between African Americans and local police in their community?

Suggested Resources

Web Sites

American Civil Liberties Union: Police Practices
http://www.aclu.org/PolicePractices/PolicePracticesList.cfm?c=118

Domelights.com: Racial Profiling
http://www.domelights.com/

Police Foundation
  www.policefoundation.org

Racial Profiling Data Collection Resource Center at Northeastern University
  http://www.racialprofilinganalysis.neu.edu/

Publications

Cussak, Lance, and Milton Heumann. *Good Cop, Bad Cop: Racial Profiling and Competing Views of Justice in America.* New York: P. Lang, 2003.

Demmer, Valerie L. "Civil Liberties and Homeland Security." *Humanist* 62, no. 1 (January/February 2002): 7–9.

Dutta, Sunil. "Sometimes Cops Profile by Race: So What? It's Not a Big Deal Unless There's Abuse." *Los Angeles Times,* October 30, 2001, p. B13.

Frederickson, Darin D., and Raymond P. Siljander. *Racial Profiling: Eliminating the Confusion between Racial and Criminal Profiling and Clarifying What Constitutes Unfair Discrimination and Persecution.* Springfield, Ill.: Charles C Thomas, 2002.

Glasser, Ira. "Racial Profiling and Selective Enforcement: The New Jim Crow." *The Brief* 30, no. 4 (Summer 2001): 31–39.

Harris, David A. *Profiles in Injustice: Why Racial Profiling Cannot Work.* New York: New Press, 2002.

Knight, Elizabeth A., and William Kurnik. "Racial Profiling in Law Enforcement: The Defense Perspective on Civil Rights Litigation." *The Brief* 30, no. 4 (Summer 2001): 16–23, 44.

Leitzel, Jim. "Race and Policing." *Society* 38, no. 3 (March/April 2001): 38–42.

Lowry, Richard. "Profiles in Cowardice." *National Review* 54, no. 1 (January 28, 2002): 32, 34, 36.

Mac Donald, Heather. *Are Cops Racist?* Chicago: I. R. Dee, 2003.

———. "The War on the . . . Police . . . and How It Harms the War on Terrorism." *Weekly Standard* 7, no. 16 (December 31, 2001): 26–30.

Meeks, Kenneth. *Driving While Black — Highways, Shopping, Taxicabs, Sidewalks: How to Fight Back If You Are Victims of Racial Profiling.* New York: Broadway, 2000.

Schultz, Evan P. "Whatever It Takes? There's No Good Way to Profile a Turk from a Pashtun from an Arab. Even If There Were, We Cannot Afford Another Racial Wound." *Legal Times,* October 1, 2001, pp. 51, 53.

Taylor, Stuart, Jr. "1984 No More: This Time, Uncle Sam Isn't Big Brother." *Legal Times,* October 8, 2001, p. 60.

U.S. Cong., Senate. *Racial Profiling within Law Enforcement Agencies.* Hearing before the Subcommittee on the Constitution, Federalism, and Property Rights of the Committee on the Judiciary, 106th Cong., 2d Sess., March 30, 2000.

U.S. General Accounting Office. *Racial Profiling: Limited Data Available on Motorist Stops.* Report to the Honorable James E. Clyburn, chairman, Congressional Black Caucus/United States General Accounting Office. Washington, D.C.: General Accounting Office, 2000.

6

Should the Death Penalty Be Abolished?

The Eighth Amendment to the Constitution forbids "cruel and unusual punishments" but does not specify what makes a punishment cruel or unusual. When the Bill of Rights was adopted, the death penalty, or capital punishment, as it is called, was not considered cruel or unusual. But particularly since the nineteenth century, there has been continuing controversy about the morality of capital punishment, not only in the United States but throughout the world. The global trend has been away from capital punishment. Today the United States is the only Western industrial country that allows the death penalty.

The death penalty has been brought before the Supreme Court on a number of occasions. In 1972, the Supreme Court decided in *Furman v. Georgia* to bar the death penalty as it was imposed under statutes at the time, objecting to the randomness of procedures.[1] As a result of the decision, most state legislatures enacted new laws complying with the *Furman* decision so that capital punishment could still be used as a punishment for major violent crimes.

The Supreme Court again considered capital punishment in 1976 in *Gregg v. Georgia.* In that case and in four related cases it accepted the constitutionality of the death penalty under certain conditions.[2]

The death penalty is under continuous legal challenge. One related issue the Supreme Court considered involved racism. In 1987, the Court rejected a challenge that capital punishment was more likely to be inflicted on African American defendants than whites and therefore violated the Equal Protection Clause of the Fourteenth Amendment.[3]

The death penalty is also under consideration in the executive and legislative branches. In the late 1980s and 1990s, political leaders sought to be "tough on criminals" by making punishments more severe: expanding the coverage of existing criminal laws, making it more difficult for prisoners to get parole, and strengthening capital punishment laws. Advocates of capital punishment also objected to the long time between sentencing and execution. Between 1976, when the death penalty was reinstated, until February 26, 2003, 834 people in the United States received the death penalty.[4] An estimated 3,692 people were on death row on January 1, 2003.[5] Many death row inmates die from natural causes while awaiting execution.

The slow progress of appeals through the court system is the principal reason for the delay. To speed the process, Congress directed in the Antiterrorism and Effective Death Penalty Act of 1996 that prisoners be barred from filing a second writ of habeas corpus unless a three-judge appeals court panel approves. (A habeas corpus writ orders a state to produce a prisoner before the court so that the inmate can make his or her case.)

This decision cannot be appealed. In addition, the statute expands the federal death penalty to more than fifty crimes. The law was enacted in response to outrage at the bombing of the World Trade Center and the Oklahoma City federal building. In 1996, the Supreme Court unanimously upheld the provision of the antiterrorism law restricting habeas corpus petitions.[6]

As of 2003, twelve states and the District of Columbia ban capital punishment. A number of proposals have been put forward for a moratorium on the death penalty at both the state and the national level. In January 2000, Illinois governor George Ryan appointed the Illinois Commission on Capital Punishment and halted all executions pending its report. He did so after Illinois had released thirteen innocent inmates from prison who had been on death row in the same time period that twelve had been put to death. In April 2002, the commission called for reforms, such as reducing the number of crimes subject to the death penalty and improving the procedures for appointing competent attorneys to represent individuals accused of crimes involving the death penalty.

On January 11, 2003, Ryan, who was about to complete his term as governor, commuted the sentences of all 167 of the Illinois inmates who were on death row, primarily to life in prison. He found the death penalty to be a flawed system of punishment because it was arbitrary and capricious, and therefore immoral.

At the federal government level, in 2001 U.S. Senator Russ Feingold from Wisconsin, a Democrat, proposed a National Death Penalty Moratorium Act. The proposed law would create a national commission to study the death penalty at the state and federal levels and would impose a moratorium on federal executions.

In the debate below, Senator Feingold argues for an end to the death penalty. He notes:

1. Many people convicted of heinous crimes and subject to a death penalty punishment had their convictions reversed. In some cases, innocent people on death row went to their death although they were innocent of the crimes for which they were tried.
2. The American system of justice requires that it is better to have many guilty people go free than for one innocent person to suffer.
3. The nation should interpret the Eighth Amendment provision of the Constitution forbidding no cruel and unusual punishment to mean no death penalty.

4. The majority of the world's nations have outlawed the death penalty, and the United States increasingly stands isolated in the civilized world because of this fact.
5. The death penalty varies in many respects. For the same crime, people who have money are less likely to receive the death penalty than people who do not.
6. The death penalty is applied unfairly to people of minority races, and it is applied differently to people of different parts of the country.
7. A look at the statistics shows that the death penalty does not deter crime. European countries that have outlawed the death penalty have a lower murder rate than the United States.
8. The taking of a human life oversteps the boundaries that should limit the powers of government.

Matthew T. Mangino, district attorney of Lawrence County, Pennsylvania, supports the death penalty. He is particularly critical of efforts aimed at establishing a moratorium on this sentence. He contends:

1. The death penalty is not racist.
2. Alternative punishment, such as life without parole, will easily be more costly to the government than the current system of capital punishment.
3. The death penalty is a deterrent to crime.
4. Without a doubt, the death penalty process in the United States is one of the most accurate criminal justice sanctions in the world so that the chances of an innocent person being subjected to the death penalty is infinitesimal.
5. A moratorium on the death penalty will do nothing more than put the lives of true innocents at risk.

NOTES

1. *Furman v. Georgia*, 498 U.S. 238 (1972).
2. *Gregg v. Georgia*, 428 U.S. 153 (1976).
3. *McCleskey v. Kemp*, Supreme Court docket no. 84–6811 (April 22, 1987).
4. Death Penalty Information Center at www.deathpenaltyinfo.org, accessed March 3, 2003.
5. NAACP Legal Defense Fund, *Death Row USA*, January 1, 2003, as cited in www.deathpenaltyinfo.org, accessed March 3, 2003.
6. *Felker v. Turpin*, 116 S. Ct. 2533 (1996).

✓ *YES*

Should the Death Penalty Be Abolished?

RUSS FEINGOLD

A New Millennium:
Time to Stop Tinkering with the Machinery of Death

When Anthony looked at the calendar, he could see that he had only two more days to live. Where must your thoughts run when you can taste your own death in your mouth?

Do they turn, to paraphrase the lyricist Jonathan Larson: To sunsets, to midnights, to cups of coffee? To inches, to miles, to the roads you will not travel? To laughter, to strife, to the smiles you will not see? To mothers, to loves, to the children you won't embrace? To two thousand, eight hundred, eighty minutes? Of what do you ponder, when you think of your last two days on earth?

Anthony Porter came to that place in September 1998, on death row, in Cook County, Illinois. Sadly, in the United States of America at the turn of the 21st century, the organized citizenry of 38 states and our Nation itself will almost certainly this year put a hundred people in that same place, wondering of what to think, with just two days to live. And the story was sadder still, because Anthony was innocent.

At the dawn of a new millennium, after five thousand years of recorded history, the time has come to reconsider whether government-sponsored killing should stop.

Society can take few more momentous decisions than to bring about the death of another human being. The decision takes from that person simply everything, alpha and omega, all that is or ever could be. In duration, the decision continues forever, irrevocably, without the remotest possibility of turning back.

Justice demands that where the consequences are so complete and final, the decision must be completely certain. When the destination is "the undiscover'd country from whose bourn no traveler returns," one must hesitate to step.

For Anthony Porter, when the calendar said that he had only two more days to live, the Illinois Supreme Court stayed his execution. A team of Northwestern University journalism students and their professor then tracked down the truth. They obtained a confession from another man, on videotape, that he had actually committed the crime. An Illinois judge ordered Anthony released from prison, after nearly 17 years in prison, separated from his mother, separated from his six children.

And then there's Ronald Jones, whom the people of Illinois had sentenced to die for the rape and murder of a Chicago woman. DNA evidence was found that exonerated Ronald.

And Anthony and Ronald are not really exceptional cases. Since the Supreme Court reinstated the death penalty in 1973, the people of Illinois have executed 12 people, and have lifted the death sentence from the shoulders of 13 people who had been on death row. The manifest uncertainty with which Illinois has been convicting defendants and sentencing them to die has led Governor George Ryan to impose a moratorium on carrying out the death penalty while he examines the system.

And Illinois is not alone in its predicament. Nationwide, since the Supreme Court reinstated the death penalty in 1973, courts have freed 85 people from death rows throughout the country. Even after prosecutors, juries, and courts decided beyond a reasonable doubt that each of these defendants deserved to die, other courts on reexamination found errors in judgment sufficient to reverse that decision. These reviews have freed one death row inmate from execution for every seven inmates executed. Just as the proverbial 13th stroke of a clock calls into question not only itself but the 12 other chimes that preceded it, this scandalously large number of demonstrated errors calls into question the certainty of the entire enterprise of killing.

A 1987 study found that between 1900 and 1985, 350 people convicted of capital crimes in the United States were innocent of the crimes charged. Many of those people came to that place where they had only two days to live. Some escaped execution by minutes. Regrettably, according to researchers Radelet and Bedau (in their 1992 work *In Spite of Innocence*), 23 had their lives taken from them in error.

The Marquis de Lafayette once said, "I shall ask for the abolition of the death penalty until I have the infallibility of human judgment demonstrated to me."

And when, in the wake of the Boston Massacre, John Adams defended the British soldiers accused of committing the killings there, he said:

> [I]t [is] more beneficial that many guilty persons should go unpunished than one innocent person should suffer. . . . [W]hen innocence itself is brought to the bar and condemned, especially to die, the subject will exclaim, "It is immaterial to me whether I behave well or ill, for virtue itself is no security."

This is the central pillar of the American system of justice, that it is better that many guilty should go free than that one innocent should suffer. Sadly, history has demonstrated that time and again, America has brought innocence itself to the bar and condemned it to die. That history now demonstrates that even in America, innocence itself has provided no security from the ultimate punishment.

Leonel Herrera may have been innocent, but he could not demonstrate it to the satisfaction of the Supreme Court. A former Texas judge submitted an affidavit swearing that another man had confessed to the crime for which Leonel faced execution. But the Supreme Court said that at the late stage of his appeal, Leonel needed an extraordinary amount of proof to stop his execution. The people of Texas put him to death in 1993.

In response to the decision, Justice Harry Blackmun warned: "The execution of a person who can show that he is innocent comes perilously close to simple murder."

Because as long as there are executions, fallible humans will never to a certainty be able to avoid executing the innocent, the killing must stop.

From the beginning of memory, our species has debated the morality of killing. From the time of Hammurabi, nearly four thousand years ago, humans organized as a government have made killing an offense against the state. We think of Hammurabi as a great lawgiver for introducing proportionality to punishment.

But as much as we credit Hammurabi the lawgiver, his code also prescribed punishments from which civilized society came to shrink. Hammurabi literally calling for an eye for an eye — not just the metaphorical eye for an eye to which the Bible alludes. Hammurabi's code called for breaking the bone of an aristocrat who broke another aristocrat's bone, for cutting off the hand of a son who struck his father. And among the 282 legal paragraphs in Hammurabi's code were 30 capital offenses, including death for the thief who could not afford to make restitution, and including death for an aristocrat's daughter whose father killed another aristocrat's daughter. I am thankful that, over the long millennia, the human race has moved to reject many of the cruel punishments from our ancient past.

The framers of the American Constitution wrote into that document that: "Excessive bail shall not be required, nor excessive fines imposed, nor cruel and unusual punishments inflicted." Even at that time, such leaders as Benjamin Rush of Pennsylvania, a signer of the Declaration of Independence and a Member of the Continental Congress, wrote in opposition to the death penalty. Benjamin Rush warned of the death penalty: "It lessens the horror of taking away human life, and thereby tends to multiply murders."

And in the 1972 case of *Furman v. Georgia*, the Supreme Court held that, at least as it was then administered, the imposition and carrying out of the death penalty in the cases then before the Court constituted cruel and unusual punishment in violation of the Eighth and Fourteenth Amendments.

In his concurrence in *Furman*, Justice [William O.] Douglas wrote: "It would seem to be incontestable that the death penalty inflicted on one defendant is 'unusual' if it discriminates against him by reason of his race, religion, wealth, social position, or class, or if it is imposed under a procedure that gives room for the play of such prejudices."

Justice Douglas continued:

[T]he words ["cruel and unusual"], at least when read in light of the English proscription against selective and irregular use of penalties, suggest that it is "cruel and unusual" to apply the death penalty — or any other penalty — selectively to minorities whose numbers are few, who are outcasts of society, and who are unpopular, but whom society is willing to see suffer though it would not countenance general application of the same penalty across the board.

Justice [William J.] Brennan, in his concurrence, wrote:

If a punishment is unusually severe, if there is a strong probability that it is inflicted arbitrarily, if it is substantially rejected by contemporary society, and if there is no reason to believe that it serves any penal purpose more effectively than some less severe punishment, then the continued infliction of that punishment violates the command of the Clause that the State may not inflict inhuman and uncivilized punishments upon those convicted of crimes.

Justice Brennan concluded: "Under these principles and this test, death is today a 'cruel and unusual' punishment."

Justice [Potter] Stewart wrote: "These death sentences are cruel and unusual in the same way that being struck by lightning is cruel and unusual. For, of all the people convicted of rapes and murders in 1967 and 1968, many just as reprehensible as these, the petitioners are among a capriciously selected random handful upon whom the sentence of death has in fact been imposed."

Justice [Byron R.] White concluded that "the death penalty is exacted with great infrequency even for the most atrocious crimes and . . . there is no meaningful basis for distinguishing the few cases in which it is imposed from the many cases in which it is not."

And Justice Thurgood Marshall wrote in his concurrence: "I cannot believe that at this stage in our history, the American people would ever knowingly support purposeless vengeance. Thus, I believe that the great mass of citizens would conclude on the basis of the material already considered that the death penalty is immoral and therefore unconstitutional."

But then four years later in the 1976 case of *Gregg v. Georgia,* the Court held that the death penalty does not invariably violate the Constitution. Thirty-eight states and the federal government have since found ways to draft death penalties that meet with the Supreme Court's approval, but as Judge Irving Kaufman wrote, "One generation's dissents have often become the rule of law years later."

I remember the day, after the Supreme Court reinstated the death penalty, the first execution took place in 1977 in Utah, when Gary Gilmore aggressively sought his own death by a firing squad. But I more vividly remember the day in May 1979 when the first involuntary execution took place. That morning, I finished my last law school exam. Later that day, I turned on the television and saw the news report that Florida had just executed John Spenkelink. I was overcome with a sickening feeling. The education in law that I had just completed had filled me with the belief that our legal system was advancing inexorably through the latter quarter of the 20th century. Instead, to my great dismay, I beheld a throwback to the electric chair, the gallows, and the routine executions of our Nation's violent past. I will never forget that experience. I will never forget that day.

Today, throughout our Country, people of conscience are questioning the killing by the state that is carried out in our name. The Nebraska legislature passed a moratorium, although the governor vetoed it. Legislators in Alabama, Maryland, New Jersey, Oklahoma, Pennsylvania, and Washington state have introduced moratorium legislation. And last month, the New Hampshire House became the first legislative body in the Nation to vote to abolish an existing capital punishment law since the Supreme Court reinstated it in 1976. This February, Philadelphia's City Council became the eighth municipality to urge a halt to executions.

I have introduced legislation in the United States Senate to abolish the federal death penalty. In the House of Representatives, Congressman Jesse Jackson Jr. has also introduced a moratorium bill. Representative Jackson and I have met with administration officials to press for a moratorium on the application of the federal death penalty.

In 1997, the American Bar Association adopted a resolution calling for a moratorium. And late last year, the National Jewish/Catholic Consultation — a joint effort of the National Conference of Catholic Bishops and the National Council of Synagogues — issued a joint statement calling for the end of the death penalty, drawing on both ancient religions' teachings, from second-century rabbis to Pope John Paul II.

And the balance of the world has distinctly moved away from the death penalty. By Amnesty International's count, over a hundred countries — the majority of countries in the world — have now abolished the death penalty in law or practice.

Since 1985, more than 35 countries have abolished the death penalty or, having previously abolished it for ordinary crimes, have abolished it for all crimes. These countries span the globe, from Angola to Azerbaijan, from Canada to Cambodia, from Moldova to Mozambique. During the same period only four countries reintroduced the death penalty, and one of those — Nepal — abolished it again.

It used to be that the United States stood with only the Soviet Union and South Africa in the industrialized world in its embrace of capital punishment. But Russia's former President Boris Yeltsin imposed a moratorium on all executions in August 1996. And South Africa's Constitutional Court declared the death penalty unconstitutional in 1995 and then its parliament voted to abolish it.

In 1998, the United States was one of just four countries that together accounted for 86 percent of all executions recorded by Amnesty International worldwide. We now stand in the company of China, the Democratic Republic of Congo, and Iran. Amnesty International has also received reports of hundreds of executions in Iraq, but could not confirm the reports.

In 1989, the United Nations General Assembly adopted the Second Optional Protocol to the International Covenant on Civil and Political Rights, which provides for the peacetime abolition of the death penalty. At least 40 countries have now ratified the Protocol.

At least 33 European states have now ratified Protocol Number 6 to the European Convention for the Protection of Human Rights and Fundamental Freedoms, which also abolishes the death penalty in peacetime.

Three international conventions prohibit sentencing to death anyone who was under 18 years old at the time of their crime. The United Nations Subcommission on the Promotion and Protection of Human Rights adopted a resolution that condemned the United States, along with Iran, Nigeria, Saudi Arabia, Pakistan, and Yemen, for executing juvenile offenders. A report to the United Nations Commission on Human Rights also criticized the United States for breaching international standards in executing mentally handicapped defendants, a practice allowed in 28 of the 38 American states that have capital punishment.

Last year [1999], the United Nations Human Rights Commission voted in favor of a resolution supporting a worldwide moratorium on executions. The United States voted against the resolution along with 10 other countries, including China, Bangladesh, Botswana, Indonesia, Pakistan, Rwanda, Sudan, and Qatar.

The European Union has passed a resolution calling for the immediate and unconditional global abolition of the death penalty, and called on all states within the United States to abolish the death penalty. Germany announced that it would sue the United States in the International Court of Justice in The Hague for violating international laws and treaties by executing two German nationals last year in Arizona without consular access and notification of German authorities. German Justice Minister Herta Daeubler-Gmelin criticized the United States, saying, "Respecting international law cannot be a one-way street."

I traveled to ten countries in Africa at the end of last year, and I would often raise human rights issues with government officials with whom I met. I can remember that I questioned the minister of one government about its detaining journalists. The minister replied: "You can hardly criticize us for imprisoning journalists when you have people sitting on death row for 20 years."

Because our use of the death penalty increasingly isolates us in the civilized world, the killing must stop.

Other nations criticize the United States for the way in which our Nation has applied the punishment disparately by class and race.

The columnist Sydney Harris wrote in the *Chicago Daily News:* "One of the oldest Russian proverbs remains as inexorably true in modern America: 'No one is hanged who has money in his pocket.' Or as one might say, capital punishment is only for those without capital."

As well, the application of the death penalty also varies dramatically from one part of the country to another, or even within different areas of the same state. For example, a *USA Today* study found that those who commit a murder in upstate New York are more likely to receive a death sentence than those arrested here in New York City or its three largest suburban counties.

Most insidiously, the evidence mounts that the United States applies the death penalty differently to people of different races. Look at the numbers: Although African-Americans constitute only 13 percent of the American population, since the Supreme Court reinstated the death penalty in 1976, African-Americans account for 35 percent of those executed, 43 percent of those who wait on death row nationwide, and 67 percent of those who wait on death row in the Federal system. Although only 50 percent of murder victims are white, fully 84 percent of the victims in death penalty cases were white. Since 1976, America has executed 11 whites for killing a Black, but has executed 144 Blacks for killing a white.

The ghosts of institutional racism still haunt our courthouses. They intrude when lawyers select jurors, during the presentation of evidence, when the prosecutor contrasts the race of the victim and defendant, and when juries deliberate. The numbers tell the story: no matter how hard most of us try to exorcize the demons of our Nation's past, we cannot seem to overcome their hold.

Because the risk appears substantial that people are dying because of the color of their skin, the killing must stop.

Some will say that the death penalty deters crime. Were that so, Europe would have a higher murder rate than the United States. But it doesn't, and it's not even close. The murder rate in the United States is six times that in Britain, seven times that in France, and five times that in Sweden.

But we don't even need to look across the Atlantic to see that capital punishment fails to deter crime. When Canada abolished the death penalty for murder, the homicide rate per 100,000 population fell from a peak of 3.09 in 1975, the year before abolition, to 2.41 in 1980, and has remained relatively stable since. Canada's abolition of the death penalty has not led to more murders.

Even closer to home, compare Wisconsin and Texas. I'm proud that my state of Wisconsin was the first in this Nation to abolish the death penalty completely, when it did so in 1853. Wisconsin has been death penalty–free for nearly a century and a half. In contrast, Texas is the most prodigious user of the death penalty, having executed about 200 people since 1976. But from 1995 to 1998, Texas has had a murder rate nearly twice that in Wisconsin. The deterrent value of the death penalty is more fable than fact.

Because the death penalty does not deter crime, the killing must stop.

Indeed, as George Bernard Shaw wrote, "It is the deed that teaches, not the name we give it. Murder and capital punishment are not opposites that cancel one another, but similars that breed their kind."

Just as parents who beat their children often raise children who grow up to beat their own children, the death penalty teaches the appropriateness of killing. Death begets death. For from the days of the Flood, we have known the wisdom that "Whoso sheddeth man's blood, by man shall his blood be shed."

Society breeds a casual attitude toward killing and death when through its government it sanctions the death penalty. With each new death penalty statute enacted and each execution carried out, our governments add to a culture of violence and killing. With each person executed, society teaches our children that the way to settle scores is through violence, even to the point of taking a human life.

Let me be clear. I believe that we must severely punish murderers and other violent offenders. I do not seek to open the prison doors and let murderers rush out into our communities. This is not about letting criminals off the hook. The question is not whether to free them. The question is whether our society should kill them.

William Randolph Hearst said, "What is murder in the first degree? It is cruel, calculated, cold-blooded killing of a fellow human man. It is the most wicked of crimes and the State is guilty of it every time it executes a human being."

Or, as the mathematician Blaise Pascal said, "Must we kill to prevent there being any wicked? This is to make both parties wicked instead of one."

Because the institution of the death penalty declares on behalf of all of us that killing is right, the killing must stop.

And should there not be some limit to the powers that the government can arrogate to itself in the name of the people?

Juan Raul Garza, who sits on death row in the Federal system, has exhausted his appeals. Sometime soon, he could become the first prisoner that the Federal Government has executed since 1963. What right does the Nation that represents us all have to kill this man in the name of us all, including those of us who live in the 12 states and the District of Columbia that have chosen to abolish the death penalty?

George Bernard Shaw said: "Assassination on the scaffold is the worst form of assassination, because it is invested with the approval of society."

Let it not be said that this is the will of the people. There should be some things beyond the power of a simple majority to elect. It should be beyond their power, to make us all complicit.

The philosopher Nicholas Berdyaev wrote: "Capital punishment is murder pure and simple. . . . It is the most striking instance of the state overstepping its legitimate boundaries, for human life belongs to God and not to man."

Think of the hubris. We mortals, when we put on black robes and employ uniformed men who carry guns, take upon ourselves the power of life and death. We cannot create a life, but we arrogate to ourselves the power to end it. As Benjamin Rush wrote, the death penalty is a "usurpation of the prerogative of heaven." At the least, it is a lack of due humility.

Because "Vengeance is mine . . . saith the Lord," the killing must stop.

Regardless of their crimes, those who wait on death row are still people.

Those who wait on death row are people, people who love, people who hope, people who feel pain. Many are fathers and mothers to children. Each one is some mother's child.

Because the condemned are people too, this government-sponsored killing must stop.

Among the Ten Commandments, the sages linked the commandment "Thou shalt not kill" to the first commandment about the identity of God, for when one destroys any single person, one effaces the divine image, which every person bears.

Because killing cheapens the value of life, the killing must stop.

This February [2000], Betsy Wolfenden of Carrboro, North Carolina, wrote the *Washington Post* about those whom she called "the other victims of murder: the children of the men and women on our death rows." Betsy wrote:

> My husband — who is on death row — and I have four children. Our children have suffered greatly because of the actions of their father. Although our children recognize that their father did something terribly wrong, they still love and need their dad.
>
> The . . . children whose parents are on death row . . . suffer in silence. I know of one 9-year-old who writes on his calendar, "Daddy dies today," each time his father receives a new execution date. . . .
>
> . . . I would like to tell the families who have been harmed by the murders committed by our loved ones that we understand the pain they are feeling because we feel that pain, too. Their children are innocent victims — but so are ours. I pray that all children whose parents have been murdered will find comfort and peace. But my children may also lose their dad to murder, and I wonder who will weep for them.

That's what Betsy Wolfenden wrote.

Now, of course, I do not seek to absolve this man, or any murderer, for the wrongs that he or she did. But neither can our righteous anger with those wrongs blind us to the unnecessary further wrong that will be done these innocent children.

Because we should always strive, in this imperfect world, that no innocent child should have to bewail the loss of a parent to killing, the killing must stop.

The great lawyer Edward Bennett Williams summarized: Capital punishment "is inhuman because its deterrent effects are now recognized as myth. It is unjust because it leaves no remedy for mistake. It is unequal because it is exacted almost exclusively of the poor and the ignorant. It is, in effect, a relic of the barbarous days when our law demanded an eye for an eye."

Because the death penalty has become, in Justice Benjamin Cardozo's words, "an anachronism too discordant to be suffered, mocking with grim reproach all our clamorous professions of the sanctity of life," the killing must stop.

Because, as Martin Luther King Jr. said, "The old law of an eye for an eye leaves the whole world blind," the killing must stop.

When he retired from his long career of supporting the death penalty, after voting against suspending it in *Furman v. Georgia,* and after voting to reinstate it in *Gregg v. Georgia,* the late Justice Lewis Powell told his biographer in 1991: "I have come to think that capital punishment should be abolished." Justice Powell came to find that the decision he most regretted was that in *McCleskey v. Kemp,* which held that statistical evidence of disparate racial application was insufficient to overturn the death penalty.

And in his 1994 dissent in the case of *Callins v. Collins,* the late Justice Harry Blackmun wrote:

> From this day forward, I no longer shall tinker with the machinery of death. For more than 20 years I have endeavored — indeed, I have struggled — ... to develop procedural and substantive rules that would lend more than the mere appearance of fairness to the death penalty endeavor. Rather than continue to coddle the Court's delusion that the desired level of fairness has been achieved ..., I feel morally and intellectually obligated simply to concede that the death penalty experiment has failed. ... The problem is that the inevitability of factual, legal, and moral error gives us a system that we know must wrongly kill some defendants. ...

Like Justices Powell and Blackmun, let us too reconsider our Nation's position, and stop the tinkering with the machinery of death. Let us stop the killing to protect the innocent who have all too often been condemned to die. Let us stop the killing to join the civilized world in its progress from the barbaric past. Let us stop the killing so as not to reopen again and again the ancient wounds of racial discrimination. Let us stop the killing to honor the value of human life. And let us stop the killing to demonstrate once and for all that, not just with our eyes, we finally can see.

☑ *N O*

Should the Death Penalty Be Abolished?

MATTHEW T. MANGINO
Death Penalty Moratorium

Frustrated by overwhelming and persistent public support for the death penalty, opponents of the death penalty are using a nationwide call for a moratorium as a strategy to stop executions. Capital punishment has inflamed supporters and opponents since the Supreme Court addressed the issue during the Nixon administration.

In 1972, the High Court in *Furman vs. Georgia* invalidated the death penalty, finding it discriminatory. In the years that followed, thirty-eight states and the federal government rewrote their respective sentencing statutes. The death penalty was not gone for long. Currently, more than three out of four states have the ability to execute convicted murders.

Thirty years after the *Furman* decision, the state of Illinois imposed a moratorium on the death penalty. Illinois has created the Ryan Commission on Capital Punishment. The committee's eighty-five suggested reforms have just become public. This month [June 2002], Maryland joined Illinois in imposing a moratorium on the death penalty.

Death penalty opponents and moratorium supporters provide various reasons for promoting a temporary hiatus. They suggest race, cost, execution of innocents and the lack of a deterrent effect. These "concerns" are not founded in reality. A close review of their arguments is telling.

I. RACE

Death penalty opponents argue that 42 percent of death row inmates are black. Blacks make up 13 percent of the population. Therefore, they conclude the system is prejudiced.

However, this argument assumes that people are executed by some random selection process like a court jury pool. According to the latest Bureau of Justice statistics, blacks commit 51 percent of all murders in this country. According to undisputed statistics, white murderers are twice as likely to be executed in the United States, as are black murderers. In addition, white murderers are executed twelve months quicker, on average, than their black counterparts.

In the early 1970s, the NAACP sponsored a study of the new death penalty statute in Georgia. The study was led by Dr. David Baldus, an ardent death penalty opponent. Baldus looked hard for evidence that black killers are more likely to be executed than white killers. He concluded, "What is most striking about these results is the complete absence of any race-of-defendant effect."

II. COST

The savings, if any, that would result from fewer trials and appeals without the death penalty, will certainly be surpassed by the cost of life without parole. The cost of geriatric and medical care will easily surpass the cost we currently expend on the appeals of capital convictions.

The strategy of the anti-death penalty movement is apparent. First, run up the cost of capital punishment by promoting costly never ending appeals. Then, after engaging in endless delaying appeals, come back and argue that the whole process is too expensive.

The Ryan Commission has proposed additional training for judges in capital cases, [and] two trained, competent attorneys for each capital defendant and two equally competent prosecutors.

How much will that cost and who is going to bear the burden? Dual "competent" counsel will cost dramatically more. Should we also suppose that a defendant sentenced to life without the possibility of parole would not file endless appeals and requests for post conviction review?

III. DETERRENTS

The assertion that the death penalty doesn't deter killers flies in the face of everyday common sense. Significantly, not even the anti-death penalty studies have been able to say that no one is deterred by the death penalty.

Two independent studies released over the past two years have found to the contrary. The first study by economists at Emory University found that for each murderer executed there were eighteen less murders. The second, the Cloninger and Marchesini study at the University of Houston, concluded that the 1996 de facto moratorium on the death penalty in Texas resulted in 200 more homicides. Why is there no hue and cry for those two-hundred wholly innocent citizens who, unlike their killers, did not deserve to die?

IV. INNOCENTS EXECUTED

Death penalty opponents have argued that 101 innocent people have been released from death row since 1972, the most recent from Lawrence County, Pennsylvania.

A close review of those cases would provide only thirty factually innocent situations. That equates to less than one-half of one percent of the 7,000 defendants sentenced to death.

Barry Scheck, co-founder of the Innocence Project, stated that he had no proof of an innocent being executed in the United States since the *Furman* decision.

Some commentators have suggested that the death penalty phase of a trial should be tied to some unattainable standard or burden of proof like mathematical perfection. However, the United States Supreme Court has already stated that those subject to the death penalty in the United States receive Super Due Process. From 1973 to 2000, six-thousand nine-hundred and thirty (6,930) people were sent to death row. Two-thousand four-hundred and one (2,401) of those cases, or 35 percent, were overturned on appeal. Six-hundred eighty-three, or 9.4 percent, were executed after an average of ten years of review. The United States death penalty process is without doubt the most accurate criminal justice sanction in the world.

In Pennsylvania, since 1976 only three death row inmates were executed, all at their own request. Twelve had died of natural causes. By far the greatest threat today is not the death of an innocent on death row but the death of a true innocent as a result of a moratorium on the death penalty.

Recently, escaped murderers murdered at least three innocent people. That is three more than we have proof of innocents executed since 1973. According to Capital Punishment 2000, at least 8 percent of those on death row had committed one or more murders prior to the murder which put them on death row. This suggests that those sent to death row had murdered six-hundred additional innocent people after the system failed to properly restrain them following their previous murders.

With the Super Due Process afforded to defendants sentenced to death, death penalty defendants are the least likely to be wrongly executed. If we are to focus on the wrongly convicted, the more likely tragedy is that an innocent sentenced to life in prison will die in jail after spending his life behind bars.

A moratorium will do nothing more than put true innocent lives at risk. Will a temporary moratorium turn death penalty opponents into death penalty supporters? It is unlikely. Will a temporary moratorium save innocent lives on death row? There has yet to be an innocent executed since 1973. Will a moratorium cause truly innocent deaths? Yes, eighteen innocent citizens for every murderer not executed. Who will benefit most by a moratorium? The most cold-blooded murderers in America, rightly convicted and scheduled for execution.

Questions for Discussion

1. How would you evaluate whether capital punishment serves as a deterrent to murder?
2. How could you determine whether the death penalty is an instrument of racial oppression?

3. If the death penalty is acceptable, in what kinds of cases should it be applied? Why?
4. What effect would public executions have on violent crimes?
5. What effect would public executions have on arguments for and against the abolition of the death penalty?
6. What role does possible arbitrariness of capital punishment sentences play in your evaluation of this issue?

Suggested Resources

Web Sites

American Bar Association
    http://www.abanet.org/

Campaign to End the Death Penalty
    http://www.nodeathpenalty.org

Death Penalty Information Center
    http://www.deathpenaltyinfo.org

Pro-death Penalty.com
    http://prodeathpenalty.com

Publications

Banner, Stuart. *The Death Penalty: An American History.* Cambridge, Mass.: Harvard University Press, 2002.

Bedau, Hugo Adam, ed. *The Death Penalty in America: Current Controversies.* New York: Oxford University Press, 1997.

Berns, Walter. *For Capital Punishment: Crime and the Morality of the Death Penalty.* Lanham, Md.: University Press of America, 1991.

Bessler, John D. *Kiss of Death: America's Love Affair with the Death Penalty.* Boston, Mass.: Northeastern University Press, 2003.

Cole, David. *No Equal Justice: Race and Class in the American Criminal Justice System.* New York: New Press, 1999.

Dow, David R., and Mark Dow, eds. *Machinery of Death: The Reality of America's Death Penalty Regime.* New York: Routledge, 2002.

Fein, Bruce. "The Death Penalty, but Sparingly." *Human Rights* 28, no. 3 (Summer 2002): 18–19.

Gillespie, L. Kay. *Inside the Death Chamber: Exploring Executions.* Boston, Mass.: Allyn & Bacon, 2003.

Jackson, Jesse L., Sr., Jesse L. Jackson Jr., and Bruce Shapiro. *Legal Lynching: The Death Penalty and America's Future.* New York: New Press, 2001.

Jost, Kenneth. "Rethinking the Death Penalty." *CQ Researcher* 11, no. 40 (November 16, 2001): 945–68.

Martinez, J. Michael, William D. Richardson, and D. Brandon Hornsby, eds. *The Leviathan's Choice: Capital Punishment in the Twenty-First Century.* Lanham, Md.: Rowman & Littlefield, 2002.

Nathanson, Stephen. *An Eye for an Eye: The Immorality of Punishing by Death*, 2d ed. Lanham, Md.: Rowman & Littlefield, 2001.

Radelet, Michael L., Hugo Adam Bedau, and Constance E. Putnam. *In Spite of Innocence: Erroneous Convictions in Capital Cases.* Boston: Northeastern University Press, 1992.

Sievert, Ronald J. "Capital Murder: A Prosecutor's Personal Observations on the Presentation of Capital Cases." *American Journal of Criminal Law* 27, no. 1 (Fall 1999): 105–16.

Solotaroff, Ivan. *The Last Face You'll Ever See: The Private Life of the American Death Penalty.* New York: HarperCollins, 2001.

Taylor, Stuart, Jr. "Pondering the Penalty: Does It Change the Debate If Capital Punishment Really Does Save Lives?" *Legal Times*, May 28, 2001, p. 68.

Tucker, William. "Capital Punishment Works." *Weekly Standard* 6, no. 45 (August 13, 2001): 27–29.

Zimring, Franklin E. *The Contradictions of American Capital Punishment.* New York: Oxford University Press, 2003.

7

Should the Doctrine of Separation between Church and State Be Interpreted in a Way That Is Favorable to Public Worship and Acknowledgment of God?

The American people have a strong religious faith. According to Norman Redlich, former dean of New York University Law School, as a percentage of the population, "There are more members of organized churches in the United States than any other country in the world."[1] But Americans practice different religious faiths. To protect religious freedom, the constitutional system upholds the separation of church and state. The First Amendment to the Constitution states: "Congress shall make no law respecting an establishment of religion, or prohibiting the free exercise thereof."

Where the line is drawn between what government can or cannot do in matters of religion has long been controversial. Even when the Constitution was submitted to the states for ratification, Anti-Federalists complained that the word "God" did not appear in the document. Nor did the word "Christian" appear, although the country was composed mostly of people who were Christians.

Congress begins each day with a prayer, and the Supreme Court starts each session with a prayer. Since 1863, the currency of the United States carries the words, "In God We Trust." And in 1954, the Pledge of Allegiance was changed to include the words "under God." A long-term practice in public schools was the recitation of prayers at the beginning of the school day and at assemblies. In 1962, however, the Supreme Court held in *Engel v. Vitale* that a New York State law giving school officials the option of mandating a daily prayer was unconstitutional. In 1963, the Court invalidated laws in Pennsylvania and Maryland that compelled daily Bible reading and prayer in public schools.[2]

The issue of church-state relations has often been contentious as the courts have had to reconcile the law — and particularly the Constitution's First Amendment provision in which Congress "shall make no law respecting an establishment of religion, or prohibiting the free exercise thereof" — with religious practices. Some of the noteworthy church-state cases have involved such issues as whether children of Jehovah's Witnesses could be excused from saluting the American flag, whether parochial schools or students attending those schools could be given government funds, and whether religious symbols and statements could be displayed in government buildings or offices and at certain public ceremonies.

In recent years, the issue of school vouchers has received much attention. In a system of school vouchers, money is distributed to parents of school-age children, usually in inner-city school districts. Parents could then use the funds to pay for the tuition of the children at private schools, which can be religious or secular. Vouchers can be funded and administered by government, private organizations, or by some combination of both.

This issue elicited litigation and public comment in which the subject of church-state relations was a matter of great public concern. On June 27, 2002, the Supreme Court, in *Zelman v. Simmons-Harris*, upheld a school voucher program in Cleveland.[3]

Church-state issues were also at center stage in the administration of President George W. Bush. During the presidential campaign of 2000, candidate Bush promised to help religious organizations compete for federal money to run charitable programs, such as soup kitchens, homeless shelters, and drug-treatment programs. Once elected, he established a White House Office of Faith-Based and Community Initiatives to fulfill his campaign pledge. As of March 2003, however, no legislation on this matter resulted from the effort.

The role of religion in society remains a central concern in American politics. Some individuals argue that the government should encourage religious belief and practice and that some existing policies and court rulings have undermined religious faith. But other individuals say that the First Amendment separation of church and state does not mean that the nation is antagonistic to religion; rather, it signifies a respect for religious belief.

The sensitivity of these concerns is expressed in both articles of this debate. Roy S. Moore, a judge in Alabama, argues that public worship should have a prominent place in political life. He contends:

1. The American justice system is firmly rooted in the Judeo-Christian tradition.
2. Constitutional issues regarding public worship and the public acknowledgment of God should be resolved in support of religious faith.
3. Thomas Jefferson's phrase "wall of separation," which is so often used to prevent public displays of faith, is not mentioned in the Constitution, Declaration of Independence, or any other official American document.
4. What Jefferson and other Framers meant by separation of church and state was that government may never dictate one's form of worship or articles of faith. They did not mean that all public worship should be halted.
5. The Framers believed it was the duty of civil government to encourage public professions of faith.

6. Historical precedent shows that the federal government acknowledged God, so it is illogical to believe that the federal government could prohibit the states from doing the very same thing.
7. Putting God in the public square by displays of faith would help solve some of the great social problems that Americans face.

In a sermon delivered before the Fox Valley Unitarian Universalist Fellowship in Appleton, Wisconsin, Rev. Roger Bertschausen argues for a high wall of separation between church and state. He contends:

1. Madison and Jefferson believed that if there is a wall of separation, then it is clear that governmental support of religion — whether preferential to one religious sect or not — is never acceptable.
2. In fact, nonpreferential treatment of religion is a fantasy since it is doubtful that the government would really support the social service programs of a religious organization against which there is strong popular enmity.
3. The wall of separation between church and state saves us from the quicksand of trying to figure out which religions deserve and do not deserve governmental support.
4. The wall of separation is good for religious diversity, which enriches the nations.
5. The wall of separation is good for religion.
6. Current proposed policies that should be opposed because they erode the wall of separation between church and state include President Bush's faith-based initiative, school vouchers, tax-exempt status for congregations that engage directly in partisan politics, and religious symbolic practices, such as posting the Ten Commandments in courthouses of schools, recitation of school prayer, portraying religious scenes like the Nativity in public spaces, and the making of "God Bless America" our official or de facto national anthem.

NOTES

1. Quoted in Laurie Goodstein, "Religious Freedom Amendment Pressed; Conservatives Cite Need at Hill Hearing," *Washington Post*, June 9, 1995, p. A12.
2. *Engel v. Vitale*, 307 U.S. 421 (1962); *School District of Abington Township v. Schempp*, 374 U.S. 203 (1963).
3. *Zelman v. Simmons-Harris*, 536 U.S. ___(2002).

☑ *YES*

Should the Doctrine of Separation between Church and State Be Interpreted in a Way That Is Favorable to Public Worship and Acknowledgment of God?

ROY S. MOORE
Putting God Back in the Public Square

In his first official act, Pres. George Washington did something that would be unthinkable today: He prayed in public! Specifically, during his inaugural address, he made "fervent supplications to that Almighty Being who rules over the universe, who presides in the councils of nations, and whose providential aids can supply every human defect, that His benediction may consecrate to the liberties and happiness of the people of the United States a Government instituted by themselves for these essential purposes. . . . No people can be bound to acknowledge and adore the Invisible Hand which conducts the affairs of men more than the people of the United States. Every step by which they have advanced to the character of an independent nation seems to have been distinguished by some token of providential agency."

If that were not enough, Washington added: "We ought to be no less persuaded that the propitious smiles of Heaven can never be expected on a nation that disregards the eternal rules of order and right which Heaven itself has ordained."

More than 200 years later, few government officials are bold enough to make earnest professions of faith. It seems that politicians can do just about anything in public but pray, unless it is obligatory (say, during an annual prayer breakfast at the White House). They can survive scandal and immoral conduct, but they suffer ostracism and worse once they are labeled members of the "Religious Right."

Even the American justice system, which is firmly rooted in the Judeo-Christian tradition, has developed a bias against public worship and the public acknowledgment of God that ought to give the most militant atheist cause for concern. If judges can deny Christians and Jews the right to express their beliefs in the public square, they can surely deny secular humanists (devout believers of a different sort) the same right.

- In California, creches and crosses have been removed from downtown Christmas and Easter displays.
- In Kansas, city hall monuments featuring religious symbols have been torn down.
- In Rhode Island, high school graduation invocations and benedictions have been banned.
- In Alabama, students have been prohibited by Federal court order from praying, distributing religious materials, and even discussing anything of a devotional or inspirational nature with their classmates and teachers.

- In Ohio, an appellate court has overturned the sentence of a man convicted of raping an eight-year-old child 10 times. Why? Because the judge who pronounced the sentence quoted from the 18th chapter of Matthew: "But whoso shall offend one of these little ones which believe in me, it were better for him that a millstone were hanged about his neck, and that he were drowned in the depth of the sea."

In the courtroom in which I preside, the public display of the Ten Commandments and voluntary clergy-led prayer prior to jury organizational sessions have sparked not only a national controversy, but an epic legal battle. In 1995, I was sued in Federal court by the American Civil Liberties Union and the Alabama Freethought Association. Just prior to that case being dismissed for lack of standing (the ACLU and Alabama Freethought Association failed to show that they had been or were about to be injured), a separate lawsuit was filed in Alabama state court requesting a ruling on whether the First Amendment to the Constitution prohibits the display of the Ten Commandments and voluntary prayer in the courtroom. A state circuit court judge presiding in Montgomery County, Ala., held that the practices in Etowah County were unconstitutional under the First Amendment's "Establishment Clause," which reads, "Congress shall make no law respecting an establishment of religion. . . ." It would appear that the circuit court judge and others were not impressed when the members of the House of Representatives and the Senate passed a resolution stating that: "the Ten Commandments are a declaration of fundamental principles that are the cornerstones of a fair and just society; and the public display, including display in government offices and courthouses, of the Ten Commandments should be permitted."

The state circuit court's ruling was appealed to the Alabama Supreme Court, which set it aside in 1998. Nevertheless, Federal constitutional issues regarding public worship and the public acknowledgment of God remain unresolved.

In a 1997 law review article, Brian T. Collidge expressed the opinion of many in the legal profession when he claimed that the mere display of the Ten Commandments in the courtroom is a "dangerous" practice. Although Collidge concedes that the Commandments reflect universal teachings that are beneficial to a civil society, they make explicit references to God, and, in his view, this is an unconstitutional breach of the "wall of separation between church and state."

This now-famous "wall of separation" phrase does not appear in the Constitution, Declaration of Independence, Articles of Confederation, or any other official American document, yet millions of Americans have been led to believe that it does and that, in the words found in a 1947 Supreme Court decision, "The wall must be kept high and impregnable."

The phrase is actually mentioned for the first time in a letter Pres. Thomas Jefferson wrote in 1802 in reply to an inquiry from the Danbury Baptist Association: "Believing with you that religion is a matter which lies solely between man and his God; that he owes account to none other for his faith or his worship; that the legislative powers of the government reach actions only, and not opinions, I contemplate with sovereign reverence that act of the whole American people which declared that their legislature should make no law respecting an establishment of religion, or prohibiting the free exercise thereof, thus building a wall of separation between church and state."

Yet, did Jefferson mean that the government should in no way support religion? To find the answer, we must go back more than 100 years before he wrote to the Danbury Baptist Association. Jefferson was strongly influenced by John Locke, a well-known English philosopher, who published "A Letter Concerning Toleration" in 1689 wherein he clearly defined the proper church-state relationship. Locke stated that "The magistrate has no power to enforce by law, either in his own Church, or much less in another, the use of any rites or forms of worship by the force of his laws."

Herein lies the true meaning of separation between church and state as the concept was understood by Jefferson and the other Founding Fathers: Government may never dictate one's form of worship or articles of faith. Not all public worship of God must be halted; on the contrary, freedom to engage in such worship was the very reason for creating a doctrine of separation between church and state.

Two days after he wrote to the Danbury Baptist Association, Jefferson attended a church service conducted by John Leland, a prominent Baptist minister, in the halls of the House of Representatives. Throughout his presidency, Jefferson attended similar services, which were often held in the north wing of the Capitol. From 1807 to 1857, church services were held in a variety of government buildings where Congress, the Supreme Court, the War Office, and the Treasury were headquartered.

Obviously, neither Jefferson nor any other officials in the early Republic understood separation between church and state to mean that the Federal government was precluded from recognizing the necessity of public worship or from permitting active support of opportunities for such worship. Indeed, they plainly recognized that the duty of civil government was to encourage public professions of faith. Perhaps this is why John Jay, the first chief justice of the Supreme Court, specifically authorized the opening of jury sessions over which he presided with voluntary prayer led by local clergy of the Christian faith.

Many believe that James Madison, as chief architect of the Constitution and the Bill of Rights, led the fight to keep religion out of politics. In truth, he was more interested in protecting religion from politics. In 1785, two years before the Constitutional Convention, he wrote a *Memorial and Remonstrance* opposing a Virginia bill to establish a provision for teachers of the Christian religion. He stated that man's first duty is to God, and that "religion, or the duty which we owe to our Creator, and the manner of discharging it," was a right and a duty, "precedent both in order of time and degree of obligation, to the claims of a civil society. Before any man can be considered as a member of civil society, he must be considered as a subject of the Governor of the Universe."

Madison championed the First Amendment's Establishment Clause with one overriding purpose — to keep one sect from gaining an advantage over another through political patronage. This is a far cry from denying public worship or the public acknowledgment of God. Madison also made sure that the Establishment

Clause was followed by the "Free Exercise Clause," so that the First Amendment would read, in relevant part, "Congress shall make no law respecting an establishment of religion, or *prohibiting the free exercise thereof. . . ."* (Emphasis added.)

Both Jefferson and Madison would have agreed with Supreme Court Justice Joseph Story's definitive *Commentaries on the Constitution of the United States* (1833) in which he posed the question of whether any free government could endure if it failed to provide for public worship. They would have concluded, as did Story, that it could not. He explained that "The promulgation of the great doctrines of religion, the being, and attributes, and providence of one Almighty God; the responsibility to him for all our actions, founded on moral freedom and accountability; a future state of rewards and punishments; the cultivation of all the personal, social, and benevolent virtues; these never can be a matter of indifference in any well ordered community. It is, indeed, difficult to conceive, how any civilized society can well exist without them."

HISTORICAL PRECEDENT

When the Federal legislature met in 1789, one of its first actions was to appoint chaplains in both houses of Congress. (Congress still recognizes God by appointing and paying chaplains who open each session with a prayer — even the session devoted to the impeachment proceedings against Pres. [Bill] Clinton.)

On the very day that Congress approved the wording of the First Amendment, its members resolved to request of Pres. Washington a day of public thanksgiving and prayer for the peaceful manner in which the Constitution was formed.

A month earlier, Congress had passed the Northwest Ordinance, one of the most important documents in American history. Article III of the Ordinance declared, "Religion, morality, and knowledge, being necessary to good government and the happiness of mankind, schools and the means of education shall forever be encouraged."

Every president of the U.S. (with only one possible exception) has been administered the oath of office with his hand on the Bible, ending with the words "so help me God." The Supreme Court begins every proceeding with the ringing proclamation, "God save the United States and this Honorable Court."

Throughout our history, the executive and legislative branches have decreed national days of fasting and prayer. Public offices and public schools close in observance of religious holidays. U.S. currency bears our national motto, "In God We Trust."

Also by law, the Pledge of Allegiance to the Flag affirms that we are "one nation under God." Congress would not even allow a comma to be placed after the word "nation" in order to reflect the basic idea that ours is a "nation founded on a belief in God."

It is ludicrous and illogical to believe that it is constitutionally permissible for all three branches of the Federal government to acknowledge God openly and publicly on a regular basis, and yet, at the same time, accept the notion that the Federal government can strictly prohibit the states from doing the very same thing. Have we become so ignorant of our nation's history that we have forgotten the reason for the adoption of the Bill of Rights? It was meant to restrict the Federal government's power over the states, not to restrict them from doing what the Federal government can do.

It is no wonder that Supreme Court Justice William Rehnquist observed in a 1985 dissenting opinion that "the wall of separation between church and state is a metaphor based upon bad history, a metaphor which has proved useless as a guide to judging. It should be frankly and explicitly abandoned."

Rehnquist added that "the greatest injury of the 'wall' notion is its mischievous diversion of judges from the actual intention of the drafters of the Bill of Rights." He is right. The doctrine of separation between church and state has been abused, twisted, and taken out of context in recent court decisions in order to prevent the public worship and acknowledgment of God.

The Pharisees demanded of Jesus, "Is it lawful to give tribute unto Caesar, or not?" He asked them to produce a coin and tell him whose image was inscribed on its face. When they replied, "Caesar's," Jesus gave his answer: "Render therefore unto Caesar the things that are Caesar's, and unto God the things that are God's."

We have to render an awful lot to Caesar these days, but we do not and should not surrender our freedom of conscience. The state can't tell us how we ought to think or what we ought to believe. As Jefferson testified, "Almighty God hath created the mind free."

Nevertheless, since the latter half of the 20th century, the state is trying to take by force the unalienable rights freely given to us by God, declared in the Declaration of Independence to be "self-evident." Caesar is trying to tell us when, where, and how we can profess our faith.

In 1962 the Supreme Court outlawed a simple, 22-word, nondenominational prayer devised by the New York Board of Regents and used in the New York public schools: "Almighty God, we acknowledge our dependence upon thee, and we beg thy blessings upon us, our parents, our teachers, and our country."

A year later the Court issued another ruling declaring that reading the Bible and reciting the Lord's Prayer in Pennsylvania and Maryland public schools was unconstitutional, thus outlawing "without the citation of a single case" practices that had existed in American schools for over 170 years. Writing for the majority, Justice Tom C. Clark asserted, "In the relationship between man and religion, the state is firmly committed to a position of neutrality." Justice Potter Stewart pointed out in his lone dissent that this was false neutrality indeed, designed to stifle public professions of faith. Stewart also noted, "We err in the first place if we do not recognize, as a matter of history and a matter of the imperatives of our free society, that religion and government must necessarily interact in countless ways."

Both decisions represented a major turning point in U.S. history. Judges were no longer interested in the "original intent" of the Founders or in legal precedents (which they unapologetically and arrogantly failed to cite). They were eager to embrace the new doctrine of "judicial activism," that would allow them the opportunity to use their power to reshape society according to the attitudes and whims of the changing times.

DESTROYING THE DISTINCTION

Since the 1960s, judicial activists have made a concerted effort to banish God from the public square. They have done this by deliberately destroying the distinction between "religion" and "religious activity." These terms may sound similar, but, in fact, they are very different. Religious activities may include many actions that would not themselves constitute religion. For example, prayer and Bible reading might be characterized as religious activities, but they do not constitute religion, and they are not limited to any specific sect or even to religious people. One may read the New Testament to gain wisdom, and school students may pray before a big exam. Neither activity was intended to be, is, or should be proscribed by the First Amendment, even if practiced in public.

However, it seems that the judicial activists are winning the war. Consider the 1997 case in DeKalb County, Ala. There, a Federal district court determined that a student's brief prayer during a high school graduation ceremony was a violation of the First Amendment because it allegedly coerced unwilling citizens to participate in religious activity. We have evidently forgotten that nothing in the Constitution guarantees that an individual won't have to see or hear things that are disagreeable or offensive to him. We have also failed to realize that peer pressure and public opinion are not the types of coercion against which the Framers were seeking to safeguard.

No student should ever be forced by law to participate in prayer or in other religious activity. However, to outlaw the public acknowledgment of God simply because another student might have to witness it is as illogical as abandoning a school mascot or motto because it might not be every student's favorite or because some might not believe in "school spirit."

In this context, Justice Story is again worth quoting. He said that the "duty of supporting religion, and especially the Christian religion, is very different from the right to force the consciences of other men, or to punish them for worshiping God in the manner, which, they believe their accountability to him requires." Even more to the point, Supreme Court Justice William O. Douglas once wrote that forbidding public worship discriminates in favor of "those who believe in no religion over those who do believe."

October, 1997 — Pearl, Miss.; December, 1997 — Paducah, Ky.; March, 1998 — Jonesboro, Ark.; April, 1998 — Edinborough, Pa.; May, 1998 — Fayetteville, Tenn.; April, 1999 — Littleton, Colo. These dates and places — these outbreaks of mass violence and needless loss of young lives — serve as a cruel reminder of something gone wrong, desperately wrong, in a nation founded upon faith in God and a respect for His eternal commandments.

Liberal commentators in the media, academe, and the justice system deride the notion that restoring prayer and posting the Ten Commandments can help stem the tide of violence and bloodshed. They prefer secular solutions, especially ones that involve more Federal spending and regulation. In effect, they favor more concertina wire, metal detectors, and armed security guards instead of the simple and effective teaching of moral absolutes.

Yes, teaching moral absolutes is out of the question. "We don't want to trample on the civil rights of students," they cry. "We don't want to teach that one creed or one code of conduct or one lifestyle is better than another." When will they understand that secular solutions will never solve spiritual problems?

Tragically, as in the days of the Roman Empire, we have become accustomed to "bread and circuses." With our stomachs full and our minds preoccupied with the pleasures of this world, we fail to ponder seriously the reason for the tragedies that are regularly occurring before our very eyes. We rarely contemplate the significance of the judiciary's usurpation of power and suppression of religious liberty. When and if we do, we too often are afraid to take a stand — somehow ashamed of our faith in God, afraid to hazard the notion of putting God back into the public square.

We must not wait for more violence, for a total breakdown of our schools and our communities. We must not be silent while every vestige of God is removed from our public life and while every public display of faith is annihilated. The time has come to recover the valiant courage of our forefathers, who understood that faith and freedom are inseparable and that they are worth fighting for.

In the words of that great Christian and patriot, Patrick Henry, "We must fight! I repeat it, sir, we must fight! An appeal to arms and to the God of Hosts is all that is left us! . . . Why stand we here idle? What is it that the gentlemen wish? What would they have? Is life so dear, or peace so sweet, as to be purchased at the price of chains and slavery? Forbid it, Almighty God! I know not what course others may take; but as for me, give me liberty or give me death!"

Should the Doctrine of Separation between Church and State Be Interpreted in a Way That Is Favorable to Public Worship and Acknowledgment of God?

ROGER BERTSCHAUSEN
Rethinking the Separation between Church and State

Call to Gather: from Paul Robeson

> I shall take my voice wherever there are those who want to hear the melody of freedom or the words that might inspire hope and courage in the face of despair and fear. My weapons are peaceful, for it is only by peace that peace can be attained. The song of freedom must prevail.[1]

Readings: from a letter from Thomas Jefferson to the Baptist Association of Danbury, Connecticut

Believing with you that religion is a matter which lies solely between man and his God, that he owes account to none other for his faith or his worship, that the legislative powers of government reach actions only, and not opinions, I contemplate with sovereign reverence that act of the whole American people [the First Amendment] which declared that their legislature should "make no law respecting an establishment of religion, or prohibiting the free exercise of thereof," thus building a wall of separation between Church and State.[2]

From Justice Hugo Black in the 1947 *Everson vs. Board of Education* decision

The "establishment of religion" clause of the First Amendment means at least this: Neither a state nor the Federal Government can set up a church. Neither can pass laws which aid one religion, aid all religions, or prefer one religion over another. Neither can force nor influence a person to go to or remain away from church against his will or force him to profess a belief or disbelief in any religion. No person can be punished for entertaining or professing religious beliefs or disbeliefs, for church attendance or non-attendance. No tax in any amount, large or small, can be levied to support any religious activities or institutions, whatever they may be called, or whatever form they may adopt to teach or practice religion. Neither a state nor the Federal Government can, openly or secretly, participate in the affairs of any religious organizations or groups and vice versa. In the words of Jefferson, the clause against establishment of religion by law was intended to erect "a wall of separation between church and state." . . . That wall must be kept high and impregnable.[3]

One of the miracles of our whole remarkable system of government is that it is based on a relatively short document written in a vastly different era. But while the Constitution is largely fixed and unchangeable — amending it is a difficult and rare occurrence — the government it creates is incredibly flexible and changeable. This is surely part of the great genius of the Constitution.

You can see this process in the constant evolution of the relationship between church and state. An important part of the fuel for this evolution is built right into the First Amendment itself. The First Amendment contains two clauses. The first states that the government shall take no action "respecting the establishment of religion." The second states that the government shall not prohibit the "free exercise" of religion. The first clause, in other words, says that the government can do nothing to establish religion; the second says that the government can also do nothing to bar people from practicing their chosen religion. The Constitution charges the government with neither encouraging nor discouraging religion. There is a balance to be struck, and this balance has been the focal point of the evolution of church/state relations over the centuries.

Central to this balance over the years has been this question: Is it acceptable for the government to aid religion if it does so in ways that don't aid particular sects over other sects? This question goes back to the beginning of the republic. Some answered yes, some no. The leader of one side was Patrick Henry. He answered this question "Yes": it is acceptable for the government to give aid to religion as long as it doesn't favor one religion over another. His fierce opponents James Madison and Thomas Jefferson answered "No." They argued that there should be, in Jefferson's words, a wall of separation between church and state. If there is a wall of separation, then it is clear that governmental support of religion — whether preferential or non-preferential — is never acceptable.

Right now we are in a relatively intense period of rethinking the relationship between church and state. A focal point of this reconsideration is the question Henry, Madison and Jefferson first debated.

For much of the twentieth century, the Jefferson/Madison interpretation of a strict wall of separation between church and state held sway — especially in Supreme Court decisions. You can see this in the Hugo Black decision that I quoted earlier. In the last decade or two, as the Court has become increasingly more conservative, Patrick Henry's view has gained ground. When it comes to church/state issues, the Supreme Court is now rather evenly divided between followers of Jefferson and Madison on the one hand, and followers of Patrick Henry on the other. In fact, in general there are four justices on each side, with Sandra Day O'Connor in her customary position of being the decisive vote in the middle. With the Court so evenly divided, no wonder this issue is particularly intense right now.

As citizens and as religious people, this period of rethinking the church/state relationship provides us with a good opportunity for focusing our attention on this important issue. Today I want to share my view of the church/state relationship in hopes that it might help each of you come up with your own view.

In church/state issues, I side with Jefferson and Madison. Since they were so central in the drafting of the Constitution — unlike Patrick Henry, who bitterly opposed the Constitution — I think their view of a wall of separation is more in keeping with the spirit of the Constitution. I do not support any governmental support of religion — regardless of whether support is conferred on particular religions or is non-preferential.

Actually I don't think non-preferential treatment of religion is even possible. To me this truth is already very evident in President [George W.] Bush's faith-based initiative. The faith-based initiative is designed to promote federal aid to religious groups that provide social services and to create church-state partnerships to deal with social problems.

Are we really willing to support social service programs of *all* religions with our federal tax dollars? Is our government really willing to support Wiccan, atheist, Muslim, white supremacist or Unitarian Universalist social service programs, to name a few of the more controversial faiths? If we say that the program is non-preferential — which we have to say if governmental support of religion is to have any chance at all of passing Constitutional muster — then we have to be ready to support *all* religious organizations. Is Jerry Falwell really going to abide his tax dollars supporting a Wiccan social service ministry? Or a Unitarian Universalist ministry? Am I going to want my tax money supporting the Nation of Islam or Jerry Falwell's social service initiatives? No way! Non-preferential treatment of religion is a fantasy. It ain't gonna happen!

You can already see this in the faith-based initiative. President Bush has announced that he would not allow funding for Nation of Islam social service programs because in his view the Nation of Islam preaches hatred. Well, I happen to agree with his assessment of the Nation of Islam. But who gets to decide which religion is worthy of governmental support and which isn't? Who decides who's in and who's out? Who decides that the government shouldn't support the Nation of Islam? Well, the government, of course. Suddenly the faith-based initiative is a preferential program, favoring one religion over another. Catholic Social Services and Lutheran Social Services would get federal money; the Nation of Islam would not. Suddenly whatever Constitutional support could be mounted for the faith-based initiative evaporates. If the faith-based initiative truly is non-preferential, then the Nation of Islam would have to be eligible for funding, too.

Thankfully, the wall of separation between church and state saves us from the quicksand of trying to figure out which religions deserve and do not deserve governmental support. It says simply that we should support none.

I think the wall of separation is good for other reasons, too. Most importantly, I believe it is good for our nation. Our government is based on the premise that individuals should have the freedom to make choices about important matters. And what could be more important — and personal — than one's choice of faith? This is why many immigrants over the years — starting with the Pilgrims — came to this land: to be able to freely practice their faith. It is a precious part of our heritage. Government support of religion flies in the face of this free religious heritage.

A huge part of what makes the United States such a great nation is our religious diversity. Though it is not always easy — whoever said democracy is easy? — I think the burgeoning diversity of religion in our nation is a wonderful thing. Just look around the Fox Valley. You can now see thriving Christian, Islamic, Jewish, Baha'i, Native American and Unitarian Universalist communities, to name a few. These diverse communities are a tremendous source of the richness of our area.

I know in these past six months I have developed an even deeper appreciation for the presence of the Fox Valley Islamic Society in our community. Because of this congregation's presence, Islam in the Fox Valley is more than an abstract, media-sensationalized idea. Here Islam has the face not of distant fanatics depicted in the media, but of friends and neighbors and co-workers and classmates. When our Coming of Age youth wanted to learn about Islam, they didn't have to learn second-hand through books or videos. Instead they visited the mosque in Neenah and had face-to-face conversations with Muslim neighbors. What a wonderful gift from our community's diversity!

Our nation's and our community's growing religious pluralism is a wonderful thing because it helps all of us learn more about the diverse world in which we live. It helps us speak and act out of understanding rather than ignorance. This thriving religious pluralism in our community and nation would not be possible without religious freedom. And a key linchpin of religious freedom is the separation between church and state. Once the state gets involved in religion, our religious freedom inevitably erodes.

I also support Jefferson's wall of separation because it is good for religion. I think it is incredibly illuminating to note that religion is languishing in countries where it enjoys state support, and thriving in countries like the United States in which there is little or no state support. Why is this? The answer is simple: because religious freedom is necessary for religion to thrive. A lack of choice — or the sense that because the state supports the church I don't have to — saps religion of its vitality and energy.

I ran across some interesting data lately on religion in colonial America. I was amazed to learn that only one in five people in colonial New England belonged to a church. One in fifteen in the middle colonies belonged to a church, and even less in the South. Religion in colonial America — which enjoyed state support — was just like state-supported religion in Europe, then and now: lethargic and unpopular. Only with independence and religious freedom did religion take off in the United States.[4]

Today there are many hot-spots in the evolving relationship between church and state. I want to examine a few of these.

The first, already alluded to, is President Bush's faith-based initiative. This initiative was of course a major plank in Bush's campaign and is a priority in his administration. I am against the faith-based initiative because I believe it significantly erodes the wall between church and state. As the Rev. Barry Lynn of Americans United for Separation of Church and State observes, "Forcing taxpayers to subsidize religious institutions they may or may not believe in is no different from forcing them to put money in the collection plates of churches, synagogues and mosques."[5] Forcing me to subsidize a ministry that discourages reproductive freedom and opposes gay and lesbian rights is a horrible violation of my freedom of conscience, just as forcing a fundamentalist Christian to support a ministry that encourages reproductive freedom and gay rights would be a violation.

I have nothing against religious organizations working to help individuals in need and our society to become more just. In fact, through the Unitarian Universalist [UU] Service Committee among other organizations, I support such programs with my money. The UU Service Committee and other organizations do a lot of good, and I am grateful for them. But my support is voluntary. Social service ministries should be supported by voluntary contributions, not government subsidies.

Another current hot-spot in church/state relations is school vouchers. The United States Supreme Court is currently considering the landmark case of Cleveland's school-voucher program. In the 1999–2000 school year, 96 percent of the 3,800 students who received vouchers in Cleveland attended religious schools. The Cleveland program — like programs in Milwaukee and elsewhere — shifts tax dollars from public schools to private, mostly religious schools. During the six years of the Cleveland program's existence, nearly forty-six million dollars has been transferred from public school coffers to private, mostly religious schools.

Everybody in Cleveland is supporting religious schools with their tax dollars, regardless of their religious affiliation.

The Cleveland case will likely decide the constitutionality of school vouchers. I hope the Supreme Court preserves rather than tears down the wall of separation between church and state by finding vouchers unconstitutional. Again, I have nothing against religious schools. Some families within this Fellowship have opted to send children to religious schools, and I totally respect their choice. But they — not all of us — should pay for their choice. Our tax dollars should go to the tremendous challenge of making public schools the best schools they can possibly be, not to private schools.[6]

A third hot issue right now involves whether congregations should engage directly in partisan politics. Since the 1950s, a law has punished congregations that engage directly in partisan politics by taking away their tax-exempt status. This law has a dubious origin: then Senator Lyndon Johnson pushed it through Congress in order to lessen the support conservative Christian churches could give to a potential opponent. In spite of this dubious origin, I think the law is a good law. It strengthens the wall between church and state without restricting basic freedoms. A church can decide to engage in partisan politics (and therefore also pay taxes). Individuals within a church community can still get together to engage in politics; they just can't do their political work in the name of the church. And of course the church can — and should, I believe — remain a place where politics are discussed and individual political actions are encouraged.

A final church/state hot-spot focuses on the largely symbolic issues. These include things like posting the Ten Commandments in courthouses or schools, school prayer, portraying religious scenes like the Nativity in public spaces, and the effort to make "God Bless America" our official or de facto national anthem. Once again, I opt for a clear wall of separation between church and state. Posting the Ten Commandments, for example, privileges Judaism and Christianity and symbolizes more than anything else that these religions are or should be the official, state-supported religions of our country. This is very potent symbolism. I join those who work against symbols that attempt to unify rather than keep divided church and state.

From Patrick Henry to George Bush, our country has always had people who seek to erode the wall of separation. And we have always had people like Thomas Jefferson and James Madison who toil tirelessly to keep the wall of separation strong and high. I find inspiration in Jefferson and Madison, and in many less famous Americans who have been willing to lay it on the line to preserve the wall of separation.

I find inspiration in Emily Lesk, a high school student who objects to a Virginia law requiring public schools to have a moment of silence each day. She believes that the moment of silence is the beginning of bringing prayer into the public schools. Every day, Emily conducts a sixty-second protest by leaving her classroom and standing in the hall. A practicing Jew, Emily believes that our personal faiths don't need the support of the state in order to thrive.[7]

I find inspiration in a youth member of our Fellowship who had the courage to stand up to a high school teacher who pushed religion on his students. When the teacher dismissed this student's objections, she shared her concern with her parents, with me and with her principal. As a result, the teacher was told to quit pushing religion on his students.

I find inspiration from Robert Nordlander, a member of our Fellowship with whom I disagree more often than I agree. But Robert works tirelessly and consistently to shine the light of our community's attention on violations of church/state separation. I am grateful for Robert's work.

These folks show me my duty as a concerned citizen: to be vigilant about church/state separation and to be willing to speak and act on my convictions. Eternal vigilance is truly the price of freedom.

NOTES

1. Reading #462 in *Singing the Living Tradition* (Boston: Beacon Press, 1993).
2. Quoted in Edd Doerr, "Jefferson's Wall," *The Humanist*, vol. 62 (1), January/February 2002, p. 10.
3. Ibid., p. 10.
4. Sidney M. Goetz, "Would the Freethinking Jefferson Be Elected Today?" *The Humanist*, vol. 62 (1), January/February 2002, p. 14.
5. Press release from Americans United for Separation of Church and State, February 20, 2001, http://www.commondreams.org/news2001/0220-03.htm.
6. Warren Richey, "Voucher Case Tests Church-State Wall," *Christian Science Monitor*, February 20, 2002, pp. 1, 10; and Gail Russell Chaddock, "Key Case in Future School Choice," *Christian Science Monitor*, February 19, 2002, pp. 1, 4.
7. Emily Lesk, "My 60-Second Protest from the Hallway," *Newsweek*, June 11, 2001, p. 13.

Questions for Discussion

1. Is the practice of saying a prayer at the beginning of each day in Congress a violation of the First Amendment? What are the reasons for your answer?
2. Is there a cause-and-effect relationship between the Supreme Court's decisions on such matters as school prayer and posting the Ten Commandments, and the kinds of social problems that exist in the United States? What are the reasons for your answer?
3. Is the wall of separation between church and state breached if government funds are used for students who are attending religious schools? What are the reasons for your answer?
4. What are the advantages and disadvantages of providing government assistance to religious institutions that are engaged in such practices as providing medical care for the sick, education for the poor, and social assistance for the elderly?
5. What effect does putting God in the public square have on people who do not believe in religion?

Suggested Resources

Web Sites

Americans United for Separation of Church and State
   http://www.au.org

Anti-Defamation League
   http://www.adl.org/adl.asp

Liberty Counsel
   http://www.lc.org

National Reform Association
   http://www.natreformassn.org/

Publications

Boston, Rob. *Why the Religious Right Is Wrong about Separation of Church and State,* 2d ed. Amherst, N.Y.: Prometheus Books, 2003.

Brown, Steven Preston. *Trumping Religion: The New Christian Right, the Free Speech Clause, and the Courts.* Tuscaloosa: University of Alabama Press, 2002.

Cookson, Catharine. *Regulating Religion: The Courts and the Free Exercise Clause.* New York: Oxford University Press, 2001.

Curry, Thomas J. *Farewell to Christendom: The Future of Church and State in America.* New York: Oxford University Press, 2001.

Davis, Derek. "Separation, Integration, and Accommodation: Religion and State in America in a Nutshell." *Journal of Church and State* 43, no. 1 (Winter 2001): 5–17.

Dionne, E. J., Jr., and Ming Hsu Chen, eds. *Sacred Places, Civic Purposes: Should Government Help Faith-Based Charity?* Washington, D.C.: Brookings Institution Press, 2001.

Doerr, Edd. "Jefferson's Wall." *Humanist* 62, no. 1 (January/February 2002): 10–11.

Fisher, Louis. *Religious Liberty in America: Political Safeguards.* Lawrence: University Press of Kansas, 2002.

Hamburger, Philip. *Separation of Church and State.* Cambridge, Mass.: Harvard University Press, 2002.

Kramnick, Isaac, and Laurence Moore. *The Godless Constitution: The Case against Religious Correctness.* New York: W. W. Norton, 1996.

Marshall, Patrick. "Religion in Schools." *CQ Researcher* 11, no. 1 (January 11, 2001): 1–24.

McCollister, Betty. "No 'Faith' in the Constitution." *The Humanist* 6, no. 3 (May 2001): 40–42.

Perry, Michael J. *Under God? Religious Faith and Liberal Democracy.* New York: Cambridge University Press, 2003.

U.S. Cong., Senate. *Religious Liberty.* Hearing before the Committee on the Judiciary, 106th Cong., 1st Sess., 1999.

Wallace, J. Clifford. "The Framers' Establishment Clause: How High the Wall?" *Brigham Young University Law Review* 2001, no. 2 (2001): 755–72.

Willis, Ellen. "Freedom from Religion." *Nation* 272, no. 7 (February 19, 2001): 11–12, 14–16.

Wilson, John F., and Donald L. Drakeman, eds. *Church and State in American History: The Burden of Religious Pluralism,* 3d ed. Boulder, Colo.: Westview Press, 2002.

Is Affirmative Action
a Desirable Policy
to Remedy Discrimination
in Higher Education?

In the decades following World War II, the civil rights movement in the United States achieved notable successes. The Supreme Court ruled that racially discriminatory practices were unconstitutional, and laws were adopted at the national, state, and local level ending practices of segregation and other forms of discrimination.

The civil rights movement focused initially on political gains — voting rights, school integration, and access to public accommodations. Although resistance was strong, the movement achieved legal guarantees of equal treatment. Achieving equal economic opportunity proved to be a more intractable problem. As many African Americans pointed out, it is all well and good to have the legal right to go to any fine restaurant or hotel, as civil rights laws required, but the legal right does not make much practical difference to the people who cannot afford to pay.

Civil rights legislation did not secure economic equality. Many companies hired only a few African Americans, and often the jobs they held were low level. Few African Americans rose to top positions in business. Many departments in colleges and universities had few African American teachers or administrators. And even professional sports — baseball, basketball, and football — which welcomed African Americans to their teams as athletes, hired few African Americans as coaches or executives. Many people in the civil rights movement saw this economic and social disparity between African Americans and whites as just another form of discrimination. They called upon government to guarantee equal employment opportunities.

Government responded in two ways: by enforcing antidiscrimination laws, and by adopting affirmative action programs, which required employers to take special measures to recruit, hire, train, and upgrade members of groups that have suffered harm from past discrimination. Both policies were not limited to African Americans but were applied to other racial minorities and to women.

Support for the enforcement of antidiscrimination laws was broad. Government agencies sought to ensure that employers made job information available to all groups, did not use tests or create standards that were unrelated to performance of jobs as an unfair screening device against minority groups, and placed no discriminatory barriers to advancement within an organization.

Affirmative action was — and remains — controversial. It is based on the idea that special measures are needed to benefit groups of people who suffered from a long history of discrimination. In this view, affirmative action is needed to make previously excluded groups of people more competitive in economic and professional life.

When a government agency or court determines that a private or public organization is engaged in discriminatory hiring practices, it may require the organization to end those practices. But detecting discrimination in hiring practices is difficult. At times, the government relies on a statistical analysis based on the composition of either the work force in an organization or the number of applicants to particular jobs there. Government agencies sometimes require employment "guidelines" or "targets," which the organizations are expected to follow to comply with civil rights regulations. But critics of affirmative action complain that these guidelines are actually "quotas" in which specific percentages are allotted to targeted groups.

In matters of higher education, quotas are illegal in the United States. According to a landmark case, *Regents of the University of California v. Bakke,* the Supreme Court decided that an affirmative action program using quotas for medical school admissions violates the Civil Rights Act of 1964. The Court, however, declared that admissions committees can consider race as one of a complex of factors involved in admissions decisions.[1] Critics of affirmative action say that guidelines inevitably become quotas, while supporters of the policy say that they do not.

Since *Bakke,* affirmative action has increasingly come under attack in judicial and political arenas. In 1995, the Supreme Court decided in *Adarand Constructors v. Pena* that the federal government must adhere to the same strict constitutional standards that states had to obey when implementing affirmative action programs designed to benefit minorities and other groups that had suffered discrimination.[2] The Court applied a "strict scrutiny" test for federal programs, as already existed with states. This decision reversed earlier Supreme Court decisions that gave the federal government broader discretion than states had to implement affirmative action programs. *Adarand* was the first case in which the Supreme Court refused to uphold a federal affirmative action program.

In response, President Bill Clinton ordered a review of affirmative action policies in the federal government. In October 1995, the Department of Defense ended a program designed to help minority-owned firms win defense contracts. It was the first significant action by the Clinton administration following a review of affirmative action. President Clinton, however, remained committed to affirmative action. In a speech on July 19, 1995, he said: "We should reaffirm the principle of affirmative action and fix the practices. We should have a simple slogan: mend it, but don't end it."[3]

Many developments in affirmative action in 1995 and 1996 dealt blows to the program. In March 1996, in *Hopwood v. Texas,* a federal appeals court invalidated a race-based admissions policy at the University of Texas School of Law. The court held that race or ethnicity could not be used as a factor in admissions even to correct a perceived racial imbalance in the student body. The court also determined that the university had failed to identify past discrimination at the law school as a justification for a remedy that gives preferences to racial minorities.[4] And in April 1996, Georgia Attorney General Michael Bowers asked the state's thirty-four government-sponsored colleges and universities to change admissions policies that give preference to racial minorities. He did so, he said, to comply with decisions of federal judges in recent cases.

Legal challenges to affirmative action have continued. In May 2001, the Supreme Court decided to let stand a federal court decision upholding the use of race as a factor in admission at the University of Washington Law School. But in June 2001, the Supreme Court declined to decide whether an affirmative action program favoring minority students to the University of Texas Law School was unconstitutional. In doing so, it let stand a ruling in 2000 by the U.S. 5th Circuit Court of Appeals in New Orleans that had struck down the policy.

In May 2002, the United States Court of Appeals for the Sixth Circuit upheld the constitutionality of the University of Michigan Law School's race-conscious admissions policy. On December 2, 2002, the Supreme Court announced that it would consider affirmative action in this case and in another one, also involving the University of Michigan, before the end of its current term in June 2003.[5]

Stanley Fish, dean of the College of Liberal Arts and Sciences at the University of Illinois in Chicago, argues that affirmative action is needed in higher education. He contends:

1. It is needed because not much has changed to benefit minorities and women in the workplace and universities in recent years.
2. It is working, and arguments that deny this fact serve as a rationale for the status quo.
3. It is fair because minorities have not had the privileges that others have had by birth.
4. It is based on merit if the term *merit* is properly understood.
5. It is not racist because it is a self-defense response to the discriminatory practices that the white majority inflicted on minorities and women in the past.
6. Black people were discriminated against as a group and not as individuals; hence, it is wrong for opponents of affirmative action to say that they are champions of treating persons as individuals.

7. Quotas are not bad if they are designed to admit minority students, not to keep them out as the old system of quotas required, and to select qualified minority members for admission.
8. The argument that affirmative action lowers self-esteem on its beneficiaries is false because affirmative action is a weak predictor of self-esteem.
9. To say that affirmative action provokes racism is false because it is part of a blame-the-victim strategy.

Roger Clegg, vice president and general counsel of the Center for Equal Opportunity, opposes affirmative action. In testimony before the United States Commission on Civil Rights, he argues:

1. Affirmative action based on race and ethnicity is discriminatory and should be stopped because: (a) students who are less qualified than other students are admitted to universities as a consequence of affirmative action, (b) quotas exist in affirmative action programs even when they are not rigid targets, (c) racial and ethnic preferences are more irrational, more divisive, more stigmatizing, and more constitutionally problematic than any other criteria.
2. Affirmative action is not needed in higher education to keep college admissions officers from discriminating against blacks and Hispanics. The admissions officers are not engaged in such discriminatory practices today.
3. Affirmative action does not provide remedial benefits because: (a) college admissions officers are already receptive to minority applicants, (b) minority applicants today are unlikely to have suffered the systematic discrimination against them that would justify systematic discrimination in their favor, and (c) past discrimination against racial and ethnic groups is a weak justification for affirmative action.
4. The argument for the educational benefits of diversity are weak because: (a) it falsely assumes that bigots or potential bigots will be less biased if they are surrounded by students from racial and ethnic minorities who are beneficiaries of affirmative action, and (b) it is the diversity of intellectual thought rather than race or ethnicity that is important in a university.
5. The costs of affirmative action are not worth the remedies because: (a) affirmative action discriminates on the basis of race, (b) it creates resentment among those who lose out because of discrimination, (c) it stigmatizes the beneficiaries of the preferences, (d) it compromises the mission of the university, and (e) it is breaking the law.
6. The argument that without affirmative action, certain groups would be underrepresented at universities is without merit because: (a) the argument is based on nothing more than "discrimination for its own sake," (b) the students rejected would still go to a different university,

and (c) students from racial and ethnic minorities would still be admitted to top-tier universities although the number of those students might be fewer than would be admitted under affirmative action.

NOTES

1. *Regents of the University of California v. Bakke,* 438 U.S. 265, 57 (1978).
2. *Adarand Constructors v. Pena,* 115 S. Ct. 2097 (1995).
3. Quoted in "Excerpts from Clinton Talk on Affirmative Action," *New York Times,* July 20, 1995, p. B10.
4. *Hopwood v. Texas,* 116 S. Ct. 2581 (1996).
5. *Grutter v. Bollinger* 288 F.3d 732 (6th Cir.2002) and *Gratz v. Bollinger,* 122 F. Supp.2d 811 (ED Mich. 2000).

 YES

Is Affirmative Action a Desirable Policy to Remedy Discrimination in Higher Education?

STANLEY FISH

Affirming Affirmative Action

The arguments against affirmative action are now rehearsed so routinely that you can tick them off in a verbal shorthand and be immediately understood. Here they are:

- it's not needed.
- it's not working.
- it's not fair.
- it's not merit.
- it's reverse racism.
- it's group-think.
- it's quotas.
- it lowers self-esteem.
- it provokes race consciousness.

There are many who believe these arguments to be unanswerable because they have never heard anyone attempt to answer them. Here is my attempt.

The argument that affirmative action is not needed comes in two versions: (1) it's not needed because discrimination is already illegal and nothing more is required; and (2) it's not needed because the pendulum has already swung too far in the direction of women and minorities. The first version falls before the undoubted facts of systematic discrimination — glass ceilings and redlining practices that keep neighborhoods all white and deny loans to well-qualified African Americans; the second version is belied by every statistical survey that shows the pendulum just where it has been for years. As a *Los Angeles Times* news story recently put it: "The prevailing public sentiment that . . . preferences have had a huge effect on the workplace or in universities . . . is flatly untrue."[1]

The argument that affirmative action is not working also comes in two (contradictory) versions: (1) it's not working because the problems of the underclass have more to do with economics than with race; and (2) it's not working because the gap between blacks and whites is genetic, not cultural, and we are only throwing good money after bad. The first version collapses under its own weight: if the problem has multiple causes then a multiple strategy is required and it makes no sense to discard one prong of it. The second version is what many think of as *The Bell Curve* argument (although the authors insist that their thesis is about intelligence, not race).[2] It says that blacks occupy inferior social and economic positions because they are naturally inferior. The fact that many believe this, despite the overwhelming scientific consensus that the concept of race has no biological foundation and cannot be correlated with anything, is a tribute to the appeal of any argument that can serve as a rationale for the status quo.

The third argument is a favorite. It's not fair because those who pay the penalty did not inflict the injury. Why should white males in 1995 be taxed for acts performed fifty or one hundred or two hundred years ago by people long dead? The question is its own answer: if today's white males do not deserve the (statistically negligible) disadvantages they suffer, neither do they deserve to be the beneficiaries of the sufferings inflicted for generations on others; they didn't earn the privileges they now enjoy by birth and any unfairness they experience is less than the unfairness that smooths their life path irrespective of their merit.

Merit is the heart of the fourth argument. It goes like this: people should get jobs and places in college because they merit them, and neither race nor gender could be a component of merit. The trick here is to define merit narrowly — with test scores or examination results — and then stigmatize any other consideration as unwarranted preference or bad social engineering. But merit is just a word for whatever qualifications are deemed desirable for the performance of a particular task and there is nothing fixed about those qualifications. Some medical schools now decline to certify aspiring doctors who have proven themselves technically but lack the skills that enable them to relate to patients. These schools are not abandoning merit, but fashioning an alternative conception of it rooted in an alternative notion of what the job requires. In the same way, it may be a qualification for a policeman or policewoman in the inner city to be black or Hispanic; and it may be part of the merit of a worker in a rape crisis center that she is a woman. Merit is not one thing but many things, and even when it becomes a disputed thing, the dispute is between different versions of merit and not between merit and something base and indefensible.

The fifth argument is the big one and the most specious. If it was wrong for Jim

Crow laws to penalize people just for being black, then it is equally wrong to give preference to some people just for being black. It's reverse racism. But the reasoning works only if the two practices are removed from their historical contexts and declared to be the same because they both take race into consideration. According to this bizarre logic, those who favor minority set-asides are morally equivalent to Ku Klux Klanners. It is just like saying (what no one would say) that killing in self-defense is morally the same as killing for money because in either case it is killing you're doing. When the law distinguishes between these two scenarios, it recognizes that the judgment one passes on an action will vary with the motives informing it. It was the express purpose of some powerful, white Americans to disenfranchise, enslave, and later exploit black Americans. It was *what they set out to do,* whereas the proponents of affirmative action did not set out to deprive your friend's cousin's son of a place at Harvard.

The sixth argument — it's group-think — says that by focusing on group harms and remedies, affirmative action runs contrary to the American tradition of regarding persons as individuals. The "group perspective" is rejected both as a way of assigning responsibility — it is individuals who discriminate, not society or patterns of history — and as a way of identifying the victimized — it is individuals not groups who are harmed. But this insistence on what the *Adarand* decision calls an "individualized showing" of harm[3] does not correspond to the manner in which the harms were inflicted and experienced. Blacks were not historically discriminated against one by one, but as a group, by persons who had the entire African-American population, not particular members of it, in mind. And those who experienced discrimination did not do so as the result of being individually targeted (although that of course happened more than occasionally) but as the result of living in a society whose general and impersonal structures worked ceaselessly to their disadvantage. It is ironic that after practicing "societal discrimination" for so long, the society would now decide to make amends by proceeding piecemeal and leaving the larger patterns of exclusion it had fashioned firmly in place. If "group-think" is a problem, it is not one originated by the proponents of affirmative action but by those who oppose it.

The seventh argument — it's quotas — is on one level easily dismissible because quotas are illegal. What is permitted under current affirmative action law are ranges, targets, and goals. But, reply those who oppose affirmative action, ranges, targets, and goals amount to quotas in the end because they require employees and school administrators to move toward proportions numerically defined. This is in fact a strong argument which should be answered not by reinvoking the distinction between quotas and goals, but by asking the question, "What's wrong with quotas anyway?" What's wrong with quotas, presumably, is that they require taking race into consideration when making hiring or admissions decisions. But that is precisely what affirmative action is all about. The objection against quotas is really an objection to the word *affirmative* in the phrase affirmative action; and as the historical record surely shows, without *affirmative* action the inequalities and inequities produced by massive legal and cultural racism would not be remedied. But isn't a quota that reserves a number of places for women and minorities the same as the old, now despised, quotas that prevented all but a few Jews and even fewer African Americans from entering colleges, law schools and medical schools? The answer is no because the objection fails to distinguish between quotas imposed to keep people out (what is often called "first order" discrimination) and quotas designed to let previously excluded persons in, which might in some small measure have the secondary — not intended — effect of marginally disadvantaged members of the majority. Finally, the case against quotas is often misrepresented as the case against "strict racial quotas." But that is a misnomer; there are no strict racial quotas in the sense that a contractor or chairman or college admissions officer is told to go down to the mall and pick out the first ten minority-looking persons he sees whether or not they are qualified. In fact, when quotas — or ranges or goals or targets — are in place, their implementation always occurs in relation to a pool of already qualified applicants. No one is telling anyone to hire or admit persons who are unqualified; rather, employers and admissions officers are being told that when the pool of qualified workers or applicants has been assembled (and new ways of assembling it are also a part of affirmative action imperatives), choices within it can take minority status into consideration in cases where gross, disparate representation is obvious and long-standing. The last sentence of mine is wordy and unwieldy and doesn't have the quick impact of "it's racial quotas," but at least it is accurate.

The eighth argument — affirmative action lowers the self-esteem of its clients — has little statistical support and is dubious psychology. Some beneficiaries of affirmative action will question their achievements; others will be quite secure in them; and many more will manage to have low self-esteem no matter what their history. Affirmative action is a weak predictor of low self-esteem, and even if there were a strong correlation, you might prefer the low self-esteem that comes along with wondering if your success is really earned to the low self-esteem that comes with never having been in a position to succeed in the first place. At any rate, low self-esteem is at least in part the product of speculation about it. People who never would have thought of questioning their accomplishments might begin to do so if the question was raised every night on the evening news.

The ninth argument — affirmative action provokes race consciousness — is a variation on the blame-the-victim strategy. If there were no affirmative action, it tells us, whites would not be resentful and racial hostility would be dissipated. This might make sense were it not for the little fact that racial hostility antedates affirmative action, which is a response to its effects. To say that as a response it only creates more of what it would redress is like saying, "don't complain or agitate or we will hit you again." The affirmative action backlash is certainly real but it reflects discredit on the backlashers and not on those who continue to press for justice.

There they are, the nifty nine arguments and the counter-arguments you may not have heard elaborated. Use them the next time the question of affirmative action comes up. But don't be surprised if some of those you talk to persist even when the reasons they have always relied on are challenged by reasons equally powerful and by the facts. Sometimes the reasons people give for taking a position are just window dressing, good for public display but only incidental to the heart of the matter, which is the state of their hearts.

NOTES

1. Cathleen Decker, "Affirmative Action Is under Fire," *Los Angeles Times*, Feb. 19, 1995, at A1, A24.
2. *See* Richard J. Herrnstein and Charles A. Murray, *The Bell Curve: Intelligence and Class Structure in American Life* (1996).
3. *Adarand Constructors, Inc., v. Pena*, 115 S. Ct. 2097, 2118 (1995).

Is Affirmative Action a Desirable Policy to Remedy Discrimination in Higher Education?

ROGER CLEGG

Not a Close Question: Preferences in University Admissions

I am glad that the Commission [on Civil Rights] is having this briefing, and indeed I think it is long overdue. For many years, colleges and universities in the United States have used racial and ethnic preferences in the admissions process. My organization has collected strong evidence of such discrimination and published it in studies of public colleges and universities in California, Colorado, Michigan, North Carolina, Washington, and Virginia, as well as the service academies at West Point and Annapolis. I am submitting copies of those studies today to the Commission, and they are also available on our website, <www.ceousa.org>.

The purpose of the Commission on Civil Rights, according to the letter of invitation I received for this briefing, is to investigate discrimination. There is no longer any doubt that many, many schools discriminate on the basis of race and ethnicity in ways that cannot be squared with the decisions of the Supreme Court, let alone the plain language of Title VI of the Civil Rights Act of 1964, which bars any recipient of federal money — and this includes most colleges and universities — from "subject[ing] to discrimination" any "person in the United States . . . on the grounds of race, color, or national origin." That's why I say this briefing is long overdue — assuming, of course, that the Commission is still opposed to racial and ethnic discrimination.

This is the fundamental question before the Commission today: whether college admission programs should discriminate on the basis of race and ethnicity. In framing the issue in these terms, I do not mean to suggest that the answer has to be "No"; but I do think that we have to be honest in admitting that the question is whether to discriminate or not. That is the only kind of "affirmative action" that's in dispute.

BE HONEST

Frankly, those favoring such discrimination frequently resist being honest about what they want. If accused of advocating discrimination, they will respond, for instance, by saying that race or ethnicity is "only one factor among many that should be considered." But that hardly means that discrimination on these grounds won't take place. To the contrary: even if these considerations are "only one factor," there will be some cases — in fact, there are many such cases — in which they make the difference between whether someone is admitted to a college or not. If that is not true, then why consider these factors at all, right? And in those cases where race or ethnicity has been the deciding factor, then someone has been discriminated against because of that immutable characteristic. If he or she had different melanin content or ancestors, he or she would have been treated differently.

Another favorite ploy of the apologists for this kind of discrimination is to respond that they "are opposed to unqualified applicants being admitted." But, again, this hardly means that there is no discrimination. The question is whether someone who is less qualified — even if not unqualified — is being admitted because of race or ethnicity. If so, then there has been discrimination.

Or the apologist will argue that they are not favoring discrimination because they "are not favoring quotas." And, of course, quotas then are defined in such a narrow way that no one could favor them. But, once more, the absence of such quotas hardly means that there is no discrimination. It is easy to have discrimination without there being an absolutely rigid numerical target; a general or flexible target can result in discrimination just as easily.

Defenders of preferences also will frequently point out that written tests are not perfect predictors of future performance at college and that other admission criteria frequently used — like being the offspring of an alumnus or being a good tennis player — are even less predictive. But none of this makes the consideration of race or ethnicity any less discriminatory. If schools are using selection devices that are defective for whatever reason, go ahead and criticize them, but don't think for a minute that such criticisms answer the objection to using race and ethnicity factors that are, in any event, more irrational, more divisive, more stigmatizing, and more constitutionally problematic than any other criteria.

A good way to tell whether discrimination has occurred is to ask what the reaction would be if the shoe were on the other foot. This is a good test to keep in mind whenever someone proposes a justification for discriminating in favor of a particular group: ask yourself how persuasive it would be if it were offered as a justification for discriminating against that group. For instance, suppose that, just after *Brown v. Board of Education,* a college in Mississippi had said that, while it was not going to have an absolute ban on admitting blacks to a particular school, nonetheless race was going to be "a factor" of unspecified weight. Or suppose that this school said that it was not discriminating because only "qualified" whites were being admitted. Or suppose that the school denied it was discriminating because the low ceiling it set on blacks was just a general and flexible target, or that it was permissible to consider race because the school also used other, equally irrational criteria in its decisionmaking. I don't think that any of us would hesitate to label those denials of discrimination as specious. Maybe the discrimination was not as categorical or as absolute as total segregation, but no one would doubt that discrimination was taking place.

THE REAL QUESTION

So, we are dealing with discrimination — the real question is, is the discrimination worth it? That is, are the costs of discrimination outweighed by the benefits? (I'm not talking only, or even principally, about economic costs here; I mean to include all social costs.)

I am not going to argue that there are no conceivable benefits to granting preferences. But, too often, the apologists will state the justifications and then, not only will they not answer the criticisms of those justifications, they will not even consider the fact that, even if those justifications have some merit, we must consider the costs of preferences before anyone can conclude that they are a good idea.

Again, let's put the shoe on the other foot. Suppose an apologist for pre-*Brown* segregation had said, well, segregation makes sense because it improves school spirit. Now, there are two ways to attack that argument. First, you can argue that it doesn't improve school spirit, or at least not as much as the apologist says. But, second, you would argue that maybe it does, maybe it doesn't, but even if it does you don't stop the inquiry there. There are costs to segregation that make it a bad idea even if it means school spirit won't be improved. The chance that maybe school spirit will be improved just isn't worth the likely costs.

The costs and benefits of discrimination must each be weighed, and they must be weighed against one another at the same time on the same scale. By that, I mean that you should not adopt a credulous, "Well, there might be a benefit," mindset for considering arguments in favor of discrimination and a highly skeptical, "But there might be some exceptions to that general rule, maybe," mindset for considering the arguments against discrimination.

So, let us consider, first, the benefits that preferences might have, and then weigh them against their costs.

THREE BENEFITS

The claimed benefits for the use of preferences fall into three categories: prophylactic, remedial, and diversity. The prophylactic justification is that we must affirmatively discriminate in favor of a group's members lest we fall into discriminating against them. The remedial justification is that discrimination now in favor of members of a group can help make up for discrimination against members of that group in the past. And the diversity rationale is that there are benefits to having certain groups represented in some substantial way at the school.

The justifications for preferences almost always fall into one of these three categories — and not only for higher education, but for employment, government contracting, voting, and other areas as well. But sometimes a justification is more plausible in one context than in another.

Prophylactic Benefits

Consider, for example, the prophylactic argument. If we were dealing with a recalcitrant employer who had over and over tried to circumvent a court order that he stop discriminating against blacks for a relatively unskilled, entry-level position, then the prophylactic argument in favor of the judge ordering him to set and meet certain hiring goals has some power. That employer really is likely to discriminate against blacks unless such goals are in place. In this situation, the aim is to create the same nondiscriminatory result that would have come about anyway had the employer not been a bigot.

But the prophylactic rationale has very little plausibility in American higher education today. Do we really need to set goals and timetables to keep college admission officers from discriminating against blacks and Hispanics? That seems very unlikely. The admission officers at the University of Texas law school, for instance, cheerfully ran an illegally segregated admission system for years to ensure that blacks and Mexican Americans would be given heavily preferential treatment.

Remedial Benefits

There is also an obvious pitfall with the second, remedial rationale: discrimination in favor of today's individuals in group X does nothing to help the different individuals in group X who suffered discrimination in the past. The justification, then, must argue one or both of the following: (a) the very individuals who suffered discrimination against them are the ones who now will be receiving discrimination in their favor, or (b) the discrimination suffered in the past has had discriminatory results still being felt by those in group X.

As to the first justification, bear in mind that, in the context of college admissions, we are dealing mostly with 18-year-olds, born around 1981 or 1982. They probably have not participated much in the workforce; if they have, the laws prohibiting discrimination against them on the basis of race or ethnicity have been in effect since long before they were born. Nor have they suffered discrimination in education. Public schools are no longer segregated by race or ethnicity, nor are most private schools.

I can hear the objections. Yes, there are exceptions to the statements in the preceding paragraph. Some teenagers may have suffered employment discrimination because of their race or ethnicity; some public schools may receive less funding because of the color of the children who go there. But the point is that an

18-year-old today is unlikely to have suffered the kind of systematic discrimination against him or her that would justify systematic discrimination in his or her favor. Something as dramatic as a preference has to be based on likelihoods, not bare possibilities.

The Present Effects of Past Racial and Ethnic Discrimination.

So, under the remedial rationale, we are left to consider preferences for race and ethnicity because of the historical effects of discrimination being felt by the descendants of those who suffered the discrimination firsthand. Whether such preferences make sense will hinge on how good a "fit" there is between the class of people who have a particular color or ethnicity and the class of people who are suffering because of past discrimination against their ancestors.

The fit is a poor one. There are, to mix a metaphor, too many false negatives and too many false positives. That is, there are many people who are descended from past sufferers of discrimination who are not eligible for preferences, and many who are not so descended who will be eligible. For instance, not only blacks and Hispanics but also Jews, Asians, American Indians, and Americans of Irish, Italian, Polish, and German origin have all been subjected to discrimination at one time or another in this country, yet probably no college would grant a preference to all these groups. Conversely, some blacks are descendants of recent immigrants and can hardly claim to have suffered even indirectly from slavery and the Jim Crow laws; a high percentage of Hispanics are immigrants or descended from recent immigrants. It is also unclear why the only relevant discrimination to consider is that which occurred in the United States. If a college wants to right the wrongs of past discrimination that it did not itself commit, then why does it matter where the discrimination occurred? This really would open the floodgates, since many, many immigrants — especially the early WASPs, whose descendants everyone hates — were fleeing religious or some other kind of persecution in their native countries.

Some have suggested that preferences ought to be limited to blacks — a special case of particularly heinous discrimination (although no black was interned during World War II, like Japanese Americans, or shunted off to reservations, like American Indians). But, again, not all blacks have slave ancestors. And not every black was confronted with discrimination or the same kind of discrimination (among the most obvious variables are geography and occupation).

It is likewise dangerous to generalize among the many different subgroups who make up the group "Hispanic," a social-scientist construct. And many blacks and many Hispanics do not suffer a depressed socioeconomic status even though they or their ancestors may have suffered discrimination — which makes it impossible to justify a preference for them on the assumption that they do.

It is also a non sequitur to assert that those blacks and Hispanics who did suffer a depressed socioeconomic status and who also may have suffered discrimination became or remained impoverished because of racism. Intervening and independent decisions probably had a greater impact. Illegitimacy, substance abuse, and poor work habits can mire an individual in poverty just as racism can. I understand the argument that racism leads to despair and that despair makes bad lifestyle choices more likely, but this is a tenuous sequence — overcome by many — and the additional connection between this sequence and an entitlement to racial preferences is more tenuous still.

There is also the problem of mixed ancestry. If a wealthy white doctor marries a nurse who belongs to a discriminated-against minority, are their children entitled to a full preference, or no preference, or a half preference? There is no way to avoid this question. Either you say that one drop of minority blood entitles some-one to a full preference, or you draw the line Nuremberg-fashion somewhere else, or you award weighted preferences. All are unattractive choices.

Finally, it would be desirable if those now penalized by the use of preferences also happened to be the beneficiaries of past discrimination against those now receiving the preferences. There is, however, little if any correlation in this regard. Recent immigrants and children of recent immigrants, descendants of working-class northerners, Midwest farmers' sons, Hasidic Jews, and so on — none of them is likely to have benefited in more than a very indirect way from discrimination against blacks or Hispanics, yet each of them is placed at a competitive disadvan-tage with them by admission preferences.

Diversity

The final justification for the use of preferences is, to quote Justice Lewis Powell's opinion in *Regents of the University of California v. Bakke,* "the educational bene-fits that flow from an ethnically diverse student body."

Since Justice Powell's opinion is relied on so heavily by the advocates for diver-sity — legally, there is nothing else they can rely on — it is worth quoting at the outset a paragraph from the opinion that makes clear what the "diversity" argu-ment cannot justify, at least as far as Justice Powell was concerned:

> If [the university's] purpose is to assure within its student body some speci-fied percentage of a particular group merely because of its race or ethnic ori-gin, such a preferential purpose must be rejected not as insubstantial but as facially invalid. Preferring members of any one group for no reason other than race or ethnic origin is discrimination for its own sake. This the Consti-tution forbids.

My own suspicion is that this is a fair description of what most colleges are doing. They have decided that they want to have a particular mix of students, and they have asked their lawyers to come up with a rationale, any rationale, that will allow them to achieve that mix. Diversity is one such rationale, and it has been one of the few successful ones as a matter of law, but it remains a pretext.

Justice Powell also rejected the argument that preferences could be justified on the grounds that minority graduates (in the case of *Bakke,* minority doctors) would be more likely to serve minority communities. Eight years later, in *Wygant v. Jack-son Board of Education,* he also rejected the so-called role model argument — that preferential treatment was justified because minority children needed role models (in that case, teachers) to look up to. As he wrote in *Wygant,* "Carried to its logical extreme, the idea that black students are better off with black teachers could lead to the very system the Court rejected in *Brown v. Board of Education. . . ."*

The "Educational Benefits" of Diversity.

But let's assume then that colleges really believe that there is something educationally beneficial about diversity. The first problem to note is that this belief is a two-edged sword. If diversity can justify preferences in favor of certain groups that are "underrepresented," then surely it can justify negative weights on those that are "overrepresented." There is simply no way to justify the former without justifying the latter. Recall the unhappy history of the Ivy League's ceilings on overrepresented Jews.

Well, let's press on. What might the "educational benefits" to diversity be? There are two basic possibilities. First, it might be that there is something desirable simply about being with people who have a different color or ethnic background, even if they do not otherwise differ. Or, second, it might be that because of the difference in color or ethnicity, people are different inside, too. For instance, they might be more likely to hold particular views or beliefs, or to reflect different cultures or ways of thinking, or to have had particular experiences.

The first possibility hinges on the ability to show students that race and ethnicity don't matter. The idea is that a bigot or potential bigot, if he is forced to see that people of other colors are really not so different from himself, will conclude that bigotry is wrong. But this plan will work only if the bigot is surrounded by students who really are similar to him in ability. If the minorities admitted into the school are less qualified than the nonminorities, the bigot's attitudes will be reinforced, not eroded. And, of course, the first possibility is inconsistent with the second — that is, the argument that minorities are in fact different inside from nonminorities.

So let's turn to this second possibility. This is what Justice Powell had in mind in *Bakke*. The critical passages in his opinion there read as follows:

- [T]he nation's future depends upon leaders trained through wide exposure to the ideas and mores of students as diverse as this Nation of many peoples.
- [U]niversities must be accorded the right to select those students who will contribute the most to the robust exchange of ideas. . . .
- [A] student with a particular background . . . may bring [to the school] . . . experiences, outlooks, and ideas that enrich the training of its student body and better equip its graduates to render with understanding their vital service to humanity.

To decide how plausible this rationale is, we must decide: (a) what the desired inner differences are and (b) whether the best way to find them is by considering race or ethnicity.

On the first point, not every difference is important. Maybe some groups, as a whole, have a particular "outlook" or "experience" when it comes to food, but so what? The desired differences ought to relate to the intellectual discipline being taught. Thus, for instance, it is unclear to me how any cultural difference is relevant to graduate work in mathematics. On the other hand, having experienced discrimination firsthand may well give one insights for sociology and law. Are schools making these distinctions?

The Dangers of Proxies.

The second point is the most critical: Given that we might want some particular inner qualities or experiences represented at the university, does it make sense to use race or ethnicity as a proxy for them? Instead, why not select directly for the quality or experience rather than assuming that everyone with a particular race or ethnicity has it and that others can't?

In the passages quoted from Justice Powell's opinion, he stressed the importance of having students with particular "ideas and mores" and, later, "experiences, outlooks, and ideas," who will "contribute the most to the robust exchange of ideas." Well, if we want students with particular ideas, mores, outlooks, and experiences, then why not select those students — rather than assuming that, because a student has a particular color or ancestry, he or she will meet the admission officer's conception of, for instance, a typical Hispanic woman? And why assume that only certain racial and ethnic groups — and not, for example, religious groups — have a special perspective?

This is also a good time to put the shoe on the other foot. How persuasive would most affirmative-action apologists find it if a college were to limit the enrollment of blacks and Hispanics by using race or ethnicity as a proxy? Not very, I'm sure. There's not much difference in this context between a proxy and a stereotype. Suppose a university were to deny admission to women into a military history program on the grounds that women were unlikely to appreciate matters of military camaraderie? Or to grant a preference to persons of European descent in a European Studies program? Or, on grounds of diversity, to limit the number of Hispanics admitted into its Spanish graduate program?

Let us go through the items on Justice Powell's list and consider how persuasive the claim is that race or ethnicity are the best way to select students. Can we make blanket generalizations about the "ideas," "outlooks," and "mores" of people by looking at their color and ancestors? The answer is no. Indeed, that used to be the required answer among liberals.

What about "experience"? I would be reluctant to generalize much about the kind of life a person had lived simply by looking at him. Moreover, there is no monolithic "black" or "Hispanic" culture that is part of every black or Hispanic. It is certainly invalid to assume that everyone in some racial or ethnic group is economically disadvantaged — invalid and unnecessary since, if you want to grant a preference for those who have suffered economic disadvantage, you can do so without introducing race into the equation.

At the end of the day, the diversity rationale boils down to an argument that the firsthand experience of discrimination is one that ought to be represented in the study of certain disciplines, like law and sociology. Certainly this is the strongest case for the use of race or ethnicity as a proxy. But the weakness in this claim is essentially the same as the weakness in the claim for "remedial benefits" based on these characteristics: we are dealing, after all, with teenagers, born around 1981 or 1982. We are being asked to believe that all, or nearly all, of these teenagers — regardless of other particulars in their backgrounds — have suffered discrimination to the extent and of the sort that will give them special insights lost to other 16-, 17-, and 18-year-olds. I am very skeptical of this claim.

IS IT WORTH IT?

Still, I am not prepared to say that the claims for benefits from preferences are ludicrous, although obviously I believe each claim is riddled with holes. As I warned earlier, however, the inquiry cannot end with the conclusion that there might be something to the claim that the use of preferences has some benefits. The inquiry must proceed to ask, is it likely that those benefits outweigh the costs?

And what are those costs? Unlike the claimed benefits, the costs are clear and undeniable.

To begin with, you are discriminating on the basis of race or ethnicity. You are making generalizations about people on the basis of these immutable characteristics. You are then rewarding or punishing them because they happen to have a certain color or ancestors. This is a bad thing to do. You set a bad precedent and give up a lot when you give up the principle of colorblindness. It is an especially dangerous activity for a state or state-run institution.

Next, you create resentment among those who lose out because of your discrimination. And this resentment is unlikely to be limited in time or scope to the one instance in which it occurs. It is also unlikely to be limited to the immediate victim: his parents, friends, and family will be resentful, too. So will his or her spouse and children, if any.

You will stigmatize the so-called beneficiaries of the preferences — both in the eyes of others and in their own eyes. Where preferences are used, people will assume that a person in the preferred group who was admitted was less qualified than other people who were admitted. And, of course, that is a fair assumption. The whole purpose of the preferences is, after all, to admit those who would otherwise have been rejected as less qualified. And this lesson is taken to heart by the beneficiaries of the preference, too, as Shelby Steele has discussed. They will then begin to doubt their own ability to succeed without preferences, or they will conclude that they do not lack the ability but that the system must lack fairness. Both lessons are unfortunate and untrue.

You will compromise the mission of the university. You will be making intellectual ability a secondary attribute. Your graduates will not be as good. You will be tempted to discriminate in your grading, retention, and graduation policies. The school's graduates will be less competent, with all the attendant social and economic costs of that.

And, finally, as a lawyer I must point out the obvious: You will be breaking the law. The court of appeals in *Hopwood v. Texas* has ruled, correctly, that the Fourteenth

Amendment (which applies to all state schools) and Title VI of the Civil Rights Act of 1964 (which applies to all schools, private and state, that receive federal money) forbid the use of preferences, too. Other courts have rejected the diversity rationale in other contexts. And the Supreme Court has ruled that section 1981 of Title 42 of the U.S. Code bars racial discrimination even by private schools that do not receive federal money. Finally, section 1983 of Title 42 creates broad civil liability for such discrimination, and sections 241 and 242 of Title 18 provide criminal punishment.

THE LAST ARGUMENT

The last argument made by those favoring discrimination is that, whether or not the preferences can be justified, we must use them because otherwise certain groups will be dramatically "underrepresented" at our colleges and universities. There are several responses to this argument.

The first is that this is precisely the rationale that Justice Powell rejected. This justification is nothing more than "discrimination for its own sake."

The second response is that the claim is exaggerated. The students who otherwise got into top-tier schools might now go to second-tier schools — where, incidentally, they will be surrounded by students whose qualifications they more closely match. Not a bad thing — indeed, a good thing.

But what about those top-tier schools? Isn't it the case that for them there may be, for instance, fewer blacks or Hispanics — even if other criteria are used in addition to standardized test scores? Fewer, but not none. Besides, if a school is using the best criteria it can devise to select the best qualified students, then why should anyone object to the school's demographic makeup? Suppose there are no blacks admitted to Harvard Medical School one year. So what? Is it rational for black people to conclude from this fact that America is racist or that they have no stake, or less of a stake, in our nation? Only a Harvard intellectual could believe that. Different professions favor different interests, talents, and inclinations, which may not be perfectly mirrored at every point in time among our nation's many demographic groups. Again, so what?

CONCLUSION

So, tally up the costs and benefits. Maybe there is something to the diversity rationale in some cases, and maybe there is something to the remedial and prophylactic rationales in some cases, too, although we have seen that all three rationales are riddled with holes. But let's suppose that there is something left, in each case, greater than zero. You then are obliged to consider what's on the other side of the scale: the fact that you are discriminating, the resentment, the stigmatization, the compromising of the mission of the university, and the illegality. Which way does the scale tip? To anyone who is intellectually honest, it is not a close question. Preferences should not be used.

The Commission should condemn this discrimination, just as it has condemned other discrimination in the past.

Questions for Discussion

1. What criteria should be used in deciding which groups should be included in a category warranting affirmative action?
2. Can an affirmative action policy exist without a quota system? What are the reasons for your answer?
3. What criteria should be used by a university admissions committee of a prestigious college or university in selecting students for admission? What is the relevance of your answer to the issue of affirmative action?
4. What impact does racial and ethnic diversity in admissions have on a university campus?
5. What effect does affirmative action have on its beneficiaries?
6. How would you determine whether an affirmative action program for university admissions should be ended?
7. Are people who oppose affirmative action based on race and ethnicity bigots? Are people who support affirmative action based on race and ethnicity bigots? What are the reasons for your answer?

Suggested Resources

Web Sites

Affirmative Action and Diversity Project: A Web Page for Research
http://aad.english.ucsb.edu/

American Association for Affirmative Action
http://www.affirmativeaction.org/

Center for Equal Opportunity
http://www.ceousa.org

Coalition to Defend Affirmative Action and Integration and Fight for Equality by Any Means Necessary
http://www.bamn.com

National Center for Public Policy Research: Affirmative Action Information Center
http://www.nationalcenter.org/AA.html

Publications

Bowen, William G., and Derek Bok. *The Shape of the River: Long-Term Consequences of Considering Race in College and University Admission.* Princeton, N.J.: Princeton University Press, 1998.

Cahn, Steven M., ed. *The Affirmative Action Debate,* 2d ed. New York: Routledge, 2002.

Cohen, Carl. "Race Preference and the Universities — A Final Reckoning." *Commentary* 112, no. 2 (September 2001): 31–39.

Cokorinos, Lee. *The Assault on Diversity: An Organized Challenge to Racial and Gender Justice.* Lanham, Md.: Rowman & Littlefield, 2003.

Crosby, Faye J., and Cheryl VanDeVeer, eds. *Sex, Race, and Merit: Debating Affirmative Action in Education and Employment.* Ann Arbor: University of Michigan Press, 2000.

Guerrero, Andrea. *Silence at Boalt Hall: The Dismantling of Affirmative Action.* Berkeley: University of California Press, 2002.

Guinier, Lani, and Susan Sturm. *Who's Qualified?* Boston: Beacon Press, 2001.

Jost, Kenneth. "Affirmative Action." *CQ Researcher* 11, no. 32 (September 21, 2001): 737–60.

"Look What Happens When Affirmative Action Is Banned: Black Students Are Pushed Down into Second- and Third-Tier Institutions." *Journal of Blacks in Higher Education* no. 34 (Winter 2001/2002): 82–94.

McWhorter, John H. "The Campus Diversity Fraud." *City Journal* 12, no. 1 (Winter 2002): 74–81.

Milem, Jeffrey F. "Why Race Matters." *Academe* 86, no. 5 (September/October 2000): 27–29.

Orfield, Gary, with Michael Kurlaender, eds. *Diversity Challenged: Evidence on the Impact of Affirmative Action.* Cambridge, Mass.: Harvard Education Publishing Group, 2001.

Pincus, Fred L. *Reverse Discrimination: Dismantling the Myth.* Boulder, Colo.: Lynne Rienner, 2003.

Thernstrom, Abigail. "Diversity Yes, Preferences No." *Academe* 86, no. 5 (September/October 2000): 30–32.

Popular Participation

Democracies pride themselves on the freedom of people to participate in the political process. Such participation takes many forms, including forming private associations known as interest groups, getting involved in political campaigns, voting, working for political parties, and expressing ideas through speech or the mass media.

The traditional definition of an interest group is a collection of people with common interests who work together to achieve those interests. When a group becomes involved in the activities of government, it is known as a political interest group.

More than a century ago, Alexis de Tocqueville observed that the people of the United States have a propensity to form associations. This observation is as valid a description of our time as it was of the 1830s. The United States has a large number of political interest groups — business, labor, professional, religious, and social reform. Interest groups engage in a variety of activities, including making financial contributions to candidates for public office and to political parties, getting their viewpoints known to the general public and to other groups, organizing demonstrations, and influencing government officials. Legitimate political behavior in a democracy allows for great freedom to participate in these ways. The First Amendment of the Constitution is often cited as the basis for such political behavior. That amendment states:

> Congress shall make no law respecting an establishment of religion, or prohibiting the free exercise thereof; or abridging the freedom of speech, or of the press; or the right of the people peaceably to assemble, and to petition the government for a redress of grievances.

One form of political activity is involvement in political campaigns and elections. In a democracy people are free to support candidates of their choice. Such support may consist of merely voting in an election, but it may also include organizing meetings, soliciting support for candidates, raising and spending money for candidates, and publicizing issues.

An effective democracy requires that information be widely disseminated. The same First Amendment that protects the rights of individuals and groups to engage in political activities also safeguards the press and other media such as television, radio, and magazines. Television, particularly, has become the chief source of news for many people.

What people do and what they think are of vital importance to government officials. In democracies (and even in many dictatorships) government makes every effort to know what public opinion is on many issues. Sometimes government leads and sometimes it follows public opinion.

Although modern dictatorships rely on political participation, that participation is generally controlled by the ruling elite. Interest groups are not spontaneous organizations designed to be independent from government but are linked to government primarily through government-controlled leadership. And so, for example, trade unions are not free to strike or engage in protest activities — at least not legitimately. People are not free to form competitive political parties, and often there is only one political party that dominates elections. That party is regarded as having a special role in mobilizing the masses.

In many modern dictatorships elections do take place, but they are generally rigged. Where opposing candidates are permitted to compete, there is generally no significant difference between the candidates on issues. Protest movements and mass demonstrations are broken up, sometimes ruthlessly, unless those movements are controlled by the government. To be sure, protest movements and demonstrations do exist in some modern dictatorships, but government tries to control or suppress them.

In modern dictatorships, moreover, the media are not free to report the news in an objective manner. Instead, the media reflect the wishes of the ruling dictators. News is suppressed; opposition newspapers are closed down. There is only one truth — that of the government — disseminated through television, radio, magazines, and newspapers.

Although democracies are fundamentally different from dictatorships, even democracies do not always live up to the standards of freedom they cherish. In this regard, the political behavior of private individuals and groups in the United States poses problems for those interested in protecting democratic processes. Although it is relatively easy to discuss democracy in the abstract, actual practices raise thorny questions. Part III considers five issues pertaining to popular participation in the democratic process in the United States: the political power of big corporations, the voting choices that individuals make, the method of financing campaigns for public office, the utility of the Electoral College in electing the president, and whether the mass media have a liberal bias.

9

Do Big Corporations
Control America?

In 2002, stories of wrongdoing by corporations were a common feature in the media. Insider trading and corrupt accounting practices became a regular subject of the news. And pictures of former corporate executives pleading guilty to charges of illegality made executive officers anathema to many people in American society. Enron, Arthur Andersen, and WorldCom were but a few corporations in the news for criminal investigations. And major stock companies paid millions of dollars to settle charges of manipulating stocks. What was particularly striking to many were the pictures of workers in some of those companies who lost their jobs partly or wholly because of the economic consequences that followed from corporate wrongdoing.

Bad publicity for corporations is not new in American life. In the early twentieth century, for example, Upton Sinclair's novel *The Jungle* exposed the unsanitary and harsh working conditions of the big meatpackers in the Chicago stockyards.

Popular attitudes toward corporations are shaped not only by what corporations do as a consequence of their commercial operations but also by their connections with government. Corporations are heavily involved in American political life, for they are keenly aware that governmental decisions, such as tax policy, can affect their financial situations. Some corporations are heavily dependent on getting contracts from government for the products they make or the services they perform. Among these are corporations that manufacture military equipment and build highways and bridges.

The influence of government on corporations is found in many areas of public policy. Specifically, environmental protection laws directly affect the way that automobiles are manufactured. Tariffs are a concern of corporations fearing competition from abroad. Pharmaceutical companies worry about patent legislation. Giant corporations worry about antitrust prosecution.

And so corporations in the United States engage in much political activity. They contribute to corporate political action committees that give campaign contributions to political parties. They employ lobbyists to influence legislation and administrative policies. They try to influence the naming of political appointees who are sympathetic to policies they would like to see adopted. They sponsor compelling television, radio, and newspaper commercials promoting views they want government to follow.

In recent decades, corporations have become bigger and bigger, as companies in many industries have merged. Some observers feel that the economic power is being translated into political power for the benefit of the corporations at the expense of ordinary Americans.

Do corporations have such political power that they actually control America? In an interview by Ruth Conniff for *The Progressive*, Richard Grossman, an advocate for democratic control of corporations, argues that corporations control America. He says:

1. Giant corporations take over government decision making, which in a democracy is supposed to belong to the people.
2. Corporations shape elections and the development of ideas. They write the laws and structure public debate.
3. The corporate class has used law and the Constitution for its own benefit rather than for the people.
4. Eventually people must change the culture so that corporate values do not dominate the American political system.

Economist James Rolph Edwards argues that big corporations do not control America. He contends:

1. Business interests in America are diverse and have conflicting goals.
2. Government imposes high personal taxes on wealthy people who derive their income from corporations, and government enacts corporate income taxes, too. If the corporations controlled America, they would not have let such laws be enacted.
3. Because competition remains a central feature of American capitalism, turnover in dominant companies in particular industries is high. If the big corporations controlled America, that feature of the economic system would not exist.
4. Small- and medium-size firms have competed successfully against the big corporations and have increased their market share of many industries — a development that shows the limitations of power of big corporations.

 YES

Do Big Corporations Control America?

RICHARD GROSSMAN

Big Corporations Undermine Democracy:
An Interview by Ruth Conniff

I first met Richard Grossman when I was following Ralph Nader on the campaign trail through New England. Grossman lives in New Hampshire, and Nader brought him along on a visit to the state capitol, introducing him to lawmakers as "the preeminent historian of corporations" and a "treasure" right there in their home state.

Grossman co-directs the Program on Corporations, Law, and Democracy, which describes its mission as "instigating democratic conversations and actions that contest the authority of corporations to govern."

The group came together in the early nineties, he says, when a dozen activists who had spent much of their lives working on issues of peace, labor, women's rights, and the environment decided that something more had to be done.

"It's funny, we did not set out to become experts on the corporation," he says. "We set out to try to discover why it is that the activist work of so many good and able people around the country for so many decades had not brought about the kinds of changes that people had been hoping for. Why is it — after so many years of so many groups fighting toxic chemicals and winning, passing laws, and closing dumps, and doing all kinds of good things — that every day more toxic chemicals are produced than the day before? We saw that power was being concentrated even more in corporate boardrooms. The ideal of democracy was moving further out of reach. And by most objective criteria — the wealth gap, public health, the environment, workers' rights — things were getting worse."

In a recent book published by the group, *Defying Corporations, Defining Democracy* (Apex Press, 2001), Grossman and his colleagues argue that corporate power has grown unchecked. "Following the Civil War and well into the twentieth century, appointed judges gave privilege after privilege to corporations," the book notes. One of the worst cases early on was the 1886 Supreme Court decision *Santa Clara County v. Southern Pacific Railroad Co.,* which ruled that a corporation was a "person" under the Constitution, sheltered by the Fourteenth Amendment. This legal doctrine spawned modern corporations — commercial Frankensteins — with all the rights of real people, and immortality, too. In one stroke, the Court killed future efforts by states and local governments to rein in corporate behavior.

It's time people took back control over corporations, Grossman says. I spoke to him by phone as the Enron debacle was generating front-page news coverage.

Q Do you think Enron is going to be a mass consciousness-raising exercise? How about Dick Cheney refusing to release the list of corporations that helped shape energy policy because it would have a chilling effect on shaping policy in the future?

Richard Grossman: Who's going to be surprised at Dick Cheney's list of corporate executives who participated in the energy plan? We've seen the plan. We know what it's about, we know whose values are represented there, whose ideas. It's not a big question.

The real issue is that Enron's DNA was to do what it did. Enron basically created a new market that wasn't about goods or services that people need; it was about making money. The executives figured out where they wanted to go, what laws they had to change, how they had to reframe the debate about energy, and then within ten or twelve years they accomplished a huge amount of what they set out to do. And that didn't happen because they were the most brilliant people in the world, but because they had all the tools they needed. Enron took advantage of a process that has been going on for the last 200 years, which made it very easy for them. They could use the law, the regulatory agencies, and the Supreme Court doctrine that money is a form of speech. They spread their money around to Congress, to state legislators, to think tanks, the press — all the places where ideas are influenced in this country.

And most of the stuff that they did along the way was perfectly legal. All the money they gave to the elected officials, that was all legal, lobbying in the Federal Trade Commission, that was all legal. Enron executives essentially said, "Well, we've got to go into state legislatures and persuade these guys that the existing state-regulated energy system is inefficient and wrong, and we're going to throw it out, and we're going to go to the federal government and get all kinds of changes, and start creating a federal grid that we can milk more effectively."

Q So you don't think that any illegalities or any particular political scandal is going to be the point of Enron?

Grossman: What comes out of this depends on how the issues are framed. It seems to me the job of a political movement, of activists, is to think in a different way, to use what's happening now to help people see the underlying questions: What is a corporation? Where does it come from? How can it be that our elected officials create and enable entities like Enron, which fundamentally take over the decision-making, which in a democracy is supposed to belong to the people?

Q How do they take over democratic decision-making?

Grossman: As soon as a corporation is chartered — corporations are chartered in the states — at the very moment of conception, the corporate form is endowed with certain rights and privileges. They can shape elections, shape the development of ideas, write the laws, and shape public debate. They can do what Enron did — transform thinking at the federal level about energy, and shut people up and out at the state and local level.

Look at the next steps. Why is it that people in communities, municipalities, and states believe they can't pass laws that ban corporations from spending any money on election campaigns, or that they can't pass laws that even ban particular products of corporations from their communities? If a community set out today to say "within our jurisdiction, no genetically modified food is allowed to enter," or if it passed a law that banned any corporate contribution to public discussion of ideas or to referenda, the corporations' lawyers would run right to federal court. The court would end up throwing the laws out, claiming constitutional rights and privileges of the corporation dating back to the Commerce Clause, the First Amendment, and the Fourteenth Amendment.

Q It sounds almost conspiratorial to say that corporations shape how we think. How does that work?

Grossman: Well, I'm not sure what conspiratorial means. There's a corporate class that has enormous wealth, and the power of law behind it, and it dominates the way issues are framed. I mean, is it really true that the majority of the American people over the last twenty-five years didn't want a major transition in energy to move to efficiency and solar, didn't want universal health care, but wanted pig genes in fish?

Isn't it extraordinary that despite shelves and shelves of books and all kinds of practical experience on all these issues, the dominant view on everything from energy to corporate agriculture is that big technology, chemicals, and the most complex energy systems possible are the best? Where do these ideas come from, and how are they sustained? They're surely not the ideas that people believe are going to make their communities more harmonious, democratic places.

Q What's the big picture we're not getting?

Grossman: Look, why was it so easy for GM and Firestone in the 1940s to buy up electric trolley systems all over the country? Destroy the tracks, destroy the trains, and basically set the nation's transportation policy as highways and cars and trucks? That was a scandal, too. There were hearings and trials, and in the end they were fined $5,000. But the whole transportation system, the elaborate intercity electric trolley system, that existed in so many places across the country had been literally destroyed. And the policy of the federal government was to put public wealth into highways and trucks and buses and not rapid transit.

The same thing happened with agriculture. The public wealth and public resources since the beginning of the twentieth century have been behind the notion that the largest farms were the most efficient farms. So, as with Enron, you have private entities created by the state, enabled with vast powers and privilege, and given the authority to make the governing decisions. And they're able to use the coercive force of law — the courts, the police, the regulatory agencies — to get their way. And sometimes they're not clever enough, like Enron, and things fall apart. But it's naive to believe that out of this will come some major legal or societal transformation without a significant movement, a significant uprising of folks who are clear about what's happening here.

Q You say it's important how this Enron thing is framed. So what is the twenty-five-word summary that would be a really salutary message that could get out?

Grossman: That's a challenge. I think there are many people working towards the bumper-sticker message. I don't have it in twenty-five words, but in general it's about the history of this country, the laws and culture that govern us today. My colleagues and I were really unaware, we were misinformed, we were uninformed, we were ignorant about so much in U.S. history that made what's happening today — what Enron is — totally logical.

People in previous generations were much more aware than people today of what was going on and how the reality of the structure from the beginning disadvantaged the majority of people. So it's about the lack of real democracy from the beginning, the fact that the law and the Constitution have been used to privilege first a propertied class and then a corporate class, and that we've all been taught that the corporation is the only vehicle we can rely on for jobs, for goods, for services, to be "competitive" in the world. And our elected officials don't have to be bought to believe that. Essentially, that's what they believe. They don't see any alternative. They believe they have to turn everything over to these giant corporations.

State legislators don't even know the extent to which they have authority to write the state corporate codes in ways that make corporations subordinate. I would suspect that an awful lot of Senators and Representatives don't know that history.

For example, in the analysis I'm seeing of Enron, I haven't seen a schematic of the 3,500 corporate entities under the Enron umbrella. Where are they chartered? Apparently, there are quite a few chartered out in the Cayman Islands or the Bahamas, offshore. But they're also chartered in Texas and Oregon and other states. Attorneys general and governors of states give what's called a certificate authority for a corporation to do business in a state. They have the authority to prevent — in fact, they have the responsibility to prevent — these corporations from doing what they're doing.

I think that all the attorneys general should be throwing themselves into this Enron situation, seizing assets, setting out to revoke the charters of these entities, throwing themselves into the fight.

Q Do you see the battle against corporate power as something akin to the civil rights movement where there's a big defining struggle taking place in the courts?

Grossman. No. I think the big defining struggle is going to take place in the culture. And the courts will come last. In a sense, *Brown v. Board of Education* wasn't worth much until the civil rights struggle really moved into the culture in a very significant way, forced by this extraordinary grassroots-based, multigenerational civil rights movement. It took another twenty years of really serious grassroots mobilizing, agitation in the culture. And that's where this has to happen, and it is happening: in Seattle, or at the demonstrations outside both of the parties' conventions last year, or recently in New York at the World Economic Forum. Those are the visible aspects of a growing ferment in community after community.

It's interesting how ideas form and shape and what takes root and what doesn't. It's not pure chance. If there's a social movement that's trying to inject new ideas into the culture, it takes generations. Look at desegregation. Look what it took to move that idea through society. And that idea is still not totally accepted in this society.

Q So is this the same case for what you're trying to do? It's going to take generations?

Grossman: I think so. And it's more complicated because it's not a single, tangible issue. It's not about the rights of a single class of people. It's about how people become self-governing. How do almost 300 million people come together in all these different jurisdictions to make the rules and to live as harmoniously as possible? If the ideal in this country has always been that the people rule, well, how are we going to do that? And can we do that if the Constitution and the law prevent us from doing that because they are enabling the few and disabling the many?

If the government had been neutral on slavery, if the slave owners could not rely on the fugitive slave clause in the Constitution to return runaway slaves or indentured servants, and the militia couldn't be called out to put down slave rebellions, and it was just the slave owners against the slaves, slavery would have been gone very quickly. The same is true of segregation. If the police wouldn't have come out and enforced all the Jim Crow laws, segregation would not have lasted.

What we have now is a system where the coercive force of government and the culture that goes along with it enable a few people through the law and through their institutions called corporations to dominate the governing of this country. Many people don't want to acknowledge that. Because to do something about it means to change this country in very significant ways. If this country were really a country of democratic self-governance where the people actually were the source of all political and legal authority, it would be a very different country. And the people who govern today wouldn't govern. The class that governs today wouldn't govern.

Q So what can people do right now?

Grossman: Compared to five or six years ago there's so much more going on. Activists are investing their energies beyond regulatory proceedings, beyond reform laws that basically choose paper or plastic.

In Pennsylvania, nine townships have passed laws banning the corporate ownership of farms. The issue was big corporate hog farms coming in. And so people decided there that they weren't going to do regulations about hog manure, and how many hogs per square feet, which activists are doing in North Carolina and many other states. They're saying, "In our jurisdiction, no corporations can own farms."

So that issue is being totally reframed. It's not about the science of hog odor and hog manure. It's about municipalities exercising their authority to define what goes on within their jurisdictions. That's the kind of confrontation that needs to take place in communities around the country, and at the state level, in order to drive this movement eventually into national struggles over who gets to decide and who sets the values in this country. A few people behind the shield of giant corporations empowered by our elected officials? Or the public through directly elected officials not chosen by the corporate class?

On a couple levels, it's working. So far, no corporate hog farms have come into those communities. And agribusiness corporations and the Farm Bureau have launched the lawsuit we anticipated. They are suing one of the townships, and the lawsuit is very clear. It basically says, "This township does not have the legal and constitutional authority to pass such a law." All that did was infuriate folks. And every time the head of the Farm Bureau in Pennsylvania writes an article saying he's trying to talk about efficiency and the consumer and this and that, more and more people who are getting involved with the issue through neighbors and friends see it as absolute nonsense. Because you don't have to read too carefully in a 400-word article where the main themes are the corporations know best, the Constitution says that the corporations have all these rights, and you people have no rights. It just drives these folks to be stronger and clearer and more determined.

And that's a lesson for activists around the country. If you frame the issue about who's in charge, about power, and not around six parts per million or eight parts per million or how many kilowatts here versus kilowatts there, that's what arouses people. That's what educates people. That's what pushes some people on their own to say, "I didn't know any of this history, let's check it out."

Q What's the ultimate goal?

Grossman: The abolitionists eventually had to take their struggle into the Constitution and write the Thirteenth, Fourteenth, and Fifteenth amendments because the ownership of humans as property and the denial of human rights had been imbedded in the Constitution. The women's suffrage movement also had to go into the Constitution. The same is true with what we're talking about. Eventually, when the culture changes, when there's been enough contesting, revealing, and educating, these issues will either be driven into the Constitution or they won't. Eventually, the fundamental law of the land will change or it won't. And our job and the job of the next generation is not to be diverted into paper versus plastic, but to keep our focus on that fundamental work.

$$☑\ N\ O$$

Do Big Corporations Control America?

JAMES ROLPH EDWARDS
Do Big Corporations Control America?

Since the mid-eighteenth century the development of market-based societies in America and elsewhere, with constitutional protections of property and freedom, has had startling effects. Well over 90 percent of the improvement in the material living standards of ordinary persons that has occurred in the 6,000 years of recorded human history has occurred in that last 250 years and in those nations. Mean life expectancy in the United States rose from 35 years in 1800 to 50 in 1900, and around 76 in 2000. Famine in such nations disappeared and many diseases were conquered. All this resulted from replacing the caste and status relationships of medieval society with contract relationships between mutually consenting adults, while restricting the power of government to enforcing contracts, providing national defense, preventing crime, and a few other basic functions.

Despite the enormous gains this form of social organization generated for ordinary people, particularly in America, a political and ideological reaction began after the Civil War, when industrialization was proceeding rapidly, and lasted more than a century. A key claim of the partisans of this view — who originally called themselves Progressives — is that large corporations not only dominate capitalist society economically, essentially abolishing market competition, but also dominate the political system. So most, if not all legislation, serves the wealthy corporate interests. Karl Marx may have originated this argument, but to this day, shorn of its Marxist metaphysics, it is the majority perspective among the intellectual and political classes in America. Even many conservatives, and a few libertarians, adhere to this perspective.

Most staunch free-market advocates and political libertarians argue, to the contrary, that the dominant political and ideological impulse of the twentieth century in America and the West has been statist and anti-capitalist. In this view the "corporate domination" argument is simply a key element in that statist ideology, used to justify legislation enhancing governmental power and reducing human freedom. In an essay published several decades back, Ayn Rand made the connection clear when she wrote: "Every movement that seeks to enslave a country, every dictatorship or potential dictatorship, needs some minority group as a scapegoat which it can blame for the nation's troubles and use as a justification of its own demands for dictatorial powers. In Soviet Russia, the scapegoat was the bourgeoisie; in Nazi Germany, it was the Jewish people; in America, it is the businessmen."[1] Rand went on to claim, with some justification, that businessmen, big businessmen in particular, were America's most persecuted minority, using the inequities of the antitrust laws to illustrate her argument.

Certainly, things are somewhat more complicated than Rand claimed in that essay. One need not believe that an all powerful conspiracy of international bankers and wealthy capitalists lies behind the statist movements of our day to recognize that businessmen have often supported extensions of state power. This was particularly so in the decades after World War I. Woodrow Wilson had centralized power in Washington during the war and exercised regulatory command and control over the economy. He drew many corporate executives into the government to operate the bureaus he created, and many of them found they preferred issuing and enforcing orders over attempting to motivate and manage voluntary, contractual employees, who could quit at will.

Thus some big-business executives came to the same elitist, technocratic view held by most intellectuals and academics: that ordinary people are too ignorant to run their own lives, much less largely determine, through their consumption and employment choices, the allocation of resources in society. It follows, in this view, that experts should run things by fiat, maintaining only a thin veneer of democracy and free markets. Franklin Roosevelt drew heavily on this pool of statist business executives to staff his administrations during the Great Depression.

Economists have also found reason to recognize that businessmen often act to extend government power and attenuate market competition. George Stigler developed the economic theory of regulation in the late 1960s, arguing that, instead of regulation being imposed on industries in genuine democratic response to the desires of oppressed and abused consumers, firms often actually seek government regulation in an effort to gain monopoly or cartel powers they cannot obtain by market methods. The historian Gabriel Kolko, in a detailed study of the Progressive era, made a similar argument a few years before Stigler. Rand herself, in many of her works, recognized the existence of such corrupt businessmen. Thus statist and corporate interests and ideology may converge at least to some degree, leaving a limited-government, free-market perspective as the only logical opposition.

TEMPORARY ALLIES

Still, businessmen and statists can at best be temporary and uneasy allies. The majority of businessmen are honest, and unlike the intellectual, academic, and bureaucratic classes in America, where a statist view dominates, business interests are too diverse to generate a consistently statist legislative impulse. Some import-competing businesses, for example, will lobby for government to pass a tariff to raise the price of a product they sell domestically. Other businesses that use that product as an input, however, will oppose the tariff. Also, attitudes of firms toward regulation sometimes reverse. The airline industry sought the creation of the Civil Aeronautics Board [CAB] and the airline cartel in the 1930s. But when their profits were absorbed by airline unions in the 1970s and many airlines were frustrated by the CAB in their efforts to compete on particular routes, much of the industry supported deregulation. Business groups donate to all influential parties and political groups, unlike labor unions, which donate exclusively to statist groups. Much business lobbying is essentially defensive, aimed at staving off oppressive and costly regulation, often unsuccessfully.

Most of the basic legislative structure in America conflicts with the view that legislation is dominated by wealthy corporate interests. Consider the tax structure. If such interests dominated, would the Sixteenth Amendment ever have been adopted? Would the personal income tax it allowed Congress to establish have become progressive, with a top rate that at times has been as high as 90 percent? Would over 70 percent of all revenue collected through the personal income tax come from the top 20 percent of income-earning families, as it has since the mid-1990s?

Again, if the wealthy corporate interests dominated government and legislation, would there ever have been a corporate income tax? Such a tax, levied on the net income of firms *before* distribution to investors, actually taxes the incomes of stockholders twice. That is because all the net income of the firm is generated by capital supplied by those investors, whose incomes are then taxed again, through the personal income tax, *after* distribution through stock dividends. As a result, the actual tax rate on investor income is enormously higher than the stated personal income tax rate. Certainly, rational capitalists would not have allowed such a grossly unfair and costly law to pass had they the power to stop it. The corporate income tax *disadvantages* corporations relative to other forms of business organizations, such as partnerships and proprietorships, which suffer no such double taxation. If wealthy corporate interests dominated our political system, would they ever have allowed such a thing?

Similarly, would they have accepted a law compelling businesses to withhold the taxes of employees? Income-tax withholding forces firms to act as tax collectors for the government at their own expense. This is done without compensation of any kind, in violation of the Fifth Amendment takings clause of the Constitution, and against their wills, in violation of the Thirteenth Amendment injunction against involuntary servitude. Withholding imposes an economic burden that corporate or other business interests would not have willingly accepted had they the power to prevent it. Do not such policies in fact reflect an anti-capitalist animus?

CORPORATE CONTROL?

The notion that a corporate elite dominates the nation politically presumes also that large corporations are able to control prices, output, and entry in their industries on an enduring basis, as John Kenneth Galbraith has long claimed. Though in some industries this has clearly occurred, precisely through corporate lobbying to secure franchises and monopoly or cartel protection (the electric utilities are a good example), there is precious little evidence of any successful system-wide abolition of competition. Precisely the opposite seems to be the case. The turnover of dominant firms in particular industries is far too high, and the market shares of firms in concentrated markets far too unstable year to year, to support any view that being top dog guarantees continued dominance. Add to this the rapid and constant innovation we observe, and such turnover and market-share instability indicates that most firms gain large market shares by satisfying customers with lower priced and/or higher quality products than their competitors, and lose share when they stop doing so.

The evidence regarding macro concentration points to the same conclusions. Any simple comparison of the Fortune 500 lists of the largest industrial corporations in 1980, 1990, and 2000, for example, will impress an observer with the impermanence of corporate domination. Likewise, Gary Quinlivan recently compared the *Wall Street Journal* lists of the world's top 100 firms ranked by market value for 1990 and 1999, and found that there were 66 new firms in the 1999 list. He also reports that the United Nations, comparing lists of the top 100 nonfinancial multinational corporations for 1990 and 1997, found a 25 percent turnover. This is less impressive than the *Wall Street Journal* comparison, but still an enormous turnover of top firms in just a few years.[2]

Using data available in the 1986-to-1996 editions of the *Statistical Abstract of the United States,* I recently found some remarkable changes in U.S. macro concentration between 1980 and 1993. The 500 largest industrial corporations in the

United States employ a large fraction of American workers, embody a large part of our productive assets, and produce a large share of our aggregate output. Over those 13 years, however, the assets of the top 500 industrial firms, as a share of total corporate assets, fell by over 20 percent. Employment in the top 500 firms, as a share of total employment in the country, fell even more, by 29 percent. And most amazing of all, the share of gross domestic product generated by those firms fell by an astonishing 39 percent over that short period.[3]

Clearly, the turnover in any list of the largest corporations is inconsistent with the naïve view that large firms are able to abolish competition and insure their continued dominance. So is the evidence on the output, employment, and assets of large firms in the aggregate. Assets, employment, and market share have clearly shifted significantly to small- and medium-sized firms in the last two decades. Such firms have competed with increasing success against larger corporations in a computerized and internationally integrated economic environment. Would any economically and politically dominant class of wealthy capitalists in big corporations have allowed such an enormous decline in their relative wealth and power to occur if they could have stopped it?

In fairness, it should be noted that these economic events are also not entirely consistent with the view that the statist and anti-capitalist ideology held by most members of the intellectual, academic, bureaucratic, and media elites still dominates the legislation process. Certainly that was true for most of the twentieth century, as illustrated in the graph showing both federal government expenditures (FGE) as a fraction of gross national product and the sum of federal and state expenditures as a fraction of GNP from 1929 to 1990. The data come from various volumes of *The Economic Report of the President,* which is issued annually by the President's Council of Economic Advisers. The growth in FGE/GNP, from about .025 (or 2.5 percent) in 1929 to .233 in 1990, nearly ten times as large, clearly, if imperfectly, documents the size and growth of the leviathan state.

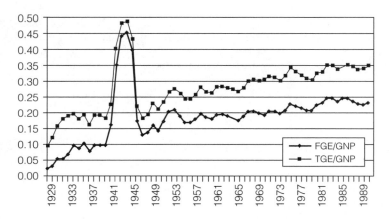

Figure 9.1 Federal and Total Government Expenditures as Fractions of GNP, 1929–1990

Since about 1980, however, the ideological and political grip of statism has begun to loosen. Statist policies of regulation and income redistribution have visibly failed. Slowly, some of the statist fetters have been lifted from the economy, allowing entrepreneurship and economic growth to continue. Federal outlays actually fell from 21 percent of gross domestic product in 1994 to only 18.8 percent in 1999 (GDP replaced GNP in the National Income and Product Accounts after 1990). This nearly 10.5 percent decline in the relative size of government, and commensurate release of resources to the private sector, more than any other thing, accounted for the rapid economic growth of the late 1990s. Many statist policies still advance, of course. Things hang in the balance, but the tide seems to have incrementally turned toward restoration of a freer society. Whether that trend will continue or be deflected in a statist direction again by the terrorist attack of September 11 remains to be seen.

NOTES

1. Ayn Rand, "America's Persecuted Minority: Big Business," in Ayn Rand, ed., *Capitalism: The Unknown Ideal* (New York: Signet, 1967), p. 45.

2. Gary Quinlivan, "Multinational Corporations: Myths and Facts," *Religion and Liberty,* November and December 2000, pp. 8–10.

3. James Rolph Edwards, "The Myth of Corporate Domination," *Liberty,* January 2001, pp. 41–42.

Questions for Discussion

1. What are the strengths of big corporations in projecting their power in American political life?
2. What are the weaknesses of big corporations in projecting their power in American political life?
3. To what extent does the political culture of the American people influence the political power of big corporations?
4. Do environmental protection laws demonstrate the political strength or weakness of big corporations on the American political system? What are the reasons for your answer?
5. What role should government play in limiting the power of big corporations? What are the reasons for your answer?

Suggested Resources

Web Sites

Federal Trade Commission
   http://www.ftc.gov/

Program on Corporations, Law & Democracy
   http://www.poclad.org/

ReclaimDemocracy.org
  http://www.reclaimdemocracy.org/

United States Chamber of Commerce
  http://www.uschamber.com/default

Publications

Aronowitz, Stanley. *How Class Works: Power and Social Movement.* New Haven, Conn.: Yale University Press, 2003.

Casper, Barry M. *Lost in Washington: Finding the Way Back to Democracy in America.* Amherst: University of Massachusetts, 2000.

Derber, Charles. *Corporation Nation: How Corporations Are Taking over Our Lives and What We Can Do about It.* New York: St. Martin's Press, 1998.

Domhoff, G. William. *Who Rules America? Power and Politics,* 4th ed. Boston: McGraw Hill, 2002.

Draffan, George. *The Elite Consensus: When Corporations Wield the Constitution.* New York: Apex Press, 2003.

Dye, Thomas R. *Who's Running America? The Bush Restoration,* 7th ed. Upper Saddle River, N.J.: Prentice Hall, 2002.

Fox, Loren. *Enron: The Rise and Fall.* New York: Wiley, 2003.

Gonzalez, George A. *Corporate Power and the Environment: The Political Economy of U.S. Environmental Policy.* Lanham, Md.: Rowman & Littlefield, 2001.

Green, Mark. *Money Shouts: Democracy for Sale from Washington to Enron.* New York: Regan Books, 2002.

Jacobs, David C. D. *Business Lobbies and the Power Structure in America: Evidence and Arguments.* Westport, Conn.: Quorum Books, 1999.

Parenti, Michael. *Democracy for the Few,* 7th ed. Boston: Bedford/St. Martin's, 2002.

Ritz, Dean, ed. *Defying Corporations, Defining Democracy: A Book of History and Strategy.* New York: Apex Press, 2001.

Slivinski, Stephen. "The Corporate Welfare Budget: Bigger Than Ever." *Cato Policy Analysis,* no. 415, October 10, 2001.

Smith, Mark A. *American Business and Political Power: Public Opinion, Elections, and Democracy.* Chicago: University of Chicago Press, 2000.

Watkins, Michael, Mickey Edwards, and Usha Thakrar. *Winning the Influence Game: What Every Business Leader Should Know about Government.* New York: Wiley, 2001.

10

Should You Vote for the "Lesser Evil" from a Major Party over a Minor Party Candidate You May Prefer?

For most of the nation's history, a two-party system has been a feature of American political life. In spite of this fact, third parties have also been around for two centuries. In recent years, some third parties nominated candidates for the presidency. Although they did not win, they attracted some support. Among these candidates were George Wallace in 1968 and John Anderson in 1980. Ross Perot ran as an independent in 1992 and as a Reform Party candidate in 1996. Third-party candidates have also competed in state and local contests. One of the recent successes was the victory of Jesse Ventura of the Reform Party in the election for governor of Minnesota in 1998.

Popular support for each of the major parties comes with a variety of groups across the political spectrum. Particularly in presidential contests but in many other contests as well, candidates of the major parties try to put together a platform that is acceptable to groups reflecting different interests. In doing so, they are forced to make compromises. For example, a candidate may want to support environmental protection, but if his or her constituency contains powerful economic interests — both business and labor — that would be hurt by a proposed environmental program, that candidate may seek some compromise that may not satisfy either interest.

Since a candidate of one of the two major parties usually wins an election, a voter with strong convictions about a particular issue often has great difficulty in making a choice. That voter could vote for a candidate from one of the major parties that is not really his or her choice but is, rather, better on the issue of greatest importance to the voter than is the other major party candidate. The "better" candidate is really the "lesser evil" of the majority party candidates who are running. The voter may, however, conclude that it really makes no difference which of the two major party candidates wins because neither of them is really good on the most important issue. As a result of thinking this way, that individual may decide not to vote at all. But if there is a third-party candidate who represents the views of the voter on the issue of greatest importance, then the voter can cast his or her ballot for that candidate. If the third-party candidate attracts enough votes from those who would ordinarily vote for a major party candidate to influence the election outcome — to be viewed as a "spoiler" — then the result may be that the "greater evil" will win. Both Democrat and Republican candidates in national, state, and local elections have been hurt by spoilers.

The issue of a spoiler effect came up in the presidential election of 2000 in which Democratic Party candidate Al Gore faced Republican Party candidate George W. Bush. In that contest, however, liberal activist Ralph Nader ran as a candidate of the Green Party. Democrats feared that Nader would take votes away from Gore. But Pat Buchanan, a lifelong Republican, abandoned his party and became the Reform Party candidate for president. Republicans feared that he would take votes away from Bush. (See Chapter 12.)

The debate below reflects an argument among two liberals just before the presidential election of 2000. Michael Lerner, editor of *Tikkun* magazine, argues that people should vote for the candidate who best represents them and not for the lesser evil. In addressing his concerns directly to his readers whatever their views, he contends:

1. Your vote for the lesser evil signifies a moral and spiritual corruption of your soul.
2. For Democrats, lesser evilism disempowers liberal and progressive forces.
3. Minor party candidates can win.
4. You don't know the consequences of your lesser evil winning.
5. Lesser evilism weakens faith in democracy.
6. Lesser evilists ignore how policies get shaped.
7. Voting for a lesser evil entails abandoning and helping to dispirit those who share your principles.

Representative Barney Frank, a Democrat from Massachusetts, takes issue with Michael Lerner. The congressman contends:

1. A voter ignoring the consequences of his or her vote may contribute to the strengthening of policies that the voter detests.
2. People who decide to vote for Al Gore in spite of their more liberal preferences do not lose their commitment to liberal values.
3. Voting in a manner that would increase the chances of George W. Bush to win the presidency in the 2000 election would undermine the liberal values that Lerner holds, such as human rights, abortion rights, gay rights, gun control, the minimum wage, Social Security, a prescription drug program, and blocking tax cuts for the wealthy.
4. It really will make a difference whether Gore or Bush makes Supreme Court appointments over the next four or eight years.

☑ *Y E S*

Should You Vote for the "Lesser Evil" from a Major Party over a Minor Party Candidate You May Prefer?

MICHAEL LERNER

Don't Vote Lesser Evil Politics!

I know that many people in our community feel divided in themselves about whether to support Al Gore or one of the various protest candidates like Ralph Nader or John Hagelin. I respect whatever position you take. And as a non-profit magazine, of course, we do not ever endorse candidates. But we do want to encourage a national debate about the morality and social consequences of what could best be described as "lesser evilism" in politics.

Many people talk about the presidential elections of 2000 with a mixture of indifference, contempt, and despair. They tell us that they are not excited about voting for Al Gore given their perception of his slavish subordination to corporate interests, his cheerleading for the military, his flip-flops and lack of a moral center, and his betrayal of environmental causes for the sake of political self-interest. Yet, although they do not feel that Gore represents their own worldview or that he is likely to fight for most of the things they believe in, they nevertheless feel that they have no alternative: in their eyes, George W. Bush is even worse and would enact policies and make appointments which are dangerous and must be avoided.

Many people on the Right feel a similar tension supporting Bush.

When we challenge lesser evilism we are not addressing or critiquing those who feel that Gore or Bush do in fact represent them. They should enthusiastically support their candidate. By "lesser evilism" we refer to the proposition that you must choose the candidate most likely to win who will do the least harm, rather than choosing the candidate who comes closest to expressing your own views and attitudes.

You are choosing the lesser evil if some candidate who the media and the polls indicate has little chance to win actually represents your own views or comes very close to them on many issues (for example, Ralph Nader or John Hagelin or David McReynold) but you don't vote for that candidate because the media has convinced you that he can't win and you are scared of what will happen if the worse of the two "front runners" does win.

So let me make it clear that if, for example, you think that Al Gore or George W. Bush comes closer to actually representing your ideas and attitudes in this campaign than any of the "minority candidates," nothing in what I'm writing here is meant to be an argument against that conclusion. But if that is not the case, then I want to present some arguments for why you shouldn't throw your vote away by authorizing someone you don't believe in to represent you:

MORAL AND SPIRITUAL CORRUPTION OF OUR SOULS

When we become used to accepting the lesser evil, we begin to give our stamp of approval to a social reality that we in fact deplore. This is a slippery slope that leads us to accommodate ourselves to moral corruption in other aspects of our lives. Many people perceive that the "reality" of our economic marketplace is that people are willing to cheat and hurt others and make environmentally destructive or morally insensitive choices to advance themselves. The more you teach people to make their major electoral choices on the basis of accommodating a reality that they detest, the more likely they are to similarly accommodate themselves to morally insensitive ways of acting in the world of work and in other aspects of daily life.

Powerlessness corrupts. To the extent that we come to believe we have no alternative but to accept the lesser evil, we lose the inner quality of soul that makes it possible to fight for anything against the odds. In short, we become idolaters, bowing to reality rather than asking how we can change reality. And that inevitably leads us to accommodate evil everywhere. We may take a cynical attitude toward the current world, but as long as we've adopted the attitude that we can't really fight it and must accept its terms, we have cast our vote in favor of keeping what is.

Not surprisingly, as people become used to making this choice in daily life, they become most angry not at the forces of evil to which they accommodate, but at those who retain their commitment to fight for their highest ideals.

LESSER EVILISM DISEMPOWERS LIBERAL AND PROGRESSIVE FORCES

Because liberals and progressives consistently accept the lesser evil argument, the Democratic Party focuses all of its energy on accommodating those who might otherwise vote Republican. Instead of imagining democratic politics as a counterweight to the incredible power of corporations, the logic of lesser evilism turns the Democratic Party into a second wing of the pro-corporate Property Party, ensuring that the major difference between Gore and Bush will be how quickly their knees hit the floor when called upon by their corporate funders.

YOU DON'T KNOW WHO CAN WIN

As Jesse Ventura showed in the last election, calculations about who is likely to win can be deeply mistaken. The two leading candidates are shoo-ins because the corporate-dominated media gives them disproportionate time to present their case to us, tells us that anyone who doesn't share the dominant corporate agenda is marginal, and tells us that no one else can be considered a realistic alternative. By not voting your conscience, you are giving the media the justification it seeks to ignore significant alternative views. If your own views get marginalized in future national debate, the media can say "the one time you were consulted — the election booth — you indicated that the issues that you cared about were those that were articulated by your candidate, so why should we give attention to views that have been demonstrated to be so marginal?" You become the author of your own marginalization.

YOU DON'T KNOW THE CONSEQUENCES OF YOUR LESSER EVIL WINNING

Our country may have lunged further to the right under Bill Clinton and the right-wing Congress elected in reaction to him than it would have under [George H. W.] Bush and a Democratic Congress elected to constrain him. Better to vote your conscience than your calculations, since outcomes can be very uncertain.

A good friend of mine was deeply angry at me in 1998 when I questioned his lesser evil choice of voting for Gray Davis for governor of California. Though on most issues there was little difference between Davis and his opponent, my friend assured me that Davis would make a big difference when it came to appointing better judges than his opponent. For the sake of those facing the criminal justice system, I was told, we must vote for Davis.

As it turned out, Davis has become one of the most rabid "law and order" governors the state has seen for many decades. Prisoners' rights have deteriorated and Davis has demanded that judges who do not share his view of tough sentencing resign their judicial positions. Our Democratic legislature would have made a powerful counterweight to measures of this sort had they come from a Republican, but they have been less energetic in opposing the excesses of a governor of their own party. My friend now admits that he was snookered by fears of lesser evilism.

And this happens over and over and over again.

In the Clinton years, the gap between the rich and the poor has increased and the social supports for the poor have decreased. The dominant discourse in our society has become "How do I get rich?" rather than "How do we create a better world together?" This reality was created because in 1976 and then again in 1992 the Democrats selected as their candidate for the presidency men who represented their most pro-corporate wing, knowing that the rest of us would go along with this choice.

But didn't Clinton (some will argue) go in the direction he did because of the Republican ascendancy in Congress?

No.

That Republican ascendancy was a consequence of Clinton himself abandoning the idealism he momentarily articulated during the 1992 elections, and instead articulating very similar values to those of the Republicans. I know the dominant media story: Clinton was too liberal and visionary in his first two years in office. For those of us who were there in the heart of the administration's battles, however, the reality was just the opposite: Clinton's health care proposal failed because the protections he put in to satisfy the medical profiteers and insurance industry turned what could have been a clear "single payer" plan like the one that operates in Canada today into a crazy bureaucratic maze which excited nobody.

The story would have been very different in 1994 had Clinton fought a valiant fight for a single payer health care plan and made his commitment to universal health care the central issue of the 1994 congressional election. Had Clinton stood for something clear and mobilized support for that vision, it is unlikely that Republicans would have become the majority party in Congress.

On the other hand, had Bush been reelected in 1992, the mood of the country would likely have led to a continued dominance of Democrats in Congress, and a Democratic Congress could have blocked the kind of dismantling of the public sector which actually took place in the 1990s, presided over by a Democratic president. The "corporate interest uber alles" mentality of the 1990s might have faced greater restraints in a society with a Republican president countered by a Democratic Congress than by a corporate-cheerleading Democrat (an assessment shared by many on Wall Street who have found themselves unrestrainedly filling the coffers of the Democrats).

Similarly, Bush might have been better for the Jews. It has been the contention of this magazine that it is in the best interest of the Jewish people and of Judaism to have an Israel which has ended its oppression of the Palestinian people. George Bush stood up to Israel's right wing in 1991 and refused to go along with guarantees of loans that Israel sought to facilitate the influx of Soviet Jews. He made the loan guarantee contingent on a halt in West Bank construction. That remarkable act of political courage, in the face of outrage by establishment Jewry (who slavishly subordinated themselves to Israeli Prime Minister Shamir's policies), caused a political shift in Israel and contributed to the electoral victory of Yitzhak Rabin in 1992.

The Clinton/Gore team has never been willing to pressure Israel toward peace. As a result, in the ensuing years the number of West Bank settlers has increased, and the Oslo accord was not fully implemented. Al Gore, whose closest advisor on these issues is the rabidly anti-Palestinian Martin Peretz (the owner and chief ideologue of the *New Republic*), is likely to be even less willing to pressure Israel toward the kinds of steps which could lead to real reconciliation with the Palestinian people. . . .

The general point is this: don't be so sure that you know the consequences of voting for your candidate and whether they will in fact turn out to be the lesser evil. There are moments in history where the differences are so great that I would suspend this argument (e.g., if we were facing a Hitler). Some might even argue that lesser evilism is justified during elections like that of 1980, between Reagan and Carter, where the immediate outcome is so lastingly destructive as to outweigh all other considerations.

But look at 1968; even the election of Richard Nixon looks less clear in retrospect. Nixon in office was mean and repressive (and he personally supervised the federal indictment against me for organizing anti-war demonstrations, an indictment which led to my imprisonment for "contempt of court," caused me to be fired from my teaching job at the University of Washington, and made it impossible for me to get other academic employment). Yet it was Nixon who ended the policy, upheld under the Democrats, of demonizing China (a policy which provided the intellectual foundation for the war in Vietnam); it was Nixon who helped create the Occupational Safety and Health Administration; and it was Nixon who helped push the first environmental laws (which have been significantly weakened subsequently, including under the Clinton administration). The configuration of political forces restraining a Republican president sometimes can lead them to take more progressive steps than certain kinds of Democrats who feel the need to placate their Right.

And don't forget the potential impact on the entire public discourse of having a powerful third party enter the political arena. Congressional Democrats who largely played "dead" rather than confront Ronald Reagan might be far more likely to constrain a Republican president like Bush (for example, blocking any rabidly "pro-life" appointments to the federal judiciary in the same aggressive way that the Republicans have blocked many of Clinton's nominees) if they feared a growing progressive alternative to their Left. If progressives vote for Gore on lesser evil grounds, eliminating the pressure on Democrats from the Left, and Bush wins anyway, the Democrats are likely to feel overwhelming pressure to give in to Bush's programs and nominees no matter how venal.

LESSER EVILISM WEAKENS FAITH IN DEMOCRACY

If people consistently vote for candidates in whom they do not believe, they end up feeling they are without representation, and hence our government itself feels less legitimate. Many stop voting altogether. Others feel dirtied by a process in which they have authorized through their vote the actions of an elected official who, acting in their name, supports policies they find morally and environmentally reprehensible.

LESSER EVILISTS IGNORE HOW POLICIES GET SHAPED

Whether it is Supreme Court appointees or legislation, the key factor determining what happens in politics is the relative balance between corporate power and popular mobilization for progressive ideals. Democratic senators could block bad appointees to the Supreme Court and the judiciary, just as conservatives have consistently done, but they feel no pressure to do so as long as they know that they can count on liberals and progressives to always vote for them as the lesser evil. For that same reason, a Democrat might make far more conservative appointments than you'd expect, just to placate the Right.

I do not want to underestimate the legitimacy of progressives' concern about Supreme Court appointees. Ultimately, however, that concern is based on the view that progressives will remain demobilized, and will have to count instead on friendly elites to ensure the outcomes they seek. Why should that be the case? The right wing in the United States has built a mobilized political movement, and it is that movement which led George W. Bush to select right-winger Dick Cheney as his vice-presidential candidate.

Couldn't we learn this lesson from them: if we want to put pressure on politicians to respect our perspectives, the best way is to mobilize mass movements, not to throw away our vote by automatically giving it to politicians who actually don't even share our ideals.

VOTING FOR A LESSER EVIL ENTAILS ABANDONING AND HELPING TO DISPIRIT THOSE WHO SHARE YOUR PRINCIPLES

The next time you look around for allies for some visionary idea or moral cause that inspires you, you will find fewer people ready to take risks, because when they stood up for their ideals at election time you weren't willing to support them. Don't underestimate how much your vote for the lesser evil makes others feel depressed about ever changing anything.

In short, it's not some "other" who is keeping us from getting the world we want, but our own internalized powerlessness and depression — what I describe, in *Spirit Matters,* as a pathogenic belief that no one else will ever really share our values or fight for a better world, so we had better not risk doing so ourselves.

It's true that there are those who share the politics of meaning or spiritual politics perspective who find that none of the candidates, including Nader and Hagelin, share our core notion that the most important task is to "change the bottom line" from materialism and selfishness to a definition of productivity or efficiency that would validate love and caring, awe and wonder as central criteria. With respect to the spiritual transformation we seek, they argue, the differences between Gore and Nader are slight. In that case, the vote for Gore is not much different than a vote for Nader or any of the other candidates, since none of them are even in the same ballpark with us on these issues.

This is the kind of evaluation we don't intend to make one way or the other. Our interest is not in which candidate you choose today, but in how your decision to choose affects the choices we have in the future.

One thing about which we feel fairly certain: we will never win a society we believe in unless we are willing to stand up and fight for it, even if in the short run we lose some of our battles.

I still have great respect for those who believe that this election threatens the dismantling of abortion rights and other important advances of past decades. Though they realize that if Nader gets enough votes, the Green Party will receive federal funding and be able to contend much more seriously in the next election, they don't want to help elect Bush. Some people in this mindset have suggested the following: wait until the day before the election to see what the vote is in your own state. If either of the two leading candidates has a solid lead, you can then vote for a third party candidate without fearing that your vote will undermine the chances of your lesser evil. On the other hand, if it's too close to call in your state (because elections are determined state by state in our electoral system) then you might choose to vote for your lesser evil candidate.

However you vote, we do hope that you will take some time to discuss with others the moral/spiritual issues I've raised here — that discussion might be the most lasting impact of this election.

☑ *NO*

Should You Vote for the "Lesser Evil" from a Major Party over a Minor Party Candidate You May Prefer?

BARNEY FRANK

Response to Lerner on Lesser Evil Politics!

Michael Lerner blends two arguments. He begins by arguing that one should vote for the candidate with whom one agrees the most without regard to the consequences. He criticizes those who fail to vote for their ideal candidate "because they are scared of what will happen if some other candidate does win."

But what if the "other candidate" will oppress minorities, or worsen the situation in life of the most vulnerable, whereas the "lesser evil" candidate would try to help these two groups, albeit less completely than you prefer? To say that this is irrelevant is a very stark statement of your right to ignore the consequences of your own actions. Given the perennially imperfect state of democratic politics, it is a license for moral irrelevance.

How can people who are committed to improving the world insist on their right to ignore the results of their actions? Lerner's main defense of this position betrays its logical and factual weakness. He asserts, "To the extent that we come to believe that we have no alternative but to accept the lesser evil, we lose the inner quality of soul that makes it possible to fight for anything against the odds. In short, we become idolaters, bowing to reality rather than asking how we can change reality. And that inevitably leads us to accommodate evil everywhere."

No, it doesn't. There is nothing at all inconsistent between deciding to choose the lesser evil at a given point in time, and simultaneously continuing to work so that the next time a choice has to be made, one may be able to choose an even lesser evil, or a greater good. This is in fact the essence of thoughtful, principled participation in politics.

Lerner is simply wrong to suggest that the committed liberals who are working hard to elect Al Gore are somehow deficient in our commitment also to changing American political reality. It is precisely those of us who work hardest at "changing reality" who disagree most vehemently with the argument that we should ignore it when election time comes. Take the example of Jesse Jackson, who, unlike Ralph Nader, has chosen to work with great force to improve the Democratic Party. Does Lerner seriously argue that by working hard for Al Gore, Jesse Jackson is losing "the inner quality of soul that makes it possible to fight for anything against the odds"?

It is not simply liberal Democratic politicians who are making this fight. The leading advocates for gay and lesbian rights, the right of women to have abortions without governmental permission, and the right of society to regulate gun ownership in the interest of public safety all strongly support Al Gore over George W. Bush. None of us think Al Gore perfect. All of us have been working before this year to improve our society and will continue to work very hard for that afterwards. Neither empirically nor logically does it make sense to argue that those of us who will be supporting Al Gore in part because we are "scared of what will happen if . . . [George Bush] does win" have in any way been corrupted or lost our willingness or ability to fight for a reality that will mean better choices the next time around.

As a morally serious man committed to fighting for social justice, Lerner does not seem comfortable with his assertion that we should vote for the ideal candidate without regard to the consequences, so he spends most of his essay in an effort to show that liberal values will not be worse off if George Bush wins. It is to his credit that he realizes that he cannot convincingly make the case for helping Ralph Nader unless he shows that a resulting win for Bush will not damage liberal values. But the case cannot be made and Mr. Lerner's effort is an example of polemical necessity being the mother of intellectual invention.

Among the consequences of a Bush win are those that have convinced the Human Rights Campaign, the National Abortion Rights Action League, Sarah Brady, and others to be passionately committed to a Gore victory.

It is not the case that Gore is the lesser evil. There are two aspects to the Gore versus Nader debate. On economic issues, Nader is in many respects better than Gore. But Gore is significantly better than Bush, and since one or the other of them will win, I believe that support for raising the minimum wage, protecting Social Security, having a real prescription drug program for older people through Medicare, and blocking large tax cuts for the wealthy are reasons to vote for Gore. And with regard to abortion, gun control, and gay rights, Gore is not only far better than Bush, he is far superior to Nader, who has simply ignored these issues throughout his distinguished career.

These issues are especially relevant to the weakest part of the "it makes no difference" view — the Supreme Court. It would be honest for Nader and his supporters to argue that their dislike of Al Gore and the current state of the Democratic Party is so great that they are prepared to live with Supreme Court appointments that will move that institution significantly to the Right. It is completely inaccurate to argue that it really won't make any difference whether Gore or Bush makes Supreme Court appointments over the next four or eight years.

Bill Clinton's two appointments, Stephen Breyer and Ruth Bader Ginsburg, have been solid supporters of the rights of women to choose abortions and of the rights of gay and lesbian people to be free from discrimination. On gay and lesbian rights, the Court is now five to four on the negative side; on abortion rights it is five to four positive. No one seriously believes that the Supreme Court appointments to be made over the next four years will have a negligible impact on both of these issues. The age and health of the current justices make it overwhelmingly likely that between two and four appointments will be made by the next president, and they are likely to be evenly drawn from each of the ideological sides.

One of the great paradoxes that I find in today's debate is the willingness of many on the Left to disregard the views of the people most affected when it comes to their own electoral interests. It is not simply the leading advocates of gun control, gay rights, and abortion who are strongly for Gore. While James Hoffa of the Teamsters has not endorsed Gore, partly because of his own anger at the administration's support for his opponent in the last Teamster elections, and the UAW [United Auto Workers] is also holding out, the rest of the labor movement is enthusiastically for Gore.

Even those industrial unions which are very unhappy with Gore's trade posture understand that there are enormous differences between Gore and Bush on a whole range of economic issues, and they are not prepared to ignore the consequences of a Bush win. Why do Nader and his followers give so little credence to the strong support for Gore from those who have fought hardest on this range of issues? Is Lerner arguing that the Human Rights Campaign, the National Abortion Rights Action League, Handgun Control, and John Sweeney have somehow suffered some "corruption of the soul" and lost their willingness to fight for fundamental change?

Rather, it is the case that as part of the very tough, principled fight they are all engaged in, they understand that a Gore presidency rather than a Bush presidency means important gains for the people and causes they represent. This does not mean that they will, on the day of Al Gore's inauguration, stop fighting. It does mean that they are committed not simply to verbalizing their ideals, but to acting on them in the most effective way possible.

Questions for Discussion

1. Did it matter whether George Bush or Al Gore won the presidential contest in 2000? What are the reasons for your answer?
2. Is a vote for a third-party candidate a "throw-away" vote? What are the reasons for your answer?

3. What impact do third parties have on the public debate of issues in a political campaign?
4. What impact do third parties have on the major political parties?
5. What are the factors that contribute to the success of a third-party candidate in an election? How is third party "success" defined?

Suggested Resources

Web Sites

Center for Voting and Democracy
   http://www.fairvote.org/

Political Resources on the Net
   http://www.politicalresources.net/usa1.htm

Project Vote Smart
   http://www.vote-smart.org/

Voter Information Services
   http://www.vis.org/

Publications

Disch, Lisa Jane. *The Tyranny of the Two-Party System.* New York: Columbia University Press, 2002.
Domhoff, G. William. *Changing the Powers That Be: How the Left Can Stop Losing and Win.* Lanham, Md.: Rowman & Littlefield, 2003.
Flanigan, William H., and Nancy H. Zingale. *Political Behavior of the American Electorate.* Washington, D.C.: CQ Press, 2002.
Herrnson, Paul S., and John C. Green, eds. *Multiparty Politics in America: Prospects and Performance.* Lanham, Md.: Rowman & Littlefield, 2002.
Lerner, Michael. *Spirit Matters.* Charlottesville, Va.: Walsch Books, 2000.
Maisel, L. Sandy. *Parties and Elections in America: The Electoral Process,* 3d ed. Lanham, Md.: Rowman & Littlefield, 2002.
Nader, Ralph. *Crashing the Party: Taking on the Corporate Government in an Age of Surrender.* New York: Thomas Dunne Books/St. Martin's Press, 2000.
———. "So You Want to Run for President? Ha! Barriers to Third Party Entry." *National Civic Review* 90, no. 2 (Summer 2001): 163–72.
Patterson, Thomas E. *The Vanishing Voter: Public Involvement in an Age of Uncertainty.* New York: Alfred A. Knopf, 2002.
Political Staff of the Washington Post. *Deadlock: The Inside Story of America's Closest Election.* New York: Public Affairs, 2001.
Scheele, Paul E., ed. *"We Get What We Vote for — Or Do We?" The Impact of Elections on Governing.* Westport, Conn.: Praeger, 1999.

Schier, Steven E. *You Call This an Election? America's Peculiar Democracy.* Washington, D.C.: Georgetown University Press, 2003.

Sifry, Micah L. *Spoiling for a Fight: Third Party Politics in America.* New York: Routledge, 2002.

Wattenberg, Martin P. *Where Have All the Voters Gone?* Cambridge, Mass.: Harvard University Press, 2002.

Wayne, Stephen J. *Is This Any Way to Run a Democratic Election? Debating American Electoral Politics,* 2d ed. Boston, Mass.: Houghton Mifflin, 2003.

11

Is Campaign Finance Reform Desirable in the American Political System?

For most of U.S. history the funding of political campaigns was left entirely to private sources. Unlike the practice in countries where the government underwrites the expense of campaigning, in the United States political parties and candidates have had to attract donations from individuals and groups.

In the twentieth century, campaign contributions came under greater government regulation. In 1907 Congress passed a law prohibiting corporations from using their own funds in federal election campaigns. A similar prohibition was enacted for labor unions in 1943. Between 1947 and 1962 the law governing campaign expenditures forbade both corporate and union contributions and expenditures in federal primaries, general elections, and nominating conventions.

A number of laws were passed in the 1970s to deal with campaign finance. Many resulted from the revelations of illegal corporate contributions to the Committee to Reelect the President, the campaign organization for the reelection of President Richard Nixon in 1972. Challenges to provisions in these laws resulted in Supreme Court decisions invalidating some restrictions on campaign finance in federal elections.

Today, campaign laws require that all federal candidates must disclose their campaign contributions. For presidential contests, a system of matching grants and public financing was established, and expenditure limits were set. But a presidential candidate who uses only his or her own personal funds in a campaign is not subject to any spending limits. Independent Ross Perot used his own funds in his unsuccessful attempt to win the presidency in 1992. But when he ran again on the Reform Party ticket in 1996, he relied on government financing and, consequently, was subject to the kinds of restrictions faced by his Democratic and Republican Party presidential opponents. No limits are placed on how much a congressional candidate's campaign committee can spend on the candidate's campaign.

One of the consequences of the campaign reform legislation of the 1970s was the growth of political action committees (PACs). A PAC is a private organization concerned with promoting economic, social, or ideological goals in public policy through electoral and other forms of political activity.

PACs contribute money to candidates for public office. In addition, some of them help with voter registration and turnout. For the election cycle of 1977–78, PACs contributed $35.2 million to all federal candidates. In the 1999–2000 election cycle, the PAC contribution figure rose to $259.8 million.[1]

Critics of campaign finance practices complain about the influence of private money on the American political system. In past years, they attacked PACs and "soft money" — donations for costs and activities that help state, local, and federal candidates with party advertising and voter mobilization campaigns. In March 2002, President George W. Bush signed into law the Bipartisan Campaign Finance Reform Act of 2002. (The law is also known as McCain-Feingold campaign finance law, named for Senators John McCain of Arizona and Russ Feingold of Wisconsin.) The law bans unregulated, unrestricted soft money contributions. It also places restrictions on the broadcast of "issue ads" before elections. The law is currently being challenged in the courts on constitutional grounds.

Both before and after the newest campaign reform bill became law, the desirability of campaign finance reform in general and specific proposed reform versions have been controversial. In speaking before the U.S. Senate in its consideration of the McCain-Feingold bill in 2001, Joseph I. Lieberman, a Democratic U.S. Senator from Connecticut, supports campaign finance reform. He contends:

1. Under the current campaign system, a person's wealth is leading in the direction of having more importance than a person's views or votes.
2. The current system of campaign finance money is undermining our political system, breeding cynicism among our citizens, and compromising democracy.
3. Because of the importance of money in political campaigns, many Americans no longer trust our government or even bother to vote.
4. The McCain-Feingold campaign finance proposal would actually enhance free speech rights in the United States.

Bradley A. Smith, who was a law professor and is currently a commissioner on the Federal Election Commission, argues against campaign finance reform. He contends:

1. Campaign finance reform is unnecessary because: (a) Too much money is not spent on campaigns. (b) Large contributions are necessary to provide enough money to finance campaigns at a level that informs the electorate. (c) Higher levels of contributions to a candidate may stem simply from the desire of donors to contribute to candidates who are likely to win, and they may also reflect a level of public support that is manifested later at the polls. (d) Campaign contributions affect very few votes in the legislature.

2. Campaign finance reform has had several negative consequences: It has: (a) entrenched the status quo, (b) made the electoral system less responsive to popular opinion, (c) strengthened the power of elites, (d) favored wealthy candidates, and (e) limited opportunities for grassroots political activity.

NOTE

1. Federal Election Commission news releases, "PAC Activity Shows Little Growth over 1992 Level, Final FEC Report Finds," November 1995, and "PAC Activity Increases in 2000 Election Cycle," May 31, 2001.

☑ YES

Is Campaign Finance Reform Desirable in the American Political System?

JOSEPH I. LIEBERMAN
Campaign Finance Reform

In taking up this proposal today, the Senate is embarking on a historic journey. Over the next couple of weeks, we will have an opportunity to do something that is really quite rare around here: that is, to debate, consider, and ultimately vote on the essential nature of our political system. That vote I believe will have a significant effect on the vitality and, indeed, on the viability long term of our democracy.

No less than our forefathers who drafted the Constitution, we will be asked in the days ahead to take a stand on how we believe our Government should work and to whom its leaders should be held accountable.

These are the questions we will be considering and debating in this proposal:

Do we want a government in which power comes from the people, and those who are privileged to exercise that power are ultimately accountable to the people?

Will we uphold the ideal of our democracy so that the passion and force with which people articulate their views and the votes that they cast on Election Day are the means through which they influence our Government's direction? Or do we want a system where the size of a person's wallet or the depth of an interest group's bank account count more than a person's views or votes?

I do not believe that anyone in this body would embrace the latter vision of our Republic. But that is precisely, I believe, where our Government is headed if we do not enact the bill we are debating today. For too many years, we have allowed money and the never ending chase for it to undermine our political system, to breed cynicism among our citizens, and to compromise the essential principle of our democracy. For, after all, America is supposed to be a country where every citizen has an equal say in the Government's decisions, and every citizen has an equal ability, in the words of the Constitution, to petition the Government for a redress of grievances.

As that great observer of America's democratic genius Alexis de Tocqueville put it when he analyzed our Nation's political system during the nineteenth century:

> The people reign in the American political world as the Deity does in the universe. They are the cause and the aim of all things; everything comes from them, and everything is absorbed in them.

How far we have come. I question whether any current observer of American politics could repeat de Tocqueville's statement with a straight face.

Look at what has become of our system. Virtually every day in this city an event is held where the price of admission far exceeds what the overwhelming majority of Americans can ever dream of giving to a candidate or a political party. For $1-, $5-, $10-, $50- or $100,000, wealthy individuals or interest groups can buy the time of candidates and elected officials, gaining access and thereby influence that is far beyond the grasp of those who have only their voice and their votes to offer.

Our national political parties publicly tout the access and influence big donor donations can buy. One even advertises on its web site that a $100,000 donation will bring meetings and contacts with Congressional leadership throughout the year, and tells us it is "designed specifically for the Washington-based corporate or PAC representative" a donor group whose entry price is $15,000.

For that amount, the party's web site tells us, donors get into a club whose agenda "is simple — bringing the best of our party's supporters together with our congressional leadership for a continuing, collegial dialogue on current policy issues."

Needless to say, the political parties selling these tickets to access and influence have found buyers aplenty. In 1997, I spent the better part of a year participating in the Governmental Affairs Committee's investigation into campaign finance abuses during the 1996 campaign. Our attention was riveted by marginal hustlers such as Johnny Chung who compared the White House to a subway, saying, "You have to put in coins to open the gates," and Roger Tamraz, who told us that he did not even bother to register to vote because he knew that his donations would get him so much more.

Appalling as these stories were, they, in the end, obscured a far greater scandal; that is, the far more prevalent collection of big soft dollar donations comes not from opportunistic hangers on but from mainstream corporations, unions and individuals.

Staggering amounts have gone to both political parties. During the election cycle that just ended, the parties collectively raised $1.2 billion, almost double the amount raised in 1998, and 37 percent more than in the last Presidential cycle.

The bulk of those increases came in the form of soft money — the unlimited large dollar donations from individuals and interest groups. Republicans raised $244.4 million in soft money while Democrats raised $243 million. For Republicans, it was a 73 percent increase over the last cycle, and for Democrats it nearly doubled what they raised during the last cycle.

When compared to election cycles further back, the numbers become all the more jolting. The 1996 soft money record that was blown away by this cycle's fund-raising was itself 242 percent higher than the 1992 soft money fund-raising in the case of Democrats and in the case of Republicans 178 percent higher. The roughly $262 million in party soft money raised in 1992, itself, dwarfed the approximately $19 million raised in the 1980 cycle, and the $21.6 million raised in the 1984 cycle was also dwarfed by those numbers.

The bottom line is that since soft money, and the loophole that allowed it into our political system, entered the system some 20 years ago, it has grown exponentially in each cycle, from barely $20 million in total in 1980 to nearly $500 million — a half a billion dollars — last year. And it is difficult to see any end in sight to this exponential growth of soft money except S. 27, the McCain-Feingold campaign finance reform proposal.

Is it any wonder, with these numbers, that the American people — they who are supposed to be the true source of our Government's authority — have been so turned off by politics that many of them no longer trust our Government or even bother to vote?

This must end or our noble journey in self-government will veer further and further from its principled course. When the price of entry to our democracy's discussions starts to approach the average American's annual salary, something is terribly wrong. When we have a two-tiered system of access and influence — one for the average volunteer and one for the big contributor — something is terribly wrong. And when the big contributor's ticket is for a front-row seat, while the voter's is for standing room only, something is most definitely terribly wrong.

Our opponents will continue, I understand, to see the situation differently. Money, they tell us, is just speech in another form. And the outlandish increases we have seen in political giving, they say, are actually signs of the vibrancy of our marketplace of ideas. It is a marketplace all right, but what is for sale is most certainly not ideas, and what is threatened most certainly is not free speech.

Free speech is a principle we all hold dear. But free speech is about the inalienable right every American has to express his or her views without Government interference. It is about the vision the framers of our Constitution enshrined in that great document, a vision that ensures both we in Congress and those outside — every citizen — will never be forced to compromise our American birthright to offer opinions, even and particularly when those are unpopular or discomforting to those in power.

That simply is not at issue in this debate, not at issue as a result of the McCain-Feingold proposal. Absolutely nothing in this bill will do anything to diminish or threaten any American's right to express his or her views about candidates running for office or about any problem or any issue in American life. Indeed, if more money in the system were a sign of more Americans speaking and more Americans being better informed, then we would have significantly more vibrant elections, dramatically more informative campaigns, increasingly larger voter turnout, and better and better public debates than we had 20 years ago before soft money exploded onto the scene.

I challenge anyone in this body or outside to say that is the case. It most certainly is not. To the contrary, this campaign finance reform proposal would actually enhance our polity's free speech rights. Under the current system, the voice of monied interests drowns out the voice of average Americans, often preventing them from being truly heard in our public policy debates. In that sense, it is the current system, with its addiction to soft money and all its maleffects, that limits free speech, and it is this bill, the McCain-Feingold bill, that will restore Americans' true ability to exercise their rights of expression without limit and with full effect.

In short, Mr. President, what would be threatened by this bill is not speech but something entirely different, the ever increasing and disproportionate power that those with money have in our political system. That is threatening a principle that I would guess all of us hold just as dearly — perhaps more dearly — as the principle of free speech, and that is the principle of democracy, that literally sacred ideal that shaped our Republic and still does, which promises that each person has one vote and that each and every one of us, to paraphrase the words from the Bible, from the heads of the tribes to the priests of the temple to the hewers of wood and the bearers of water, each of us has an equal right and an equal ability to influence the workings of our government.

As it stands now, it is that sacred principle — I use that adjective intentionally — that is under attack. It is that sacred principle that will remain under attack until we do something to protect it. That something, I submit, is campaign finance reform.

Unless we act to reform our campaign finance system, people with money will continue, as they give it, to have a disproportionate influence in our system. The American people will continue to lose faith in our government's institutions and their independence, and the genius of our Republic, that it is our citizenship, not our status, that gives each of us equal power to play a role in our country's government, will be lost. . . .

The bottom line is this: For too long we have watched as our Nation's greatest treasure, its commitment to democracy, has been pillaged by the ever escalating chase for money. It is time for this Senate to say that enough is enough, to remove the disproportionate power of some over our political system, and to restore the political influence and confidence to where our Nation's founding principles say it should be — with the people, with the voters.

☑ *NO*

Is Campaign Finance Reform Desirable in the American Political System?

BRADLEY A. SMITH

Campaign Finance Reform: Faulty Assumptions and Undemocratic Consequences

The agenda of the campaign finance reform movement has been to lower the cost of campaigning, reduce the influence of special interests, and open up the political system to change. In 1974, reformers gained their greatest victory, passing major amendments to the Federal Elections Campaign Act. Nevertheless, by 1996, Congressional campaign spending, in constant dollars, nearly had tripled.

Congressional election contributions by political action committees (PACs) increased from $20,500,000 in 1976 to $189,000,000 in 1994. Since 1974, the number of PACs has risen from 608 to more than 4,500. House incumbents outspent challengers in 1996 by almost four to one. Meanwhile, incumbent reelection rates in the House reached record highs in 1986 and 1988, before declining slightly in the 1990s. What went wrong?

The problem is that reform has been based on faulty assumptions and is, in fact, irretrievably undemocratic. Reform proposals inherently favor certain political elites. support the status quo, and discourage grassroots political activity.

FAULTY ASSUMPTIONS

Too Much Money Is Spent on Campaigns

The language in which political campaigns are described in the press reinforces the perception that too much money is spent on them. Candidates "amass war chests" with the help of "special interests" which "pour their millions" into campaigns. "Obscene" expenditures "careen" out of control or "skyrocket" upwards. Yet, to say that too much money is spent on campaigning is to beg the question, "compared to what?" For instance, Americans expend two to three times as much money each year on potato chips as on political campaigns.

In the two-year period ending in November, 1996, approximately $800,000,000 was spent by all Congressional general election candidates. Although this set a record for Congressional races, it amounts to about $4 per eligible voter, spent over a two-year period. Total direct campaign outlays for all candidates for local, state, and Federal elections over the same period can be estimated around $2,500,000,000, or about $12 per eligible voter over the two-year cycle. By comparison, Procter & Gamble and Philip Morris, the nation's two largest advertisers, budget roughly the same amount on advertising as is laid out by all political candidates and parties.

Increased campaign spending does translate into a better informed electorate, and voter understanding of issues grows with the quantity of campaign information received. Candidate ads are the major source of voter information. Lower campaign spending will result in less public awareness and understanding of issues. Considering the importance of elections to any democratic society, it is hard to believe that direct expenditures of approximately $10 per voter for all local, state, and national campaigns over a two-year period is a crisis requiring government regulation and limitations on spending.

Campaigns Based on Small Contributions Are More Democratic

As many as 18,000,000 Americans make some financial contribution to a political party, candidate, or PAC in an election cycle. No other system of campaign funding anywhere in the world enjoys so broad a base of support. Yet, this amounts to just 10% of the voting-age population. Even though this figure represents a far broader base of contributors than historically has existed, it made the political system more democratic and responsive.

In many cases, those candidates who best are able to raise campaign dollars in small contributions are those who are most emphatically out of the mainstream. Republican Barry Goldwater's 1964 presidential campaign, for example, garnered $5,800,000 from 410,000 small contributors before he suffered a landslide defeat. On his way to an even more crushing defeat in 1972, Democrat George McGovern raised almost $15,000,000 from small donors, at an average of approximately $20 per contributor.

Assuming that reliance on numerous small contributions makes a campaign in some way more democratic, the most "democratic" campaign of recent years was the 1994 Senate race of Republican Oliver North. He amassed approximately $20,000,000, almost entirely from small contributors, and outspent his nearest rival by nearly four-to-one. Yet, he lost to an unpopular opponent plagued by personal scandal.

With the exception of the occasional candidate such as McGovern or North, Americans are unwilling, individually, to contribute enough money in small amounts to run modern campaigns. The likelihood that what any individual does will matter simply is too small to provide most voters with the incentive to give financially to candidates. If large contributions were banned totally, there would not be enough money available to finance campaigns at a level that informs the electorate.

Money Buys Elections

A candidate with little or no money to spend is unlikely to win most races. Furthermore, the one expending the most wins more often than not. The correlation between spending and victory, though, may stem simply from the desire of donors to contribute to candidates who are likely to win, in which case the ability to win attracts money, rather than the other way around. Similarly, higher levels of campaign contributions to a candidate may reflect a level of public support that is manifested later at the polls.

A greater outlay does not necessarily translate into electoral triumph. Having money means having the ability to be heard; it does not mean that voters will like what they hear. In 1994 House of Representative races, for example, 34 Republicans defeated Democratic incumbents, spending on average two-thirds as much as their opponents. In 1996, several Senate candidates won despite being outspent. Republican Michael Huffington spent nearly $30,000,000 of his own money in the 1994 California senatorial race, only to come up empty-handed.

Money Is a Corrupting Influence on the Legislature

A substantial majority of those who have studied voting patterns on a systemic basis agree that campaign contributions affect very few votes in the legislature. The primary factors in determining a legislator's votes are party affiliation, ideology, and constituent views and needs. Where contributions and voting patterns intersect, this is largely because donors contribute to candidates believed to favor their positions, not the other way around.

These empirical studies often cut against intuition. Experience and human nature suggest that people are influenced by money, even when it does not go directly into their pockets, but into their campaigns. Yet, there are good reasons why the impact of contributions is not so great. First, people who are attracted to public office generally have strong personal views on issues. Second, there are institutional and political incentives to support party positions. Third, large contributors usually are offset in legislative debate by equally well-financed interests that contribute to a different group of candidates. Large PACs and organizations frequently suffer enormous losses in the legislative process.

Moreover, money is not the only political commodity of value. For instance, the National Rifle Association has a large PAC, but also has nearly 3,000,000 members who focus intently, even solely, on NRA issues in their voting. The NRA's power would seem to come less from dollars than from votes. To the extent that it comes from dollars, that, too, is a function of votes — *i.e.,* the group's large membership. Groups advocating gun control frequently complain that the NRA outspends them, but rarely mention that the NRA outvotes them as well.

Campaign finance reformers often pose as disinterested citizens, merely seeking "good government." In fact, there is ample evidence that they have targeted certain types of campaign activities closely tied to political agendas reformers oppose. They therefore favor regulation that would tilt the electoral process in favor of preferred candidates, against popular will.

NEGATIVE CONSEQUENCES

Campaign finance reform has had several negative consequences, which broadly can be labeled "undemocratic." Reform has entrenched the *status quo* and made the electoral system less responsive to popular opinion, strengthened the power of elites, favored wealthy individuals, and limited opportunities for "grassroots" political activity.

Entrenching the Status Quo

Contribution limits favor incumbents by making it relatively harder for challengers to raise money to run their campaigns. The need to solicit cash from a large number of small contributors benefits incumbent candidates who have in place a database of past givers, an intact campaign organization, and the ability to raise funds on an ongoing basis from political action committees.

Newcomers with low name recognition have the most difficulty raising substantial sums from small contributors, who are less likely to give to unknowns. Well-known public figures challenging the *status quo* traditionally have relied on a small number of wealthy patrons to fund their campaigns. Theodore Roosevelt's 1912 Bull Moose campaign was funded almost entirely by a handful of wealthy supporters. Eugene McCarthy's 1968 anti-war campaign relied for seed money on a handful of six-figure donors, including industrialist Stewart Mott, who gave approximately $210,000, and Wall Street banker Jack Dreyfus, Jr., who may have contributed as much as $500,000.

More recently, John Anderson probably would have had more success in his independent campaign for the presidency in 1980 had his wealthy patron, Mott, been able to give unlimited amounts to his campaign. Whereas Ross Perot's 1992 presidential campaign was made possible by the Supreme Court's holding that an individual may spend unlimited sums to advance his own candidacy, contribution limits make it illegal for Perot to bankroll the campaign of another challenger, such as Colin Powell, in the same manner. The Reform Party, started in 1996, was able to get off the ground, in large part, thanks to Perot's money.

Beyond making it harder for challengers to raise cash, contribution limits indirectly reduce spending. This further works against challengers. Incumbents begin each election with significant advantages in name recognition. They are able to attract press coverage because of their office and often receive assistance from their office staffs and government-paid constituent mailings. Through patronage and constituent favors, they can add to their support.

To offset these advantages, challengers must expend money. Studies have found that the effect of each dollar spent is much greater for challengers than for incumbents because most voters already have some knowledge about incumbents and their records. Since spending is so much more important for challengers than incumbents, lower limits tend to hurt the former more.

Set low enough, contribution and spending limits make it almost impossible for challengers to attain the critical threshold of name recognition at which point a race becomes competitive. The bills introduced unsuccessfully in the last two Congresses by Senators John McCain (R.-Ariz.) and Russell Feingold (D.-Wis.) included spending limits. In 1994 and 1996, every challenger who spent less than the limits in the McCain-Feingold bill lost, but each incumbent who expended less than the proposed limits won.

Influence Peddling and Accountability

Like all political activity, the purpose of campaign contributions is to influence public policy. Contributors may adopt a legislative strategy, attempting to influence votes in the legislature, or an electoral strategy, aimed at influencing who wins elections. Influence peddling only becomes a problem when legislative strategies are pursued; under an electoral strategy, groups are trying to persuade the public to vote for a preferred candidate, and there is nothing wrong with that. Yet, contribution limits — the most popular reform measure — encourage legislative strategies by PACs and other monied interests.

Campaign contributors must weigh the costs and benefits of each strategy. Normally, they prefer an electoral strategy, aimed at convincing voters to elect like-minded candidates to office. Money given to a losing challenger is not merely a waste, it can be counterproductive, since such contributions increase the enmity of the incumbent. Because incumbents win most races, an electoral strategy of supporting challengers is a very high risk.

The alternative is to give to the incumbent in the hope that a legislative strategy might succeed, at least by minimizing otherwise hostile treatment aimed at the contributor's interests. When contributions are limited to an amount unlikely to change the result of an election, rational donors are forced into a legislative strategy. Thus, to the extent that campaign contributions influence legislative policy-making, limits are likely to make the situation worse.

Furthermore, PACs — and the interests they represent — play an important role in monitoring an office-holder's record. In most cases, it will not be rational for individuals to devote considerable time to monitoring the performance of elected officials, but, by banding together with others having similar concerns, they can perform that function at a reasonable cost. PACs are an important part of this process. Thus, contribution limits may reduce legislative monitoring, leading to a legislature ever more isolated from the people.

Favoring Select Elites

Campaign finance reform usually is sold as a populist means to strengthen the power of "ordinary" citizens against "big money" interests. In fact, campaign finance reform has favored select elites and further isolated individuals from the political process.

There are a great many sources of political influence. Hollywood personalities, by virtue of their celebrity, may receive an audience for their political views they would not have otherwise. They may be invited to testify before Congress, despite their lack of any particular expertise, or use their celebrity to assist campaigns through appearances at rallies. Successful academics may write powerful articles that change the way people think about issues. Labor organizers have at their disposal a vast supply of manpower that can be used to support favored candidates. Successful entrepreneurs may amass large sums of money, which can be applied for political purposes. Media editors, reporters, and anchors can shape not only the manner in which news is reported, but what is reported. Those with marketing skills can raise funds or produce advertising for a candidate or cause.

Newspapers, magazines, and TV and radio stations can spend unlimited sums to promote the election of favored candidates. Thus, Katherine Graham, the publisher of the *Washington Post*, has at her disposal the resources of a media empire to promote her views, free from the campaign finance restrictions others are subjected to. News anchor Peter Jennings is given a nightly forum on national TV on which to express his opinions.

Media elites are not the sole group whose influence is heightened by campaign spending and contribution limits. Restricting the flow of money into campaigns increases the relative importance of in-kind contributions, and so favors those who are able to control large blocks of manpower, rather than dollars. Limiting contributions and expenditures does not particularly democratize the process, but merely shifts power from people who give money to those whose primary contribution is time, media access, or some other attribute — *i.e.*, from small business groups to labor unions and journalists. Other beneficiaries of campaign finance limitations include political middlemen; public relations firms conducting "voter education" programs; lobbyists; PACs, such as Emily's List, which "bundle" large numbers of $1,000 contributions; and political activists. These individuals probably are less representative of public opinion than the wealthy philanthropists and industrialists who financed campaigns in the past.

Campaign finance restrictions do not make the system more responsive to the interests of the middle and working class. Efforts to assure equality of inputs into the campaign process are less likely to guarantee popular control than is the presence of multiple sources of political power. Campaign finance regulation reduces the number of voices and increases the power of those groups whose form of contribution remains unregulated.

Favoring Wealthy Candidates

Though campaign finance restrictions aim to reduce the role of money in politics, they have helped to renew the phenomenon of the "millionaire candidate," of whom Huffington and Perot arguably are the most celebrated examples. The Supreme Court has held that Congress may not limit constitutionally the amount a candidate can spend on his or her own campaign. Access to unlimited amounts, coupled with restrictions on raising money, favors those candidates who can contribute large sums to their own campaigns from personal assets. A Michael Huffington, Herb Kohl, or Jay Rockefeller becomes a particularly attractive candidate precisely because personal wealth provides a direct campaign advantage that cannot be offset by a large contributor to the opposing candidate.

At the same time that contribution limits help wealthy candidates, they tend to harm working-class political interests. A candidate with many supporters who can afford to give the legal limit may be relatively unscathed by "reform" legislation. However, candidates with large constituencies among the poor and working class traditionally have obtained their campaign funds from a small base of wealthy donors. By limiting the ability of wealthy individuals such as Stewart Mott or Augustus Belmont to finance these efforts, working-class constituencies may suffer.

FAVORING SPECIAL INTERESTS

Campaign finance regulation also is undemocratic in that it favors well-organized special interests over grassroots political activity. Limitations on campaign contributions and spending require significant regulation of the campaign process. They favor those already familiar with the regulatory machinery and people with the money and sophistication to hire the lawyers, accountants, and lobbyists needed to comply with complex filing requirements. Such dynamics naturally will run against newcomers to the political arena, especially those who are less educated or less able to pay for professional services.

As opportunities to gain an advantage over an opponent through use of the regulatory process are created, litigation has become a major campaign tactic. One can expect such tactics to be used most often by those already familiar with the rules, and there is some evidence that campaign enforcement actions are directed disproportionately at challengers, who are less likely to have staff familiar with the intricacies of campaign finance regulation.

Perhaps those most likely to run afoul of campaign finance laws — and thus to be vulnerable to legal manipulations aimed at driving them from the political debate — are those engaged in true grassroots activities. For instance, in 1991, the *Los Angeles Times* reviewed Federal Election Commission files and found that one of the largest groups of campaign law violators consisted of "elderly persons . . . with little grasp of the federal campaign laws."

Even sophisticated interest groups have found campaign finance laws a substantial hindrance to grassroots campaign activity and voter education efforts. In 1994, the U.S. Chamber of Commerce and American Medical Association decided not to publish and distribute candidate endorsements to thousands of their dues-paying members, under threats of litigation from the Federal Election Commission [FEC]. Under FEC regulations, just 63 of the Chamber of Commerce's 220,000 dues-paying members qualified as "members" for the purposes of receiving the organization's political communications. Similarly, the FEC had held that it would be unlawful for the AMA to distribute endorsements to about 44,500 of its members.

The First Amendment was based on the belief that political speech was too important to be regulated by the government. Campaign finance laws operate on the directly contrary assumption that campaigns are so important that speech must be regulated. Campaign finance laws constitute an arcane web of regulation that has led to citizens being fined for distributing homemade leaflets and trade groups being prohibited from communicating with their members.

The solution to the campaign finance dilemma is to recognize the flawed assumptions of the campaign finance reformers, dismantle the Federal Elections Campaign Act and the FEC bureaucracy, and take seriously the system of campaign finance "regulation" that the Founding Fathers wrote into the Bill of Rights: "Congress shall make no law . . . abridging the freedom of speech."

Questions for Discussion

1. What impact do private campaign contributions have on legislation? Provide evidence for your answer.
2. What is the impact of private campaign funding on voter turnout?
3. Who are the opponents of campaign finance reform? Why do they oppose reform?
4. Who would be the principal beneficiaries of public financing for congressional campaigns? Why?
5. What effect would the denial of private funding have on First Amendment rights?

Suggested Resources

Web Sites

Campaign Finance Information Center
   http://www.campaignfinance.org

Center for Responsive Politics
   http://www.opensecrets.org

Common Cause
   http://www.commoncause.org

Public Campaign
   http://www.publiccampaign.org

Real Campaign Reform
   http://www.realcampaignreform.org

Publications

Baker, Paula, ed. *Money and Politics*. University Park: Pennsylvania State University Press, 2002.

Bauer, Robert F. "Going Nowhere, Slowly: The Long Struggle over Campaign Finance Reform and Some Attempts at Explanation and Alternatives." *Catholic University Law Review* 51, no. 3 (Spring 2002): 741–83.

Birnbaum, Jeffrey H. *The Money Men: The Real Story of Fund-raising's Influence on Political Power in America*. New York: Crown, 2000.

Gross, Donald A. *The States of Campaign Finance Reform*. Columbus: Ohio State University Press, 2003.

Kobrak, Peter. *Cozy Politics: Political Parties, Campaign Finance, and Compromised Governance*. Boulder, Colo.: Lynne Rienner, 2002.

Magleby, David B., ed. *Financing the 2000 Election*. Washington, D.C.: Brookings Institution Press, 2002.

Redish, Martin H. *Money Talks: Speech, Economic Power, and the Value of Democracy.* New York: New York University Press, 2001.

Schneider, Jerrold E. *Campaign Finance Reform and the Future of the Democratic Party.* New York: Routledge, 2002.

Smith, Bradley A. "Some Problems with Taxpayer-Funded Political Campaigns." *University of Pennsylvania Law Review* 148, no. 2 (December 1999): 591–628.

————. *Unfree Speech: The Folly of Campaign Finance Reform.* Princeton, N.J.: Princeton University Press, 2001.

Taylor, Stuart, Jr. "Same Old Story." *Legal Times,* January 21, 2002, p. 38.

U.S. Cong., House of Representatives. *Constitutional Issues Raised by Recent Campaign Finance Legislation Restricting Freedom of Speech.* Hearing before the Subcommittee on the Constitution of the Judiciary Committee, 107th Cong., 1st Sess., June 12, 2001.

U.S. Cong., Senate. *Constitution and Campaign Reform.* Hearings before the Rules and Administration Committee, 106th Cong., 2d Sess., March 22, 29, April 5, 12, 26, and May 3, 17, 2000.

12

Should the Electoral College Be Abolished?

When the popular vote was tallied in the 2000 presidential election, Democratic presidential candidate Al Gore had won 539,897 more popular votes than his Republican Party opponent George W. Bush. And yet Bush was declared the victor and assumed office on January 20, 2001. Usually in presidential elections, the candidate with the most popular votes wins the presidency, but this is not always the case because of the mechanism used to determine presidential contests: the Electoral College.

When citizens vote in U.S. presidential elections, they do not cast their ballot for presidential candidates but for electors who are pledged to support particular candidates. These electors constitute the Electoral College, which officially elects the president.

The Framers of the Constitution created an Electoral College because they feared popular election as the means for filling the nation's highest office. Instead, they hoped that wise electors would make independent judgments. Today electors are committed to supporting their party's candidate, but they are not uniformly required to do so. Still, citizens can generally be certain that electors will vote as pledged.

In the Electoral College the number of electors for each state is equal to the number of senators and representatives from that state. Heavily populated states have more electors than sparsely populated states because they have more representatives. In all but two states the slate of electors that gets the largest number of popular votes (a plurality or a majority) gets all the Electoral College votes of that state. This is a winner-take-all system. In Maine and Nebraska, where electors represent congressional districts and two electors are selected at-large, it is possible to have a divided electoral vote. To become president, a candidate must win a majority of the votes in the Electoral College. If no candidate wins a majority, the House of Representatives makes the choice from the three candidates with the largest number of electoral votes. In this runoff election state delegations vote as units, each state having one vote.

It is possible for a person to lose the popular vote and win the presidential election, as the election of George W. Bush shows. But similar results occurred in the elections of John Quincy Adams in 1824, Rutherford B. Hayes in 1876, and Benjamin Harrison in 1888.

The electoral contest between Bush and Gore was particularly controversial. The outcome depended on the vote count in Florida because the winner of that state's popular vote would have enough Electoral College votes to win the election. The vote count in Florida was close, with Bush leading, but a recount was ordered. Five weeks after the election, the Supreme Court voted to end recounts in Florida, thus resulting in the Bush victory.

The effect of the Electoral College system on the distribution of power has been to give advantages to the heavily populated states, like New York, California, and Illinois, because these states have large electoral votes. Presidential candidates usually devote their attention to these more populous states because of the Electoral College's winner-take-all system.

During the last two centuries more than seven hundred proposals to change the Electoral College system have been introduced in Congress. Several new proposals were made in the session of Congress following the 2000 presidential election, but none were successful. Some of the more prominent examples of proposals for changes are:

- Require electors to vote for the candidate to whom they are pledged. (Some electors have failed to vote in this manner.)
- Replace the winner-take-all system with a system in which candidates get the same proportion of a state's electoral vote as they receive in its popular vote.
- Adopt the district-type system used by Maine and Nebraska in which each congressional district chooses an elector and two electors are chosen at large. A divided vote is then possible.
- Eliminate the Electoral College and establish direct popular vote of the president. One version of this form would be to require that if the election produced no candidate who had received at least 40 percent of the popular vote, then a runoff popular election between the top two vote-getters would be conducted.

Senator Richard J. Durbin, a Democrat from Illinois, wants to abolish the Electoral College. He contends:

1. The Framers had no philosophical underpinnings for establishing the Electoral College. The Electoral College was a contrived institution created to appeal to a majority of the delegates to the Constitutional Convention in 1787 who were divided by the issues of federal versus state powers, big state versus small state rivalries, the balance of power between branches of government, and slavery.
2. The Electoral College is undemocratic and unfair because it distorts the election process, with some votes by design having more weight than others.

3. While it appears that smaller and more rural states have an advantage in the Electoral College, the reality of modern presidential campaigns is that these states are generally ignored.
4. The Electoral College system totally discounts the votes of those supporting the losing candidate in their state.
5. The winner-take-all rules greatly increase the risk that minor, third-party candidates will determine who is elected president.
6. The Electoral College is clearly a more risky system than a direct popular vote, providing ample opportunity for manipulation, mischief, and litigation.

Testifying before the Subcommittee on the Constitution of the Judiciary Committee of the House of Representatives, political scientist Judith A. Best argues for maintaining the Electoral College system. She contends:

1. The abolition of the Electoral College system would get rid of the federal principle, which is one of the two fundamental structural principles of our Constitution (the other being the separation of powers).
2. The federal principle in presidential elections forces presidential candidates to build broad cross-national political coalitions, thus producing a strong national consensus.
3. Under direct nonfederal elections, contingency, or runoff, elections would become the rule.
4. The proposed amendments to change the Electoral College system would threaten the legitimacy of the system for Senate and House elections.

Should the Electoral College Be Abolished?

RICHARD J. DURBIN

Abolish the Electoral College

For those who want to defend the current electoral college system, I want to ask, What are the philosophical underpinnings that lie at its foundation? I submit there are none. Instead, the electoral college was a contrived institution, created to appeal to a majority of the delegates to the Constitutional Convention in 1787, who were divided by the issue of Federal versus State powers, big State versus small State rivalries, the balance of power between branches of Government, and slavery.

James Madison was opposed to any system of electing the President that did not maintain the South's representational formula gained in an earlier compromise that counted three-fifths of the African American population toward their State totals. A direct popular election of the Chief Executive would have diluted the influence of the South and diluted the votes based on the slave population.

Many delegates opposed a direct popular election on the grounds that voters would not have sufficient knowledge of the candidates to make an informed choice. Roger Sherman, delegate from Connecticut, said during the Convention: I stand opposed to the election by the people. The people want for information and are constantly liable to be misled.

Given the slowness of travel and communication of that day, coupled with the low level of literacy, the delegates feared that national candidates would be rare and that favorite sons would dominate the political landscape. James Madison predicted that the House of Representatives would end up choosing the President 19 times out of 20.

Also, this system was created before the era of national political parties. The delegates intended the electoral college to consist of a group of wise men — and they were all men at that time — appointed by the States, who would gather to select a President based primarily on their individual judgments. It was a compromise between election of the President by Congress and election by popular vote. Certainly, it is understandable that a young nation, forged in revolution and experimenting with a new form of government, would choose a less risky method for selecting a President.

Clearly, most of the original reasons for creating the electoral college have long since disappeared, and after 200 years of experience with democracy, the rationale for replacing it with a direct popular vote is clear and compelling.

First, the electoral college is undemocratic and unfair. It distorts the election process, with some votes by design having more weight than others. Imagine for a moment if you were told as follows: We want you to vote for President. We are going to give you one vote in selection of the President, but a neighbor of yours is going to have three votes in selecting the President.

You would say that is not American, that is fundamentally unfair. We live in a nation that is one person — one citizen, one vote.

But that is exactly what the electoral college does. When you look at the States, Wyoming has a population of roughly 480,000 people. In the State of Wyoming, they have three electoral votes. So that means that roughly they have 1 vote for President for every 160,000 people who live in the State of Wyoming — 1 vote for President, 160,000 people. My home State of Illinois: 12 million people and specifically 22 electoral votes. That means it takes 550,000 voters in Illinois to vote and cast 1 electoral vote for President. Comparing the voters in Wyoming to the voters in Illinois, there are three times as many people voting in Illinois to have 1 vote for President as in the State of Wyoming.

On the other hand, the philosophical underpinning of a direct popular election system is so clear and compelling it hardly needs mentioning. We use direct elections to choose Senators, Governors, Congressmen, and mayors, but we do not use it to elect a President. One-person, one-vote, and majority rule are supposedly basic tenets of democracy.

I am reminded of the debate that surrounded the Seventeenth Amendment which provides for the direct election of Senators. It is interesting. When our Founding Fathers wrote the Constitution, they said the people of the United States could choose and fill basically three Federal offices: The U.S. House of Representatives, the U.S. Senate, and the President and Vice President. But only in the case of the U.S. House of Representatives did they allow the American people to directly elect that Federal office with an election every 24 months.

I suppose their theory at the time was those running for Congress lived closer to the voters, and if the voters made a mistake, in 24 months they could correct it. But when it came to the election of Senators in the original Constitution, those Founding Fathers committed to democracy did not trust democracy. They said: We will let State legislatures choose those who will serve in the Senate. That was the case in America until 1913. With the Seventeenth Amendment, we provided for the direct election of Senators. So now we directly elect Senators and Congressmen, but we still cling to this age-old electoral college as an indirect way of electing Presidents of the United States. The single greatest benefit of adopting the Seventeenth Amendment and providing for the direct election of Senators was that voters felt more invested in the Senate as an institution and therefore able to have more faith in it.

In my State, in that early debate about the Seventeenth Amendment, there was a Senator who was accused of bribing members of the State legislature to be elected to the Senate. There were two different hearings on Capitol Hill. The first exonerated him. The second found evidence that bribery did take place. That was part of the impetus behind this reform movement in the direct election of Senators.

Second, while it appears smaller and more rural States have an advantage in the electoral college, the reality of modern Presidential campaigns is that these States are generally ignored.

One of my colleagues on the floor said: I will fight you, Durbin, on this idea of abolishing the electoral college. I come from a little State, and if you go to a popular vote to elect a President, Presidential candidates will pay no attention to my little State.

I have news for my colleagues. You did not see Governor Bush or Vice President Gore spending much time campaigning in Rhode Island or Idaho. In fact, 14 States were never visited by either candidate during the campaign, while 38 states received 10 or fewer visits. The more populous contested States with their large electoral prizes, such as Florida, Pennsylvania, Ohio, and Wisconsin, really have the true advantage whether we have a direct election or whether we have it by the electoral college.

Third, the electoral college system totally discounts the votes of those supporting the losing candidate in their State. In the 2000 Presidential race, 36 States were never really in doubt. The average percentage difference of the popular vote between the candidates in those States was more than 20 percent. The current system not only discounts losing votes; it essentially adds the full weight and value of those votes to the candidate those voters oppose.

If you were on the losing side in a State such as Illinois, which went for Al Gore, if you cast your vote for George Bush, your vote is not counted. It is a winner-take-all situation. All 22 electoral votes in the State of Illinois went to Al Gore, as the votes in other States, such as Texas, went exclusively to George Bush.

Fourth, the winner-take-all rules greatly increase the risk that minor third party candidates will determine who is elected President. In the electoral college system, the importance of a small number of votes in a few key States is greatly magnified. In a number of U.S. Presidential elections, third party candidates have affected a few key State races and determined the overall winner.

We can remember that Ross Perot may have cost President [George H. W.] Bush his reelection in 1992, and Ralph Nader may have cost Al Gore the 2000 election. In fact, in 1 out of every 4 Presidential elections since 1824, the winner was one State away from becoming the loser based on the electoral college vote count.

This is a chart which basically goes through the U.S. Presidential elections since 1824 and talks about those situations where we had a minority President, which we did with John Adams in 1824, with Rutherford B. Hayes in 1876, and Benjamin Harrison in 1888. These Presidential candidates lost the popular vote but won the election, which is rare in American history. It may happen this time. We do not know the outcome yet as I speak on the floor today.

In so many other times, though, we had very close elections where, in fact, the electoral vote was not close at all. Take the extremely close race in 1960 to which many of us point: John Kennedy, 49.7 percent of the vote; Richard Nixon, 49.5 percent. Look at the electoral college breakdown: 56 percent going to John Kennedy; 40 percent going to Richard Nixon. The electoral college did not reflect the feelings of America when it came to that race.

The same thing can be said when we look at the race in 1976. Jimmy Carter won with 50.1 percent of the vote over Gerald Ford with 48 percent of the vote. Jimmy Carter ended up with 55 percent of the electoral college and Gerald Ford with 44 percent. Again, the electoral college did not reflect that reality.

In comparison, under a direct popular vote system where over 100 million votes are cast, third party candidates generally would have a much more difficult time playing the spoiler. For instance, there have only been two elections since 1824 where the popular vote has been close enough to even consider a recount. Those were 1880 and 1960. In today's Presidential elections, a difference of even one-tenth of 1 percent represents 100,000 votes.

Fifth, the electoral college is clearly a more risky system than a direct popular vote, providing ample opportunity for manipulation, mischief, and litigation.

The electoral college provides that the House of Representatives choose the President when no candidate receives a majority of electoral votes. That happened in 1801 and 1825.

The electoral system allows Congress to dispute the legitimacy of electors. This occurred several times just after the Civil War and once in 1969.

In 1836, the Whig Party ran different Presidential candidates in different regions of the country. Their plan was to capitalize on the local popularity of the various candidates and then to pool the Whig electors to vote for a single Whig candidate or to throw the election to Congress.

In this century, electors in seven elections have cast ballots for candidates contrary to their State vote. Presidents have received fewer popular votes than their main opponent in 3 of the 44 elections since 1824.

In the 2000 election, I ask why the intense spotlight on Florida? The answer is simple: That is where the deciding electoral votes are. More disturbing is the fact that anyone following the election knew that Florida was the tightest race of those States with large electoral prizes. Those wishing to manipulate the election had a very clear target.

In contrast, under a direct popular vote system, there is no equivalent pressure point. Any scheme attempting to change several hundred thousand votes necessary to turn even the closest Presidential election is difficult to imagine in a country as vast and populous as the United States. Similarly, as I previously mentioned, recounts will be much more rare under a direct popular vote system given the size of the electorate.

Some people have said to me: Durbin, if you have a direct popular vote — here we have Gore winning the vote this time by 250,000 votes — wouldn't you have contests all across the Nation to try to make up that difference? Look what happened in Florida. The original Bush margin was about 1,700 votes. It is now down to 500 votes after 4 weeks of recount efforts and efforts in court, not a very substantial change in a State with 6 million votes. So to change 250,000 votes nationwide if we go to a popular vote would, of course, be a daunting challenge.

Throughout American history, there has been an inexorable march toward one citizen, one vote. As the Thirteen Colonies were debating if and how to join a more perfect Union, only a privileged few — those with the right skin color, the right gender, and the right financial status — enjoyed the right to cast votes to select their leaders. The people even gained the right to choose their Senators by popular vote with the ratification of the Seventeenth Amendment in 1913.

As one barrier after another has fallen, we are one step away from a system that treats all Americans equally, where a ballot cast for President in Illinois or Utah or Rhode Island has the same weight as one cast in Oregon or Florida. The electoral college is the last barrier preventing us from achieving that goal. As the world's first and greatest democracy, it is time to fully trust the people of America and allow them the right to choose a President.

We would like to say, when this is all over, that the American people have spoken and chosen their President. The fact is that is not the case. With the electoral college, the American people do not make the choice. The choice is made indirectly, by electing electors in each State, on a winner-take-all basis.

I leave you with a quote from Representative George Norris of Nebraska, who said the following during the debate in 1911 in support of the direct election of U.S. Senators. I quote:

It is upon the citizens that we depend for stability as a government. It is upon the patriotic, common, industrious people of our country that our Government must always lean in time of danger and distress. To this class of people then, we should give the right to control by direct election the selection of our public officials and to permit each citizen who is part of the sinew and backbone of our Government in time of danger to exercise his influence by direct vote in time of peace.

Mr. President, I will be introducing this proposal to abolish the electoral college and to establish the direct election of a President as part of our agenda in the next Congress. I sincerely hope it will be debated and considered. This time is the right time for us to take the time and look at the way we choose the President of the United States. It will not change the outcome of what happened on November 7 in the year 2000. But if history is our guide, I hope we will learn from this past experience and make our election machinery more democratic and more responsive.

Part of my proposal will also include the requirement that anyone to be elected President has to win 40 percent of the popular vote. Failing that, the top two candidates would face a runoff election. I think it is reasonable to suggest that leading this country requires at least the approval of 40 percent of the popular vote. That is why it would be included.

I hope my colleagues in the Senate, even those from the smaller States, will pause and take a look at this proposal.

I hope, before I yield the floor to my colleague from Minnesota, to make one other comment. There is a lot of talk about how this contest is going to end when it comes to this last election and the impact it will have on the Presidency.

I continue to believe that the American people want a strong President. They want a strong leader in the White House. They want our President to succeed. Whoever is finally declared the winner in the November 7, 2000, election, that person, I believe, deserves the support not only of the American people but clearly of Congress, too. We have to rally behind our next President in support of those decisions which really do chart the course for America. I think that force, coupled with the Senate equally divided 50–50, is going to be a positive force in bringing this Nation back together after this session of Congress comes to a close.

☑ *NO*

Should the Electoral College Be Abolished?

JUDITH A. BEST
In Defense of the Electoral College

Critics of the electoral vote system believe that the principle of democratic legitimacy is numbers alone, and therefore they think the system is indefensible. On the contrary, the electoral vote system is a paradigm — the very model — of the American democracy, and thus is quite easy to defend. For all practical purposes it is a direct popular federal election. (The Electors are mere ciphers, and the office of elector, but not the electoral votes, can be abolished.) The critics' principle of democratic legitimacy is inadequate because it is apolitical and anti-federal. Logically it boils down to: the majority must win and the minority must lose no matter what they lose. It is a formula for majority tyranny. But majority rule is not the principle of our Constitution. Rather it is majority rule with minority consent. The critics, however, think that because the system does not follow an arithmetical model it may produce the "wrong" winner. In fact, I contend, because it is federal it produces the right winner. . . .

In this country, it requires a federal political process. The federal principle is one of the two fundamental structural principles of our Constitution (the other being the separation of powers). The proposals to abolish the electoral college are proposals to abolish the federal principle in presidential elections. All of our national elective offices are based on the federal principle — they are state-based elections for we are a nation of states. Thus our national motto: E Pluribus Unum.

The federal principle in presidential elections forces presidential candidates to build broad cross-national political coalitions. Thereby it produces presidents who can govern because of their broad cross-national support. In politics as well as in physics there is such a thing as a critical mass. In presidential elections numbers of votes are necessary but not sufficient. To create the critical mass necessary for a president to govern, his votes must be properly distributed. This means he must win states and win states in more than one region of the country.

Under the federal presidential election system, a successful candidate can't simply promise everything to one section of the country and neglect the others. Analogy: Why are professional football teams required to win games in order to get into the playoffs and win the Super Bowl? Why not simply select the teams that scored the most points during the regular season? Any football fan can tell you why. Such a process wouldn't produce the right winner. Teams would run up the score against their weakest opponents, and the best teams in the most competitive divisions would have the least chance to get into the playoffs. Such a system isn't the proper test of the team talent and ability. A nonfederal election is not a proper test of support for the president.

If we abandon the federal principle in presidential elections we will be abandoning a national consensus building device by allowing candidates to promise everything to the populous Eastern megalopolis, or to promise everything to white Christians, or to suburbanites who are now half of all the voters. These are formulas for inability to govern or even civil war. And a system, like direct popular election, based on raw unstructured numbers alone rather than on the structuring federal principle, would effectively reduce the influence of minorities who often are the swing votes in closely divided states — groups like farmers who are only 2 percent of national population or blacks who are only 12 percent.

We need to remember that when we change the rules, we change the game and the game strategy and the skills needed to win. Under the federal principle successful candidates must have consensus-building skills. The goal of politics in this country is harmony — majority rule with minority consent. But when and why would a minority consent to majority rule? The answer is only if the minority can see that on some occasions and on some vital issues it can be part of the majority. It is irrational to consent to a game in which you can never win anything at all. To gain minority consent the Framers created many devices to allow minorities to be part of the majority, devices that give minorities more influence than their raw numbers would warrant including the state equality principle for representation in the Senate and the state districting principle for the House of Representatives. (The majority party in the House is often "over-represented" if our measure is raw numbers of votes nationally aggregated.) Then, of course, there is the state equality principle in voting on constitutional amendments. And there is the three-fourths requirement for passage of amendments. Such devices are designed to give minorities an influential voice in defining the national interest. The president is a major player in defining the national interest, and therefore it is necessary that the presidency be subjected to the moderating influence of a federal election system.

An equally important outcome of a state-based election system is that it serves to balance local and national interests. It is not just racial, religious, ethnic or occupational minorities that must be protected, there are local minorities whose consent must be sought. The people in small states must be protected against misuse of the phrase "the national interest." My favorite example is the problem of nuclear waste which none of us want in our backyards — not in my state. The rest of us can outvote Utah — so let's turn Utah into our national nuclear waste dump. This is majority tyranny in action. Nuclear waste is a national problem and the burden of solving it should not be placed on the people of one state without their consent. Since the president is a major player in making national policy, it is just as important that he be sensitive to balancing national and local interests, and the federal election system is designed to make it so. The right winner is a presidential candidate who recognizes the necessity and often the justice in balancing national and local interests. As [Thomas] Jefferson said, "the will of the majority to be rightful must be reasonable." The federal principle even and especially in presidential elections is a device for building reasonable majorities.

The opponents of the electoral vote system are head counters who confuse an election with a census. In a census our goal is mere accuracy. We want to know how many people are married or divorced, or have incomes over or under $20,000, or are Catholic or Protestant etc. In short, we want to break down the population into its multiple individual parts. In an election, especially a presidential election, we want to bring the people together. We want to build consensus, to build the support necessary and sufficient for our president to govern.

The proponents of direct national election think their system solves problems, but in fact it creates problems that are addressed or avoided by the federal election system. Presidential elections have multiple goals. Obviously we want to fill the office with someone who can govern, but we also want a swift, sure decision, and we want to reduce the premium on fraud, and most of us want to support the two-party system — a major source of national stability and a consensus, coalition building system.

From this perspective, the current system has been very successful. Since 1836 with the almost universal adoption of the state unit rule, awarding all of a state's electoral votes to the winner of the popular plurality, we have never had a contingency election. That's a proven record of 160 years. And we know the reason why: the magnifier effect of the state unit rule, a.k.a. the winner-take-all system. The victor in the popular vote contest for president will have a higher percentage of the electoral vote. The magnifier effect does not exaggerate the mandate — popular vote percentages are widely reported, not electoral vote percentages. The magnifier effect is not like a fisherman's story in which the size of the fish grows with the telling. Rather it is like the strong fishing line that serves to bring the fish, whatever its size, safely to shore. It supports the moderate two-party system, and balances national and state interests. And it makes the general election the only election.

Of course, there would be no magnifier effect under direct non-federal election, and the result is that contingency elections would become the rule. Under one proposal there would be a national runoff if no candidate received 50 percent of the popular vote. This provision would turn the general election into a national primary, proliferate candidacies and weaken or destroy the two-party system. It would also increase the potential for fraud and result in contested general elections with every ballot box in the United States having to be reopened and recounted under court supervision. Even the Left-handed Vegetarians Party could bring a court challenge because 1 percent or less of the popular vote could trigger a runoff election. And there would be a reason to challenge. In a runoff election even candidates who are not in the contest can win something by making a deal with one of the remaining two in return for support in the runoff. Not only would this mean an extended period of uncertainty about who the president will be — a temptation to foreign enemies — but also little time for the orderly transfer of power.

Most proponents of direct election, recognizing that to require a majority of the popular votes would produce these problems, suggest a 40 percent instead of a 50 percent runoff rule. The fact that most supporters of direct election are willing to make this concession indicates the seriousness of the problems attending contingency elections. This is a compromise of their principle — the arithmetical majority principle. Logically, on their principle, whenever no one polls 50 percent plus one vote there should be a runoff election.

And 40 percent is not a magical figure. It could be 42 or 44 percent with similar result — frequent runoffs. It is true that only one president, [Abraham] Lincoln (who was not on the ballot in 10 states), failed to reach the 40 percent plurality figure. However, history under the current system cannot be used to support the 40 percent figure because when you change the rules you change the game. Under the current rules we have had 17 minority presidential terms — presidents who came to the office with less than 50 percent of the popular vote. The last two are [Bill] Clinton's terms. The list includes some of our best presidents, not only Lincoln, but also [Woodrow] Wilson (twice), [James K.] Polk and [Harry] Truman. Seventeen minority presidential terms out of 42 presidents! The unit rule magnified their popular pluralities into electoral vote majorities because they won states.

But under direct nonfederal election there would be no magnifier effect. Potential candidates would recognize that multiple entries would be likely to trigger a runoff wherein one losing candidate could win a veto promise, another a Supreme Court nomination and a third a special interest subsidy in return for an endorsement in the runoff. And there is no reason to believe all such deals would be struck in the open. There would be no incentive for coalition building prior to the general election. The two major national parties would lose all control over the presidential nomination process — their life blood. Factional candidates, single-issue candidates, extremist candidates would serve as spoilers. As one commentator noted, on the day prior to the election, the *New York Times* would have to publish a twenty-page supplement simply to identify all the candidates.

Add to this the second-chance psychology that would infect voters, and you have the formula for a national ordeal. Second-chance psychology arises from the recognition that a popular vote runoff is a real possibility. Many a voter, thinking he will have another chance to vote in a runoff, will use his general election vote to protest something or other — to send a message.

Recounts would be demanded not only to determine who won, but also whether any candidate actually polled the 40 percent minimum, and if not which two candidates would be in the runoff. Under the unit rule magnifier effect which discourages multiple candidacies, we have already had five elections in which the popular vote margin was less than one percent. In the 1880 election the margin was one tenth of one percent. If such could happen under the current system where it is unlikely to trigger a runoff, it surely will happen under a 40 percent rule with a hair trigger runoff system. Weeks or months could pass with the outcome in doubt. One candidate could claim victory and start naming his cabinet only to be told some weeks later that he would have to participate in a runoff.

Further, the electorate wearies of prolonged elections. Even in the sports world players as well as fans reach a point where they want an end to it, and so accept sudden death rules. It is so important to fill the office on a timely basis that we have even had one president, Gerald Ford, who was not confirmed by a national election. Ford succeeded to the office on the resignation of his predecessor, Richard Nixon, but unlike vice presidents who had succeeded before him, he had been nominated by Nixon and confirmed by congressional vote under the provisions for filling vice presidential vacancies in the Twenty-fifth Amendment.

No election system is perfect, but the current system has borne the test of time. It has never rejected the winner of a popular vote majority. In every case but one it gave the victory to the winner of the popular plurality. And that one case proves the rule. [Grover] Cleveland, who lost in the electoral vote, won the popular vote while running a sectional campaign. He did not seek to broaden his support; he focused his message on one section of the country. Unintentionally, he thereby sent a message about the current system to all future presidential candidates: Remember 1888! Don't run a sectional campaign! Further, he won the popular vote by only eight tenths of one percent! This was an election that verged on a tie. Since a timely decision is so important, a reasonable tie breaker is the win states' federal principle.

The proposed amendments would deform not reform the Constitution. It is not just the presidency that is at risk here. If the federal principle is illegitimate in presidential elections, why isn't it illegitimate for Senate and House elections? Why should a state with half a million people have the same representation in the Senate as a state with twenty million people? Why should every state have at least one representative in the House? Why shouldn't states with very small populations have to share a representative with folks in another state? And why should each state regardless of its population size have an equal vote on constitutional amendments? The Framers knew the answer to these questions — the federal principle. It is true that the electoral vote system did not work out in precisely the fashion that the Framers anticipated, but it did evolve in conformity to the federal principle and the separation of powers. I have no doubt that they would recognize this if they were here today. It evolved in conformity with the federal spirit of the constitution, the "great discovery" the Framers themselves made.

For this, let us turn to Alexis de Tocqueville, who commenting on the federal principle in the Constitution, called it "a wholly novel theory, which may be considered as a great discovery in modern political science." He goes on to explain that it combines the best of both worlds. He says that its advantage is to unite the benefits and avoid the weaknesses of small and large societies. He learned this not only from observation, but also from reading James Madison in *Federalist 39,* who said that our form of government "is, in strictness, neither a national nor a federal Constitution, but a combination of both."

Madison's word "combination" is the key. The federal principle is a "great discovery," because it is a combination like an alloy — my term not his. We create alloys because we want to combine the advantages and avoid the weaknesses of two different things. We fuse copper and zinc to create brass because brass is harder, more malleable and more ductile than copper. We create steel alloys for the same reason. The federal system is an alloy. It not only makes us strong as a nation, it also allows us to be diverse and flexible, to experiment. It thereby increases our freedom without destroying our national unity. Tocqueville was right: it was a "great discovery" of modern political science. Let us preserve it.

Questions for Discussion

1. What effect did the failure of George W. Bush to win a majority of the popular vote in the presidential election of 2000 have on his presidency?
2. How would direct election of the president affect the two-party system?
3. How would direct election affect the power of racial minorities in the United States?
4. How would a system of direct election of the president affect the political campaigning strategy of presidential campaigns?
5. Which groups benefit and which are hurt by the Electoral College system?

Suggested Resources

Web Sites

Federal Election Commission
http://www.fec.gov/pages/ecmenu2.htm

Freedom Works
http://freedom.house.gov/electoral/

National Archives and Record Administration
http://www.archives.gov/federal_register/electoral_college/electoral_college.html

U.S. Supreme Court:
Florida Election Cases Involving the 2000 Presidential Election
http://supremecourtus.gov/florida.html

Publications

Ackerman, Bruce, ed., *Bush v. Gore: The Question of Legitimacy.* New Haven, Conn: Yale University Press, 2002.

Barbash, Fred. *The Founding: A Dramatic Account of the Writing of the Constitution.* New York: Linden Press/Simon & Schuster, 1987.

Best, Judith. *The Choice of the People: Debating the Electoral College.* Lanham, Md.: Rowman & Littlefield, 1996.

Dover, E. D. *The Disputed Presidential Election of 2000: A History and Reference Guide.* Westport, Conn.: Greenwood Press, 2003.

Dworkin, Ronald, ed. *A Badly Flawed Election: Debating Bush v. Gore, the Supreme Court, and American Democracy.* New York: New Press, 2002.

"Electoral College: Anachronism or Bulwark of Democracy?" *Congressional Digest* 80, no. 1 (January 2001): entire issue.

Glennon, Michael J. *When No Majority Rules: The Electoral College and Presidential Succession.* Washington, D.C.: Congressional Quarterly, 1992.

Gregg, Gary L., II, ed. *Securing Democracy: Why We Have an Electoral College.* Wilmington, Del.: ISI Books, 2001.

Hardaway, Robert M. *The Electoral College and the Constitution: The Case for Preserving Federalism.* Westport, Conn.: Praeger, 1994.

Jefferson-Jenkins, Carolyn. "Who Should Elect the President? The Case against the Electoral College." *National Civic Review* 90, no. 2 (Summer 2001): 173–81.

Jost, Kenneth, and Gregory L. Giroux. "Electoral College." *CQ Researcher* 10, no. 42 (December 8, 2000): 977–1008.

Longley, Lawrence D., and Neal R. Peirce. *The Electoral College Primer 2000.* New Haven, Conn.: Yale University Press, 1999.

Political Staff of the *Washington Post. Deadlock: The Inside Story of America's Closest Election.* New York: Public Affairs, 2001.

Schlesinger, Arthur M., Jr. "Not the People's Choice." *American Prospect* 13, no. 6 (March 25, 2002): 23–27.

Schumaker, Paul D., and Burdett A. Loomis, eds. *Choosing a President: Electoral College and Beyond.* New York: Chatham House, 2001.

U.S. Cong., House of Representatives. *Proposals for Electoral College Reform.* Hearing before the Subcommittee on the Constitution of the Committee on the Judiciary, 105th Cong., 1st Sess., September 4, 1997.

Do the Mass Media Have a Liberal Bias?

B y most accounts the mass media — television, newspapers, magazines, and the radio — play a central role in the U.S. political system. Some observers believe that the media's influence is so powerful that they function as the fourth branch of government. The media's perception of political leaders, events, and policies affects what people believe, so that political leaders neglect the media at their peril. After the aircraft hijacking and attack on the World Trade Center and the Pentagon on September 11, 2001, the administration of President George W. Bush took great care to use the media to make its case for taking strong measures against terrorists at home and abroad.

On domestic matters, too, media accounts influence opinion. After Trent Lott, a U.S. senator from Mississippi, made a public statement honoring Senator Strom Thurmond of South Carolina, media accounts highlighted that part of the statement indicating that the United States would have avoided many problems had Thurmond been elected president in 1948. Since Thurmond ran as a segregationist in the election, media reporting of the statement played a role in the resignation of Lott as the Republican leader of the U.S. Senate. For his part, Lott apologized for the statement he had made but felt obliged to withdraw from his position as his party's leader in the Senate because of mounting public criticism.

The media's influence is derived not only from the stories presented but from the prominence given them. An analysis of the media's reporting on a single day will show a diversity of emphases. News, or the importance of particular items of news, is not so self-evident that everyone in the profession of journalism agrees on what is, and what is not, significant. Some critics of the media have noted the importance of emphasis in coverage of the Vietnam War, coverage they claim was detrimental to U.S. foreign policy interests. Television news reporting that highlighted the killing by U.S. soldiers of Vietnamese civilians or the use of drugs by GIs was biased, these critics argue, because the enemy's actions and problems were not also exposed. Not only was the coverage unbalanced, the critics added, but it was much less sensitive to U.S. government needs than news reporting during World War II. Supporters of the media counter that these critics simply do not like the news and so are "killing the messenger." Reporters are simply doing their job, media supporters contend, and political leaders who try to dominate the news are always going to be annoyed when news stories cast them in an unfavorable light.

Media critics often claim that the media have a bias, but they differ about what the bias is. *Boston Globe* columnist Jeff Jacoby argues that the media have a liberal bias. In pointing out that some observers are wrongly saying that the media have a conservative bias, he notes:

1. Although there are some media sources that are conservative, liberals by far outnumber conservatives and dominate the media.
2. Reporters and editors overwhelmingly hold liberal views. Such views make it easy for newsrooms to ignore conservative opinions.

Bernie Sanders, an independent member of the U.S. House of Representatives from Vermont, makes the case that the U.S. media are conservative rather than liberal. He notes:

1. The media are controlled by a few giant conglomerates that determine what Americans see, hear, and read. These corporations have interests that they seek to protect through their control of the media.
2. Issues that have the support of liberals, such as increased health care for the poor, long hours and low wages for American workers, unfair distribution of wealth and income in the United States, and a high rate of poverty, are often ignored in the media.
3. Dozens of conservative right-wing talk shows espouse an antiliberal viewpoint.

☑ YES

Do the Mass Media Have a Liberal Bias?

JEFF JACOBY
U.S. Media Retain Their Liberal Bias

A groaning shelf of evidence bears out what many people know intuitively: the American mass media suffer from a left-wing slant. The data come in a variety of forms: classic studies such as *The Media Elite* (first published in 1986) and William McGowan's *Coloring the News* (2001), insider exposés like CBS veteran Bernard Golberg's recent bestseller *Bias,* and a thick sheaf of industry studies and public opinion polls.

Yet some liberals have always claimed that liberal media bias is a shibboleth.

"It's one of the great political myths," insisted Dan Rather in 1995. "Most reporters don't know whether they're Republican or Democrat, and vote every which way. . . . And also, let me say that I don't think that 'liberal' or 'conservative' means very much any more."

Peter Jennings offered much the same argument last year.

"I think it's just essential to make the point," he told Larry King, "that we are largely in the center, without particular axes to grind, without ideologies which are represented in our daily coverage." Likewise, Geraldo Rivera, to take just one more example, contends that "people who pretend the media has a liberal bias aren't really listening or reading."

Comes now an even more cockeyed claim: Not only does Big Media not tilt left, it is in fact being shoved to the right.

"The media is kind of weird these days on politics, and there are some major institutional voices that are, truthfully speaking, part and parcel of the Republican Party," former vice president Al Gore recently declared. "Fox News [Channel], *The Washington Times,* Rush Limbaugh — there's a bunch of them, and some of them are financed by wealthy ultra-conservative billionaires. . . . Most of the media has been slow to recognize the pervasive impact of this fifth column in their ranks — that is, day after day, injecting the daily Republican talking points into the definition of what's objective as stated by the news media as a whole."

Gore's motion was seconded by a number of prominent media liberals. Paul Krugman of *The New York Times* pronounced it "so clearly true." *The Washington Post*'s E. J. Dionne averred that conservatives have won a "genuine triumph" — "a media heavily biased toward conservative politics and conservative politicians." After all, he noted, when Senate Democratic Leader Tom Daschle publicly denounced Rush Limbaugh, two cable TV talk shows took the unheard-of step of interviewing Limbaugh.

One thing to be said about this "new" argument is that it's not new. The idea that conservative operatives are turning the media into a GOP echo chamber goes back at least six years, when it was an article of faith in the Clinton administration.

Everyone recalls Hillary Clinton sneering away reports of an affair between her husband and Monica Lewinsky as the ravings of a "vast right-wing conspiracy." What most forget is just how gripped by conservatives-are-taking-over-the-media panic the Clinton White House was. In 1995 it produced a 332-page report purporting to prove — I am not making this up — that Republican politicians, conservative think tanks, certain "British tabloids," *The Wall Street Journal*'s editorial page, and *The Washington Times* were all linked in a plot, funded by the heir to the Mellon fortune, to get scandalous "fringe stories" about Bill Clinton "bounced into the mainstream media."

Well, conspiracy thinking is something of an American tradition. Some people believe the CIA [Central Intelligence Agency] funneled cocaine to the Los Angeles slums; others believe Richard Mellon Scaife is the root of all evil. It somehow comes as no surprise to find Al Gore resurrecting the Clinton-era fable about the right-wing tentacles that manipulate CNN, *Time, The New York Times, USA Today,* National Public Radio, NBC, and all the other influential outlets that make up the national mainstream media. It's not the only dotty theory cherished by the former vice president.

The hard reality, though, is that the media's few conservative institutional voices cannot hope to overpower the liberal bias that permeates the rest of the media. It is a simple matter of arithmetic. As Michael Kelly noted last week, Fox News Channel's viewers add up to about 3 percent of the ABC-CBS-CNN-NBC-PBS news audience. *The Washington Times* has one-eighth the circulation of *The Washington Post*. In the media world, power comes from numbers.

And so does media bias. The national media are largely left-of-center because those who go into the national media are largely left-of-center. "Everybody knows that . . . there's a heavy liberal persuasion among correspondents," Walter Cronkite has said. Inevitably, that liberal persuasion colors reporters' and editors' work. How could it not? When everyone in the newsroom shares a liberal worldview, conservative opinions become easy to dismiss. The result is that on a host of topics from capital punishment to tax cuts, Big Media usually speaks with one voice. It's hard to believe Al Gore can't hear it.

 N O

Do the Mass Media Have a Liberal Bias?

BERNIE SANDERS
Corporations Have Chokehold on U.S. Media

One of our best-kept secrets is the degree to which a handful of huge corporations control the flow of information in the United States. Whether it is television, radio, newspapers, magazines, books or the Internet, a few giant conglomerates are determining what we see, hear and read. And the situation is likely to become much worse as a result of radical deregulation efforts by the Bush administration and some horrendous court decisions.

Television is the means by which most Americans get their "news." Without exception, every major network is owned by a huge conglomerate that has enormous conflicts of interest. Fox News Channel is owned by Rupert Murdoch, a right-wing Australian who already owns a significant portion of the world's media. His network has close ties to the Republican Party, and among his "fair and balanced" commentators is Newt Gingrich.

NBC is owned by General Electric, one of the largest corporations in the world — and one with a long history of anti-union activity. GE, a major contributor to the Republican Party, has substantial financial interests in weapons manufacturing, finance, nuclear power and many other industries. Former CEO Jack Welch was one of the leaders in shutting down American plants and moving them to low-wage countries like China and Mexico.

ABC is owned by the Disney Corp., which produces toys and products in developing countries where they provide their workers atrocious wages and working conditions.

CBS is owned by Viacom, another huge media conglomerate that owns, among other entities, MTV, Showtime, Nickelodeon, VH1, TNN, CMT, 39 broadcast television stations, 184 radio stations, Paramount Pictures and Blockbuster Inc.

The essential problem with television is not just a right-wing bias in news and programming, or the transformation of politics and government into entertainment and sensationalism. Nor is it just the constant bombardment of advertising, much of it directed at children. It's that the most important issues facing the middle-class and working people of our country are rarely discussed. The average American does not see his or her reality reflected on the television screen.

The United States is the only industrialized nation on earth that does not have a national healthcare program. Yet, despite 41 million people with no health insurance and millions more underinsured, we spend far more per capita on healthcare than any other nation. Maybe the reason is that we are seeing no good programs on television, in between the prescription drug advertisements, discussing how we can provide quality healthcare for all at far lower per capita costs than we presently spend.

Despite the great "economic boom" of the 1990s, the average American worker is now working longer hours for lower wages than 30 years ago, and we have lost millions of decent-paying manufacturing jobs. Where are the TV programs addressing our $360 billion trade deficit, or what our disastrous trade policy has done to depress wages in this country? And while we're on economics, workers who are in unions earn 30 percent more than non-union people doing the same work. There are a lot of programs on television about how to get rich by investing in the stock market. But have you seen any "specials" on how to go about forming a union?

The United States has the most unfair distribution of wealth and income in the industrialized world, and the highest rate of childhood poverty. There's a lot of television promoting greed and self-interest, but how many programs speak to the "justice" of the richest 1 percent owning more wealth than the bottom 95 percent? Or of the CEOs of major corporations earning 500 times what their employees make?

If television largely ignores the reality of life for the majority of Americans, corporate radio is just plain overt in its right-wing bias. In a nation that cast a few million more votes for Al Gore and Ralph Nader than for George Bush and Pat Buchanan, there are dozens of right-wing talk show programs. Rush Limbaugh, G. Gordon Liddy, Bob Grant, Sean Hannity, Alan Keyes, Armstrong Williams, Howie Carr, Oliver North, Michael Savage, Michael Reagan, Pat Robertson, Laura Schlessinger — these are only a few of the voices that day after day pound a right-wing drumbeat into the heartland of this country.

And from a left perspective there is — well, no one. The Republican Party, corporate owners and advertisers have their point of view well represented on radio. Unfortunately, the rest of America has almost nothing.

As bad as the current media situation is, it is likely to be made much worse by a recent decision in the District of Columbia Court of Appeals that responded to a suit by Fox, AOL Time Warner, NBC and Viacom. That decision struck down a federal regulation limiting companies from owning television stations and cable franchises in the same local markets. The court also ordered that the Federal Communications Commission either justify or rewrite the federal rule that limits any one company from owning television stations that reach more than 35 percent of American households.

The bottom line is that fewer and fewer huge conglomerates are controlling virtually everything that the ordinary American sees, hears and reads. This is an issue that Congress can no longer ignore.

Questions for Discussion

1. What criteria should be used in determining whether a newspaper or television program is biased in presenting the news?
2. If there is a media bias, what is it? What is your evidence?
3. How do political leaders attempt to shape the news? Are they successful?
4. How does corporate ownership affect the presentation of the news?
5. How do the attitudes of the journalists, producers, and executives affect the shape of the news?

Suggested Resources

Web Sites

Accuracy in Media
   www.aim.org

Center for Media and Public Affairs
   www.cmpa.com

Fairness and Accuracy in Reporting
   www.fair.org

Media Research Center
   www.mediaresearch.org

Pew Research Center for the People and the Press
   www.people-press.org

Publications

Alterman, Eric. *What Liberal Media? The Truth about Bias and the News.* New York: Basic Books, 2003.

Fallows, James. *Breaking the News: How the Media Undermine American Democracy.* New York: Pantheon Books, 1996.

Goldberg, Bernard. *Bias: A CBS Insider Exposes How the Media Distorts the News.* Washington, D.C.: Regnery, 2001.

Jamieson, Kathleen Hall, and Paul Waldman. *The Press Effect: Politicians, Journalists, and the Stories That Shape the Political World.* New York: Oxford University Press, 2002.

Kuypers, Jim A. *Press Bias and Politics: How the Media Frame Controversial Issues.* Westport, Conn.: Praeger, 2002.

Lichter, S. Robert, Stanley Rothman, and Linda S. Lichter. *The Media Elite.* Bethesda, Md.: Adler & Adler, 1986.

McGowan, William. *Coloring the News: How Crusading for Diversity Has Corrupted American Journalism.* San Francisco: Encounter Books, 2001.

Mindich, David T. Z. *Just the Facts: How Objectivity Came to Define American Politics.* New York: New York University Press, 1998.

Murray, David, Joel Schwartz, and S. Robert Lichter. *It Ain't Necessarily So: How Media Remake Our Picture of Reality.* New York: Penguin Books, 2002.

Niven, David. *Tilt? The Search for Media Bias.* Westport, Conn.: Praeger, 2002.

Sanford, Bruce W. *Don't Shoot the Messenger: How Our Growing Hatred of the Media Threatens Free Speech for All of Us.* New York: Free Press, 1999.

Policy-Making Institutions

As indicated in Part I, the Framers of the Constitution established a system of powers and checks and balances constituted in three branches of government — legislative, executive, and judicial. The Framers feared that the concentration of powers in the hands of one branch would be a danger to liberty.

The Constitution, as has so often been said, is a living document, and it has changed over time through formal constitutional amendment, statutes, political practices, and customs. In part because of the ambiguities in some provisions of the Constitution and in part because of historical developments, power has shifted in different eras from one branch to another.

Constitutional amendments have modified the major branches of government. For example, the Seventeenth Amendment, adopted in 1913, changed the method of choosing U.S. senators from election by the state legislatures, as provided in Article I of the Constitution, to direct popular election in each state. Statutes have also changed the Constitution. Congress passed numerous laws in the nineteenth and twentieth centuries establishing new departments and government agencies. When the Constitution was adopted, the role of government in society was minimal, but through statutes passed, particularly in the twentieth century, Congress has given executive agencies — the bureaucracy — vast powers in both domestic and foreign policy.

The formal constitutional actors in the U.S. political system have had their own impact on constitutional development. The Constitution says nothing about the power of judicial review, but the Supreme Court, under John Marshall, asserted that power in *Marbury v. Madison* in 1803. Today the power of judicial review is an accepted principle of the U.S. political system. The Constitution, moreover, says nothing about the organization of Congress into committees, but congressional committees today play important roles in the enactment of legislation.

Custom, too, influences the Constitution. George Washington left office at the end of his second term, and a two-term tradition was widely accepted over time until Franklin D. Roosevelt was elected to a third term in 1940 and a fourth term in 1944. Adopted in 1951, however, the Twenty-Second Amendment limited presidential terms to two, thus giving formal constitutional sanction to what had been a custom until Roosevelt's third term.

The power of the principal institutions of government depends, then, on a variety of factors. The Constitution and laws provide the basic structure and define the formal powers of the major actors in the political system. The relationship of policy makers over time, however, depends on the personalities of the policy makers, the ties between the president and influential members of Congress, the character of judicial decisions, the astuteness of top bureaucrats, and historical developments.

Part IV deals with some of the important issues about the power, role, and behavior of policy makers in the national government today. The debates consider the adoption of a parliamentary system for the United States, presidential war powers, the use of ideological considerations in confirming Supreme Court nominees, the role of the government bureaucracy, and the judicial doctrine of strict constructionism.

14

Should the United States Adopt a Parliamentary System of Government?

Two principal forms of government in democratic societies are presidential and parliamentary systems. The United States has a presidential system in which power is deliberately dispersed among different institutions. The Framers of the Constitution were influenced by the eighteenth-century French philosopher Baron de Montesquieu, who believed in the dividing of political power. In the words of James Madison, an architect of the Constitution, "The accumulation of all powers legislative, executive, and judiciary in the same hands . . . may justly be pronounced the very definition of tyranny."[1]

And so, the presidential system is marked by a system of separation of powers and checks and balances. According to the Constitution, separation of powers means that each of the branches is equal to and independent from the other branches. The Constitution gives primary legislative power to the Congress, primary executive power to the president, and primary judicial power to the Supreme Court.

A system of checks and balances encourages further fragmentation. In that system each branch of government has some powers over the other branches. Because of separation of powers and checks and balances, Congress has some executive powers (such as the power to create federal agencies) and some judicial powers (such as the power to control the number of people on the Supreme Court). The president has some legislative power (such as the power to propose legislation) and some judicial power (the power to nominate judges to federal courts). The Supreme Court can declare laws enacted by Congress and actions taken by the president to be unconstitutional. The method of election of president and Congress further emphasizes divided power. The president is elected by the Electoral College. Initially, the Senate was chosen by the states, although since the adoption of the Seventeenth Amendment in 1913 it is elected by popular vote. The House of Representatives is elected by popular vote. Terms of office vary, too. The term of office for the president is four years, for House members two years, and for Senate members six years. Members of the Supreme Court can serve for life.

Although political parties in the United States emerged after the Constitution was adopted, they play an important role in the political process. But the major political parties in the United States are largely decentralized. State and local party organizations have greater control over nominating candidates than do the central party organization. It is not uncommon for some members of the same political party in Congress to vote against the proposed legislation supported by their congressional party leaders.

The parliamentary system is different from the presidential system. Although parliamentary systems vary somewhat among countries, if we take the British system as an example for purposes of the debate discussion we can see notable differences. Parliament is composed of a House of Lords and a House of Commons. The power of the House of Lords, which is composed of bishops of the Church of England and hereditary and life peers, is minimal. It is the House of Commons that holds the effective legislative power, and its members are elected by the people.

Executive power is in the hands of the monarch, prime minister, and cabinet. The monarch is a figurehead, who has ceremonial power but no political power. The prime minister and cabinet are members of the House of Commons. The prime minister is chosen by the majority party or a coalition of majority parties in the House of Commons, and voting on legislation is usually done along party lines.

An act of Parliament is supreme and cannot be declared invalid by a court. If a British government loses a vote of confidence — that is, members of the House of Commons fail to approve one of its major proposals — then new elections for all the members of the House of Commons must soon be conducted. There is no fixed term of office for members of the House of Commons. To be sure, an election must be held within five years, but other than losing a vote of confidence, a prime minister can call an election at any time during the period of five years.

Political parties are centralized in Great Britain. Members of the House of Commons usually vote along party lines. If they do not do so, then the majority party may lose a vote of confidence, causing a new election. The central party organization, moreover, can deny a sitting member of the House of Commons from that party the opportunity to run for office with that party's designation if the member votes against his or her party in the House of Commons.

Key features of the parliamentary system, then, are the supremacy of Parliament, the fusion of executive and legislative powers, and strong, centralized political parties. These are features that are quite different from the presidential system with its separation of powers, checks and balances, and decentralized political parties.

A number of scholars have suggested that the United States adopt a parliamentary type system. Using the British-type model as an example of a parliamentary system for purposes of discussion, Herbert M. Levine presents the pros and cons of the issue. Arguments supporting such a change to a parliamentary system are:

1. Government would become more accountable and democratic.
2. Government would become more efficient.
3. Traditional powers, presently assumed by the executive, would be restored to the legislature.

Arguments opposing a parliamentary system for the United States are:

1. A presidential system is even more accountable than the British parliamentary system because of the separation of powers.
2. The American political system is efficient.
3. There is no evidence to indicate that legislative power in a parliamentary system would increase with respect to the executive compared to legislative power in a presidential system.

NOTE

1. James Madison, *Federalist* no. 47, in Alexander Hamilton, James Madison, and John Jay, *The Federalist Papers*, ed. Clinton Rossiter (New York: New American Library, 1961), p. 301.

 ☑ *YES*

*Should the United States Adopt
a Parliamentary System of Government?*

HERBERT M. LEVINE
The Case for a Parliamentary System

Throughout the twentieth century many writers, including such notables as the political scientist and president Woodrow Wilson and the journalist Walter Lippmann, have called for major structural changes in the American political system so that it will more closely resemble British parliamentary government. We concur with this position and contend that the American system should be restructured so as to allow for the designation of two separate officials: a chief of state who would be a ceremonial leader, and a prime minister who would be a member of the legislative body. We would also eliminate the system of federalism and put government power completely into the hands of a newly formed Congress. That Congress would be unicameral and would select the prime minister and cabinet. The American prime minister would have much the same powers that his or her British counterpart possesses today. A strong, centralized, two-party system would assure party discipline, and the loss of a vote of confidence in Congress would bring on a general election. The American prime minister could be dismissed by his or her party without the necessity of going through a general election. The prime minister's cabinet would be composed of members of Congress. Each cabinet member would be in charge of an executive department. The Supreme Court would no longer have its power of judicial review, although it could interpret the law as enacted by Congress.

Such structural changes are essential in the American political system. With such alterations, the system would achieve the following advantages: (1) government would become more accountable and democratic; (2) government would become more efficient; and (3) traditional powers, presently assumed by the executive, would be restored to the legislature. We would then have a government that would be streamlined enough to carry us through the twenty-first century.

ACCOUNTABILITY AND DEMOCRACY

Representative democracy is a system of government in which elected public officials represent the people. Advocates of democracy differ as to the particular character of the representative. Some view the representative as a delegate — a person who must represent the interests of his or her constituency whether or not he or she agrees with those interests. Others view the representative as a trustee — a person who votes on the basis of conscience in legislative considerations for those principles in which he or she believes. Either theory, however, implies that representatives must in some way be accountable to the people who elect them.

If a Labour government is in power in Great Britain, then Labour is held accountable for what happens to the society. If the inflation rates rise rapidly or foreign policy setbacks are experienced, then it is Labour's fault. Accountability is clear in a system in which the legislative and executive power are fused.

In the United States, however, power and authority are dispersed. "The splitting of sovereignty into many parts amounts to there being no sovereign," the nineteenth-century British writer Walter Bagehot observed.[1] Particularly in situations in which the president belongs to one party and the Congress to another, responsibility is claimed only for good news and not for bad. When Republican Gerald Ford was president, he blamed the Democratic Congress for inflation because of its spending policies. It was difficult for voters to hold elected public officials accountable in such a diffused system. Democracy requires accountability, and parliamentary reforms in the American political process along British lines would provide for that accountability.

EFFICIENCY

The American political system of government is a highly inefficient way to rule. The U.S. Constitution was created in the late eighteenth century at a time when the population of the United States totaled only about 3 million people who lived mostly in eastern coastal states. At that time, the American economy was dominated by agriculture. Moreover, the United States was a country on the periphery of power politics dominated by the big European powers.

The Constitution of 1787 created an inefficient government because government was regarded by many eighteenth-century Americans as a necessary evil. Today, strong government is necessary but not possible, given the constitutional constraints imposed by a document written for the needs of two centuries ago. "The separation of powers between the legislative and executive branches, whatever its merits in 1793," writes the Washington attorney Lloyd Cutler, "has become a structure that almost guarantees stalemate today."[2]

Today, the United States needs a structure that can provide positive government to meet the needs of a modern post–industrial society. The rapidly changing global economic situation makes necessary decisive action that only a unified government can provide. The position of the United States as a superpower, moreover, requires the country to speak with one voice rather than having the executive trying to move in one direction and the legislature trying to get the executive to move in another. A parliamentary system based on the British model, then, would allow for the positive and efficient government that our system currently lacks.

Efficiency in government would be helped by putting people with long experience in government into positions of responsibility. To become a minister requires many years of working one's way up through party ranks and developing a knowledge about government. By the time an individual becomes a prime minister in Britain, he or she has learned how to get things done in government.

The separate election of president and Congress, in contrast, means that an individual can come to the presidency with little or no experience in dealing with the Congress. Walter Bagehot commented in 1867 about the low quality of executive talent recruited to the presidency. He regarded this situation as caused by the separation of powers. He did indicate that Abraham Lincoln was an able president but noted aptly that "success in a lottery is no argument for lotteries."[3] In more modern times individuals attaining the presidency from outside the legislative branch have had to "learn on the job" while the country was being impaired by the president's inexperience.

The parliamentary system, moreover, would assure that the most talented members of Congress would retain their seats and not be ejected from the legislature because of electoral defeat. Good people could be given safe seats from which members of their party are nearly always elected so as to assure their making a continuing contribution to the government. The country benefits when it retains legislators of talent as active participants in the political process.

LEGISLATIVE ASSERTION

In 1885 Woodrow Wilson published a study of the American system of government entitled *Congressional Government,* which reflected where power resided at that time. In the twenty-first century, however, the executive branch of government has come to play a more prominent role in government decision making.

The examples are varied and include foreign policy, national security, and domestic matters. In foreign policy executive agreements (which require merely the approval of the president) have increasingly been used instead of treaties requiring Senate approval. In national security matters, moreover, the president has used his powers as commander-in-chief to involve the country in acts of war. The Constitution specifically indicates that Congress shall have the power to declare war, but American involvement in Korea in the 1950s, in Vietnam in the 1960s and 1970s, and in the Persian Gulf in the 1990s did not come about by formal declarations of war. American casualties in the first two wars were high, and the mere fact that war was not declared did not alter the high price the country paid for executive action.

Domestic matters, too, have experienced executive encroachment, as presidents have authorized government snooping, wiretapping, and surveillance of private individuals without congressional authority. Executives also have expanded their powers in the management of the economy, determining at times such matters as price and wage controls and import-export restrictions.

The high point of executive power came during the Watergate affair, when power became wrongdoing. For a period of more than a year, President Richard Nixon and his top aides struggled to ward off investigations by Congress and the courts. The conduct of government was slowed down by the struggle. Ultimately, Richard Nixon resigned. No American president had been previously thrown out of office before his term expired, and none had previously resigned. The fixed period of four years made it impossible to remove the president without a grave constitutional crisis.

Had the United States been governed by a parliamentary system, it would not have had to go through such an agonizing experience. In 1940, Prime Minister Neville Chamberlain was replaced by Winston Churchill when Chamberlain's policy of appeasement against Adolf Hitler became discredited. In 1956, moreover, Anthony Eden resigned over the failure of his policy on the Suez Canal, and he was replaced by Harold Macmillan. Both Churchill and Macmillan came to power without a constitutional crisis and without a general election. It would have been possible, and much more sensible, to remove Richard Nixon in the same way that Chamberlain and Eden were removed had the United States been governed by a parliamentary system.

The same parliamentary system would be desirable even if a president has not been guilty of wrongdoing. When Herbert Hoover was elected president in 1928, he was a popular figure. The Great Depression beginning in 1929, however, diminished his popularity. In spite of the extended period of economic devastation, Hoover remained in the White House until 1933, when Franklin D. Roosevelt came to power and promised the American people a "New Deal" to get the country out of its economic difficulties.

As the nation moves ahead in the twenty-first century, it must streamline its government to meet the even more complex challenges. A parliamentary system would allow for government to be accountable, efficient, and responsive to popular demands.

NOTES

1. Walter Bagehot, *The English Constitution*, 2d ed. (London: Oxford University Press, 1952), p. 201. The study was originally published in 1867.
2. Lloyd Cutler, "To Form a Government," *Foreign Affairs* 59 (Fall 1980): 127.
3. Bagehot, *English Constitution*, p. 28.

Should the United States Adopt a Parliamentary System of Government?

HERBERT M. LEVINE
The Case against a Parliamentary System

The argument that the United States would have better government if it adopted the British parliamentary system should be dismissed after a close examination is made of both the current British political system and the American political system. We shall leave aside for argument's sake the practical contention that such a reshuffling of powers and institutions would not be possible to implement in the United States. Even Walter Bagehot contended that the parliamentary system worked best in a limited area with uniform standards of wealth and education. He felt that it could not work for the entire American political system.

Let us take the points of accountability and democracy, efficiency, and legislative assertion to justify our case.

ACCOUNTABILITY AND DEMOCRACY

It is true that power is fragmented in the American political system. It is false, however, that government is not held accountable because of the system of separation of powers. In Great Britain the voter has little choice but to cast a ballot for a particular candidate with a party designation. In the United States, by contrast, the voter can hold a variety of public officials accountable for their actions since the voter casts a ballot separately for a representative, a senator, and the president. As the political scientist Don K. Price notes, the presidential system provides the voters with a "double-check on their government" through their president and other elected officials. Price adds that however poorly the president and Congress are carrying out their responsibilities, the voters "are not kept from exercising their controls by a system of mutual deference that results from the fear of disturbing each other's [president and Congress] tenure of office."[1]

The American system of separation of powers is in fact more accountable than the British parliamentary system, as the evidence reveals. Because of the separation of powers, the system assures an independent legislature capable of challenging the actions of the executive. The legislature may subpoena civil servants to disclose executive actions in the American system, a practice denied in the British political system. There is much more disclosure about what government is doing in the American political system than in the British system. This feature is explained in part by the fact that the laws of press freedom allow more discretion to American journalists than to their British counterparts. Another important reason for the disclosure of so much information, however, is that legislators do not have to fear that their careers will be ruined if they either vote against or organize opposition to the president, who is also a member of their political party. A people who are able to have access to vast amounts of information are in a far better position to hold government accountable for its acts, as befits a democracy.

EFFICIENCY

The American political system is far more efficient than its detractors would have us believe. Although the Constitution is more than two centuries old, it has been a document that has not put the political system into a cast-iron mold. Not only have amendments changed the Constitution to meet the needs of the times, but custom, political practices, statutes, and judicial interpretation have all contributed to the continuing success of the political system.

Even with an "antiquated" Constitution, the nation has been able to adapt to its foreign policy, national security, and domestic needs. In foreign affairs the small power of the eighteenth century became the superpower of the twenty-first century, with its orientation moving from an isolationist to an internationalist perspective. In national security matters, moreover, the country has been able to maintain its institutions and way of life in spite of threats from enemies abroad. In domestic matters the separation of powers did not prevent the growth of the welfare state, the regulation of big industry, and the protection of the environment.

The key to the success is that although the system of checks and balances may seem, on paper at least, to thwart action by government, it does not prevent patterns of cooperation between the executive and legislative branches of government. Such cooperation may be seen in foreign policy. The Senate has approved nearly a thousand treaties and turned down about twenty, and only five in the twentieth century. "In general," writes the political scientist James Q. Wilson, "the Senate tends to go along."[2]

Often we pay attention to the major conflicts between the branches in such highly dramatic cases as the defeat of the Versailles Treaty by the United States

Senate in 1919, the confrontation of President Franklin D. Roosevelt and Congress over the size of the Supreme Court, and the congressional and executive conflicts in the Watergate affair; but these cases are the exceptions rather than the rule in government. In point of fact, cooperation often characterizes the relationships of the two branches of government; if it did not, then it would be impossible for American government to function.

There is no clear case to indicate that a parliamentary system would be more or less efficient to meet the problems of the day. British governments, too, have not always coped well with their problems, as the lack of preparation for World War II and the inflationary spiral of the 1970s testify. More than mere government structure accounts for efficiency in government.

There is no assurance, moreover, that if the United States were to try to adopt a British-type parliamentary system to replace the current presidential system it would retain a two-party system. The experience of France under the Fourth Republic shows that a multiparty parliamentary system may be highly unstable and inefficient. It is wrong to tinker with the Constitution when we do not know what greater problems might result.

Efficiency in government depends, too, upon the quality of the personnel in government. The evidence does not indicate that American presidents have been unqualified to rule. Men such as Thomas Jefferson, Abraham Lincoln, Theodore Roosevelt, Woodrow Wilson, and Franklin D. Roosevelt were outstanding chief executives. Though assuming the office of president from outside the ranks of the legislature, moreover, they did not lack political experience. Wilson and both Roosevelts, for example, were state governors, and their activities at the state level provided them with sound executive experience.

The American system, moreover, allows for clearer political direction of the bureaucracy than does the British system. When a new president is elected, he brings to the administration not only cabinet secretaries but thousands of under-secretaries and other executives. Often, these are people with great experience outside government who inject fresh ideas into government so it operates more effectively. In the realm of defense, for example, Elihu Root was regarded as a superior secretary of war, and James Forrestal as an outstanding secretary of defense, although these men came to their positions from law and banking, respectively. Cabinet members, moreover, can be selected on the basis of their administrative competence, which may be tested outside of government, rather than from their skill at debate, a characteristic emphasized in the parliamentary system.

In the matter of personnel many able legislators are reelected for several terms in Congress under the current decentralized system of primaries and elections. Even if an able legislator is defeated in an election, however, that person may continue to have an influence on policy. At times, defeated legislators may be given cabinet positions or be taken into the administration as advisers to the president. The defeated legislators can run again for election. Their influence would be strong, moreover, if they merely concerned themselves with events and wrote occasional articles and books about subjects of national importance. Defeated candidates do not have to become "nonpersons" in the manner of out-of-favor political figures in totalitarian dictatorships.

LEGISLATIVE ASSERTION

It is certainly true that legislative power has declined with respect to executive power. Congress, however, has expanded its power with respect to the entire system. In years past Congress met annually for only a few months. Now its work is so vast that it is usually in session for most of the year. As government operations have expanded, so, too, has the scope of congressional activities. The enlargement of the congressional staff, moreover, has given legislators the opportunity to oversee executive actions.

Although legislative power has declined with respect to the executive throughout the world, there is no evidence to indicate that the parliamentary system is any more successful in reversing the trend toward executive dominance. When Woodrow Wilson wrote *Congressional Government,* moreover, he was critical of the undue influence of Congress on legislation and felt that a parliamentary system would strengthen the president. In fact, the British parliamentary system has experienced an increasing amount of centralized control. Some British commentators have argued that the British prime minister's power has become comparable to that of the American president. In this regard the British prime minister has the authority to make appointments to office, conclude treaties, and declare war — all without securing parliamentary consent. Geoffrey Smith observes that one dissatisfaction of British legislators is that "Parliament is thought to be merely a rubber stamp for the decisions of government."[3]

The British parliamentary system encourages a more quiescent legislature and a strong executive. When a political party is in power, the leaders of the party enforce discipline so its members do not vote against the government and thus throw the entire legislature into general elections. The legislator votes the way the party dictates as determined by the executive if he or she is the prime minister and of the same party. The point, however, should not be overstated, since party leaders take into consideration the interests of the different elements of their party. Nonetheless, the party's ability to discipline recalcitrant members of Parliament is a deterrent to "rocking the boat."

In fact, the no-confidence vote has for the most part lost any real effectiveness as an instrument of legislative control of the executive. Not since 1885 has a government commanding a majority by one party in the House of Commons been overthrown by a no-confidence vote. Governments have been toppled through no-confidence votes since then, but in those cases the government did not have majority control and needed the support of members of Parliament from other parties.

The question hour, moreover, is another overstated institution of check on the executive. As the political scientist James L. Sundquist notes, "One of the first things learned by a rising politician in a democracy is how to artfully avoid giving information he does not want to give."[4] The question hour may test the oratorical abilities of government leaders, but it is not really as significant for revealing information as its advocates pretend.

The American system of separation of powers has allowed for legislative assertion when the executive has exceeded his authority. The decade of the 1970s witnessed such legislative activity. A War Powers Act limited the power of the chief executive in the conduct of foreign policy. The Freedom of Information Act assured many Americans unprecedented access to government documents. Scholars have even relied on such previously classified documents to publish devastating indictments of executive actions.[5] Other laws of the 1970s included limitations on campaign expenditures for presidential campaigns and congressional reforms of the budgetary process. The increasing role of Congress in budgetary matters is, in fact, one of the most significant post-Watergate reforms. The entire Watergate story with its televised hearings and forced disclosures of private, taped presidential conversations in the Oval Office of the White House was revealed to the public. Watergate showed that the existing system works to deal with executive usurpation of constitutional authority. The congressional investigation of the Iran-Contra affair, moreover, again demonstrated the power of Congress to hold the president to account for illegal administration activities.

A fixed system of holding office may seem to have some drawbacks, as the cases of Herbert Hoover and Richard Nixon attest. There is, however, another side to the story. A president who is assured of the post for four years is more encouraged to take strong action and disregard the clamor from Congress. The historian Arthur Schlesinger, Jr., observes that John Adams resisted congressional agitation for war with France during his administration as president, and President Harry Truman fought the explosion of congressional wrath when he fired General Douglas MacArthur as supreme allied commander of United States forces in Korea. "Yet in retrospect," Schlesinger notes, "these two doughty Presidents never had finer hours."[6]

The case for the adoption of a parliamentary system has not been proven. It is well to heed the words of John Kennedy, who said in another context, "If it is not necessary to change, it is necessary not to change." It is, consequently, not necessary to change a system that has worked for more than two centuries.

NOTES

1. Don K. Price, "The Parliamentary and Presidential Systems," *Public Administration Review* 3 (Fall 1943): 327.

2. James Q. Wilson, "Does the Separation of Powers Still Work?" *Public Interest*, no. 86 (Winter 1987): 48.

3. Geoffrey Smith, "Parliamentary Change in Britain," in *The Role of the Legislature in Western Democracies*, ed. Norman J. Ornstein (Washington, D.C.: American Enterprise Institute for Public Policy Research, 1981), p. 37.

4. James L. Sundquist, "Parliamentary Government and Ours," *New Republic* 171 (October 26, 1974): 14.

5. For example, see William Shawcross, *Sideshow: Kissinger, Nixon and the Destruction of Cambodia* (New York: Simon & Schuster, 1979).

6. Arthur Schlesinger Jr., "Parliamentary Government," *New Republic* 171 (August 31, 1974): 14.

Questions for Discussion

1. If the United States had adopted a parliamentary system in 1787, how would it have affected the course of American history?
2. What effect would a parliamentary system in the United States have on U.S. foreign policy?
3. What effect would the absence of Supreme Court power to declare an act of the Congress in a parliamentary system to be unconstitutional have on civil liberties?
4. What effect would a parliamentary system in the United States have on the accountability of the president?
5. In order to adopt a parliamentary system for the United States, how would the Constitution have to be revised?

Suggested Resources

Web Sites

Inter-Parliamentary Union
  http://www.ipu.org/

Thomas: Legislative Information on the Internet
  http://thomas.loc.gov/

United Kingdom Parliament
  http://www.parliament.uk

Publications

Bagehot, Walter. *The English Constitution*, 2d ed. London: Oxford University Press, 1952. (Originally published in 1867.)

Cutler, Lloyd. "To Form a Government." *Foreign Affairs* 59, no. 1 (Fall 1980): 126–43.

Esberry, Joy. "What If There Were a Parliamentary System?" In *What If the American Political System Were Different?* ed. Herbert M. Levine, pp. 95–148. Armonk, N.Y.: M. E. Sharpe, 1992.

Haggard, Stephan, and Mathew D. McCubbins, eds. *Presidents, Parliaments, and Policy.* New York: Cambridge University Press, 2001.

Lijphart, Arendt, ed. *Parliamentary versus Presidential Government.* New York: Oxford University Press, 1992.

Linz, Juan J., and Arturo Valenzuela, eds. *The Failure of Presidential Democracy.* Baltimore: Johns Hopkins University Press, 1994.

Manuel, Paul Christopher, and Anne Marie Cammisa. *Checks and Balances? How a Parliamentary System Could Change American Politics.* Boulder, Colo.: Westview Press, 1999.

Scarrow, Howard A. "Parliamentary and Presidential Government Compared." *Current History* 66, no. 394 (June 1974): 264–67, 272.

Schlesinger, Arthur, Jr. "Parliamentary Government." *New Republic* 171, no. 9 (August 31, 1974): 13–15.

U.S. Cong., Joint Economic Committee. *Political Economy and Constitutional Reform.* Hearings, 97th Cong., 2d Sess., 1982.

15

Does the President Have Legal Authority to Engage in Military Action against the Nation's Enemies without the Specific Authorization of Congress?

The Constitution gives roles in military policy to *both* Congress and the president. Article I of the Constitution grants Congress the power to declare war; raise and support armies; provide and maintain a navy; make rules for the government and regulation of the land and naval forces; provide for calling forth the militia to execute the laws of the Union; and provide for organizing, arming, and disciplining the militia. Other provisions add to Congress's constitutional role. Such provisions include the Necessary and Proper Clause of Article I, Section 8, allowing Congress broad scope to carry out the powers specifically enumerated in the Constitution and its general constitutional powers of taxation and appropriation. The president's constitutional powers over military policy are set forth in Article II. That article gives the president executive power and designates that office as commander in chief.

Inherent in the Constitution itself are conflicts between the legislative and executive branches of government. One principal issue that has developed over time has involved the president's right to send military forces into actual or potential combat situations without the consent of Congress.

One of the most important reasons for the growth of executive power anywhere is the existence, or the imminent prospect, of war among nations, war within a nation, or war against terrorism. Executive power tends to increase during wartime, sometimes because the legislature grants the president emergency powers and sometimes because the executive takes action without asking for the approval of Congress.

At the outbreak of the Civil War, President Abraham Lincoln took steps that, according to the Constitution, were illegal. These included spending money that had not been appropriated by Congress and blockading southern ports. Lincoln expanded the powers of the president as commander in chief beyond the intent of the Framers of the Constitution. In 1940, President Franklin Roosevelt transferred fifty ships to Great Britain in return for the leasing of some British bases in the Atlantic — without congressional authorization to take such actions. He also ordered U.S. ships to "shoot on sight" any foreign submarine in waters that he regarded as essential for the nation's defense. In giving such an order, he was making war between the United States and Germany more likely.

Presidential power in foreign policy has also increased because of the changing character of the technology of warfare. In an age of jet aircraft, nuclear weapons, and intercontinental ballistic missiles, the president may be required to make quick decisions that cannot wait for congressional deliberation.

Since the end of World War II, the United States has become a principal actor in world politics. As a major world power, the United States has had to concern itself with global security issues in a manner unprecedented in its history.

The permanent emphasis of foreign and national security considerations has plagued executive-legislative relations since 1945. President Harry Truman sent U.S. troops to Korea without a formal declaration of war. President Dwight Eisenhower approved actions by the Central Intelligence Agency (CIA) to help bring down one government in Guatemala and put the shah in power in Iran. President John Kennedy authorized the CIA to assist a military operation planned by Cuban exiles against a communist regime in Cuba — an operation that turned out to be a foreign policy disaster for the young president. He also increased the number of military advisers to Vietnam from several hundred to about seventeen thousand.

The actions of Presidents Lyndon Johnson and Richard Nixon in the war in Indochina sparked an increasing involvement by Congress in the conduct of foreign policy. Johnson raised the number of U.S. troops to five hundred thousand. Nixon engaged in a "secret" air war in Cambodia in 1969 and sent U.S. troops into the country in 1970.

The 1970s were marked by massive congressional involvement in the conduct of foreign policy. In 1971 Congress adopted legislation forbidding the expenditures of funds to carry on the war in Cambodia. Overriding a veto by President Nixon, it passed a War Powers Resolution (1973) sharply limiting the president's ability to send troops. Under the act the president has the power on his own authority to send U.S. armed forces into an area for a period of sixty days but then must get the approval of Congress or terminate the use of armed forces. The president is also required to consult with Congress, if possible, before military intervention is ordered.

Every president since Nixon has taken the position that the War Powers Resolution is unconstitutional because a statute cannot take away powers that are traditionally the preserve of presidents in the conduct of foreign policy. But every president has complied with its provisions, even as they have used armed forces overseas. Ronald Reagan used U.S. military power against Libya. George H. W. Bush sent U.S. military force against Iraq. Bill Clinton had U.S. forces in Bosnia and Kosovo and directed U.S. aircraft to bomb Iraq. George W. Bush responded to the September 11 terrorist attacks through military intervention in Afghanistan. If and when a president refuses to comply with the War Powers Resolution, the Supreme Court will decide on its constitutionality.

Since the end of the Vietnam War, the issue of the presidential authority to use U.S. armed forces without the approval of Congress has been a matter of public concern. As the Bush administration indicated in the summer of 2002 that it was considering attacking Iraq because its leader was building weapons of mass destruction, the subject of the role of Congress in approving presidential use of the armed forces became intense. In October 2002, however, the House and Senate overwhelmingly approved a resolution authorizing President Bush to use the armed forces of the United States against Iraq if he determined that Iraq threatens U.S. national security.

Does the president have the authority to commit U.S. armed forces without the consent of Congress? John Yoo, deputy assistant attorney general in the Office of Legal Counsel of the U.S. Department of Justice in the administration of President George W. Bush, argues that the president has broad powers to introduce U.S. armed forces and that these powers are not curtailed by the War Powers Resolution. He contends:

1. The War Powers Resolution authorizes the president to use military armed forces on his own authority in certain cases, such as an attack upon the United States, its territories or possessions, or its armed forces.
2. Senate Joint Resolution 23 (Public Law 107-40) gave broad powers to the president to respond to the terrorist attacks that occurred on September 11, 2001.
3. The president's authority to control the executive power of the United States and to be commander in chief of the armed forces of the United States is spelled out in Article II of the Constitution and legally allows him to introduce U.S. armed forces into the hostilities when appropriate, with or without specific congressional authorization.
4. The fact that the United States deployed its armed forces well over a hundred times in our nation's history and that Congress has only declared war five times demonstrates that previous presidents and congresses have interpreted the Constitution as giving the president the authority to deploy armed forces without a formal congressional declaration of war.
5. The courts have never stopped the president from deploying U.S. armed forces or engaging them in hostilities.

Political scientist Louis Fisher argues that the president does not have authority to commit U.S. armed forces without the consent of Congress. He contends:

1. The Framers of the Constitution were determined to vest in Congress the sole authority to take the country from a state of peace to a state of war.
2. Presidents have often based their unilateral use of armed force on treaty obligations, such as with the United Nations (UN), the North

Atlantic Treaty Organization (NATO), and the Southeast Asia Treaty Organization (SEATO). But nothing in the history of these treaties implies that Congress gives the president unilateral power to wage war.

3. Although the War Powers Resolution was designed to limit presidential power to commit U.S. armed forces, it actually expanded it by allowing the president to unilaterally commit such forces for sixty to ninety days. So far, the courts have not dealt with this challenge to the Framers' intent.

4. Although Congress enacted a law authorizing the use of armed force against Iraq in 1991 pursuant to Security Council Resolution 678, it had no intention thereby to transfer its constitutional war powers to the Security Council.

5. The joint resolution passed by Congress on September 18, 2001, authorized President George W. Bush to use all "necessary and appropriate force" against nations, organizations, or persons that he determined planned, authorized, committed, or aided the terrorist attacks of September 11, 2001, or harbored such organizations or persons "in order to prevent any future acts of international terrorism against the United States by such nations, organizations or persons." That law authorized military action against the terrorist structure in Afghanistan. But going beyond that to fighting terrorists in other countries raises constitutional issues.

6. Although the president should consult with Congress because such consultation improves executive-legislative relations, the authority incorporated in a public law is the act that satisfies the Constitution for using U.S. armed forces.

 YES

Does the President Have Legal Authority
to Engage in Military Action against
the Nation's Enemies without
the Specific Authorization of Congress?

JOHN YOO

The President's War-Making Power

It is my honor and pleasure to come before you today, to testify on the War Powers Resolution of 1973 and presidential war powers under the Constitution. As a former general counsel of the Senate Judiciary Committee, I have long held a deep and abiding respect for this committee and all of its members. I look forward to another thoughtful exchange of ideas with the members of the committee today on this most important matter.

I currently serve as deputy assistant attorney general in the Office of Legal Counsel at the Department of Justice. As you know, that office helps the attorney general fulfill his role as legal advisor to the President, particularly in areas of constitutional law and presidential power.

As this committee is aware, legal scholars have long debated the constitutional allocation of war powers between the President and the Congress, and the effect of the War Powers Resolution on that allocation. This administration follows the course of administrations before us, both Democratic and Republican, in the view that the President's power to engage U.S. armed forces in military hostilities is not limited by the War Powers Resolution.

The sources of presidential power can be found in the Constitution itself. I shall discuss both the War Powers Resolution and the Constitution today. In doing so, I will explain in particular how the President's conduct of the war against terrorism is authorized under the Constitution and consistent with the War Powers Resolution.

First, the War Powers Resolution of 1973. Section 2 of that resolution recognizes that the President may "introduce United States armed forces into hostilities" pursuant to (1) a declaration of war, (2) specific statutory authorization, or (3) "a national emergency created by attack upon the United States, its territories or possessions, or its armed forces."

Section 2 of the resolution recognizes the President's broad power in the current circumstances. The President's decision to use armed forces to combat terrorism and respond to the attacks of September 11 fall within two of the resolution's enumerated provisions for using military force. First, the United States was attacked on September 11 by members of an international network of terrorists. That attack unequivocally placed the United States in a state of armed conflict, justifying a military response, as recognized by Congress, while NATO [North Atlantic Treaty Organization] and the United Nations recognized the U.S.' exercise of its right to self defense. In response to the September 11 attack, the President immediately issued Proclamation 7463, declaring the existence of a state of national emergency. Thus, the conditions recognized by section 2 of the resolution as justifying the use of force without any action whatsoever from Congress — an attack on the United States, and a resulting national emergency — have each been satisfied.

In addition, the President has specific statutory authorization, in the form of SJ Res 23 (Pub. L. 107-40). That resolution, which this body approved unanimously last September, states that the President may "use all necessary and appropriate force against those nations, organizations, or persons he determines planned, authorized, committed, or aided the terrorist attacks that occurred on September 11, 2001, or harbored such organizations or persons, in order to prevent any future acts of international terrorism against the United States by such nations, organizations or persons." The resolution thus recognizes that the President determines what military actions are necessary to combat those who are associated with the organizations and individuals responsible for September 11.

Thus, the President's authority to conduct the war against terrorism is recognized by Section 2 of the War Powers Resolution. Congress has specifically expressed its support for the use of the armed forces, and the United States has suffered an attack.

Moreover, the War Powers Resolution specifically provides, as it must, that "nothing in this joint resolution is intended to alter the constitutional authority of the Congress or of the President." This important language recognizes the President's constitutional authority, separate and apart from the War Powers Resolution, to engage U.S. armed forces in hostilities. That brings us to the question: what is the scope of the President's constitutional power, expressly recognized by the resolution?

Congress provided an answer when it overwhelmingly approved SJ Res 23. That resolution expressly states that "the President has authority under the Constitution to take action to deter and prevent acts of international terrorism against the United States." As Chairman [Russ] Feingold accurately explained on the Senate floor, this language plainly recognizes "that the President has existing constitutional powers."

This is quite plainly a correct interpretation of the President's war power under the Constitution. The relevant scholarly works could fill this entire room, but I will try to summarize the argument briefly here. Under Article II, Section 1 of the Constitution, the President is the locus of the entire "executive power" of the United States and, thus, in the Supreme Court's words, "the sole organ of the federal government in the field of international relations." Under Article II, Section 2, he is the "Commander in Chief" of the armed forces of the United States. These two provisions make clear that the President has the constitutional authority to introduce U.S. armed forces into hostilities when appropriate, with or without specific congressional authorization.

Notably, nothing in the text of the Constitution requires the advice and consent of the Senate, or the authorization of Congress, before the President may exercise the executive power and his authority as Commander in Chief. By contrast, Article II requires the President to seek the advice and consent of Senate before entering into treaties or appointing ambassadors. Article I, Section 10 denies states the power to "engage" in war, except with congressional authorization or in case of actual invasion or imminent danger. Article III describes the offense of treason as the act of levying war against the United States. Moreover, founding documents prior to the U.S. Constitution, such as the South Carolina Constitution of 1778, expressly prohibited the executive from commencing war or concluding peace without legislative approval. The founders of the Constitution thus knew how to constrain the President's power to exercise his authority as Commander in Chief to engage U.S. armed forces in hostilities, and decided not to do so.

Of course, as the President has the constitutional authority to engage U.S.

armed forces in hostilities, Congress has a broad range of war powers as well. Congress has the power to tax and to spend. Congress has the power to raise and support armies and to provide and maintain a navy. And Congress has the power to call forth the militia, and to make rules for the government and regulation of the armed forces. In other words, although the President has the power of the sword, Congress has the power of the purse. As James Madison explained during the critical constitutional ratifying convention of Virginia, "The sword is in the hands of the British king; the purse in the hands of the parliament. It is so in America, as far as any analogy can exist." The President is Commander in Chief, but he commands only those military forces which Congress has provided.

Congress also has the power to declare war. This power to declare a legal state of war and to notify other nations of that status once had an important effect under the law of nations, and continues to trigger significant domestic statutory powers as well, such as under the Alien Enemy Act of 1798 (50 U.S.C. § 21) and federal surveillance laws (50 U.S.C. §§ 1811, 1829, 1844). But this power has seldom been used. Although U.S. armed forces have, by conservative estimates, been deployed well over a hundred times in our nation's history, Congress has declared war just five times. This long practice of U.S. engagement in military hostilities without a declaration of war demonstrates that previous presidents and congresses have interpreted the Constitution as we do today.

As the United States rose to global prominence in the post–World War II era, Congress has provided the President with a large and powerful peacetime military force. Presidents of both parties have long used that military force to protect the national interest, even though Congress has not declared war since World War II.

President [Harry] Truman introduced U.S. armed forces into Korea in 1950 without prior congressional approval. President [John] Kennedy claimed constitutional authority to act alone in response to the Cuban missile crisis by deploying a naval quarantine around Cuba. Presidents Kennedy and [Lyndon] Johnson dramatically expanded the U.S. military commitment in Vietnam absent a declaration of war. In response to President [Richard] Nixon's expansion of the Vietnam War into Laos and Cambodia, Congress approved the War Powers Resolution, but that resolution expressly disclaimed any intrusion into the President's constitutional war power. Accordingly, Presidents [Gerald] Ford, [Jimmy] Carter, [Ronald] Reagan, and the first President [George H. W.] Bush have committed U.S. armed forces on a number of occasions. In these cases, the administration has generally consulted with, notified, and reported to Congress, consistent with the War Powers Resolution.

President [Bill] Clinton deployed U.S. armed forces in Somalia, Haiti, and Bosnia — all without prior congressional authorization. In 1999, the Clinton administration relied on the President's constitutional authority to use force in Kosovo. Assistant Secretary of State Barbara Larkin testified before Congress that April that "there is no need for a declaration of war. Every use of U.S. armed forces, since World War II, has been undertaken pursuant to the President's constitutional authority. . . . This administration, like previous administrations, takes the view that the President has broad authority as Commander-in-Chief and under his authority to conduct foreign relations, to authorize the use of force in the national interest."

In short, presidents throughout U.S. history have exercised broad unilateral power to engage U.S. armed forces in hostilities. Congress has repeatedly recognized the existence of presidential constitutional war power, in the War Powers Resolution of 1973, and more recently in SJ Res 23. And the courts have supported this view as well. As the Supreme Court noted in *Hamilton v. Dillin* (1874), it is "the President alone, who is constitutionally invested with the entire charge of hostile operations." Significantly, the courts have never stopped the President from deploying U.S. armed forces or engaging them in hostilities — most recently, in the case of *Campbell v. Clinton.*

That said, although the last administration, like its predecessors, questioned the wisdom and the constitutionality of the War Powers Resolution, it is our belief that government works best when the two branches cooperate in matters concerning the use of U.S. armed forces. Accordingly, we are committed to close consultations with Congress whenever possible regarding the need to use force to combat terrorism and to protect our national interest, whenever possible. We value the views of Congress regarding the appropriate use of military force, as evidenced by our close and meaningful consultations with Congress after the attacks of September 11, and before the introduction of U.S. armed forces into combat action in Afghanistan on October 7, 2001. In addition to the President himself addressing a joint session of Congress on September 20, senior members of the administration briefed members of Congress and their staffs on over 10 occasions in that short time period. One result of these consultations was the enactment of SJ Res 23, which the President welcomed.

At the same time, however, we must recognize that we are in a war against, to use Chairman Feingold's words again, "a loose network of terrorists," and not "a state with clearly defined borders." When fighting "a highly mobile, diffuse enemy that operates largely beyond the reach of our conventional war-fighting techniques," extensive congressional discussion will often be a luxury we cannot afford. Our enemy hides in the civilian populations of the nations of the world. As Chairman Feingold pointed out, "There can be no peace treaty with such an enemy." Likewise, there can be no formal, public declaration of war against such an enemy.

The attacks of September 11 introduced the United States into an unprecedented military situation. This administration is confident that the allocation of war powers contemplated by the Founders of our Constitution is fully adequate to address the dangers of the twenty-first century, and that, armed with the war powers conferred upon him by the Constitution and recognized by the War Powers Resolution, the President will be able to work effectively with this committee and with Congress to ensure the protection of the United States from additional terrorist attack.

☑ *NO*

Does the President Have Legal Authority to Engage in Military Action against the Nation's Enemies without the Specific Authorization of Congress?

LOUIS FISHER
The Congressional Role in War

Thank you for inviting me to testify on a most important issue: how Congress and the President commit the nation to war. Events of September 11 and the war against terrorism have brought this issue again into sharp focus. The Use of Force Act of September 18, 2001, authorized military action against the terrorist network involved in the terrorist attacks of September 11. In my judgment, however, military operations against countries other than Afghanistan can be appropriately initiated only with additional authorization from Congress. Moreover, whatever mechanisms are devised to improve consultation between the two branches will not satisfy the constitutional need for congressional authorization. The reasons for these conclusions are set forth below.

We debate the constitutionality of war power actions because of a rock-bottom belief held by the framers: It is possible to structure government in such a way to protect individual liberties and freedoms. We refer to this concept in different ways: separation of powers, checks and balances, pitting ambition against ambition. To the framers, it meant that the clash between institutions is the safest and best way of formulating national policy, whether domestic or foreign. The War Powers Resolution (WPR) relies on this same concept but uses different words: "collective judgment."

COLLECTIVE JUDGMENT

Section 2(a) of the WPR states that it is "the purpose of this joint resolution to fulfill the intent of the framers of the Constitution of the United States and insure that the collective judgment of both the Congress and the President will apply to the introduction of United States Armed Forces into hostilities, or into situations where imminent involvement in hostilities is clearly indicated by the circumstances, and to the continued use of such forces in hostilities or in such situations." 87 Stat. 555, § 2(a) (1973).

Why the emphasis on "collective judgment"? Why not let the President initiate war without congressional authority? In 1787, the existing models of government throughout Europe, particularly in England, placed the war power and foreign affairs solely in the hands of the Executive. John Locke, in his *Second Treatise on Civil Government* (1690), placed the "federative" power (what we call foreign policy) with the Executive. Sir William Blackstone, in his *Commentaries*, defined the king's prerogative broadly to include the right to send and receive ambassadors, to make war or peace, to make treaties, to issue letters of marque and reprisal (authorizing private citizens to undertake military actions), and to raise and regulate fleets and armies.

The framers studied this monarchical model and repudiated it in its entirety. They placed Locke's federative powers and Blackstone's royal prerogatives either exclusively in Congress or as a shared power between the Senate and the President (appointing ambassadors and making treaties). The rejection of the British model and monarchy could not have been more complete.

While the "original intent" of many constitutional provisions is debatable, there is no doubt about the framers' determination to vest in Congress the sole authority to take the country from a state of peace to a state of war. From 1789 to 1950, lawmakers, the courts, and the executive branch understood that only Congress could initiate offensive actions against other nations. As I will explain later, matters changed fundamentally in 1950 when President Harry Truman took the country to war in Korea without seeking congressional authority.

Admittedly, some scholars — particularly John Yoo — argue that the framers designed a system to "encourage presidential initiative in war" and that the Constitution's provisions "did not break with the tradition of their English, state, and revolutionary predecessors, but instead followed in their footsteps." This is not the place to analyze Yoo's work in detail, for that has been done elsewhere. Suffice it to say that had the framers adopted the English model, they wouldn't have written Articles I and II the way they did. Here it is unnecessary to debate the framers' intent. It is enough to look at the plain text of the Constitution. If the framers had indeed adopted "the traditional British approach to war powers," they would have written Article II to give the President the power to declare war, to issue letters of marque and reprisal, and to raise armies, along with other powers of external affairs that are reserved to Congress.

I won't repeat here the many statements of framers who believed that they had stripped the Executive of the power to take the country to war. At the Philadelphia convention, George Mason said he was "agst giving the power of war to the Executive, because not to be trusted with it. . . . He was for clogging rather than facilitating war." 2 Farrand 318–19. At the Pennsylvania ratifying convention, James Wilson expressed the prevailing sentiment that the system of checks and balances "will not hurry us into war; it is calculated to guard against it. It will not be in the power of a single man, or a single body of men, to involve us in such distress; for the important power of declaring war is vested in the legislature at large." 2 Elliot 528. The power of initiating war was vested in Congress. To the President was left certain defensive powers "to repel sudden attacks." 2 Farrand 318.

The framers gave Congress the power to initiate war because they believed that Presidents, in their search for fame and personal glory, would have too great an appetite for war. John Jay, generally supportive of executive power, warned in *Federalist* No. 4 that "absolute monarchs will often make war when their nations are to get nothing by it, but for purposes and objects merely personal, such as a thirst for military glory, revenge for personal affronts, ambition, or private compacts to aggrandize or support their particular families or partisans. These and a variety of other motives, which affect only the mind of the sovereign, often lead him to engage in wars not sanctified by justice or the voice and interests of his people."

In studying history and politics, the framers came to fear the Executive's potential appetite for war. Has human nature changed in recent decades to permit us to trust independent presidential decisions in war? The historical record tells us that what Jay said in 1788 applies equally well to contemporary times.

POWER OF THE PURSE

John Yoo recognizes that Congress has the constitutional power to check presidential wars: It can withhold appropriations. Congress "could express its opposition to executive war decisions only by exercising its powers over funding and impeachment." The spending power, he writes, "may be the only means for legislative control over war." Constitutionally, this kind of analysis puts Congress in the back seat. Yoo allows Presidents to initiate wars and continue them until Congress is able to cut off funds. The advantage to the President is striking. Executive wars may persist so long as the President has one-third plus one in a single chamber to prevent Congress from overriding his veto of a funding-cutoff.

This general issue took real form in 1973 when Congress passed legislation to deny funds for the war in Southeast Asia. After President [Richard] Nixon vetoed the bill, the House effort to override failed on a vote of 241 to 173, or 35 votes short of the necessary two-thirds majority. 119 *Cong. Rec.* 21778 (1973). A lawsuit filed by Representative Elizabeth Holtzman (D-N.Y.) asked the courts to determine that President Nixon could not engage in combat operations in Cambodia and elsewhere in Indochina in the absence of congressional authorization. District Judge Judd held that Congress had not authorized the bombing of Cambodia. Its inability to override the veto and the subsequent adoption of an August 15 deadline for the bombing could not be taken as an affirmative grant of legislative authority: "It cannot be the rule that the President needs a vote of only one-third plus one of either House in order to conduct a war, but this would be the consequence of holding that Congress must override a Presidential veto in order to terminate hostilities which it has not authorized." Appellate courts mooted the case because the August 15 compromise resolved the dispute between the two branches.

THE ROAD TO THE WAR POWERS RESOLUTION

How have Presidents acquired so much independent power to take the country to war, contrary to what the framers intended? It may be tempting to say that the reason lies in the worldwide responsibilities that moved to the United States in the twentieth century. Yet the two greatest conflagrations — World Wars I and II — were both declared by Congress pursuant to the Constitution. Other conflicts, including Iraq in 1991 and the war against terrorism in 2001, were authorized by Congress.

In 1973, lawmakers decided that a statute was necessary to curb presidential wars and protect legislative prerogatives. What created the impetus for the War Powers Resolution? At the top of the list I would put the UN [United Nations] Charter and several mutual security pacts, particularly NATO [North Atlantic Treaty Organization]. Although it was not the intent at the time, both treaties have in practice led to unilateral executive wars. Presidents sought authority not from Congress but from international and regional bodies. I have covered this development elsewhere, but will identify the main points here.

Truman in Korea, Bush in Iraq, Clinton in Haiti, Bosnia, and Kosovo — in each instance a President acted independently of Congress by relying either on the UN or NATO. Nothing in the history of the UN or NATO implies that Congress gave the President unilateral power to wage war. The legislative histories of those treaties show no such intent.

UN CHARTER

Those who drafted the UN Charter did so against the backdrop of the disaster of the Versailles Treaty and President Woodrow Wilson's determination to make international commitments without Congress. One of the "reservations" he objected to was by Senator Henry Cabot Lodge, who insisted on prohibiting the use of American troops by the League of Nations unless Congress, "which, under the Constitution, has the sole power to declare war or authorize the employment of the military or naval forces of the United States, shall by act or joint resolution so provide." 58 *Cong. Rec.* 8777 (1919).

Wilson opposed the Lodge reservations, claiming that they "cut out the heart of the Covenant" and represented "nullification" of the treaty. However, Wilson did not disagree with the substance of Lodge's language on the war power. In a letter to Senator Gilbert Monell Hitchcock on March 8, 1920, Wilson acknowledged the broad scope of congressional authority over the initiation of war: "There can be no objection to explaining again what our constitutional method is and that our Congress alone can declare war or determine the causes or occasions for war, and that it alone can authorize the use of the armed forces of the United States on land or on the sea. But to make such a declaration would certainly be a work of supererogation." In other words, Wilson objected to Lodge's language not because of its content but because it was superfluous. Both branches understood that congressional authorization was needed.

The rejection of the Versailles Treaty and Wilson's battle with Lodge remained part of the collective memory. In the meetings that led to the United Nations, the predominant view was that any commitment of U.S. forces to a world body needed prior authorization by both Houses of Congress. That attitude is reflected in the debates over the UN Charter, the UN Participation Act of 1945, and the 1949 amendments to the UN Participation Act.

During Senate debate on the UN Charter, President [Harry] Truman sent a cable from Potsdam, stating that all agreements involving U.S. troop commitments to the UN would first have to be approved by both Houses of Congress. Without any equivocation he pledged: "When any such agreement or agreements are negotiated it will be my purpose to ask the Congress for appropriate legislation to approve them." 91 *Cong. Rec.* 8185 (1945). Backed by his reassurance, the Senate supported the UN Charter by a vote of 89 to 2. This understanding was later incorporated in the UN Participation Act of 1945. Without the slightest ambiguity, Section 6 states that the agreements "shall be subject to the approval of the Congress by appropriate act or joint resolution." 59 Stat. 621, § 6 (1945).

How was it possible for Truman, five years later, to send U.S. troops to Korea without seeking or obtaining congressional authority? His Administration claimed to be acting pursuant to UN authority. On June 29, 1950, Secretary of State Dean Acheson claimed that all U.S. actions taken in Korea "have been under the aegis of the United Nations." At a news conference, Truman agreed with a reporter's description of the war in Korea as "a police action under the United Nations." If this was a UN military action, how could Truman circumvent the clear language of the UN Participation Act? The answer: The Administration chose not to enter into a "special agreement." In fact, there has never been a special agreement. The very procedure enacted to protect legislative prerogatives became a nullity.

MUTUAL SECURITY PACTS

In addition to citing the UN Charter and Security Council resolutions as grounds for using American troops in military operations, Presidents regard mutual security treaties as another source of authority. Treaties such as NATO and SEATO [Southeast Asia Treaty Organization] stipulate that provisions shall be "carried out by the Parties in accordance with their respective constitutional processes." Nothing in the legislative histories of these treaties suggests that the President has unilateral authority to act in the event of an attack. Military action by the United States would have to be consistent with "constitutional processes."

To argue that NATO and other mutual security treaties confer upon the President the authority to use military force without congressional approval would allow the President and the Senate, through the treaty process, to amend the Constitution by stripping the House of Representatives of its prerogatives over the use of military force. Scholars who examined NATO after its adoption concluded that the language about constitutional processes was "intended to ensure that the Executive Branch of the Government should come back to the Congress when decisions were required in which the Congress has a constitutional responsibility."

The NATO treaty "does not transfer to the President the Congressional power to make war."

Senator Walter George said this about SEATO: "The treaty does not call for automatic action; it calls for consultation. If any course of action shall be agreed upon or decided upon, then that course of action must have the approval of Congress, because the constitutional process is provided for." 101 *Cong. Rec.* 1051 (1955). Nevertheless, the Lyndon Johnson Administration cited SEATO as one legal justification for the Vietnam War.

The War Powers Resolution attempted to limit the effect of mutual security treaties. Authority to introduce U.S. forces into hostilities shall not be inferred "from any treaty heretofore or hereafter ratified unless such treaty is implemented by legislation specifically authorizing" the introduction of American troops. 87 Stat. 558, § 8(a) (1973). The Senate Foreign Relations Committee explained that this provision ensured that both Houses of Congress "must be affirmatively involved in any decision of the United States to engage in hostilities pursuant to a treaty." S. Rept. No. 93-220, at 26 (1973). These understandings had zero impact on requiring congressional approval for the use of U.S. forces operating in conjunction with NATO in Bosnia and Kosovo.

EISENHOWER'S MODEL OF JOINT ACTION

President Dwight D. Eisenhower thought that Truman's initiative in Korea was a mistake, both constitutionally and politically. In 1954, when Eisenhower was pressured to intervene in Indochina, he told reporters at a news conference: "I will say this: there is going to be no involvement of America in war unless it is a result of the constitutional process that is placed upon Congress to declare it. Now, let us have that clear; and that is the answer."

His theory of government and international relations invited Congress to enact "area resolutions" to authorize presidential action in such troublespots as the Formosa Straits and the Middle East. He wanted other nations — friend and foe — to understand that Congress and the President were united in their foreign policy. His chief of staff, Sherman Adams, later recalled that Eisenhower was determined "not to resort to any kind of military action without the approval of Congress."

Eisenhower emphasized the importance of executive-legislative coordination when using military force: "I deem it necessary to seek the cooperation of the Congress. Only with that cooperation can we give the reassurance needed to deter aggression." Effective policy meant not unilateral decisions by the President but "joint action by the Congress and the Executive." In his memoirs, he explained the choice between invoking executive prerogatives and seeking congressional authority. On New Year's Day, in 1957, he met with Secretary of State Dulles and congressional leaders of both parties. House Majority Leader John McCormack (D-Mass.) asked Eisenhower whether he, as Commander in Chief, already possessed authority to carry out military actions in the Middle East without congressional action. Eisenhower replied that "greater effect could be had from a consensus of Executive and Legislative opinion. . . . Near the end of this meeting I reminded the legislators that the Constitution assumes that our two branches of government should get along together."

KENNEDY AND JOHNSON INITIATIVES

Unlike Eisenhower, President John F. Kennedy was prepared to act during the Cuban missile crisis solely on what he considered to be his constitutional authority. Instead of acting under a joint resolution, he claimed "full authority" as Commander in Chief. Congress did pass a Cuba Resolution, but the resolution did not authorize presidential action. It merely expressed the sentiments of Congress.

In August 1964, President Lyndon B. Johnson asked Congress to pass the Tonkin Gulf Resolution. The resolution, authorizing military action against North Vietnam, passed the House 416 to 0 and the Senate 88 to 2. Because of the speed with which Congress debated the resolution (acting over a two-day period) and controversies as to whether the second attack in the Tonkin Gulf actually occurred, many Members of Congress came to regret their votes and support a reassertion of legislative authority. Out of this activity came the National Commitments Resolution of 1969 and the War Powers Resolution of 1973.

NATIONAL COMMITMENTS RESOLUTION

Hearings by the Senate Foreign Relations Committee in 1967 highlighted its concern for a "marked constitutional imbalance" between Congress and the President in determining foreign policy over the past 25 years. Chairman J. William Fulbright said that the President "has acquired virtually unrestricted power to commit the United States abroad politically and militarily." 1969 *CQ Almanac* 946. Two years later the Senate passed a resolution to challenge the presidential power to commit the nation without first receiving congressional authorization.

The National Commitments Resolution marked a return to Eisenhower's philosophy of interbranch cooperation and joint action. Passing the Senate by a vote of 70 to 16, the resolution defined a national commitment as the use of U.S. armed forces on foreign territory or a promise to assist a foreign country by using U.S. armed forces or financial resources "either immediately or upon the happening of certain events." The resolution provides that "it is the sense of the Senate that a national commitment by the United States results only from affirmative action taken by the executive and legislative branches of the United States government by means of a treaty, statute, or concurrent resolution of both Houses specifically providing for such commitment." 115 *Cong. Rec.* 17245 (1969). As a Senate resolution, it has no legal effect, but it represents an important expression of constitutional principles by a bipartisan Senate.

THE WAR POWERS RESOLUTION

The stated purpose of the War Powers Resolution in Section 2(a) is "to fulfill the intent of the framers of the Constitution" and to "insure that the collective judgment" of Congress and the President will apply to the introduction of U.S. troops to combat. However, both in language and implementation, the resolution has been criticized for undermining the intent of the framers and failing to insure collective judgment.

Part of the controversy associated with the War Powers Resolution stems from the incompatible versions developed by the House and the Senate. The House was prepared to recognize that the President could use military force without prior authorization from Congress, at least for 120 days. Senators, unwilling to give the President such unilateral authority, attempted to spell out the particular conditions under which Presidents could act singlehandedly. Armed force could be used in three situations: (1) to repel an armed attack upon the United States, its territories and possessions, retaliate in the event of such an attack, and forestall the direct and imminent threat of such an attack; (2) to repel an armed attack against U.S. armed forces located outside the United States, and its territories and possessions, and forestall the direct and imminent threat of such an attack; and (3) to rescue endangered American citizens and nationals in foreign countries or at sea. The first situation (except for the final clause) conforms to understandings developed by the framers. The other situations reflect the changes that have occurred in the concept of defensive war and life-and-property actions.

Pressured to produce a bill, House and Senate conferees fashioned a compromise that ended up widening presidential power. Sections 4 and 5 allowed the President to act unilaterally with military force for 60 to 90 days. He could go to war at any time, in any place, for any reason. The resolution merely required the President to report to Congress on occasion and to consult with lawmakers "in every possible instance." It is difficult to see how the breadth of that power can be squared with the framers' intent.

When the bill came out of conference committee, some Members of Congress commented on the extent to which military power was tilted toward the President. Rep. William Green (D-Pa.), after supporting the resolution because it would limit presidential power, objected that it "is actually an expansion of Presidential warmaking power, rather than a limitation." 119 *Cong. Rec.* 36204 (1973). Rep. Vernon Thomson (R-Wis.) said that the "clear meaning" of the bill pointed to "a diminution rather than an enhancement of the role of Congress in the critical decisions whether the country will or will not go to war." Id. at 36207. To Rep. Bob Eckhardt (D-Tex.), the resolution provided "the color of authority to the President to exercise a warmaking power which I find the Constitution has exclusively assigned to the Congress." Id. at 36208.

Senator Tom Eagleton (D-Mo.), having been a principal sponsor of the resolution, denounced the version that emerged from conference. Although the media continued to describe the bill as a constraint on presidential war power, Eagleton said that the bill gave the President "unilateral authority to commit American troops anywhere in the world, under any conditions he decides, for 60 to 90 days." Id. at 36177.

Beyond these issues of statutory language, implementation further expanded presidential power because of a peculiar feature in the bill: the 60–90 day clock begins to tick only if the President reports under Section 4(a)(1). Not surprisingly, Presidents do not report under 4(a)(1). They report "consistent with" the WPR. The only President to report under 4(a)(1) was President Gerald Ford in the *Mayaguez* capture, but his report had no substantive importance because it was released after the operation was over. In its operation, the WPR allows Presidents to use military force against other countries until Congress adopts some kind of statutory constraint. Federal courts are a potential check, but thus far the judiciary has decided that war power cases lack standing, ripeness, or have other qualities that place them outside judicial scrutiny.

NATO'S MILITARY OPERATIONS

President [Bill] Clinton twice relied on NATO to authorize military action, the first in Bosnia in 1994–95, and the second in Kosovo in 1999. On neither occasion did he seek authority from Congress, even though in 1993 he suggested that before using air power in Bosnia he might ask for "authority" or "agreement" from Congress. Toward the end of 1993, however, he repeatedly objected to legislative efforts to restrict his military options. His decision in 1994 to use air strikes against Serbian militias was taken without congressional authorization. Instead, the decision came in response to UN Security Council resolutions, operating through NATO's military command. He explained: "the authority under which air strikes can proceed, NATO acting out of area pursuant to U.N. authority, requires the common agreement of our NATO allies." In other words, he needed agreement from England, France, Italy, and other NATO allies, but not from Congress.

NATO air strikes began in February 1994 and continued into 1995. On September 1,1995, President Clinton explained to congressional leaders the procedures used to order air strikes in Bosnia. The North Atlantic Council "approved" a number of measures and "agreed" that any direct attacks against remaining safe areas would justify air operations as determined "by the common judgment of NATO and U.N. military commanders." On September 12, he said the bombing attacks were "authorized by the United Nations."

In 1995, President Clinton ordered the deployment of 20,000 American ground troops to Bosnia without obtaining authority from Congress. He approved NATO's operation plan for sending ground troops to Bosnia (IFOR), and followed that with the successor plan, Stabilization Force (SFOR). He welcomed NATO's decision to approve the plan and the "Activation Order that will authorize the start of SFOR's mission." Authority would come from allies, not from Congress.

Actions in Bosnia combined Security Council resolutions and NATO. When President Clinton did not have UN support for military action in Kosovo, he relied entirely on NATO. At a news conference on October 8, 1998, he stated: "Yesterday I decided that the United States would vote to give NATO the authority to carry out military strikes against Serbia if President Milosevic continues to defy the international community." The decision to go to war against another country was in the hands of one person, exactly what the framers thought they had prevented. The war against Yugoslavia began on March 24, 1999.

CONTINUED MILITARY ACTION IN IRAQ

In June 1993, September 1996, and December 1998, President Clinton ordered military operations against Iraq. U.S. military strikes in Iraq continued from 1999 to the present day. There have been no legal analyses from the Administration to justify this use of force against Iraq, but it can be argued that when Congress passed the authorization bill in January 1991, it simultaneously sanctioned future military operations authorized by the UN Security Council. Such a claim can mean: (1) delegating the war power in perpetuity, and (2) surrendering congressional power to an international body.

Here are the specifics. On January 14, 1991, in P.L. 102-1, Congress authorized the use of U.S. armed force against Iraq. Congress authorized President George [H. W.] Bush to use armed force pursuant to UN Security Council resolution 678 (1990) "in order to achieve implementation of Security Council Resolutions 660, 661, 662, 664, 665, 666, 667, 669, 670, 674, and 677." This statute is usually interpreted as congressional authority to drive Iraq out of Kuwait, which was the purpose of resolution 678, adopted on November 29, 1990. All earlier resolutions set the stage for 678. Resolution 660, passed on August 2, 1990, condemned Iraq's invasion of Kuwait and demanded immediate withdrawal. Resolution 661 imposed economic sanctions. Resolutions 662 to 677 reinforced resolutions 660 and 661 and added other restrictions.

How can one argue that Congress transferred its constitutional power to the Security Council? It depends on the interpretation of resolution 678, which authorized member states to use all necessary means "to uphold and implement 660 (1990) and all subsequent relevant resolutions and to restore international peace and security in the area." Could the phase "all subsequent relevant resolutions" mean that whatever the Security Council promulgated after January 14, 1991, is automatically sanctioned by P.L. 102-1?

What is the meaning of "subsequent"? Any resolution issued after 678, or any resolution issued after 660 but before 678? It can be read either way. The most natural reading, in terms of the purpose of P.L. 102-1, is to refer to the resolutions from 660 to 678. The statutory objective was to oust Iraq from Kuwait. President Bush did not have authority to send ground troops north to Baghdad in an effort to remove Saddam Hussein. Such an operation would have exceeded his statutory authority and fractured the alliance that joined in support.

The broadest reading is to conclude that Congress, on January 14, 1991, transferred its constitutional powers to the Security Council, and that the future scope of American military commitments is determined by UN resolutions, not congressional statutes. From this theory, whatever the Security Council decided would apparently compel Congress to vote the necessary appropriations to cover the expenses of additional military actions. There is no evidence that Congress intended such a result, or could intend such a result.

THE USE OF FORCE ACT (2001)

The joint resolution passed by Congress on September 18, 2001, authorized President George W. Bush to use all "necessary and appropriate force" against nations, organizations, or persons that he determines planned, authorized, committed, or aided the terrorist attacks of September 11, 2001, or harbored such organizations or persons, "in order to prevent any future acts of international terrorism against the United States by such nations, organizations or persons." 115 Stat. 224. No doubt the statute authorized military action against the terrorist structure in Afghanistan. Does it also authorize military operations against terrorist units in other countries?

There seems to be little constitutional objection to using U.S. forces to help train anti-terrorist organizations in other countries, such as the Philippines, Georgia, and Yemen. That kind of assistance does not represent war on those countries. U.S. troops are there at the invitation and request of the three nations.

Quite different is the use of military force against another country. That is especially so when force is used in a region that is so politically unstable that military conflict has the potential to spread beyond the target nation. The magnitude of another military operation involving a second or third country raises not merely practical but constitutional concerns, both in terms of (1) the legislative prerogative to take the country from a state of peace to a state of war, and (2) the legislative power of the purse. The principles announced by President Eisenhower and the National Commitments Resolution, calling for joint action by Congress and the President, are more than guides for good policy. They represent efforts to honor constitutional government.

THE VALUE OF CONSULTATION

Policymaking by the federal government works better when the President and executive officials consult regularly with Members of Congress on domestic issues as well as matters of foreign affairs and national security. However, consultation is not a substitute for receiving congressional authority. Congress is a legislative body and discharges its constitutional duties by passing statutes that authorize and define national policy. Congress exists to legislate and legitimate, including military and financial commitments. Consultation is a technique for improving executive-legislative relations, but authority incorporated in a public law is the act that satisfies the Constitution.

Questions for Discussion

1. Does Congress's constitutional power to declare war mean anything anymore? What are the reasons for your answer?
2. Can the War Powers Resolution be improved? What are the reasons for your answer?
3. What role should presidential consultation with Congress play in matters of sending U.S. armed forces to fight abroad?
4. If you had to rewrite the Constitution today in light of our times, would you change its provisions dealing with the president's role in committing U.S. forces abroad? If so, how and why would you do it? If not, why would you not do it?
5. What role should the courts play in dealing with presidential conduct in sending U.S. armed forces abroad?

Suggested Resources

Web Sites

Presidents of the United States: Military Use by the U.S. Presidents
http://www.presidentsusa.net/military.html

U.S. Department of State: War Powers Resolution
http://fpc.state.gov/7656.htm

White House
http://www.whitehouse.gov/

Publications

Adler, David Gray. "The Law: The Clinton Theory of the War Power." *Presidential Studies Quarterly* 30, no. 1 (March 2000): 155–68.
———. "Virtues of the War Clause." *Presidential Studies Quarterly* 30, no. 4 (December 2000): 777–82.
Boylan, Timothy S. "The Law: Constitutional Understandings of the War Power." *Presidential Studies Quarterly* 31, no. 3 (September 2001): 514–28.
———, and Glenn A. Phelps. "The War Powers Resolution: A Rationale for Congressional Inaction." *Parameters* 31, no. 1 (Spring 2001): 109–24.
Campbell, Tom. "Kosovo: An Unconstitutional War." *Mediterranean Quarterly* 11, no. 1 (Winter 2000): 1–7.

Delahunty, Robert J., and John C. Yoo. "The President's Constitutional Authority to Conduct Military Operations against Terrorist Organizations and the Nations That Harbor or Support Them." *Harvard Journal of Law and Public Policy* 25, no. 2 (Spring 2002): 487–517.

Fisher, Louis. *Congressional Abdication on War and Spending.* College Station: Texas A&M University Press, 2000.

Hallett, Brien. *The Lost Art of Declaring War.* Urbana: University of Illinois Press, 1998.

Mervin, David. "Demise of the War Clause." *Presidential Studies Quarterly* 30, no. 4 (December 2000): 770–76.

Rakove, Jack. "Who Declares a War? Congress Must Not Cede Its Power to the President." *New York Times,* August 4, 2002, p. 13.

Stern, Gary M., and Morton H. Halperin, eds. *The U.S. Constitution and the Power to Go to War.* Westport, Conn.: Greenwood Press, 1994.

Turner, Robert F. "The War on Terrorism and the Modern Relevance of the Congressional Power to 'Declare War.'" *Harvard Journal of Law and Public Policy* 25, no. 2 (Spring 2002): 519–37.

U.S. Cong., House of Representatives. *The War Powers Resolution: Relevant Documents, Reports, Correspondence.* Prepared by the Subcommittee on International Security, International Organizations and Human Rights, 103d Cong., 2d Sess., 1994.

Westerfield, Donald L. *War Powers: The President, the Congress, and the Question of War.* Westport, Conn.: Praeger, 1996.

Should the Senate Take into Consideration the Ideology of a Nominee to the U.S. Supreme Court in Its Confirmation Decision?

Article II, Section 2 of the Constitution provides that the president nominate candidates for Supreme Court justices. It also provides that for the nominees to be appointed to the Court, they must be confirmed by the Senate. The Constitution says nothing, however, about the professional and intellectual backgrounds of the nominees; nor does it say anything about the criteria that should be used by the president in nominating candidates or by the Senate in evaluating them for confirmation.

From George Washington's day to the present, presidents have nominated candidates to the Court from a variety of backgrounds, including lower court judges, cabinet members, senators, and governors. In making their choices, presidents have based their considerations on judicial background, legal philosophy, intellectual talent, personal honesty and integrity, party unity, political and ideological compatibility, and other factors.

The Senate has often confirmed the nominees. At times, however, it has rejected them. Senators, too, have used criteria similar to those of the president in voting on confirmation.

The results of the confirmation process have not always been happy for presidents. As early as 1795, the Senate rejected John Rutledge as George Washington's nominee to be chief justice of the Supreme Court. Rutledge, who had been one of the authors of the Constitution, seemed qualified. He had even served as a Supreme Court justice. But he had opposed the Jay Treaty, which would have improved relations between the United States and Great Britain. And the Federalists, who dominated the Senate, favored the treaty. The Senate, consequently, did not confirm Rutledge.

From George Washington to the present, presidents have had to be careful in nominating candidates to the Supreme Court for fear that their nominations would not win confirmation. At times, presidents have been willing to engage in major battles with the Senate for their candidates. At other times, however, presidents have made cautious nominations that resulted in quick and favorable confirmation.

For most of the twentieth century, the Senate has confirmed presidential nominees to the Court. From 1900 to 1968 only one nominee — John J.

Parker in 1930 — was rejected by the Senate. But since then, presidents have had a harder time getting their nominees confirmed. Lyndon Johnson could not get Abe Fortas confirmed as chief justice in 1968. Richard Nixon faced defeat with his nominees of Clement Haynsworth and G. Harrold Carswell. Ronald Reagan's candidate Robert Bork went down to defeat, too. One of Reagan's nominees, Judge Douglas H. Ginsberg, was forced to withdraw from consideration after revelations about his personal life brought criticisms from conservative sources.

The Senate confirmation process has become increasingly acrimonious, too. Because the Supreme Court deals with some of the most controversial political issues of our times, such as abortion, affirmative action, criminal justice, and separation of church and state, groups concerned about the outcome of policy have good reason to be vitally involved with decisions dealing with appointments to the Supreme Court. Conservatives favor conservative justices, and liberals support liberal justices — although no one can be certain about how justices will decide cases once they are appointed to the Court. Since the stakes are so high, the fight over court nominations has on occasion become fierce.

Public attention to Supreme Court nomination has been reflected in procedural changes as well as media involvement in the subject. Until the nomination of Harlan Fiske Stone in 1925, Supreme Court nominees did not even personally appear before the Senate Judiciary Committee, the unit responsible for initiating the confirmation process in the Senate. Today, all Supreme Court nominees must personally appear before the committee. The hearings, which are now televised, have given the process even greater publicity.

Some of the stormiest controversies involving nominees occurred in the Reagan and George H. W. Bush administrations. Although William Rehnquist, who was an associate justice of the Supreme Court, was confirmed as chief justice, he faced tough hearings. He won confirmation with fewer favorable Senate votes than any successful nominee for the post in the twentieth century. The Robert Bork hearings were stormy, and the Senate voted against him. And the nomination of Clarence Thomas to succeed Thurgood Marshall as associate justice produced extraordinary hearings centered on accusations of sexual harassment by a former associate, Anita Hill. Thomas won confirmation but at great cost to his reputation.

The issue of the role of ideology in confirming justices to the Supreme Court remains controversial. Harvard University law professor Laurence H. Tribe argues that ideology should play a factor in the process of Senate confirmation of Supreme Court justices. He contends:

1. The Framers of the Constitution contemplated a much more central role for the Senate in this process than merely checking the professional qualifications and the character of the president's nominees.

2. Since the administration of President George Washington, the Senate has traditionally played an active role in considering presidential nominees to the Supreme Court.

3. The identity of who serves on the U.S. Supreme Court matters not only on how the Constitution is to be approached and how its multiple ambiguities are to be addressed, but also on questions of how we lead our lives as Americans.

4. It is impossible to remove all ideological considerations in the confirmation process and make it "above politics" because (a) presidents nominate individuals to the Supreme Court who reflect the president's preferred approach to the Constitution's vast areas of ambiguity, (b) there are no unique or uncontroversial answers to dealing with areas of constitutional ambiguity, and (c) the Supreme Court is already tilted in a rightward direction.

5. Because ideology matters to the president in choosing a nominee to the Supreme Court, it should also matter to any senator who must decide whether to vote for or against confirmation of that nominee.

6. A degree of ideological oversight should also play a role in considering the confirmation of circuit court nominees.

Douglas W. Kmiec, dean of the Catholic University of America School of Law, argues that the Senate should not consider ideology as a factor in the confirmation process of Supreme Court nominees. He contends:

1. The proper Senate inquiry of a judicial candidate is demeanor, integrity, legal competence, and fidelity to the rule of law.

2. Using ideological considerations in the Senate confirmation process would undermine the very idea of an independent judiciary that is a feature of the nation's history.

3. Nominee selection is seldom sufficient to predict accurately the philosophical direction of a particular judicial candidate once appointed to a lifetime job with no salary diminution, as is shown in the appointment of Justices Earl Warren, Harry Blackmun, and David Souter. Even current members of the court who are regarded as either liberal or conservative take opinions on particular issues that are opposite to the ideological dispositions that are often attributed to them.

4. Senate use of ideological concerns in the confirmation process would undermine the legitimate role of the courts as a judicial, rather than a legislative, institution, as befits our system of separation of powers.

☑ *YES*

---

*Should the Senate Take into Consideration the
Ideology of a Nominee to the U.S. Supreme Court
in Its Confirmation Decision?*

LAURENCE H. TRIBE

*Ideology Should Be a Factor in the
Confirmation of Supreme Court Nominees*

I am honored to have been invited to appear before this Subcommittee of the Senate Judiciary Committee to shed whatever light I can on the extremely important, and hopefully not too timely, topic of the Senate's role in the consideration of presidential nominations to the Supreme Court of the United States. I say "hopefully not too timely" because I think it wise of the Senate, with such guidance as the Senate Judiciary Committee through the agency of this Subcommittee can provide, to focus its attention *now* — not when a vacancy arises or a name is put forward — on the criteria to be applied in the confirmation process, and particularly on the role of ideology in that process.

There is a difficult trade-off here, to be sure. In Washington, as elsewhere, the squeaky wheel gets the grease. Focusing meaningful attention on an issue before it becomes a problem, much less a crisis, is difficult in the best of circumstances. Doing so when the issue is as abstract and complex as that of confirmation criteria for Supreme Court justices is more difficult still. Yet waiting until the matter is upon us, complete with a name or a short list of names, with interest groups and spin-meisters formidably arrayed on both sides, assures that the discussion will resemble a shouting match more than a civil conversation, and that every remark will be filtered through agenda-detectors tuned to the highest pitch. On balance, I believe that addressing the question of the Senate's proper role under a veil of ignorance — ignorance as to precisely when a vacancy will first arise, which of the sitting justices will be the first to depart, and which name or names will be brought forth by The White House — seems likeliest to lead to fruitful reflection on how to proceed when the veil is lifted and we are all confronted with the stark reality of specific names and all that they might portend for the republic.

It is understandable that, partly because of the seemingly abstract and speculative character of such a discussion in the absence of any actual nominee, and partly because the more immediate question actually facing the Senate Judiciary Committee is how best to evaluate a group of nominees already put forward by the President to fill various vacancies in the federal courts of appeals, this Subcommittee has chosen to cast its inquiry more broadly than a focus on Supreme Court nominations would indicate and has decided to include in its charge the question of what role ideology should play in considering federal judicial nominations generally. For that reason, at the conclusion of my observations about my principal topic — that of Supreme Court nominations — I will offer a few thoughts about the broader question that is of interest to the Subcommittee. But because I want to preserve to the degree possible the distinct advantages of separating the general question of criteria from any particular nominee or set of nominees, I will carefully avoid saying anything about any pending nomination and will, until the end of my remarks, discuss only the matter of nominations to the Supreme Court.

When my book *God Save This Honorable Court* was published in 1985 defending an active role for the Senate in the appointment of Supreme Court Justices, the Court was delicately balanced, with liberals like William Brennan and Thurgood Marshall offsetting conservatives like William Rehnquist and Antonin Scalia. Yet, on the inevitable book tour, I found quite a few otherwise well informed people wondering why the composition of the Supreme Court was all that big a deal, and why it shouldn't suffice for the Senate simply to make sure that the President wasn't packing the Court with cronies and with mediocrities. Having satisfied itself of the professional qualifications and character of the President's nominee, some people wondered, why should the Senate be concerned with that nominee's philosophical leanings or ideological predispositions?

People seemed to view things differently when they were exposed to the historical background showing that the Framers contemplated a much more central role for the Senate in this process, and when they learned that it was mostly the unwieldiness of having a collective body like the Senate make the initial nomination that led the Framers, at the last minute in the drafting process, to entrust the nomination to the President and to leave the Senate with the task of deciding whether to confirm or reject; that, even in the final version of the Constitution as ratified in 1789, the Senate's task was not left wholly passive (deciding between a thumbs-up and a thumbs-down) but was cast as the role of giving its "advice and consent"; and that, with the exception of an uncharacteristic lull in the last century, the Senate has traditionally exercised its advice and consent function with respect to the Supreme Court in a lively and engaged manner, concerning itself not simply with the intellect and integrity of the nominee but with the nominee's overall approach to the task of judging, and often with the nominee's substantive views on the burning legal and constitutional issues of the day. Those who initially assumed the Senate need not concern itself with a nominee's ideology tended to view the matter in a new light when reminded that, both in the formative days of our nation's history, under presidents as early as George Washington, and in recent decades, there has been a venerable tradition in which the Senate has played anything but a deferential role on Supreme Court nominations.

All of that registered with people back in 1985, but it wasn't until the 1987 resignation of Lewis Powell and the confirmation battle later that year over Robert Bork that the concrete stakes in this otherwise abstract controversy came to life for the great majority of the American public. In retrospect, although one can lament the ways in which some interest groups and politicians — on both sides of the question, frankly — exaggerated the record bearing on Judge Bork's views and bearing on what kind of Supreme Court Justice he would have made, the fact is that his confirmation hearings represented an important education for large segments of the public on such fundamental matters as the meaning of the due process and liberty guarantees of the Fifth and Fourteenth Amendments to the Constitution, the relevance and limits of the Ninth Amendment's reference to unenumerated rights, the connection between various ways of approaching the Constitution's text and history and such particular unenumerated rights as personal privacy and reproductive freedom, the relationship between a tightly constrained and literalist reading of the Constitution in matters of personal rights and a more open-textured and fluid reading of the Constitution in matters bearing on state's rights, and a host of other topics of enduring significance.

For my own part, as one of the expert witnesses called to testify about Judge Bork's constitutional philosophy and about the consequences for the nation were he to gain an opportunity to implement that philosophy as a Supreme Court Justice, I make no apology for anything I said at the time. Knowing full well that my testimony would put me on the enemies' lists of some extremely powerful people with very long memories, I felt it my duty to testify to the truth as I understood it. I would do the same thing again today. When the Senate finally rejected the nomination of Robert Bork, many of his allies cried "foul" and have since practiced decades of payback politics. Indeed, they have even succeeded, with the aid of some revisionist history, in adding to the vocabulary the highly misleading new verb, "to Bork" — meaning, "to smear a nominee with distorted accusations about his or her record and views" — as though the predictions of the sort of justice Robert Bork would have become were in some way misleading or otherwise unfair. But the truth, as Judge Bork's post-rejection writings made amply clear, was just as his critics had indicated. Unless being confirmed would have caused him to undergo a radical conversion — something on which the nation has a right not to gamble — his rejection, and the subsequent confirmation of Justice [Anthony M.] Kennedy in his stead, meant one less member on the far right wing of the Court and left Justice Scalia (later with Justice [Clarence] Thomas) holding down the starboard alone. The nation had held a referendum on the Borkian approach to reading the Constitution of the United States, and the Borkian approach had decisively lost. And, lest it be supposed that I review this history simply to reprise a political episode that was painful for all concerned, I should make plain that my purpose is altogether different. It is to remove the fangs from the verb "to Bork" and to restore some perspective, lest anyone be misled into beginning the debate over the Senate's proper role with the erroneous premise that the Senate should be less than proud of the last instance in which it rejected a Supreme Court nominee on ideological grounds.

Today, it takes very little effort to persuade any informed citizen that the identity of who serves on the Supreme Court of the United States matters enormously — matters not simply to the resolution of these large questions of how the Constitution is to be approached and how its multiple ambiguities are to be addressed, but as well in the disposition of the most mundane, and yet basic, questions of how we lead our lives as Americans. Whether laws enacted for the benefit of the elderly or the disabled are to be rendered virtually unenforceable in circumstances where the violator is a state agency and the victim cannot obtain meaningful redress without going to federal court; whether people stopped in their cars for minor offenses like failing to have a seatbelt properly attached to a child's car seat may be handcuffed and taken by force to the police station where they are arrested and booked and held overnight; whether police may use sense-enhancing technologies like special heat detectors to peer through the walls of our homes in order to detect the details of what we do there; whether, having recognized that everything we do in the privacy of our homes counts as an intimate detail when it comes to protecting us from various kinds of search and surveillance, judges will nonetheless continue to let state legislatures regulate the most intimate sexual details of what we do behind closed doors with those we love; whether government may forbid the kind of research that might prove essential to the prevention and cure of devastating degenerative diseases whenever that research uses stem cells or other tissues from embryos created in clinics for infertile couples — embryos that would otherwise be discarded without making such life-generating new knowledge possible; what kinds of campaign finance restrictions are to be permitted when the broad values of democracy seem pitted against the specific rights of individuals and corporations to use their wealth to purchase as much media time as money can buy; who is to be the next President of the United States — these are just some of the questions whose answers have come to turn on a single vote of a single Supreme Court Justice.

The battle that was fought over the nomination of Judge Bork to become Justice Bork was fought because the general approach to constitutional interpretation that he seemed to represent attracted him to some but frightened an even larger number. Most dramatic among the anticipated consequences of his confirmation would have been the addition of his vote and voice to the far right wing of the Court on such issues as reproductive freedom, which the Constitution of course never mentions in so many words. His confirmation, people came to recognize despite his avowals of open-mindedness on all such matters, would have meant the certain demise of *Roe v. Wade,* a decision whose most recent application, in last year's "partial birth abortion" case from Nebraska, was, after all these years, still 5 to 4 — as are a large number of crucial decisions about personal privacy, gender discrimination, sexual orientation, race-based affirmative action, legislative apportionment, church-state separation, police behavior, and a host of other basic issues.

After the Supreme Court's highly controversial and I believe profoundly misguided performance last December in the case of *Bush v. Gore* — in which I should acknowledge I played a role as author of the briefs for Vice President [Al] Gore and as oral advocate in the first of the two Supreme Court arguments in the case — it's difficult to find anyone who any longer questions why it matters so much who serves on the Court. The significance of *Bush v. Gore* in this setting doesn't depend on anybody's prediction of who would have won the vote-count in Florida had the counting gone on without the Supreme Court's dramatic and sudden interruption on December 9, 2000, or of who would have been chosen the next President by Congress this January 6 [2001] if the Supreme Court had let the constitutional processes operate as designed and if competing electoral slates had been sent from Tallahassee, Florida to Washington, D.C. The great significance of the case is to underscore that, by a margin of a single vote, the branch of our government that is least politically accountable — wisely and designedly so, when matters of individual and minority rights or of basic government structure are at stake — treated the American electorate and the electoral process with a disdain that a differently composed Court would have found unthinkable. So it was that, when push came to shove, and the Supreme Court's faith in democracy was tested, the Supreme Court blinked. It distrusted the people who were doing the counting, it distrusted the state judges, it distrusted the members of Congress to whom the dispute might have been thrown if it hadn't pulled down the curtain. And the Court could get away with it, partly because nobody in the House or Senate, to be brutally honest, relished the thought of discharging the constitutional responsibility of deciding which electoral votes to count and then facing his or her own constituents — and because the people were growing weary of the no longer very sexy or novel topic of dimpled ballots and hanging chads, and Christmas was just around the corner, and, after all, everyone knew that the election was basically too close to call anyway. Lost for some in all of that realism, I fear, was the high price our democracy paid for the convenience of a Court that was willing — no, not just willing, positively *eager* — to take those burdens from our shoulders and simply decree a result. Among the results is an unprecedented degree of political polarization in the Court's favorability rating with the public — a rating that now stands roughly twice as high among Republicans as among Democrats, surely an ominous gap for the one institution to which we look for action transcending politics.

This isn't the time or place to debate the details of *Bush v. Gore,* a subject about which I have written elsewhere; I stress the case because it shows at least as dramatically as any case possibly could just how much may depend on the composition of the Court; how basic are the questions that the Court at times decides by the closest possible margins; and how absurd are the pretensions and slogans of those who have for years gotten away with saying, and perhaps have deceived even themselves by saying, that the kinds of judges they want on the Court, the "restrained" rather than "activist" kinds of judges, the kinds of judges who don't "legislate from the bench," are the kinds exemplified by today's supposedly "conservative" wing of the Court, led by Chief Justice Rehnquist and supported in area after area by Justices [Sandra Day] O'Connor, Scalia, Kennedy, and Thomas. Those are, of course, the five justices who decided the presidential election of 2000. They are, as well, the five justices who have struck down one Act of Congress after another — invalidating federal legislation at a faster clip than has any other Supreme Court since before the New Deal — on the basis that the Court and the Court alone is entitled to decide what kinds of state action might threaten religious liberty, might discriminate invidiously against the elderly or the disabled, or might otherwise warrant action by Congress in the discharge of its solemn constitutional power under Section 5 of the Fourteenth Amendment to determine what legislation is necessary and appropriate to protect liberty and equality in America.

Some might be tempted, after watching the Court perform so poorly in the pit of presidential politics, and after witnessing it substitute its policy judgments for those of Congress in one legislative arena after another, to imagine that, if we could only wave a magic wand and remove all ideological considerations from judicial selection — both on the part of the President in making nominations and on the part of the Senate in the confirmation process — somehow the Olympian ideal of a federal judiciary once again above politics and beyond partisan reproach could be restored. For several reasons, that is a dangerous illusion. First, there's no way for the Senate to prevent the President from doing what Presidents from the beginning of the republic have asserted the right to do, and what some Presidents have done more successfully than others: pick nominees who will mirror the President's preferred approach to the Constitution's vast areas of ambiguity. Second, in dealing with those areas of ambiguity, there may or may not be any right answers, but there most assuredly are no unique or uncontroversial answers; invariably, in choosing one Supreme Court nominee rather than another, one is making a choice among those answers, and among the approaches that generate them. And third, with a Supreme Court that is already so dramatically tilted in a rightward direction, anything less than a concerted effort to set the balance straight would mean perpetuating the imbalance that gave us not only *Bush v. Gore* but the myriad decisions in the preceding half-dozen years in which the Court thumbed its nose at Congress and thus at the American people.

In an accompanying memorandum that I prepared for distribution this April [2001] to a number of members of the Senate, I explore in greater detail how these recent Supreme Court encroachments on congressional authority have come about and what they signify. For purposes of my statement today, suffice it to say that such encroachments are the antithesis of judicial restraint or modesty; that the justices who have engineered them are the most activist in our history; that holding them up as exemplars of jurists who would never dream of "legislating from the bench" is, to put it mildly, an exercise in dramatic license; and that the judgments the Senate will have to make about the inclinations and proclivities of prospective members of the Supreme Court must be considerably more nuanced than the stereotypical slogans and bumper stickers about activism vs. restraint, and even liberalism vs. conservatism, can possibly accommodate.

Some scholars, including most prominently University of Chicago Law Professor Cass Sunstein, who will also be testifying before you at this hearing, have powerfully argued that an active, nondeferential, role for the Senate in evaluating Supreme Court nominees is called for, quite independent of *Bush v. Gore,* by the way in which the federal judiciary in general, and the Supreme Court in particular, have been systematically stacked over the past few decades in a particular ideological direction — a direction hostile, for example, to the enactment of protective congressional legislation under Section 5 of the Fourteenth Amendment, and hostile as well to other ostensibly "liberal" or "progressive" judicial positions, on topics ranging from privacy to affirmative action, from states' rights to law enforcement. For Professor Sunstein, who will of course speak most accurately and fully for himself, the active role the Senate ought to play is exactly as it would have been had *Bush v. Gore* never been decided.

Other scholars, most prominently Yale University Law Professor Bruce Ackerman, argue that *Bush v. Gore* has thrown the process of judicial appointment into what Professor Ackerman calls "constitutional disequilibrium," so that, instead of two independent structural checks on a necessarily unrepresentative and politically unaccountable Supreme Court, we are now down to just one. Because, in his view, the current Court must be acknowledged to have "mediated" the "President's relationship to the citizenry" — by helping put him in office by a 5 to 4 vote — "only the Senate retains a normal connection to the electorate," and this demands of that body, as Professor Ackerman sees it, that it shoulder an unusually heavy share of the burden of democratic control, by the people acting through the political branches, of the judicial branch to which we ordinarily look to hold the balance true. Translated into an operational prescription, the Ackerman position would recommend that the Senate simply refuse to confirm any new justices to the Court before President Bush, as Professor Ackerman puts it, "win[s] the 2004 election fair and square, without the Court's help." As a fallback, Professor Ackerman would urge the Senate to consider any nominations President Bush might make to the Court during his current term on their own merits, but without what Ackerman describes as "the deference accorded ordinary presidents."

Although I am intrigued by Professor Ackerman's suggestion, it seems to me the wrong way to go, either in its strongest form or in its fallback version. The strongest form would make sense, I think, only if we were convinced that the justices who voted with the majority in *Bush v. Gore* acted in a manner so corrupt and illegitimate, so devoid of legal justification, that one could say they essentially installed George W. Bush as president in a bloodless but lawless coup. But if we believed that, then the remedy of not letting the leaders of that coup profit from their own wrong — of denying them the solace of like-minded successors as they depart the scene — would be far too mild. If we thought the *Bush* majority guilty of a coup, we should have to conclude that they were guilty of treason to the Constitution, and that they should be impeached, convicted, and removed from office.

Believing that what the *Bush v. Gore* majority did was gravely wrong but not that it amounted to a coup or indeed anything like it — believing that the majority justices acted not to install their favorite candidate but out of a misguided sense that the nation was in grave and imminent peril unless they stopped the election at once — one would have to look to the Ackerman fallback position. But all it tells us is something that I argued was the case anyway as early as 1985 — that the Senate should not accord any special deference to nominations made by *any* President to the Supreme Court. Indeed, I go further than does Professor Sunstein in this respect. As I understand his position, he would have the Senate withhold such deference for reasons peculiar to the recent history of the nation and of appointments to the federal bench and especially to the Supreme Court over the past few decades. Had we not lived through a time of Republican Presidents insistent on, and adept at, naming justices who would carry on their ideological program in judicial form, sandwiching Democratic Presidents uninterested in, or inept at, naming justices similarly attuned to their substantive missions, Professor Sunstein would apparently urge that the Senate give the President his head in these matters and serve only in a backseat capacity, to prevent rogues and fools, more or less, from being elevated to the High Court.

In a world in which each position on the Supreme Court might be given to some idealized version of the wisest lawyer in the land — the most far-sighted and scholarly, the most capable of clearly explaining the Constitution's language and mission, the most adept at generating consensus in support of originally unpopular positions that come to be seen as crucial to the defense of human rights — perhaps we could afford in normal times to accept a posture of Senatorial deference, with exceptions made in special historical periods of the sort some believe we have been living through. But if we ever lived in a world where such a universal paragon of justice could be imagined, and in which the kinds of issues resolved by Supreme Court Justices were not invariably contested, often bitterly so, between competing visions of the right, that day has long since passed.

Today, regardless of whether past Presidents have acted or failed to act so as to produce a Supreme Court bench leaning lopsidedly in a rightward direction, and regardless of whether a majority of the current Court has acted in such a way as to render the President whom it helped to elect less entitled to deference than usual in naming the successors of the Court's current members, the inescapable fact is that the President will name prospective justices about whom he knows a great deal more than the Senate can hope to learn — justices whose paper trail, if the President is skillful about it, will reveal much less to the Senate than the President thinks he knows. Given his allies and those to whom he owes his political victory, as well as those on whom he will need to depend for his re-election, the incumbent President, if those constituencies expect him to leave his mark and therefore theirs upon the Court, will try to name justices who will fulfill the agenda of those constituencies — in the case of President Bush, the agenda of the right — without seeming by their published statements or their records as jurists to be as committed to that agenda as the President will privately believe them to be. Presumably, the incumbent President will look for such nominees among the ranks of Hispanic jurists, or women, or both, in order to distract the opposition and make resistance more painful. And certainly this President, like any other in modern times, will select nominees who have already mastered or can be coached in the none too difficult game of answering questions thoughtfully and without overt deception but in ways calculated to offend no-one and reveal nothing.

In this circumstance, to say that the burden is on those who hold the power of advice and consent to show that there is something disqualifying about the nominee, that there is a smoking gun in the record or a wildly intemperate publication in the bibliography or some other fatal flaw that can justify a rallying cry of opposition, is to guarantee that the President will have the Court of his dreams without the Senate playing any meaningful role whatsoever. Therefore, if the Senate's role is to be what the Framers contemplated, what history confirms, and what a sound appreciation for the realities of American politics demands, the burden must instead be on the nominee and, indeed, on the President. That burden must be to persuade each Senator — for, in the end, this is a duty each Senator must discharge in accord with his or her own conscience — that the nominee's experience, writings, speeches, decisions, and actions affirmatively demonstrate not only the exceptional intellect and wisdom and integrity that greatness as a judge demands but also the understanding of and commitment to those constitutional rights and values and ideals that the Senator regards as important for the republic to uphold.

On this standard, stealth nominees should have a particularly hard time winning confirmation. For proving on the basis of a blank slate the kinds of qualities that the Senate ought to demand, with a record that is unblemished because it is without content, ought to be exceedingly difficult. Testimony alone, however eloquent and reassuring, ought rarely to suffice where its genuineness is not confirmed by a history of action in accord with the beliefs professed. And testimony, in any event, is bound to be clouded by understandable reservations about compromising judicial independence by asking the nominee to commit himself or herself too specifically in advance to how he or she would vote on particular cases that might, in one variant or another, come before the Court. Interestingly, we do not regard sitting justices as having compromised their independence by having written about, and voted on, many of the issues they must confront year in and year out; the talk about compromising judicial independence by asking about such issues sometimes reflects unthinking reflex more than considered judgment. But on the assumption that old habits die hard, and that members of the Senate Judiciary Committee will continue to be rather easily cowed into backing away from asking probing questions about specific issues that might arise during the nominee's service on the Court, it should still be possible to formulate questions for any nominee, including tough follow-up questions, at a level of generality just high enough so that the easy retreat into "I'm sorry, Senator, I can't answer that question because the matter might come before me," will be unavailing. And, to the extent such slightly more general questions yield information too meager for informed judgment, the burden must be on the nominee to satisfy his or her interlocutors that the concern underlying the thwarted line of questioning is one that ought not to disturb the Senator. That satisfaction can be provided only from a life lived in the law that exemplifies, rather than eschewing, a real engagement with problems of justice, with challenges of human rights, and with the practical realities of making law relevant to people's needs. When a nominee cannot provide that satisfaction — when the nominee is but a fancy resume in an empty suit or a vacant dress, perhaps adorned with a touching story of a hard-luck background or of ethnic roots — any Senator who takes his or her oath of office as seriously as I know, deep down, all of you do, should simply say, "No thanks, Mr. President. Send us another nominee."

What this adds up to is, of course, a substantial role for ideology in the consideration of any Supreme Court nominee. It would be naive to the point of foolhardiness to imagine that the President will be tone-deaf to signals of ideological compatibility or incompatibility with his view of the ideal Supreme Court justice; ideology will invariably matter to any President and must therefore matter to any

Senator who is not willing simply to hand over to The White House his or her proxy for the discharge of the solemn duty to offer advise and consent.

As a postscript on the distinct subject of circuit court nominees, it seems worth noting that, although such nominees are of course strictly bound by Supreme Court precedents and remain subject to correction by that Court, and although there might therefore seem to be much less reason for the Senate to be ideologically vigilant than in the case of the Supreme Court, three factors militate in favor of at least a degree of ideological oversight even at the circuit court level.

First, well under 1 percent of the decisions of the circuit courts are actually reviewed by the Supreme Court, which avowedly declines to review even clearly erroneous decisions unless they present some special circumstance such as a circuit conflict. Especially if the circuit courts tend toward a homogeneity that mirrors the ideological complexion of the Supreme Court, that tribunal is exceedingly unlikely to use its discretionary power of review on certiorari to police lower federal courts that stray from the reservation in one direction or another; it will instead focus its firepower on bringing the state courts into line and resolving intolerable conflicts among the lower courts, state and federal.

Second, there are a great many gray areas in which Supreme Court precedents leave the circuit courts a wide berth within which to maneuver without straying into a danger zone wherein further review becomes a likely prospect. Even though no individual circuit court judge is very likely to use that elbow room in order to move the law significantly in one direction or another without a check from the Supreme Court, the overall balance and composition of the circuit court bench can have a considerable effect, in momentum if nothing else, on the options realistically open to the Supreme Court and thus to the country.

Third, in the past few decades, the circuit courts have increasingly served as a kind of "farm team" for Supreme Court nominations. On the Court that decided *Brown v. Board of Education* in 1954 there sat not a single justice who, prior to his appointment to the Supreme Court, had ever served in a judicial capacity. Governors, Senators, distinguished members of the bar, but no former judges. Today, however, rare is the nominee who has not previously served in a judicial capacity, most frequently on a federal circuit court. On the current Court, only the Chief Justice lacked prior judicial experience when he was first named a justice; and, of the other eight justices, all except Justice O'Connor, who had served as a state court judge, were serving on federal circuit courts when appointed to the Court. The reasons for this change are many; they include, most prominently, the growing recognition that ideology matters and that service on a lower court may be one way of detecting a prospective nominee's particular ideological leanings. Whatever the reasons, the reality has independent significance, for it means that any time the Senate confirms someone to serve on a circuit court, it may be making a record that, in the event the judge should later be nominated to the Supreme Court, will come back to haunt it. "But you had no trouble confirming Judge X to the court of appeals for the Y circuit," supporters of Supreme Court nominee X are likely to intone. Keeping that in mind will require the Senate to give fuller consideration to matters of ideology at the circuit court level than it otherwise might.

The primary ideological issue at the circuit court level, however, should probably remain the overall tilt of the federal bench rather than the particular leanings of
any given nominee viewed in isolation. In a bench already tilted overwhelmingly
in one direction — today, the right — a group of nominees whose ideological
center of gravity is such as to exacerbate rather than correct that tilt should be a
matter of concern to any Senator who does not regard the existing tilt as altogether
healthy.

And one needn't be particularly liberal to have concerns about the existing tilt.
Just as a liberal who recognizes that people who share his views might not have all
the right answers ought to be distressed by a federal bench composed overwhelmingly of jurists reminiscent of William J. Brennan, Jr. or William O. Douglas — or
even by a federal bench composed almost entirely of liberals and moderates and
few conservatives — and just as such a liberal should doubt the wisdom, in con-
fronting such a bench, of adding a group of judges who would essentially replicate
that slant, so too a conservative who is humble enough to recognize that people
who share her views might not have a lock on the truth should feel dismayed by a
federal bench composed overwhelmingly of jurists in the mold of Antonin Scalia
or Clarence Thomas — or even by a federal bench composed almost entirely of
conservatives and moderates and few liberals — and ought to doubt the wisdom,
in dealing with such a bench, of adding many more judges cut from that same
cloth. The fundamental truth that ought to unite people across the ideological
spectrum, and that only those who are far too sure of themselves to be comfortable in a democracy should find difficult to accept, is that the federal judiciary in
general, and the Supreme Court in particular, ought in principle to reflect and represent a wide range of viewpoints and perspectives rather than being clustered
toward any single point on the ideological spectrum.

Indeed, even those who feel utterly persuaded of the rightness of their own particular point of view should, in the end, recognize that their arguments can only
be sharpened and strengthened by being tested against the strongest of opposing
views. Liberals and conservatives alike can be lulled into sloppy and slothful
smugness and self-satisfaction unless they are fairly matched on the bench by the
worthiest of opponents. It may even be that the astonishing weakness and vulner-
ability of the Court's majority opinion in *Bush v. Gore,* and of the majority opinions in a number of the other democracy-defying decisions in whose mold it was
cast, are functions in part of the uniquely narrow spectrum of views — narrower, I
think, than at any other time in our history — covered by the membership of the
current Court — a spectrum which, on most issues, essentially runs the gamut
from A through C. On a Court with four justices distinctly on the right, two moderate conservatives, a conservative moderate, two moderates, and no liberals, it's
easy for the dominant faction to grow lazy and to issue opinions that, preaching
solely to the converted, ring hollow to a degree that ill serves both the Court as an
institution and the legal system it is supposed to lead. It is thus in the vital interest
of the nation as a whole, and not simply in the interest of those values that liberals
and progressives hold dear, that the ideological imbalance of the current Supreme
Court and of the federal bench as a whole not be permitted to persist, and that the

Senate take ideology intelligently into account throughout the judicial confirmation process with a view to gradually redressing what all should come to see as a genuinely dangerous disequilibrium.

Should the Senate Take into Consideration the Ideology of a Nominee to the U.S. Supreme Court in Its Confirmation Decision?

DOUGLAS W. KMIEC

Ideology Should Not Be a Factor in the Confirmation of Supreme Court Nominees

My proposition is simple: the proper Senate inquiry of a judicial candidate is demeanor, integrity, legal competence and fidelity to the rule of law. It is not partisanship or policy agreement. While textually the Senate is free to inquire and to reject a nominee on any ground — even a highly political, constitutionally problematic one like the nominee's views on outcomes in specific cases — it should not do so. Undertaking to make nominees carry a type of political burden of proof will over time merely invite a subservience of mind and personality that is contrary to an independent judiciary.

The significance of an independent judiciary is well-known to every school child. The point was made plain in the bill of indictment included against the English King in our Declaration of Independence. "He has made Judges dependent upon his Will alone, for the tenure of their offices," our founders complained. Any attempt to transform the Senate's advice and consent role into a similar partisan inquiry would cut deeply against our history and unnecessarily invite making federal judges dependent upon constitutionally inappropriate considerations. In the constitutional convention of 1787, great concern was expressed against having judicial appointments influenced by the Legislature out of "cabal, from personal regard, or some other consideration than a title derived from the proper qualifications." Indeed, in this past century, there has been only one other such blatant effort to subvert the independence of the federal judiciary: FDR's [Franklin D. Roosevelt] court-packing plan.

The court-packing plan, in essence, proposed that when a federal judge who had served at least ten years waited more than six months after his seventieth birthday to retire or resign, the President would add a new judge to the bench, with up to six additional slated for the Supreme Court. FDR talked about the need for "new blood" and so forth, but everyone knew that the President wanted to change the jurisprudential direction of the Court — to bend it to his will. FDR, himself, gave up the pretense soon enough. As one scholar noted, "the President virtually abandoned this line of argument and came out with his main reason: that the Court was dominated by a set of conservative justices who were making it impossible for liberal government to function." Sound familiar? These were times of great economic distress. Millions were out of work and the Court was showing little deference for FDR's regulatory initiatives to address the problem. Yet, even under these dire circumstances — which are hardly equivalent to the relative prosperity of today — "it quickly became apparent that opponents of the plan enjoyed widespread support."

Like President Roosevelt, some in the Senate today may believe the Rehnquist Court, and even the lower federal courts (even though they have recently been augmented with 377 new judges sharing the judicial philosophy of former President [Bill] Clinton) to be ideologically contrary to desired policy. Like FDR, these members of the Senate ask for a judicial population that will not weigh case or controversy by adherence to precedent or textual or structural interpretation, but by the desirability of particular outcome. This course is ill-advised and should not be pursued. The short-term political gratification of defeating one or a handful of judicial nominees on partisan or ideological grounds will harm the federal judiciary and bring dishonor to this deliberative body.

Why dishonor? Consider the words of the Senate Judiciary Committee in turning away FDR's attempt to inject partisanship into the composition of the courts. The plan was denounced for applying "force to the judiciary. It is an attempt to impose upon the courts a course of action, a line of decision which, without that force, without that imposition, the judiciary might not adopt." This assault upon judicial independence came with the following warning which unfortunately seems equally apt to the arguments being presently made to force judicial nominees to prove their ideological bona fides:

> Let us, for the purpose of the argument, grant that the Court has been wrong, wrong not only in that it has rendered mistaken opinions but wrong in the far more serious sense that it has substituted its will for the Congressional will in the matter of legislation. May we nevertheless safely punish the Court? . . . . If we yield to temptation now to lay the lash upon the Court, we are only teaching others how to apply it to ourselves and to the people when the occasion seems to warrant. Manifestly, if we may force the hand of the Court to secure our interpretation of the Constitution, then some succeeding Congress may repeat the process to secure another and a different interpretation and one which may not sound so pleasant in our ears as that for which we now contend.

In the end, the Senate Judiciary Committee in the 1930s strongly denounced the court-packing exercise as having the "initial and ultimate effect [of undermining] the independence of the courts," and [violating] "all precedents in the history of our Government and would in itself be a dangerous precedent for the future."

The future is apparently now, and sixty-four years later packing the courts on the basis of desired outcomes looks no better and is no more consistent with the spirit of the Constitution and its guarantee of judicial independence.

But more than judicial independence is at stake, because an attempt to exclude men and women of excellent credential and judgment because they don't happen to subscribe to your particular conception of federalism, or because they do not possess the right disposition toward this or that doctrinal formulation of due process, or affirmative action, or any other topical subject is a use of the vital Senatorial role of advice and consent that is either wholly random since it seeks to predict the unpredictable or deeply anti-democratic as it seeks to undo a national election and the contemplated sovereignty of the people in the selection of judges through the election of a new executive.

Nominee selection — as a matter of fact — is seldom sufficient to predict accurately the philosophical direction of a particular judicial candidate, once appointed to a lifetime job with no salary diminution. [Dwight D.] Eisenhower had his Earl Warren; [Richard] Nixon had his [Harry] Blackmun; [George H. W.] Bush had his [David] Souter. In each case, it is either popularly speculated or actually articulated that the nominee's service was at some considerable variance to the philosophy of the nominating president. A recent study for the *LBJ Journal of Public Affairs* estimates that one Justice in four disappointed his appointing president.

Whether or not presidents have been dismayed by their nominees at times, judicial behavior is certainly a hazard to predict. "Chief Justice Earl Warren, prior to his appointment, supported President Roosevelt's decision to intern United States citizens of Japanese ancestry during World War II. . . . But as Chief Justice, Warren became an icon of civil liberties organizations. . . ." Consider also just the past term of the high court. So-called conservative Justices [Antonin] Scalia and [Clarence] Thomas insisted that law enforcement observe the privacy of a home from the intrusion of a rare thermal imaging device, while claimed liberal Justice [John Paul] Stevens dissented. Meanwhile, Justice [Stephen G.] Breyer assumed by the President who nominated him, the media, and this body to have a progressive or liberal ideology at the time of his confirmation, has joined results permitting a student Bible club to use a public school classroom in the after school hours, and earlier, that would more easily exclude adult cable programming. As Professor Richard Garnett has observed: "[the] justices are neither easy to pigeonhole nor easy to predict. Their dispositions are not merely 'restrained' or 'activist.' Their decisions aren't predetermined by the ideological labels slapped on by partisan animators."

But even if there was a greater level of predictability, what possibly authorizes the Senate to substitute its judgment for that of the electorate under the disguise of inquiring into judicial fitness? Despite the disagreements that you or I may have with individual decisions of the present Supreme Court or the lower federal courts, there is little to suggest that, in the aggregate, these institutions are composed of individuals unrepresentative of the people. Quite the contrary. Five presidents have contributed to the make-up of the present Court and Presidents [Ronald] Reagan and Clinton had the opportunity to appoint virtually identical numbers of lower federal court judges over their respective terms [377 for Clinton and 382 for Reagan]. And despite the fact that the last national election may have hung by a chad, or that some academics would have preferred greater reliance upon political (rather than adjudicative) means of resolving the electoral disputes that emerged, the outcome — supported at its most basic level by seven justices (labeled conservative and liberal alike) — has vested the power to nominate judicial officers in President Bush by a majority of electoral vote. And that vote has meaning for executive and judicial appointment that ought not be undone covertly by this body.

Here it is good to recur to first principle. As the very able Northwestern legal historian Professor Stephen Presser pointed out before this body earlier this year [2001], the critics of the Constitution were particularly worried about any policy making tendencies of federal judges, especially as it might displace state authority. [Alexander] Hamilton responded to this criticism by emphasizing that it was not the job of judges to make law, that their role under the Constitution was simply to enforce the Constitution and laws as they were written, according to their original understanding. By doing so, Hamilton explained, federal judges would be acting as agents of the sovereign people themselves, and would do their part in implementing the rule of law. It was true that judges might sometimes be called upon to declare statutes invalid because of the dictates of the Constitution, but this was the role envisioned in those specific, and one might hope, rare cases. The Constitution itself sets limits on what Congress may do, Hamilton explained, and when the legislature exceeds those limits it ceases to act pursuant to the will of the people. It is then the job of the people's other agents, the Courts, to rein in the legislatures. All this is a long way of saying, as Hamilton did succinctly, that in properly deciding matters of unconstitutionality, the courts are not implementing their own preferences, but that of the people.

Professor Presser further bolstered this historical reference by mention of the separation of powers. It was well understood to our framers, pursuant to the theories of Montesquieu, that liberty could not be preserved unless judges were barred from legislating. Lawmaking was left to the legislature and the people themselves. As Hamilton wrote in *Federalist* 78, quoting Montesquieu's *Spirit of Laws* directly, "there is no liberty if the power of judging be not separated from the legislative and executive powers." And that is not just an admonition to judges to observe the boundaries of their intended role. Liberty can also be lost if judging is given over to the executive or legislative branches as well, or if prospective judges are invited to be lawmakers by the pressures of politicized confirmation.

Sadly, this is forgotten far too often today. Courts are casually discussed as merely alternative policymakers. Mr. Joseph Califano Jr. in an essay just last week, for example, accused the Congress as a whole of "political pandering," "gridlock," and "failure," and as a result argued that federal courts must become (and have become) "powerful architects of public policy." I doubt very much whether the Senate wants to indulge Mr. Califano's harsh premise of the failure of Congress. Perhaps, as a policy matter, many would support a more aggressive regulatory, perhaps even prohibitory, policy toward tobacco or hand-guns, and reading him, I suspect so would Mr. Califano. But the Congress has chosen a different path — to regulate tobacco advertising and to pursue background checks for certain weapon purchases. These are policy choices. Congress has made them. When the Supreme Court was asked to do more than Congress was willing to do — to authorize explicitly the FDA [Food and Drug Administration] to regulate tobacco products — it declined. If Congress is truly displeased with that judicial outcome, it has a far more direct and appropriate constitutional means than to smuggle a highly partisan, policy litmus-test into the judicial confirmation inquiry.

The President has the power of choice in his nomination. Textually, the Senate has unfettered power to deny that choice. But text is necessarily bounded by its historical context. History reveals that the Senate up until the 1980s largely confined its inquiries to integrity, demeanor, competence and subscription to the rule of law. "There will, of course, be no exercise of choice on the part of the Senate," wrote Hamilton in *Federalist* 66. In observing this precept over time, the Senate was observing the designed independence of the judiciary, respecting the democratic will of the people, and abiding by the separation of powers. It certainly was not attempting to escape any allegation of its own policy forfeiture, and to seek to do indirectly that which it has lacked the political courage to do directly.

If the Senate is truly interested in improving the federal judiciary, I respectfully suggest that these hearings would be better devoted to examining judicial method and fidelity to text and legislative purpose, rather than partisanship; in other words, to inquire whether nominees coming before you are willing to abide by the text of the statutory law as you have authored it. Legitimate questions can be asked whether there is a difference between statutory and constitutional interpretation, and how a prospective nominee would address that difference. The Constitution is to "endure for the ages," after all, and statutes often are intended to have a shorter life or a narrower object. But that said, what this body needs to know — especially from lower court nominees — is whether the judicial nominee proposes to observe the intended scope of statutory text given to it by the Congress, or one of his or her own making.

In brief, personal integrity, judicial temperament or demeanor, and learning in the law or competence are the primary indicia for eligibility of judicial service, and underlying them all, must be a sincere commitment to abide by the rule of law. Judicial independence from mean-spirited or shallow political posturing or inquiry is merited because in this country, citizens are still entitled to believe that lawyers called to the bench — and those receiving the confirmation of the Senate — will allow the prospective application of previously and regularly enacted rules to prevail over arbitrary power, even when they may dislike the rule at issue. Nominees should face no obstruction or delay or improper placements of political burdens so long as they believe that all people, rich and poor alike and of whatever race, are to be equally subject to generally applicable law administered by ordinary, regular courts. Yes, the Senate has a duty to inquire whether a nominee subscribes to these age-old precepts of the rule of law, well-summarized to our founders by Blackstone, and traceable to the earliest manifestations of the common law. But this inquiry bears no resemblance to the bumper-sticker like characterizations of whether one nominee or another is conservative or liberal.

If this is so well-settled, why are we invited to reconsider it now? There is little by way of a coherent response that the proponents of a heightened nominee burden of proof give. Some proponents of a reconfigured Senate role, like my friend and constitutional law colleague Laurence Tribe, propose that the ultimate purpose of the questioning is to have a balanced court. With all due respect to Professor Tribe's erudition in matters of constitutional study, a 5-4 court on the most delicate issues of the day is a fairly solid indicator of balance. Perhaps the balance "tilts" slightly to the center-right, rather than the center-left, but there is no real measure of this from term to term. So too, it is recently popular to claim that there aren't enough varieties of experience on the bench — too many former judges, as it were. This characterization, however, slights the lifetime of achievement of the present Court. Ruth Bader Ginsburg had prior appellate judicial experience, but also, led a litigation arm of a very active national organization on gender issues. Several of the justices had executive or administrative experience ([William H.] Rehnquist, Scalia and Thomas); others were teachers (Breyer and [Anthony M.] Kennedy) and still others distinguished practitioners (Stevens).

However, even if balance could be defined, another witness before you today, the distinguished Professor Sanford Levinson, says balance is the entirely wrong inquiry. Professor Levinson urges you to substantively object to the Court's Fourteenth Amendment, Commerce Clause and Eleventh Amendment jurisprudence.

Why does Professor Levinson feel comfortable substituting his view of these issues for those of the present Court, or more relevantly to today's discussion, to the views of the people as represented by the President through the appointment process? Bluntly: because, to quote him, *Bush v. Gore* is "a patently illegitimate decision, . . . monumentally unpersuasive; and . . . its illegitimacy taints Mr. Bush's own status as our President." We owe Professor Levinson a debt of gratitude for his candor, because I believe his remarks are the gravamen of this hearing.

This is not the place to re-argue *Bush v. Gore,* and I won't. However, it is clear that, unlike some academics, the overwhelming percentage of people (and seven justices of the Supreme Court) accept the proposition that equal protection when applied to ballots means at least this: if you're asked to count votes, you have to know what you're counting. When the Florida Supreme Court reflected upon the matter, five of the state justices who had previously ordered the standard-less recount affirmed that "the development of a specific, uniform standard necessary to ensure equal application and to secure the fundamental right to vote throughout the State of Florida should be left to the body we believe best equipped to study and address it, the Legislature."

Respect for the lawmaking enterprise, for legislatures, especially the Congress, is a salutary by-product of the proper exercise of advice and consent. "Limiting the judicial function to interpreting the Constitution guarantees the political branches their legitimate powers, which keeps policymaking in the hands of those who are most accountable to the people. . . . The Senate's power of advice and consent is a broad one, though it is not arbitrary. A fair interpretation of the qualities required of judicial nominees by the Constitution emphasizes legal capacity, personal integrity, and a commitment to abide by the Constitution." Obtaining commitments to abide by favored policy outcomes does not abide the Constitution.

The Senate is rightly desirous to perform its constitutional duty well. But undertaking partisan screening no matter how elegantly dressed in academic language is a default of that duty. As Hamilton explained, "the necessity of [your] concurrence would have a powerful, though, in general a silent operation. It would be an excellent check upon the spirit of favoritism in the President, and would tend greatly to prevent the appointment of unfit characters from state prejudice, from family connection, from personal attachment, or from a view to popularity."

The Senate should not place the burden of proving partisan compatibility upon judicial nominees.

Questions for Discussion

1. How has the confirmation process for Supreme Court nominees changed since the administration of President George Washington?
2. What criteria should be used in selecting a nominee to the Supreme Court? What are the reasons for your answer?
3. Is the Supreme Court a policy-making institution? What are the reasons for your answer?
4. What questions are appropriate to ask Supreme Court nominees? What are the reasons for your answer?
5. How do you account for the fact that some members of the Supreme Court decide cases in a manner that the groups who supported them in the confirmation process find disappointing?

Suggested Resources

Web Sites

Alliance for Justice
   http://www.afj.org

American Bar Association
   http://www.abanet.org/

American Judicature Society
   http//www.ajs.org

Judicial Selection Monitoring Project
   http://www.judicialselection.org

Publications

Abraham, Henry J. *Justices, Presidents, and Senators: A History of the U.S. Supreme Court Appointments from Washington to Clinton*, 4th ed. Lanham, Md.: Rowman & Littlefield, 1999.

Amar, Vikram. "How Do You Think? Ideology and the Judicial Nominee." *Legal Times*, July 9, 2001, pp. 50–51.

Binder, Sarah A. "The Senate as Black Hole: Lessons Learned from the Judicial Appointment Experience." *Brookings Review* 19, no. 2 (Spring 2001): 37–40.

Gerhardt, Michael J. *The Federal Appointments Process: A Constitutional and Historical Analysis.* Durham, N.C.: Duke University Press, 1997.

Gitenstein, Mark. *Matters of Principle: An Insider's Account of America's Rejection of Robert Bork's Nomination to the U.S. Supreme Court.* New York: Simon & Schuster, 1992.

Johnson, Dawn. "Tipping the Scale." *Washington Monthly* 34, nos. 7/8 (July/August 2002): 15–19.

Jost, Kenneth. "Judges and Politics." *CQ Researcher* 11, no. 26 (July 27, 2001): 577–600.

Kahn, Michael A. "The Appointment of a Supreme Court Justice: A Political Process from Beginning to End." *Presidential Studies Quarterly* 25, no. 1 (Winter 1995): 25–41.

Kinsley, Michael. "Borking: A Rule Book." *Washington Post*, October 4, 2002, p. A29.

Maltese, John Anthony. *The Selling of Supreme Court Nominees.* Baltimore: Johns Hopkins University Press, 1995.

Pilon, Roger. "Bench Politics." *Legal Times*, January 21, 2002, pp. 59, 61.

Schultz, Evan P. "The Case for Mudslinging." *Legal Times*, January 21, 2002, pp. 58–59, 61.

Tribe, Laurence H. *God Save This Honorable Court: How the Choice of Supreme Court Justices Shapes Our History.* New York: Random House, 1985.

U.S. Cong., Senate. *Judicial Nomination and Confirmation Process.* Hearing before the Subcommittee on Administrative Oversight and the Courts of the Committee on the Judiciary. 107th Cong., 1st Sess., 2001.

Watson, George, and John A. Stookey. *America: The Politics of Supreme Court Appointments.* New York: HarperCollins College Publishers, 1995.

Yalof, David Alistair. *Pursuit of Justices: Presidential Politics and the Selection of Supreme Court Nominees.* Chicago: University of Chicago Press, 1999.

Is the Bureaucracy
a Threat to Liberty?

When the Constitution was adopted in the late eighteenth century, only a few hundred people were employed by government at the national level. Today, however, there are nearly 2.8 million civilian federal government employees. Millions of other public employees serve in the armed forces and the agencies of state and local governments.

Government has grown remarkably in this century because of its increased activities in foreign affairs, the domestic economy, and welfare. In the late eighteenth century the United States was a small power on the periphery of the world's major powers of Europe. For more than four decades after World War II, it became one of the two strongest military powers, challenged principally by the other superpower, the Soviet Union.

Even after the disintegration of the Soviet Union, the United States was the world's only superpower. The United States still requires the services of large numbers of people in the armed forces. Government, moreover, is engaged in dispensing foreign aid, gathering intelligence information, assisting individuals and groups abroad, and helping to promote international trade.

In addition to the growth of foreign policy activities, domestic factors are responsible for government expansion. Business asks for government assistance to build highways, improve railroads, construct dams, widen waterways, and administer tariffs. It also requests government support for research in energy, transportation, medicine, and military technology. The demands of labor also increase government involvement in the economy. Labor asks for government inspection involving safety at work sites, government supervision of minimum wage laws, and government employment of those who cannot find jobs in the private sector. Labor seeks government protection of unions against the power of business.

Finally, the welfare state contributes to government growth. Individuals and groups demand government help to provide health care, Social Security, housing, and education. All these goals require programs that are administered by government, and that administration is the bureaucracy.

Big government has long been criticized. In the election of 1976, for example, Jimmy Carter ran under a campaign promise to reduce the size of the federal government. Ronald Reagan became even more identified than Carter with such a reduction. He tried to reduce the size and budget of the federal government but failed to do so. Antigovernment rhetoric is often a common feature in American political life.

In his 1996 State of the Union address, President Bill Clinton acknowledged that "the era of big government is over." His next sentence added a qualifier, however: "But we cannot go back to the time when our citizens were left to fend for themselves."[1] Whether the scope of the federal government should be reduced is still a matter of debate. Many people are opposed to big government, with its vast bureaucracy, in the abstract, but not to a reduction in services that benefit them as individuals in particular. Polls show much support for Social Security, Medicare, and environmental protection, for example.

Jacob G. Hornberger, president of the Future of Freedom Foundation, regards bureaucracy as a threat to liberty. He contends:

1. At the time of the adoption of the U.S. Constitution, Americans wanted limited government because they believed that the preservation of the individual — "and the freedom to live his life and dispose of his personal wealth as he chose" — was the highest political end. Government's sole purpose was to assist in the achievement of this end.
2. Americans today have abandoned this early view and believe in the preservation of the political bureaucracy and its unlimited power to control the lives and wealth of the citizenry. Politicians and bureaucrats see the citizenry as a means to ensure the preservation of the bureaucracy.
3. Government bureaucracies are inherently inefficient, corrupt, and power hungry, and power should be returned to the people.

Ellsworth Barnard, a retired professor of English at the University of Massachusetts at Amherst, defends government and bureaucracies — particularly at the federal government level — against their critics. He contends:

1. In order to have individual liberty and a just society, limited government is necessary.
2. The technological revolution that we live in requires national governmental involvement.
3. Government involvement is needed to keep in check the evils of the market economy.
4. The purpose of government regulations is to protect individual citizens from exploitation by a powerful minority who insist, and perhaps believe, that the market must operate without restraint, and that greed is good.

5. While it is true that the federal bureaucracy is sometimes cumbersome, the failings of the federal government are immeasurably outweighed by the benefits that it confers.
6. Taxes are not evil. Without taxes, an organized society cannot exist.

NOTES

1. President Bill Clinton, State of the Union Address, January 23, 1996, transcript.

☑ YES

Is the Bureaucracy a Threat to Liberty?

JACOB G. HORNBERGER
The Preservation of the Bureaucracy

Two hundred years ago, our American ancestors instituted the most unusual political system in history. The Constitution called into existence a government whose powers, for the first time ever, were extremely limited. Thus, unlike other people throughout history, Americans lived without such things as income taxation, welfare, licensure, immigration control, business regulation, drug laws, conscription, and passports. Generally, and with exceptions (slavery and tariffs being the most notable), laws were limited to protecting people from the violence and fraud of others.

What caused these Americans to institute this strange and novel way of life? The answer lies in the way our American ancestors perceived the relationship between the individual in society and his government. Americans of that time believed that the preservation of the individual — and the freedom to live his life and dispose of his wealth as he chose — was the highest political end. Thus, for them, government's sole purpose was to assist in the achievement of this end. Government officials were viewed as servants, and only as servants, to ensure the preservation of the individual, the freedom to live his life, and to dispose of his wealth, as he saw fit.

Although Americans of today operate under the delusion that they subscribe to the same value structure as their ancestors, the uncomfortable reality is that they have instead rejected and abandoned it. Although they will rarely admit it to themselves or others, Americans today honestly believe that the supreme end in American society is not the preservation of the individual and his freedom to choose, but rather the preservation of the political bureaucracy and its unlimited power to control the lives and wealth of the citizenry.

How do the politicians and bureaucrats, in turn, perceive the citizenry? Paying lip service to their role as "public servants," especially at election time, public officials, in reality, scoff at any such notion. In their eyes, the citizens are means, not ends, who exist solely to ensure the preservation of the bureaucracy.

This philosophical perspective — that the citizen is merely a "cog in the wheel" which can, and will, be sacrificed for the greater good of the bureaucracy — holds true, of course, with the civil bureaucracy. Usually under the guise of fighting some domestic "war," or attacking some "crisis" — poverty, drugs, illiteracy, racism, or whatever — the civil bureaucracy exercises ever-increasing control over the lives and wealth of the citizenry.

But the same holds true with the military bureaucracy. No matter what the conditions are in the world — even if peace were to break out everywhere — even if democracies were suddenly found in every nation on earth — even if American politicians and bureaucrats appointed every ruler in the world — in the mind of the military bureaucrat, crises and wars will always be a "potential threat" to "national security." And so the military bureaucracy also wields ever-increasing control over the lives and wealth of the citizenry.

All money which government has, of course, comes from the citizenry through the coercive process of taxation. Government officials understand that, in this sense, they are parasitic — that is, that they survive and flourish through the earnings that are sucked out of the pockets of the citizens. They comprehend, for example, that if the citizenry suddenly decided to stop paying taxes, the bureaucracy's lifeline would, at the same time, dry up.

The bureaucracy recognizes that, since it is a parasite, it must perform a masterful balancing act. On the one hand, it must ensure that the citizenry continue paying taxes at such a level that the bureaucracy is preserved, and hopefully expanded. But it must also ensure that the level of confiscation and plunder never gets so high that the worst fear of the bureaucracy — a tax revolt among the citizenry — materializes.

Now, the intriguing question is: if the American people decided that their ancestors were right, and that 20th-century Americans are wrong — that is, that the preservation of the individual and his freedom to choose should, in fact, be the end, and the government simply the means to ensure that end — would the politicians and bureaucrats comply with the decision of the citizenry?

The answer is in doubt. Why? Because those in the bureaucracy honestly believe that they, not the citizenry, are "the country"; that is, they actually think that the nation, and the well-being of the nation, depend on their preservation. The dismantling of the bureaucracy, in their minds, would mean the destruction of the country. Therefore, it is entirely possible that, in the midst of what the politicians and bureaucrats would consider a "national crisis," they would refuse to comply with a mandate of the citizenry to dismantle the bureaucracy and end the taxation necessary for its preservation.

One of these days, the American people will discover, much to their surprise and dismay, that which the Soviet citizens are discovering: that the bureaucracy will always tolerate the citizens' "freedom of speech" to complain about bureaucratic abuses and inefficiencies; but as soon as the bureaucracy is threatened by the citizenry with extinction, it will fight them "tooth and nail" for its "right" to be preserved.

Complaints about governmental inefficiencies and corruption have become a well-recognized and accepted part of American life: "We must get rid of waste in government programs"; "We must get 'better people' into public office." So, attempting to "correct the system" by gaining political power over their fellow citizens, Americans expend much time, money, and effort to get themselves, or their friends, elected or appointed to public office. And the results? Even when victorious, they learn that things only get worse: expanded control, greater plunder, increased waste, and more corruption — only this time by them and their friends, rather than by others.

Americans must finally come to the painful realization that their ancestors were philosophically correct: that the taking of money from one person, through the political process, in order to give it to another person is evil, immoral, and destructive; and that political interference with how a person chooses to peacefully live his life, and dispose of his wealth, is equally evil, immoral, and destructive.

Moreover, Americans must finally conclude, as painful as it may be, that waste in government programs (actually somebody's income), no matter how great an effort is expended, is impossible to eliminate. Evil and immorality, even if democratically enshrined, cannot be made to work efficiently.

And they must learn that getting "better people" into public office is not the solution either. One does not change the nature of a house of prostitution by voting in a new board of directors. And that is exactly what the American people of this century have permitted their government to become — a house of prostitution in which, for example, the principles receive "campaign contributions" and "speakers' honoraria" for "services rendered." Of course, some people, and especially those who were taught civics in their public schools and who were required to pledge allegiance every day for twelve long years, will consider this observation to be highly unpatriotic. But if it be unpatriotic to oppose a house of prostitution where once stood a great and glorious edifice, then make the most of it!

No, the answer is not to engage in a futile quest to eliminate waste in government programs. The solution is to constitutionally prohibit the programs themselves. No, the answer is not to get "better people" into public office. The solution is to constitutionally prohibit public officials, whoever they may be, from plundering the citizenry and doling out money to others. No, the answer is not to rein in the bureaucrats. The solution is to dismantle the bureaucracy and return the bureaucrats, kicking and screaming, to rewarding and productive lives as private citizens. No, the answer is not tax reform. The solution is the repeal of the Sixteenth Amendment.

In other words, the solution for America, as we enter the third century of this nation's existence, lies with the American people's recapturing the principles on which our nation was founded and limiting the power of government even more severely than our ancestors did. Not only would this restore our political system to a sound moral foundation and our society to one based on volunteerism rather than coercion, it would also unleash an economic prosperity unparalleled in history.

But the heart of the solution is to make the individual in society once again sovereign over the state. Until the American people make the preservation of the individual, as well as his liberty and property, the highest political end, they will continue living their lives in subserviency to what has been the highest political end in the 20th century: the preservation of the bureaucracy and the discord, misery, impoverishment, and destruction which it has brought in its wake.

☑ N O

Is the Bureaucracy a Threat to Liberty?

ELLSWORTH BARNARD
In Defense of Government

The greatest obstacle to America's progress toward a stable society, unplagued by social ills, is not crime or drugs or a decline in family values, but, instead, a growing hostility toward government, and particularly the federal government. The demented persons who blow up public buildings, assault the guardians of public lands, and form "militias" to oppose an imagined threat of involuntary servitude to the federal government — these are symbols of a crumbling faith among even ordinary citizens in the institutions whereby they are governed. The vociferous condemnation of government regulations; the ease with which public opinion was swayed by unprincipled propaganda against the Clinton plan for universal health insurance; the widespread sentiment for abandoning the public schools instead of improving them; the drive toward privatization of public services — these are among the phenomena that reveal a rampant distrust of "government."

Of course, rugged individualism has always been a theme in America's prideful thinking about itself. But the Great Depression compelled the country to realize that there are situations in which individual effort counts for nothing, when even the most resolutely self-reliant must reach for the helping hand of government. The ensuing onset of World War II reversed the situation, demanding the subordination of personal goals to the national need. But both crises enhanced the public perception of the necessity of a strong central government. And this mental stance was sustained by the deep-rooted fear of communism that gave birth to and continued the Cold War.

The real war in Vietnam, however, and what eventually came to be recognized as its senseless bloodshed, delivered a telling blow to the public's faith in the federal government. And what remained was further diminished by the forced resignation, unique in American history, of both a vice president and a president for having betrayed the public trust.

On the other hand, the immense personal popularity of President [Ronald] Reagan lent authority to his professed policy of "down-sizing" the federal government, based on the unquestioned assumption that the satisfaction of the desires of private persons takes precedence over the "general welfare" that it is the stated purpose of the Constitution to "promote." The resonant admonition of John F.

Kennedy — "Ask not what your country can do for you, ask what you can do for your country" — no longer echoed in the national consciousness. Moreover, the collapse of the Soviet Union freed the country from its obsessive fear of communism; and the general national prosperity erased any serious anxiety about an impending economic crisis.

The result of all this was not only a lessened trust in the federal government but also the perception of a lessened need. And from this state of mind it was only a short step to outright hostility to some undefined entity called "government," as being self-serving and incompetent, wasting "taxpayers' hard-earned dollars" on activities that, if really needed, could be better performed by the "private sector"; and, beyond this, intruding arbitrarily into the affairs of business. Government does not, it is confidently asserted, offer solutions to people's problems; it is itself the problem.

The assumption here, admirable in itself, and not less so because it clashes with most of human history, is that the proper goal of any form of social organization is the greatest possible freedom for the individual. But this freedom is, and must be, limited. What the critics of government do not see is that the relation must be reciprocal. It has never occurred to them, for instance, while vehemently asserting their right to do what they like with what is theirs, that the very concept of "private property" could not exist without some kind of government. "Ownership" means that the government has recognized and agreed to protect whatever possessions have been legally acquired. Without this guaranteed right of ownership, a person would have to defend by force everything that he calls his, in accordance with what the satirical rhyme calls:

> Nature's good old plan
> That he shall take who has the power,
> And he shall keep who can.

There would then be a genuine justification for "the right to bear arms."

It follows that since government confers the right to own property, it has at least a limited right to say how that property shall be used. If draining a wetland or clearcutting a forest area is judged to be harmful to the community as a whole, no one can rationally deny that the government has a right to prohibit such activity.

And the need to subordinate individual goals to the welfare of the group is strengthened by the technological revolution that is now taking place with astounding speed. Advances in transportation; even greater — indeed, almost miraculous — expansion of means of communication; the movement toward mergers in every area of economic activity, and the consequent vast increase in corporate power; the many motives and incentives to the geographical mobility of the population; the pressures of globalization on the perceived national interest — all these changes, irresistible and irreversible, give rise to forces that state governments are helpless to control, and whose guidance demands a national effort. Economic security, higher educational standards, the control of crime, universal access to effective health care, the preservation of the national environment — these call for a national consensus in regard to attributes and actions, to values and their implementation.

The notion that "the age of big government is over" is a delusion. Nevertheless, many persons cling to the view that, where there is a question of state or federal jurisdiction, it is the former that will best serve society's needs. And in this attitude they are following a long tradition of "states' rights" as a preferable alternative to federal authority. It is the contention of this essay, however, that this attitude is, and always has been, an impediment to progress toward the proclaimed national goal of "liberty and justice for all."

To begin with, the Constitution itself arose from the obvious need for a strong central government. The Articles of Confederation, which were the first attempt to achieve a formal and permanent union among the colonies, were shaped by the recollection of British tyranny and the fear that a strong new government might likewise trample on the painfully won freedom of states and individuals. (The Declaration of Independence speaks of "free and independent states.") Hence, there was no central executive or judiciary, and only a weak one-chamber legislative body, in which each state had one vote, and nine votes out of 13 were necessary to pass legislation — which there was no instrument to enforce. The Articles conferred no power to tax, or to regulate commerce among the states.

The inevitable result was that the new nation began to fall apart, and the conservative forces that were dominant agreed on a new Constitution that gave the central government sweeping powers to establish and maintain a unified and orderly society; while acknowledging the fears of those in whom the spirit of rebellion was still strong by setting up a system of checks and balances between the executive and legislative branches (the power of the judicial branch had yet to be asserted and accepted), and by framing a "Bill of Rights," namely, the first 10 amendments to the Constitution.

The states' rights principle, however, did not die. But whereas it was originally libertarian in spirit, it became and has remained an instrument for defending the status quo and an excuse for opposing every effort to protect and extend the basic rights of individual persons. The Southern side in the Civil War asserted that the main issue was not slavery but states' rights, and even so high-minded a person as Robert E. Lee placed loyalty to his state above loyalty to his country. Moreover, for a century after the war, the same principle supplied a facade for the denial of even the most basic human rights to the former slaves and their descendants. Federal anti-lynching laws were rejected as an unjustified usurpation of state authority, with the result that blacks could still be murdered with impunity. Likewise, the South attempted to find in this doctrine a legal defense of its continuing discrimination against blacks in every area of society. And today, as racism slowly and grudgingly dies, the principle is asserted in support of the efforts of ideological groups to impose their religious beliefs and ethical systems on those in whom conscience decrees a different creed and code. It inspires attacks on national standards in education, and tries to force the use of school textbooks that present myth as truth and faith as fact. Likewise, anti-abortionists try by the use of state statutes to limit women's constitutional right to reproductive freedom.

So much for states' rights. Another and still more powerful instance of anti-government ideology is the belief in the inevitability and desirability of a laissez-faire,

or, more euphemistically, a "freemarket" economy, in which government intervention is not merely futile but harmful. Arguments concerning the validity of this
concept have filled libraries, and cannot be repeated here. But in practice its
apostles have found it more expedient to appeal to process rather than principle.
Hence the constant complaints about the "federal bureaucracy," which is accused
of ignoring the urgent appeals of business for relief from the "regulations" that are
said to strangle individual initiative and obstruct the economic progress that
would otherwise be achieved.

As for social problems, it is argued that "Washington's" attempts to deal with
these, though sometimes grudgingly granted to be well intentioned, are often misguided because of a "one-size-fits-all" procedure, and unfamiliarity with local
conditions, which vary from region to region and state to state; whereas, state governments are more familiar with local problems and more responsive to local
needs. In short, they know better how to spend the "people's money."

In particular instances this view is valid. But as a general rule, it does not square
with reality. Whatever shortcomings may be ascribed to federal officials, these are
present in greater measure in those who handle the affairs of the separate states.
Though as individuals they may not possess less intelligence or lower moral standards than those who walk the halls of power in Washington, they are in the
nature of things more limited in their outlook and more easily swayed by powerful
"special interests." Their very closeness to those who elect them — and finance
their election campaigns — makes it harder for them to view an issue objectively
and act dispassionately for the public good.

On the other hand, Washington's relative remoteness from the heat and turmoil
of local politics, together with pressure from colleagues who represent different
states and different interests, opens to a member of Congress a clearer view of a
wider reality. To apply a trite metaphor, state legislators see only the trees, while
members of Congress are in a position to view the forest.

This, however, is only one aspect of the main issue, namely, whether "government" is the enemy or the friend of "the people." And only the unthinking can
favor the first alternative. The persons who rail against "the government in Washington" have simply taken for granted the benefits which that government supplies. Whizzing along an interstate highway, we forget that some agency had to
build it and pay for it. Buying food in a supermarket, we do not worry — except for
an occasional flurry about a particular item — about its being contaminated, or
consider who is responsible for its purity. Likewise, when taking drugs to preserve
our physical well-being, we do not question the basis of our confidence that there
will be no harmful side effects. Or, when we make a bank deposit or buy stocks,
we assume that the banker or broker can be trusted, forgetting the lesson of experience that some persons and corporations need an incentive to be honest,
namely, government oversight.

Or, passing from the realm of commerce to that in which we seek other than
material goods, we forget while enjoying the splendors of our national parks that
but for the foresight of the federal government, these natural wonders would have
been exploited purely for private profit; that Old Faithful would be surrounded by

fast food outlets and motels, with a gambling casino close by for those on whom the beauties of nature quickly pall.

And of course millions of retired persons wait with perfect confidence (not unaware of the need for prudence concerning the distant future) for the unfailing arrival of the Social Security payment that for many is their only defense against destitution.

On the other hand, taking a negative point of view, we should not ignore the thousands of workers who die each year, and the tens of thousands who suffer, from work-related accidents and illnesses that could be avoided if Congress were willing to pass stricter regulations (that obscene r-word), or the executive branch were to enforce more vigorously those that exist.

In short, we should reject the myth that government regulations are an arbitrary punishment imposed by an alien entity on a defenseless public, and recognize that their true purpose is to protect ordinary citizens from exploitation by a powerful minority who insist, and perhaps believe, that "the market" must operate without restraint, and that greed is good. Against this myth we must affirm that in a democracy, by definition, government is the people's friend.

It is true that the federal bureaucracy (another term of ill repute, though it is only a name for the mechanism of management involved in any operation, public or private) is sometimes unduly cumbersome; that small businesses, in particular, can sometimes justifiably complain of needless "paperwork"; and that government agencies, free from competitive pressure, are sometimes wasteful in spending public money, as well as unresponsive to the wishes and needs of ordinary citizens. But such faults and failings of the federal government are immeasurably outweighed by the benefits that it confers.

The foregoing factors, however — belief in states' rights, faith in a free market economy, government inefficiency — only partially explain the public's antipathy, not only to the federal government but to government in general. What most strongly sparks resentment among all ranks of the American people, overshadows their other grievances, real or fancied, and in their imagination presents government — all government — in the guise of an ogre, is taxes. Nothing is certain, opines the cynic, but death and taxes, and in the popular view they are equally unpleasant. Candidates for public office quail at the thought of being charged with the intent to "tax and spend," and the first requirement in the quest, offered early and often, is a promise to cut taxes. The assumption is that among all voters, of whatever political persuasion, there exists an ingrained conviction that taxes are always and essentially an evil — a sort of black hole into which people's money is forever being poured but which nothing ever comes out of. They are a needless burden that citizens should not be asked to bear. In the phrase "tax burden," indeed, the two words are invariably treated as a unit, uttered as automatically and matter-of-factly as the "morning mail," but always carrying a subliminal suggestion of undeserved injury.

This pervasive sentiment, however, exists in defiance of reason and reality. Without taxes, organized society could not exist. Paying taxes is no more a "burden" than paying for gasoline or groceries. Only, instead of buying things, we buy services — roads and schools and law enforcement and fire protection and vital records and — on the federal level — military security, and all the other benefits that we enjoy as members of a civilized society. It is, in fact, only the ineducable who, if they stop to think, will refuse assent to at least the second part of the famous avowal of former Supreme Court Justice Oliver Wendell Holmes, "I like to pay taxes. With them I buy civilization."

There are only three questions concerning taxes that make sense. First, how many and what services — how much civilization — do we wish to buy? Second, is the system of allocating taxes fair? Third, is the money efficiently spent? To say that taxes are "too high," or that we "cannot afford" a certain level, is meaningless. The issue is simply one of priorities. We can always afford something if we want it badly enough. And when we say that we cannot afford a particular public service, what we are really saying is that we prefer to spend the money to satisfy our private wants.

Politicians flatter prospective voters by telling them, "You can spend your money better than the government can." This is a comfortable thought for middle-class Americans. But is it true? Is it better that a household should have a TV in every room than that the owner should be taxed so that those less fortunate can have housing that is habitable? Can parents justify buying their children costly electronic games to provide them with mindless pleasure, while other children in ghetto schools are denied decent textbooks because cities "cannot afford" them? Is money spent at a gambling casino a better investment than if it were spent to provide adequate health care for those to whom such care is not a choice, those who are not poor enough to be eligible for Medicaid but for whom private health insurance is hopelessly beyond their reach? Or is money spent simply to make more money better spent than if it were spent by government to provide, let us say, a clean environment?

These are questions that most Americans do not ask. Consequently, they are able to think of "government" as an entity apart from themselves, as the antagonist in an us-against-them relationship. But in a real democracy such a state of things cannot exist. In the immortal words of Walt Kelly's *Pogo*: "We have met the enemy and he is us." We get the government that we deserve. We elect the people who make the laws, and if we do not like the laws they make, or if they do not make the laws we think they should, we can always "throw the rascals out." If we really cared, for instance, about congressional campaign finance reform, we would demand that members of Congress take action or be replaced by those who will. For better or worse, "the government" and "the people" are one and the same.

Is this a cause for hope or for despair? The thesis of this essay, as stated at the beginning, is that the widespread distrust of government in general and the federal government in particular stands in the way of a stable and orderly and — allowing for human weakness — just society. But if the public itself is responsible for government in all its aspects, including those against which its members so vociferously rebel, can there be any hope of improvement? Are we not lost in a maze from which there is no exit?

The answer is twofold. First, if we really believe in democracy, defined (can we agree?) as acceptance of a set of mutual obligations between the individual and the community, must we not also believe that the majority of Americans are persons of good will? That this is a matter of faith, affirmed in defiance of the daily news as recorded in the media, is difficult to deny. But what is the alternative? And does it not follow that this majority, when it engages in behavior that reason must decry as socially destructive, does so out of ignorance and confusion rather than with evil intent?

The second saving article of faith is that this majority, though liable to temporary error, can in the long run learn and change. Not the least of the reasons for the lasting life of the U.S. Constitution, unique in history, is the provision for amendments to meet the needs arising out of changes inevitably unforeseen, while not succumbing too easily to demands for unessential changes, however popular for the moment.

Granted this hopeful outlook toward the future, can we tentatively envision the wished-for shape of things to come: a conscious recognition and acceptance of the interdependence of the individual and the community, affirming as its goal the realization of the individual's complete potential, while acknowledging that such realization can only be achieved within a community; accepting as absolute one of the great insights of Christianity, namely, that "no man liveth unto himself alone"?

It should, but must not, go without saying that acceptance of such a union must be free. History is strewn with the wreckage of systems, admirable in themselves, whose advocates failed to see the folly of trying to implement them by force. It may seem, in contrast, that in this instance the vision is so alluring as to be self-fulfilling. But we are human beings; and, while rejecting the perverse notion that we are the automatic heirs of Adam's sin, we cannot deny what experience teaches, that we enter the world accompanied by some innate resistance — perhaps born of our evolutionary struggle for existence — to anything that looks like self-surrender, and that we need some external guidance toward the common goal.

Perhaps we can find it in the words of Thomas Jefferson concerning the "inalienable rights" — "life, liberty, and the pursuit of happiness" — with which we are "endowed": and that "to secure these rights, **governments** [emphasis added] are instituted among men."

Questions for Discussion

1. What effect would the dismantling of big government have on society in such matters as the economy, environment, health, welfare, education, and national security?
2. Which groups benefit and which groups are hurt by government bureaucracy?
3. How can waste in government be reduced?
4. What is the impact of democracy on bureaucracy?
5. What is the relationship between liberty and bureaucracy?

Suggested Resources

Web Sites

Citizens against Government Waste
  http://www.cagw.org/site/PageServer

Council for Excellence in Government
  http://excelgov.xigroup.com/

Federal Gateway
  http://www.fedgate.org/

National Academy of Public Administration
  http://www.napawash.org/

National Taxpayers Union and NTU Foundation
  http://www.ntu.org/

Office of Personnel Management
  http://www.opm.gov/

Publications

Browne, Harry. *Why Government Doesn't Work.* New York: St. Martin's Press, 1995.

DeMuth, Christopher C. "Why the Era of Big Government Isn't Over." *Commentary* 109, no. 4 (April 2000): 23–29.

Dionne, E. J., Jr. "'Political Hacks' v. Bureaucrats: Can't Public Servants Get Some Respect?" *Brookings Review* 19, no. 2 (Spring 2001): 8–11.

Gawthrop, Louis C. *Public Service and Democracy: Ethical Imperatives for the 21st Century.* New York: Chatham House, 1998.

Goodsell, Charles T. *The Case for Bureaucracy: A Public Administration Polemic,* 3d ed. Chatham, N.J.: Chatham House, 1994.

Hibbing, John R., and Elizabeth Theiss-Morse, eds. *What Is It about Government That Americans Dislike?* New York: Cambridge University Press, 2001.

Holzer, Marc, ed. *Public Service: Callings, Commitments, and Constraints.* Boulder, Colo.: Westview Press, 2000.

Kaufman, Herbert. "Major Players: Bureaucracies in American Government." *Public Administration Review* 61, no. 1 (January 2001): 18–42.

Kettl, Donald F. *The Transformation of Governance: Public Administration for Twenty-First Century Americans.* Baltimore: Johns Hopkins University Press, 2002.

Milakovich, Michael E., and George J. Gordon. *Public Administration,* 7th ed. Boston: Bedford/St. Martin's, 2001.

Orlans, Harold. "Enduring Bureaucracy." *Dissent* 48, no. 3 (Summer 2001): 62–69.

Rosen, Bernard. *Holding Government Bureaucracies Accountable,* 3d ed. Westport, Conn.: Praeger, 1998.

Weisberg, Jacob. *In Defense of Government: The Fall and Rise of Government Trust.* New York: Scribner's, 1996.

Williams, Walter E. *More Liberty Means Less Government: Our Founders Knew This Well.* Stanford, Calif.: Hoover Institution Press, 1999.

Should the Supreme Court Abide by a Strict Constructionist Philosophy?

Of the three branches of the federal government — president, Congress, and the Supreme Court — the last is the least democratic. Although representative democracy requires periodic elections, the members of the Supreme Court are appointed, never run for office in popular elections, and once on the Court, usually remain there for life or until they retire. Presidents, senators, and representatives may envy the justices' luxury of not having to run for public office.

The Supreme Court's power of judicial review is — at least on the surface — another undemocratic feature of this arm of government. Judicial review is the power of the Supreme Court to examine state and federal laws and the acts of state and federal public officials to determine whether they are in conflict with the Constitution. If these laws and acts are in conflict, then the court may declare them invalid. The fact that a majority of nine unelected members of the Court may declare null and void the laws enacted by the representatives of the majority of the people who vote seems to be a limitation on the principle of majority rule. The argument is often made, however, that the specific content of court decisions has strengthened rather than weakened democracy.

Judicial review is not the practice in all representative democracies. The British system of government, for example, permits the courts to interpret the laws but not to declare an act of Parliament void. Judicial review is not specifically mentioned in the Constitution of the United States. Debate surrounds the question of whether the Framers intended the Supreme Court to have this power over the laws of the federal government. There is general agreement, however, that the Framers understood that judicial review is applicable to acts of state legislatures in conflict with the Constitution. The Supreme Court first declared an act of Congress unconstitutional in *Marbury v. Madison* (1803). In this case the court found the Judiciary Act of 1789 to be in conflict with Article III of the Constitution.[1] Today the Supreme Court's authority to declare a statute unconstitutional is unchallenged.

Over the past century the Supreme Court has exercised its power of judicial review in a variety of cases. Those who have benefited from the Court's decisions have hailed the wisdom of the Court. The "losers" have called for a variety of responses, including limiting the jurisdiction of the Court, amending the Constitution, enlarging the size of the Court, or impeaching the chief justice.

Court decisions have not supported one group of people exclusively. In the early part of the twentieth century, for example, Court decisions were more favorable to big business, states' rights advocates, and segregationists. Since the days of the Warren Court (for former Chief Justice Earl Warren) in the mid-1950s, however, Court decisions have been more favorable to groups demanding extension of civil rights and civil liberties. The changing character of Supreme Court decisions is a reflection of such factors as the composition of the Court, legal precedents, and the political environment. One other factor that has received much attention, however, is the philosophical outlook of the judges.

Two principal philosophical outlooks have guided judicial decision making, and they are always in conflict. As we saw in Chapter 1, William Bradford Reynolds held the intentions of the Framers of the Constitution in the highest regard, while Thurgood Marshall argued that the wisdom of the Constitution lies in its adaptability to changing social needs. Strict constructionists, like Reynolds, believe that the Supreme Court should be bound by the intent of the Framers and the language in the document itself. Loose constructionists argue that strict constructionism is misconceived, impossible, or even fraudulent. At various times in U.S. history, conservatives have supported strict constructionism, but liberals, too, at times, have taken a similar philosophical approach.

The debate below elicits the main arguments of the contending schools. Federal appeals court judge J. Clifford Wallace makes a case for interpretivism — the principle that judges, in resolving constitutional questions, should rely on the express provisions of the Constitution or upon those norms that are clearly implicit in its text. He contends:

1. The Constitution itself envisions and requires interpretivist review.
2. Interpretivist review promotes the stability and predictability essential to the rule of law.
3. Judges are not particularly well suited to make judgments of broad social policy.
4. The argument put forward by noninterpretivists that certain constitutional provisions invite justices to use value judgments outside the Constitution is invalid.
5. Although the Framers' intent cannot be ascertained on every issue, interpretivism will exclude from consideration entire ranges of improper judicial responses.
6. The Fourteenth Amendment did not produce so fundamental a revision in the nature of U.S. government that the intentions of the Framers are scarcely relevant any longer.
7. The Constitution can still be changed by the only legitimate means for which it provides: formal amendment.

8. When noninterpretivists justify their actions on the basis of "doing justice," they act improperly because they are incapable of deciding what is just.
9. An activist judiciary undermines the very principles of democracy.
10. An interpretivist view shows respect for precedent.

Law professor Jeffrey M. Shaman takes the negative position on the issue. He contends:

1. History shows that whenever the Supreme Court makes a decision that someone does not like, the justices are accused of holding to their own personal views and not to the words of the Constitution or the intent of the Framers.
2. From its early history, the Supreme Court has had to go outside the written Constitution and the intent of the Framers in making some decisions.
3. The Court often must create meaning for the Constitution because the document is rife with general and abstract language.
4. There is no reason to pay greater attention to the intent of the Framers than to that of the people who ratified the Constitution or to the succeeding generations who retain it.
5. The intent of the Framers is difficult to discern.
6. The conditions that shaped the Framers' attitudes have changed in two centuries of constitutional experience.
7. The Constitution provides only the bare bones; its meaning must be augmented by the justices.
8. The Court is subject to popular constraints that keep its power limited.

NOTE

1. *Marbury v. Madison*, 5 U.S. (1 Cranch) 137 (1803).

 ☑ *YES*

Should the Supreme Court Abide by
a Strict Constructionist Philosophy?

J. CLIFFORD WALLACE
The Case for Judicial Restraint

This year [1987] we celebrate the 200th anniversary of our Constitution. This remarkable document has structured our government and secured our liberty as we have developed from 13 fledgling colonies into a mature and strong democracy. Without doubt, the Constitution is one of the grandest political achievements of the modern world.

In spite of this marvelous record, we will celebrate our nation's charter in the midst of a hotly contested debate on the continuing role that it should have in our society. Two schools of constitutional jurisprudence are engaged in a long-running battle. Some contend that the outcome of this conflict may well determine whether the Constitution remains our vital organic document or whether it instead becomes a curious historical relic. The competing positions in this constitutional battle are often summarized by a variety of labels: judicial restraint versus judicial activism, strict construction versus loose construction, positivism versus natural law, conservative versus liberal, interpretivism versus noninterpretivism.

In large measure, these labels alone are of little assistance in analyzing a complex problem. Ultimately, what is at stake is what Constitution will govern this country. Will it be the written document drafted by the Framers, ratified by the people, and passed down, with amendments, to us? Or will it be an illusive parchment upon which modern-day judges may freely engrave their own political and sociological preferences?

In this article, I intend to outline and defend a constitutional jurisprudence of judicial restraint.[1] My primary thesis is that a key principle of judicial restraint — namely, interpretivism — is required by our constitutional plan. I will also explore how practitioners of judicial restraint should resolve the tension that can arise in our current state of constitutional law between interpretivism and a second important principle, respect for judicial precedent.

INTERPRETIVISM VERSUS NONINTERPRETIVISM

What is the difference between "interpretivism" and "noninterpretivism"? This question is important because I believe interpretivism to be the cornerstone of a constitutional jurisprudence of judicial restraint. By "interpretivism," I mean the principle that judges, in resolving constitutional questions, should rely on the express provisions of the Constitution or upon those norms that are clearly implicit in its text.[2] Under an interpretivist approach, the original intention of the Framers is the controlling guide for constitutional interpretation. This does not mean, of course, that judges may apply a constitutional provision only to situations specifically contemplated by the Framers. Rather, it simply requires that when considering whether to invalidate the work of the political branches, the judges do so from a starting point fairly discoverable in the Constitution.[3] By contrast, under noninterpretive review, judges may freely rest their decisions on value judgments that admittedly are not supported by, and may even contravene, the text of the Constitution and the intent of the Framers.[4]

Interpretivist Review

I believe that the Constitution itself envisions and requires interpretivist review. To explore this thesis, we should first examine the Constitution as a political and historical document.

As people read the Constitution, many are struck by how procedural and technical its provisions are. Perhaps on first reading it may be something of a disappointment. In contrast to the fiery eloquence of the Declaration of Independence, the Constitution may seem dry or even dull. This difference in style, of course, reflects the very different functions of the two documents. The Declaration of Independence is an indictment of the reign of King George III. In a flamboyant tone, it is brilliantly crafted to persuade the world of the justice of our fight for independence. The Constitution, by contrast, establishes the basic set of rules for the nation. Its genius lies deeper, in its skillful design of a government structure that would best ensure liberty and democracy.

The primary mechanism by which the Constitution aims to protect liberty and democracy is the dispersion of government power. Recognizing that concentrated power poses the threat of tyranny, the Framers divided authority between the states and the federal government. In addition, they created three separate and co-equal branches of the federal government in a system of checks and balances.

The Framers were also aware, of course, that liberty and democracy can come into conflict. The Constitution, therefore, strikes a careful balance between democratic rule and minority rights. Its republican, representative features are designed to channel and refine cruder majoritarian impulses. In addition, the Constitution's specific individual protections, particularly in the Bill of Rights, guarantee against certain majority intrusions. Beyond these guarantees, the Constitution places its trust in the democratic process — the voice of the people expressed through their freely elected representatives.

Raoul Berger argues persuasively in *Government by Judiciary* that the Constitution "was written against a background of interpretive presuppositions that assured the Framers their design would be effectuated."[5] The importance of that statement may escape us today, when it is easy to take for granted that the Constitution is a written document. But for the Framers, the fact that the Constitution was in writing was not merely incidental. They recognized that a written constitution provides the most stable basis for the rule of law, upon which liberty and justice ultimately depend.

As Thomas Jefferson observed, "Our peculiar security is in the possession of a written constitution. Let us not make it a blank paper by construction."[6] Chief Justice John Marshall, in *Marbury v. Madison,* the very case establishing the power of judicial review, emphasized the constraints imposed by the written text and the judicial duty to respect these constraints in all cases raising constitutional questions.[7]

Moreover, the Framers recognized the importance of interpreting the Constitution according to their original intent. In Madison's words, if "the sense in which the Constitution was accepted and ratified by the Nation . . . be not the guide in expounding it, there can be no security for a consistent and stable government, [nor] for a fruitful exercise of its powers."[8] Similarly, Jefferson as President acknowledged his duty to administer the Constitution "according to the safe and honest meaning contemplated by the plain understanding of the people at the time of its adoption — a meaning to be found in the explanations of those who advocated . . . it."[9] It seems clear, therefore, that the leading Framers were interpretivists and believed that constitutional questions should be reviewed by that approach.

Next, I would like to consider whether interpretivism is necessary to effectuate the constitutional plan. The essential starting point is that the Constitution established a separation of powers to protect our freedom. Because freedom is fundamental, so too is the separation of powers. But separation of powers becomes a meaningless slogan if judges may confer constitutional status on whichever rights they happen to deem important, regardless of textual basis. In effect, under noninterpretive review, the judiciary functions as a superlegislature beyond the check of the other two branches. Noninterpretivist review also disregards the Constitution's careful allocation of most decisions to the democratic process, allowing the legislature to make decisions deemed best for society. Ultimately, noninterpretivist review reduces our written Constitution to insignificance and threatens to impose a tyranny of the judiciary.

Prudential Considerations

Important prudential considerations also weigh heavily in favor of interpretivist review. The rule of law is fundamental in our society. To be effective, it cannot be tossed to and fro by each new sociological wind. Because it is rooted in written text, interpretivist review promotes the stability and predictability essential to the rule of law. By contrast, noninterpretivist review presents an infinitely variable array of possibilities. The Constitution would vary with each judge's conception of what is important. To demonstrate the wide variety of tests that could be applied, let us briefly look at the writings of legal academics who advocate noninterpretivism.

Assume each is a judge deciding the same constitutional issue. One professor seeks to "cement a union between the distributional patterns of the modern welfare state and the federal constitution." Another "would guarantee a whole range of nontextually based rights against government to ensure 'the dignity of full membership in society.'" A third argues that the courts should give a "concrete meaning and application" to those values that "give our society an identity and inner coherence [and] its distinctive public morality." Yet another professor sees the court as having a "prophetic" role in developing moral standards in a "dialectical relationship" with Congress, from which he sees emerging a "more mature" political morality. One professor even urges that the court apply the contractarian moral theory of Professor Rawls' A Theory of Justice to constitutional questions.[10] One can easily see the fatal vagueness and subjectivity of this approach: each judge would apply his or her own separate and diverse personal values in interpreting the same constitutional question. Without anchor, we drift at sea.

Another prudential argument against noninterpretivism is that judges are not particularly well-suited to make judgments of broad social policy. We judges decide cases on the basis of a limited record that largely represents the efforts of the parties to the litigation. Legislators, with their committees, hearings, and more direct role in the political process, are much better equipped institutionally to decide what is best for society.

Noninterpretivist Arguments

But are there arguments in favor of noninterpretivism? Let us consider several assertions commonly put forth by proponents. One argument asserts that certain constitutional provisions invite judges to import into the constitutional decision process value judgments derived from outside the Constitution. Most commonly, advocates of this view rely on the due process clause of the Fifth and Fourteenth Amendments. It is true that courts have interpreted the due process clause to authorize broad review of the substantive merits of legislation. But is that what the draftsmen had in mind? Some constitutional scholars make a strong argument that the clause, consistent with its plain language, was intended to have a limited procedural meaning.[11]

A second argument asserts that the meaning of the constitutional text and the intention of the Framers cannot be ascertained with sufficient precision to guide constitutional decisionmaking. I readily acknowledge that interpretivism will not always provide easy answers to difficult constitutional questions. The judicial role will always involve the exercise of discretion. The strength of interpretivism is that it channels and constrains this discretion in a manner consistent with the Constitution. While it does not necessarily ensure a correct result, it does exclude from consideration entire ranges of improper judicial responses.

Third, some have suggested that the Fourteenth Amendment effected such a fundamental revision in the nature of our government that the intentions of the original Framers are scarcely relevant any longer. It is, of course, true that federal judges have seized upon the Fourteenth Amendment as a vehicle to restructure federal/state relations. The argument, however, is not one-sided. Berger, for example, persuasively demonstrates that the framers of the Fourteenth Amendment sought much more limited objectives.[12] In addition, one reasonable interpretation of the history of the amendment demonstrates that its framers, rather than intending an expanded role for the federal courts, meant for Congress (under section 5 of the amendment) to play the primary role in enforcing its provisions.[13] Thus, it can be argued that to the extent that the Fourteenth Amendment represented an innovation in the constitutional role of the judiciary, it was by limiting the courts' traditional role in enforcing constitutional rights and by providing added responsibility for the Congress.

Advocates of noninterpretivism also contend that we should have a "living Constitution" rather than be bound by "the dead hand of the Framers." These slogans prove nothing. An interpretivist approach would not constrict government processes; on the contrary, it would ensure that issues are freely subject to the workings of the democratic process. Moreover, to the extent that the Constitution might profit from revision, the amendment process of Article V provides the only constitutional means. Judicial amendment under a noninterpretivist approach is simply an unconstitutional usurpation.

Almost certainly, the greatest support for a noninterpretive approach derives from its perceived capacity to achieve just results. Why quibble over the Constitution, after all, if judges who disregard it nevertheless "do justice"? Such a view is dangerously shortsighted and naive. In the first place, one has no cause to believe that the results of noninterpretivism will generally be "right." Individual judges have widely varying conceptions of what values are important. Noninterpretivists spawned the "conservative" substantive economic due process of the 1930s as well as the "liberal" decisions of the Warren Court. There is no principled result in noninterpretivism.

But even if the judge would always be right, the process would be wrong. A benevolent judicial tyranny is nonetheless a tyranny. Our Constitution rests on the faith that democracy is intrinsically valuable. From an instrumental perspective, democracy might at times produce results that are not as desirable as platonic guardians might produce. But the democratic process — our participation in a system of self-government — has transcendental value. Moreover, one must consider the very real danger that an activist judiciary stunts the development of a responsible democracy by removing from it the duty to make difficult decisions. If we are to remain faithful to the values of democracy and liberty, we must insist that courts respect the Constitution's allocation of social decisionmaking to the political branches.

RESPECT FOR PRECEDENT

I emphasized earlier the importance of stability to the rule of law. I return to that theme now to consider a second principle of judicial restraint: respect for precedent. Respect for precedent is a principle widely accepted, even if not always faithfully followed. It requires simply that a judge follow prior case law in deciding legal questions. Respect for precedent promotes predictability and uniformity. It constrains a judge's discretion and satisfies the reasonable expectations of the parties. Through its application, citizens can have a better understanding of what the law is and act accordingly.

Unfortunately, in the present state of constitutional law, the two principles of judicial restraint that I have outlined can come into conflict. While much of constitutional law is consistent with the principle of interpretivism, a significant portion is not. This raises the question of how a practitioner of judicial restraint should act in circumstances where respecting precedent would require acceptance of law developed under a noninterpretivist approach.

The answer is easy for a judge in my position, and, indeed, for any judge below the United States Supreme Court. As a judge on the Ninth Circuit Court of Appeals, I am bound to follow Supreme Court and Ninth Circuit precedent even when I believe it to be wrong. There is a distinction, however, between following precedent and extending it. Where existing precedent does not fairly govern a legal question, the principle of interpretivism should guide a judge.

For Supreme Court justices, the issue is more complex. The Supreme Court obviously is not infallible. Throughout its history, the Court has at times rejected its own precedents. Because the Supreme Court has the ultimate judicial say on what the Constitution means, its justices have a special responsibility to ensure that they are properly expounding constitutional law as well as fostering stability and predictability.

Must Supreme Court advocates of judicial restraint passively accept the errors of activist predecessors? There is little rational basis for doing so. Periodic activist inroads could emasculate fundamental doctrines and undermine the separation of powers. Nevertheless, the values of predictability and uniformity that respect for precedent promotes demand caution in overturning precedent. In my view, a justice should consider overturning a prior decision only when the decision is clearly wrong, has significant effects, and would otherwise be difficult to remedy.

Significantly, constitutional decisions based on a noninterpretivist approach may satisfy these three criteria. When judges confer constitutional status on their own value judgments without support in the language of the Constitution and the original intention of the Framers, they commit clear error. Because constitutional errors frequently affect the institutional structure of government and the allocation of decisions to the democratic process, they are likely to have important effects. And because constitutional decisions, unlike statutory decisions, cannot be set aside through normal political channels, they will generally meet the third requirement. In sum, then, despite the prudential interests furthered by respect for precedent, advocates of judicial restraint may be justified in seeking to overturn noninterpretivist precedent.

CONCLUSION

It is obvious that courts employing interpretivist review cannot solve many of the social and political problems facing America, indeed, even some very important problems. The interpretivist would respond that the Constitution did not place the responsibility for solving those problems with the courts. The courts were not meant to govern the core of our political and social life — Article I gave that duty, for national issues, to the Congress. It is through our democratically elected representatives that we legitimately develop this fabric of our life. Interpretivism encourages that process. It is, therefore, closer to the constitutional plan of governance than is noninterpretivist review.

After two hundred years, the Constitution is not "broke" — we need not fix it — just apply it.

NOTES

This article is adapted from an address given at Hillsdale College, Hillsdale, Michigan, on March 5, 1986.

1. I have elsewhere presented various aspects of this jurisprudence. See, e.g., Wallace, "A Two Hundred Year Old Constitution in Modern Society," 61 *Texas Law Review,* 1575 (1983); Wallace, "The Jurisprudence of Judicial Restraint: A Return to the Moorings," *George Washington Law Review* 1 (1981).

2. Wallace, "A Two Hundred Year Old Constitution," *supra* n. 1; Ely, *Democracy and Distrust* 1 (Cambridge, Mass.: Harvard University Press, 1980).

3. Ely, *supra* n. 2, at 2.

4. See *id.* at 43–72.

5. Berger, *Government by Judiciary* 366 (Cambridge, Mass.: Harvard University Press, 1977).

6. *Id.* at 364, *quoting* Letter to Wilson Cary Nicholas (Sept. 7, 1803).

7. *Marbury v. Madison,* 5 U.S. (1 Cranch) 137, 176–180 (1803).

8. Berger, *supra* n. 5, at 364, quoting *The Writings of James Madison* 191 (G. Hunt ed. 1900–1910).

9. *Id.* at 366–367, citing 4 Elliot, *Debates in the Several State Conventions on the Adoption of the Federal Constitution* 446 (1836).

10. Monaghan, "Our Perfect Constitution," 56 *New York University Law Review,* 353, 358–360 (1981) (summarizing theories of noninterpretivists).

11. See, e.g., Berger, *supra* n. 5, at 193–220.

12. See *id.*

13. See *id.* at 220–229.

 NO

Should the Supreme Court Abide by a Strict Constructionist Philosophy?

JEFFREY M. SHAMAN

The Supreme Court's Proper and Historic Function

Considerable criticism, frequently quite sharp, has recently been directed at the Supreme Court for the way it has gone about its historic function of interpreting the Constitution. In particular, Edwin Meese, the current Attorney General of the United States [1987], has accused the Court of exceeding its lawful authority by failing to adhere strictly to the words of the Constitution and the intentions of the Framers who drafted those words.[1]

The Attorney General's attack upon the Court echoes a similar one made by Richard Nixon, who, campaigning for the Presidency in 1968, denounced Supreme Court Justices who, he claimed, twisted and bent the Constitution according to their personal predilections. If elected President, Nixon promised to appoint to the Court strict constructionists whose decisions would conform to the text of the Constitution and the intent of the Framers. (Ironically, it is some of the Nixon appointees to the Court that Meese now accuses of twisting and bending the Constitution.)

I hasten to add that it is not only politicians who sing the praises of strict constructionism; there are judges and lawyers, as well as some scholars, who join the song. Among legal scholars, though, the response to strict constructionism has been overwhelmingly negative. There are legal scholars, for instance, who describe strict constructionism as a "misconceived quest,"[2] an "impossibility,"[3] and even a "fraud."[4]

Those who criticize the Court point to rulings during the tenure of Chief Justice [Warren E.] Burger, most notably the decision in *Roe v. Wade*[5] legalizing abortion, as examples of illegitimate revision or amendment of the Constitution based upon the personal beliefs of the justices. Some years ago, similar charges were leveled at the Warren Court for its ruling requiring reapportionment along the lines of one person–one vote,[6] its decision striking down school prayer,[7] and other rulings, even including the one in *Brown v. Board of Education* outlawing school segregation.[8]

It should not be supposed, however, that strict constructionism is always on the side of conservative political values. In the 1930s it was the liberals who claimed that the Supreme Court was not strictly construing the Constitution when the justices repeatedly held that minimum wage, maximum hour, and other protective legislation violated the Fourteenth Amendment.[9] As the liberals then saw it, the conservative justices on the Court were illegitimately incorporating their personal values into the Fourteenth Amendment, which had been meant to abolish racial discrimination, not to protect the prerogatives of employers.

HISTORY LESSONS

The lesson of this bit of history seems to be that, whether liberal or conservative or somewhere in between, whoever has an ox that is being gored at the time has a tendency to yell "foul." Whenever the Supreme Court renders a decision that someone doesn't like, apparently it is not enough to disagree with the decision; there also has to be an accusation that the Court's decision was illegitimate, being based upon the justice's personal views and not the words of the Constitution or the intent of the Framers.

We can go back much further in history than the 1930s to find the Supreme Court being accused of illegitimacy. In 1810, for instance, Thomas Jefferson condemned Chief Justice John Marshall for "twistifying" the Constitution according to his "personal biases."[10]

History also reveals something else extremely significant about the Court, which is that from its earliest days, the Court has found it necessary in interpreting the Constitution to look beyond the language of the document and the intent of the Framers. In the words of Stanford Law Professor Thomas Grey, it is "a matter of unarguable historical fact" that over the years the Court has developed a large body of constitutional law that derives neither from the text of the document nor the intent of the Framers.[11]

Moreover, this has been so from the Court's very beginning. Consider, for example, a case entitled *Hylton v. United States*,[12] which was decided in 1796 during the term of the Court's first Chief Justice, John Jay. The *Hylton* case involved a tax ranging from $1.00 to $10.00 that had been levied by Congress on carriages. Mr. Hylton, who was in the carriage trade and owned 125 carriages, understandably was unhappy about the tax, and went to court to challenge it. He claimed that the tax violated section 2 of Article I of the Constitution, which provides that direct taxes shall be apportioned among the several states according to their populations. Hylton argued that this tax was a direct one, and therefore unconstitutional because it had not been apportioned among the states by population. This, of course, was years before the enactment of the Sixteenth Amendment in 1913, authorizing a federal income tax. Prior to that, Article I prohibited a federal income tax, but what about a tax on the use or ownership of carriages — was that the sort of "direct" tax that was only permissible under Article I if apportioned among the states by population?

The Supreme Court, with several justices filing separate opinions in the case (which was customary at that time), upheld the tax as constitutional on the ground that it was not direct, and therefore not required to be apportioned. What is most significant about the *Hylton* case is how the Court went about making its decision. As described by Professor David Currie of the University of Chicago Law School, the Court in *Hylton* "paid little heed to the Constitution's words," and "policy considerations dominated all three opinions" filed by the Justices.[13] In fact, each of the opinions asserted that apportioning a carriage tax among the states would be unfair, because a person in a state with fewer carriages would have to pay a higher tax. While this may or may not be unfair, the justices pointed to nothing in the Constitution itself or the intent of the Framers to support their personal views of fairness. Moreover, one of the justices, Justice [William] Paterson, went so far in his opinion as to assert that the constitutional requirement of apportioning direct taxes was "radically wrong," and therefore should not be extended to this case. In other words, he based his decision, at least in part, upon his antipathy to a constitutional provision.

While Justice Paterson went too far in that respect, he and his colleagues on the court could hardly have made a decision in the case by looking to the text of the Constitution or the intent of the Framers. The language of the document simply does not provide an answer to the constitutional issue raised by the situation in *Hylton*. The text of the document merely refers to "direct" taxes and provides no definition of what is meant by a direct tax. Furthermore, as Professor Currie points out, the records of the debates at the Constitutional Convention show that "the Framers had no clear idea of what they meant by direct taxes."[14] Thus, to fulfill their responsibility to decide the case and interpret the law, the justices found it necessary to create meaning for the Constitution.

CREATING MEANING

Indeed, it is often necessary for the Supreme Court to create meaning for the Constitution. This is so because the Constitution, being a document designed (in the words of John Marshall) to "endure for ages,"[15] is rife with general and abstract language. Those two great sources of liberty in the Constitution, the due process and equal protection clauses, are obviously examples of abstract constitutional language that must be invested with meaning. The Fourth Amendment uses extremely general language in prohibiting "unreasonable" searches and seizures, and the Eighth Amendment is similarly general in disallowing "cruel and unusual" punishment.

Even many of the more specific provisions of the Constitution need to be supplied with meaning that simply cannot be found within the four corners of the document. The First Amendment, for instance, states that Congress shall not abridge freedom of speech — but does that mean that the government may not regulate obscene, slanderous, or deceptive speech? The First Amendment also says that Congress shall not abridge the free exercise of religion — does that mean that the government may not prohibit polygamy or child labor when dictated by religious belief? These questions — which, by the way, all arose in actual cases — and, in fact, the vast majority of constitutional questions presented to the Supreme Court cannot be resolved by mere linguistic analysis of the Constitution. In reality there is no choice but to look beyond the text of the document to provide meaning for the Constitution.

There are those, such as Attorney General Meese, who would hope to find meaning for the Constitution from its authors, the beloved and hallowed Framers of the sacred text. By reputation, these fellows are considered saints and geniuses; in actuality, they were politicians motivated significantly by self-interest.

THEORETICAL DRAWBACKS

But even if the Framers do deserve the awe that they inspire, reliance on their intentions to find meaning for the Constitution still has serious theoretical drawbacks. In the first place, why should we be concerned only with the intentions of the 55 individuals who drafted the Constitution and not the intentions of the people throughout the nation who ratified it, not to mention the intentions of the succeeding generations who retain the Constitution? After all, even when finally framed, the Constitution remained a legal nullity until ratified by the people, and would be a legal nullity again if revoked by the people. The Framers wrote the Constitution, but it is the people who enacted and retain the Constitution; so if anything, it is the people's intent about the document that would seem to be the relevant inquiry.

Moreover, there are considerable difficulties in discerning what in fact the Framers intended. The journal of the Constitutional Convention, which is the primary record of the Framer's intent, is neither complete nor entirely accurate. The notes for the journal were carelessly kept, and have been shown to contain several mistakes.[16]

Even when the record cannot be faulted, it is not always possible to ascertain the Framers' intent. As might be expected, the Framers did not express an intention about every constitutional issue that would arise after the document was drafted and adopted. No group of people, regardless of its members' ability, enjoys that sort of prescience. When the Framers did address particular problems, often only a few of them spoke out. What frequently is taken to be the intent of the Framers as a group turns out to be the intent of merely a few or even only one of the Framers.

There are also constitutional issues about which the Framers expressed conflicting intentions. A collective body of 55 individuals, the Framers embraced a widely diverse and frequently inconsistent set of views. The two principal architects of the Constitution, James Madison and Alexander Hamilton, for instance, had extremely divergent political views. Madison also on occasion differed with George Washington over the meaning of the Constitution. When Washington, who had presided over the Constitutional Convention, became President, he claimed that the underlying intent of the Constitution gave him the sole authority as President to proclaim neutrality and to withhold treaty papers from Congress. Madison, who had been a leader at the Constitutional Convention, disagreed vehemently. And so, the man who would come to be known as the father of this nation and the man who would come to be known as the father of the Constitution had opposing views of what the Framers intended.[17]

These examples demonstrate that it simply makes no sense to suppose that a multi-member group of human beings such as the Framers shared a unitary intent about the kind of controversial political issues addressed in our Constitution. We can see, then, that, at best, the so-called Framers' intent is inadequately documented, ambiguous, and inconclusive; at worst, it is nonexistent, an illusion.

Even if these insurmountable obstacles could be surmounted, there are other serious problems with trying to follow the path laid down by the Framers. The Framers formed their intentions in the context of a past reality and in accordance with past attitudes, both of which have changed considerably since the days when the Constitution was drafted. To transfer those intentions, fashioned as they were under past conditions and views, to contemporary situations may produce sorry consequences that even the Framers would have abhorred had they been able to foresee them. Blindly following intentions formulated in response to past conditions and attitudes is not likely to be an effective means of dealing with the needs of contemporary society.

LOCKED TO THE PAST

Some scholars take this line of reasoning one step further by maintaining that the Framers' intent is inextricably locked to the past and has no meaning at all for the present.[18] In other words, because the Framers formed their intentions with reference to a reality and attitudes that no longer exist, their intentions cannot be transplanted to the present day. What the Framers intended for their times is not what they may have intended for ours. Life constantly changes, and the reality and ideas that surrounded the Framers are long since gone.

The futility of looking to the Framers' intent to resolve modern constitutional issues can be illustrated by several cases that have arisen under the Fourth and Fifth Amendments. The Fourth Amendment prohibits unreasonable searches and seizures, and further requires that no search warrants be issued unless there is probable cause that a crime has been committed. Are bugging and other electronic surveillance devices "unreasonable searches"? May they be used by the

police without a warrant based on probable cause? What about the current practice of some law enforcement agencies of using airplanes to fly over a suspect's
property to take pictures with a telescopic camera — is that an "unreasonable
search"? The Fifth Amendment states that no person shall be compelled to be a
witness against himself. What about forcing a suspect to take a breathalyzer test,
or a blood test, or to have his or her stomach pumped — do those procedures
amount to self-incrimination that violates the Fifth Amendment?

Whatever you may think should be the answers to these questions, you cannot
find the answers by looking to the Framers' intent. The Framers had no intent at all
about electronic surveillance, airplanes, telescopic cameras, breathalyzer tests,
blood tests, or stomach pumping, for the simple reason that none of those things
existed until well after the days of the Framers. Not even Benjamin Franklin, for all
his inventiveness, was able to foresee that in the twentieth century constables
would zip around in flying machines taking snapshots of criminal suspects
through a telescopic lens.

Many of the difficulties in attempting to resolve constitutional issues by turning
to the Framers are illustrated by the school prayer cases.[19] The religious beliefs of
the Framers ranged from theism to atheism, and among even the more devout
Framers there was a wide diversity of opinion concerning the proper relationship
between church and state. Moreover, as often happens when human beings ponder complex issues, the views of individual Framers about church and state did not
remain the same over time. As a member of Congress, James Madison, for
example, once voted to approve a chaplain for the House of Representatives, but
later decided that the appointment of the chaplain had been unconstitutional.[20]
Insofar as school prayer specifically was concerned, the Framers expressed virtually no opinion on the matter, for the simple reason that at the time public schools
were extremely rare. Thus, the Framers had no intention, either pro or con, about
prayer in public schools.

Given the theoretical deficiencies of trying to decide constitutional questions by
looking to the Framers' intent, it should come as no surprise that this approach has
been a failure when attempted by the Supreme Court. Scholars who have closely
studied the Court's use of this approach commonly agree that it has not been a sat-
isfactory method of constitutional decisionmaking, because the Court ends up
manipulating, revising, or even creating history under the guise of following the
Framers' intent.[21] The fact of the matter is that neither the Framers' intent nor the
words of the document are capable of providing much constitutional meaning.

BARE BONES

What we are left with, then, are the bare bones of a Constitution, the meaning of
which must be augmented by the justices of the Supreme Court. And that is
exactly what the justices have been doing since the Court was first established.
The overwhelming evidence of history shows that the meaning of the Constitution

has undergone constant change and evolution at the hands of the Supreme Court. Through the continual interpretation and reinterpretation of the text of the document, the Court perpetually creates new meaning for the document. Although it is formally correct that we, unlike the citizens of Great Britain, have a written Constitution, its words have been defined and redefined to the extent that for the most part we, like the citizens of Great Britain, have an unwritten Constitution, the meaning of which originates with the Supreme Court.

Strict constructionists argue that it is undemocratic for Supreme Court Justices — unelected officials who are unaccountable to the populace — to create meaning for the Constitution. Of course, using the Framers' intent to interpret the Constitution also is undemocratic; following the will of the 55 persons who supposedly framed the Constitution or the smaller group of them who actually participated in the framing is hardly an exercise in democracy.

When strict constructionists cry that the Court is undemocratic, they are ignoring that our government is not (and was not intended by the Framers) to be a pure democracy. Rather, it is a limited or constitutional democracy. What this means is that there are constitutional limits to what the majority may do. The majority may not, for example, engage in racial discrimination, even if it votes to do so in overwhelming numbers. The majority may not abridge freedom of speech or the free exercise of religion or other constitutional rights guaranteed to every individual.

Article III of the Constitution states that there shall be a Supreme Court, and in combination with Article II, decrees the Court's independence from the electorate. By its very terms, the Constitution establishes a counter-majoritarian branch of government, the Supreme Court, in juxtaposition to the more democratic executive and legislative branches. This scheme reflects one of the guiding principles that underlies the Constitution — the principle of separate powers that check and balance one another. The Supreme Court's constitutionally mandated independence functions as a check and balance upon the more majoritarian branches of federal and state governments. It thereby provides a means of maintaining constitutional boundaries on majoritarian rule.

The role of the Supreme Court is to enforce constitutional requirements upon the majoritarian branches of government, which otherwise would be completely unbridled. As dictated by the Constitution, majority control should be the predominant feature of our government, but subject to constitutional limits.

Moreover, the Supreme Court is not quite as undemocratic as the strict constructionists sometimes like to portray it to be. While it is true that the justices who sit on the Court are appointed rather than elected and that they may be removed from office only for improper behavior, it is also true that they are appointed by a popularly elected president, and their appointment must be confirmed by a popularly elected Senate. Turnover of the Court's personnel, which sometimes occurs frequently, enhances popular control of the Court. Additionally, the Court's constitutional rulings may be overruled by the people through constitutional amendment, which, though a difficult procedure, has been accomplished on four occasions.[22] Thus, while the court is not directly answerable to the public, it is not entirely immune from popular control.

THE ULTIMATE AUTHORITY

The people also have the ultimate authority to abolish the Supreme Court. That they have not done so during our two centuries of experience indicates popular acceptance of the Court's role. Admittedly, there are particular decisions rendered by the Court that have aroused considerable public outcry, but given the many controversial issues that the Court must decide, this is inevitable. More telling about the public attitude toward the Court is that the people have taken no action to curtail the Court's authority to interpret the Constitution. Indeed, the public has shown little, if any, inclination toward abolishing the Court or even restricting its powers. Despite Franklin Delano Roosevelt's overwhelming popularity, his "court-packing plan" was a dismal failure;[23] the proposal to establish a "Court of the Union" composed of state court justices which would have the power to overrule the Supreme Court evoked such widespread public disapproval that it was quickly abandoned;[24] the campaigns to impeach Justices Earl Warren and William O. Douglas never got off the ground;[25] and although various members of Congress often propose bills threatening to restrict the Court's jurisdiction, the full Congress always rebuffs those threats.[26] These experiences suggest that even in the face of controversial constitutional decisions, there has been abiding public consent to the role of the Supreme Court in our scheme of government.

The Court's role, when all is said and done, is to create meaning for a Constitution that otherwise would be a hollow document. It is perfectly appropriate for anyone to disagree with Supreme Court decisions, and to criticize the Court on that basis. But it is not appropriate to attack the Court's decisions as illegitimate on the ground that they do not follow the Framers' intent. Pretending to use the Framers' intent to impugn the legitimacy of the Supreme Court is a spurious enterprise. The Court's legitimate function is, and always has been, to provide meaning for the Constitution.

NOTES

1. Address by Attorney General Edwin Meese, III, before the American Bar Association, Washington, D.C. (July 9, 1985); "Q and A with the Attorney General," *American Bar Association Journal* 81, no. 44 (July 1985).

2. Brest, "The Misconceived Quest for the Original Understanding," *Boston University Law Review* 60, no. 204 (1980).

3. Ely, "Constitutional Interpretation: Its Allure and Impossibility," *Indiana Law Journal* 53, no. 399 (1978).

4. Nowak, "Realism, Nihilism, and the Supreme Court: Do the Emperors Have Nothing But Robes?" 22 *Washburn Law Journal* 246, 257 (1983).

5. 410 U.S. 113 (1973).

6. *Reynolds v. Sims*, 377 U.S. 533 (1964).

7. *Engle v. Vitale*, 370 U.S. 421 (1962); *Abington School Dist. v. Schempp*, 374 U.S. 203 (1963).

8. 347 U.S. 483 (1954).

9. See, e.g., Boudin, *Government by Judiciary* 433–43 (New York: W. Goodwin, 1932); Haines, *The American Doctrine of Judicial Supremacy* (Berkeley: University of California Press, 1932).

10. Ford (ed.) 9 *Writings of Thomas Jefferson* 275–76 (1902).

11. Grey, "Origins of the Unwritten Constitution: Fundamental Law in American Revolutionary Thought," 30 *Stanford Law Review* 843, 844 (1978).

12. 3 U.S. (3 Dall.) 171 (1796).

13. Currie, *The Constitution in the Supreme Court, 1789–1888* 34 (Chicago: University of Chicago Press, 1985).

14. *Id.* at 36.

15. *McCulloch v. Maryland,* 17 U.S. (4 Wheat.) 316, 414 (1819).

16. See, Rohde and Spaeth, *Supreme Court Decision Making* 41 (1976); 1 *The Records of the Federal Convention of 1787* xii–xiv (Farrand ed. San Francisco: W. H. Freeman, 1937).

17. Burns, *The Vineyard of Liberty* 101–04 (New York: Knopf, 1982).

18. Wofford, "The Blinding Light: The Uses of History in Constitutional Interpretation," 21 *University of Chicago Law Review* 502 (1964).

19. *Supra* n. 7.

20. Strokes and Pfeffer, *Church and State in the United States* 181–82 (Colorado Springs: Shepard's, 1975).

21. See, e.g., tenBroek, "Uses by the United States Supreme Court of Extrinsic Aids in Constitutional Construction," 27 *California Law Review* 399, 404 (1939); Kelly, "Clio and the Court: An Illicit Love Affair," 1965 *Supreme Court Review* 119, 122–25; Alfange, "On Judicial Policymaking and Constitutional Change: Another Look at the 'Original Intent' Theory of Constitutional Interpretation," 5 *Hastings Constitutional Law Quarterly* 603, 617 (1978).

22. The Eleventh Amendment overruled the holding of *Chisholm v. Georgia,* 2 U.S. (2 Dall.) 419 (1793); the Fourteenth Amendment nullified, in part, the decision in *Dred Scott v. Sandford,* 60 U.S. (19 How.) 393 (1857); the Sixteenth Amendment nullified the holding of *Pollack v. Farmers' Loan and Trust, Co.,* 157 U.S. 429 (1895); the Twenty-sixth Amendment neutralized *Oregon v. Mitchell,* 400 U.S. 112 (1970).

23. "Not all the influence of a master politician in the prime of his popularity was quite enough to carry a program that would impair judicial review," McCloskey, *The American Supreme Court* 177 (Chicago: University of Chicago Press, 1960). The plan was rejected vehemently by the Senate Judiciary Committee. See *Senate Comm. on the Judiciary, Reorganization of the Fed. Judiciary Adverse Report,* S. Rep. No. 711, 75th Cong., 1st Sess. 23 (1937).

24. Pfeffer, *This Honorable Court* 424–25 (Boston: Beacon Press, 1965).

25. Those who campaigned for Chief Justice Warren's impeachment were unable to have impeachment proceedings initiated against him. While impeachment proceedings were instituted against Justice Douglas, they never got beyond the subcommittee stage and were eventually forsaken. See *Special Subcomm. on H. Res., 920 of the House Comm. on the Judiciary,* 91 Cong., 2d Sess., Final Report, Associate Justice William O. Douglas (Comm. Print 1970).

26. "In the fifteen years between 1953 and 1968, over sixty bills were introduced in Congress to eliminate the jurisdiction of the federal courts over a variety of specific subjects; none of these became law." Bator, Mishkin, Shapiro and Wechsler, *Hart and Wechsler's the Federal Courts and the Federal System* 360 (Mineola, N.Y.: Foundation Press, 2d ed. 1973).

Questions for Discussion

1. What kinds of contemporary issues would the Framers have never contemplated?
2. What consequences about strict interpretivism can be drawn from your answer to Question 1?
3. How would you evaluate the qualifications of a person nominated to the Supreme Court who accepts the strict constructionist viewpoint?

4. Can the noninterpretivist view be reconciled with the U.S. system of democratic rule? What are the reasons for your answer?
5. Does the Constitution as written require the judiciary to follow the principle of judicial restraint? What are the reasons for your answer?

Suggested Resources

Web Sites

Federalist Society for Law and Public Policy Studies
  http://www.fed-soc.org/

Free Congress Foundation
  http://www.freecongress.org/

Ohio Roundtable: Judicial Activism
  http://www.ohioroundtable.org/issues/judicial/

U.S. Courts
  http://www.uscourts.gov/

Publications

Bork, Robert H. *The Tempting of America: The Political Seduction of the Law.* New York: Free Press, 1990.

Farber, Daniel A. "The Originalism Debate: A Guide for the Perplexed." *Ohio State Law Journal* 4, no. 4 (1989): 1085–106.

Graglia, Lino A. "Judicial Activism: Even on the Right, It's Wrong." *Public Interest,* no. 95 (Spring 1989): 57–74.

Lewis, Frederick P. *The Context of Judicial Activism: The Endurance of the Warren Court Legacy in a Conservative Age.* Lanham, Md.: Rowman & Littlefield, 1999.

O'Brien, David H. *Storm Center: The Supreme Court in American Politics,* 6th ed. New York: W.W. Norton, 2002.

Peretti, Terri Jennings. *In Defense of a Political Court.* Princeton, N.J.: Princeton University Press, 1999.

Perry, Michael J. "The Argument for Judicial Review — And for the Originalist Approach to Judicial Review" [Ben J. Altheimer Lecture]. *University of Arkansas at Little Rock Law Journal* 14, no. 4 (Summer 1992): 613–70.

Powers, Stephen P., and Stanley Rothman. *The Least Dangerous Branch? Consequences of Judicial Activism.* Westport, Conn.: Praeger, 2002.

Sandler, Ross, and David Schoenbrod. *Democracy by Decree: What Happens When Courts Run Government.* New Haven, Conn.: Yale University Press, 2003.

Schultz, David A., ed. *Leveraging the Law: Using the Courts to Achieve Social Change.* New York: P. Lang, 1998.

Shaman, Jeffrey M. *Constitutional Interpretation: Illusion and Reality.* Westport, Conn.: Greenwood Press, 2001.

Tushnet, Mark V. *Taking the Constitution Away from the Courts.* Princeton, N.J.: Princeton University Press, 1999.

U.S. Cong., Senate. *Judicial Activism: Defining the Problem and Its Impact.* Hearing before the Subcommittee on the Constitution, Federalism, and Property Rights of the Committee on the Judiciary, 105th Cong., 1st Sess., 1997.

Wolfe, Christopher. *Judicial Activism: Bulwark of Freedom or Precarious Security?* rev. ed. Lanham, Md.: Rowman & Littlefield, 1997.

Part V

Public Policy

P olitical democracy involves a contest over public policy. An element of that contest includes convincing individuals, private groups, and political leaders that particular policies are wise and just. An underlying theme of democratic rule is that conflicts should be resolved peacefully through discussion, freedom of association, and agreed-upon procedures for determining policy outcomes.

People who choose sides on different issues of public policy do so for many reasons. Sometimes, the choice is based on self-interest, as when a manufacturer or trade union favors protectionism so as to reduce competition from abroad. At other times, the choice is based on a perception of justice, as in issues relating to the elimination of racism or the protection of the environment. Often, choices derive from a combination of self-interested and altruistic impulses.

Part V deals with some contemporary issues in domestic and foreign policy matters of concern to the people of the United States. Specifically, the debate questions consider gun control, drug decriminalization, "smart growth," and globalization.

19

Should the Federal Government's Prohibition of Drugs Be Ended?

In the 1960s the culture of drugs won some popular approval — particularly among the young. In the minds of some advocates of drugs at that time, rational decision making had brought the United States involvement in the Vietnam War, a high military budget when other national priorities were neglected, and the rigidities of a conformist society. Timothy Leary, a former Harvard instructor, supplied the drug culture with its motto: Turn on, tune in, drop out.

The drug culture of the 1960s was in the spotlight with Haight-Ashbury, a section of San Francisco where "hippies" pursued their way of life, and Woodstock, a small town in New York that hosted a huge rock concert, with much drug use. But drugs began to take their toll. Many performers, including some who performed at Woodstock, died of overdoses and addictions: John Belushi, Jimi Hendrix, Janis Joplin, Elvis Presley. Hundreds of thousands of men and women from all social strata suffered death and physical and mental disabilities.

By the 1980s drug use was no longer a subject of comic quips by entertainment figures anxious to get quick laughs, and Americans were overwhelmingly hostile to drug abuse and drug pushers — the people who sold drugs. Elected public officials declared wars on drugs, and funding to fight against drug use was provided at all levels of government.

Although the term "drugs" is used here to mean illegal drugs, it is important to remember that not all drugs are illegal. People who are ill use drugs prescribed by physicians that otherwise would be illegal, although these are also sometimes given to abuse. Alcohol and tobacco are drugs that are legal and available to most adults. But the major drugs of most concern are cocaine (and its derivative "crack") and heroin. Marijuana, too, has been increasingly considered to be unsafe because today's variety of that substance is many times more powerful than the "grass" hippies smoked in the 1960s.

As public awareness and government action have increased, actual drug use has declined since the 1960s. Even use of alcohol and tobacco declined as Americans became increasingly concerned about good health and physical fitness. From a health point of view, tobacco and alcohol take a greater toll on the lives and health of American people than do the major illegal drugs.

Still, the problem of drug use remains serious. The *2001 National Household Survey on Drug Abuse,* a report of the Substance Abuse and Mental Health Services Administration of the U.S. Department of Health and Human Services, shows:

- In 2001, an estimated 15.9 million Americans age 12 years or older used an illicit drug during the month immediately prior to the survey interview. These people are identified as current drug users. This estimate represents 7.1 percent of the population 12 years or older. By comparison, in 2000 the survey found that 6.3 percent of this population were current users of illicit drugs.
- When the population is examined by age groups, the survey disclosed that 10.8 percent of youths 12 to 17 in 2001 were current drug users compared, with 9.7 percent in 2000. Similarly, among adults age 18 to 25 years, current drug use increased between 2000 and 2001 from 15.9 to 18.8 percent. There were no statistically significant changes in the rates of drug use among adults age 26 or older.[1]

Criminal activities and street deaths that drug abuse spawns remain a serious problem also. And there is no agreement on a solution to reducing illicit drug use. One approach is to intensify criminal punishment. Some would do so by increasing police budgets, working harder with governments of foreign countries where drugs are produced, and imposing the death penalty on drug dealers. Another approach is to provide increased public awareness for treatment.

Many West European countries are moving away from regarding drug abusers as criminals. As early as the 1970s, the Netherlands allowed use of marijuana, or cannabis, as it is generally known in Europe. More recently, Portugal decriminalized all drug use. Spain, Italy, and Luxembourg have decriminalized possession of most drugs. Some other European countries have in effect decriminalized drug use by not applying criminal penalties for addicts who are not dealers. In 2002, the British Home Office announced that it would treat possession or use of cannabis as it would a parking ticket. The focus in many countries that have modified or eliminated their tough drug laws is on treatment rather than punishment. Not all European countries have adopted these changes, however. For example, Sweden and Greece have tough drug laws.

In the United States, eight states have adopted initiatives legalizing marijuana use for medical purposes. These states are Arizona, Alaska, California, Colorado, Maine, Nevada, Oregon, and Washington. In 2000, Hawaii became the first state to legalize medical marijuana through legislation. In terms of federal law, however, the use of marijuana is illegal.

David Boaz, executive vice president of the Cato Institute, argues that the federal government's drug prohibition should be ended and that state governments should deal with drug sales and use in the same way that they deal with alcohol. He contends:

1. The federal laws on drug prohibition are constitutionally dubious.
2. Drug prohibition creates high levels of crime.
3. Drug prohibition channels over $40 billion a year into the criminal underworld.
4. Drug prohibition is a classic example of throwing money at a problem.
5. The drug laws are responsible for widespread social upheaval.
6. The drug laws break up families.
7. Drug prohibition leads to civil liberties abuses.
8. Drug prohibition undermines the use of medical marijuana for sick people with severe illnesses.
9. Drug prohibition attacks the principle of federalism, which is supposed to respect states' rights.

Donnie Marshall, a former administrator of the Drug Enforcement Administration, supports the federal government's active attack on drugs. He argues:

1. Legalization would boost drug use.
2. It would contribute to a rise in crime.
3. Most drug-related crimes are committed by people under the influence of mind-altering drugs rather than by people who are looking for money to buy drugs.
4. It would have adverse consequences in accidents, domestic violence, illness, and work opportunities.
5. It would present a law enforcement nightmare.
6. Drug enforcement works to undermine drug abuse.

NOTE

1. Substance Abuse and Mental Health Services Administration, U.S. Department of Health and Human Services, *2001 National Household Survey on Drug Abuse*, at http://www.samhsa.gov/oas/nhsda/2klnhsda/vol1/highlights.htm (accessed September 12, 2002).

 ☑ *YES*

---

*Should the Federal Government's
Prohibition of Drugs Be Ended?*

DAVID BOAZ

Drug Legalization, Criminalization, and Harm Reduction

Ours is a federal republic. The federal government has only the powers granted to it in the Constitution. And the United States has a tradition of individual liberty, vigorous civil society, and limited government: just because a problem is identified does not mean that the government ought to undertake to solve it, and just because a problem occurs in more than one state does not mean that it is a proper subject for federal policy.

Perhaps no area more clearly demonstrates the bad consequences of not following such rules than drug prohibition. The long federal experiment in prohibition of marijuana, cocaine, heroin, and other drugs has given us unprecedented crime and corruption combined with a manifest failure to stop the use of drugs or reduce their availability to children.

In the 1920s Congress experimented with the prohibition of alcohol. On February 20, 1933, a new Congress acknowledged the failure of alcohol Prohibition and sent the Twenty-First Amendment to the states. Congress recognized that Prohibition had failed to stop drinking and had increased prison populations and violent crime. By the end of 1933, national Prohibition was history, though in accordance with our federal system many states continued to outlaw or severely restrict the sale of liquor.

Today Congress confronts a similarly failed prohibition policy. Futile efforts to enforce prohibition have been pursued even more vigorously in the 1980s and 1990s than they were in the 1920s. Total federal expenditures for the first 10 years of Prohibition amounted to $88 million — about $733 million in 1993 dollars. Drug enforcement cost about $22 billion in the [Ronald] Reagan years and another $45 billion in the four years of the [George H. W.] Bush administration. The federal government spent $16 billion on drug control programs in FY 1998 and has approved a budget of $17.9 billion for FY 1999. (See Figure 19.1.) The Office of National Drug Control Policy reported in April 1999 that state and local governments spent an additional $15.9 billion in FY 1991, an increase of 13 percent over 1990, and there is every reason to believe that state and local expenditures have risen throughout the 1990s.

Those mind-boggling amounts have had some effect. Total drug arrests are now more than 1.5 million a year. There are about 400,000 drug offenders in jails and prison now, and over 80 percent of the increase in the federal prison population from

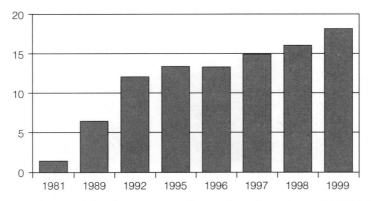

Figure 19.1 Federal Drug Control Spending, FY 1981 to FY 1999, in Billions

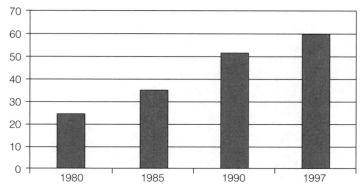

Figure 19.2 Percentage of Drug Offenders in Federal Prisons, 1980–1997

1985 to 1995 was due to drug convictions. Drug offenders constituted 59.6 percent of all federal prisoners in 1996, up from 52.6 percent in 1990. (See Figure 19.2.) (Those in federal prison for violent offenses fell from 18 percent to 12.4 percent of the total, while property offenders fell from 14 percent to 8.4 percent.)

Yet as was the case during Prohibition, all the arrests and incarcerations haven't stopped the use and abuse of drugs, or the drug trade, or the crime associated with black-market transactions. Cocaine and heroin supplies are up; the more our Customs agents interdict, the more smugglers import. In a letter to the *Wall Street Journal* published on November 12, 1996, Janet Crist of the White House Office of National Drug Policy claimed some success:

> Other important results [of the Pentagon's anti-drug efforts] include the arrest of virtually the entire Cali drug cartel leadership, the disruption of the Andean air bridge, and the hemispheric drug interdiction effort that has captured about a third of the cocaine produced in South America each year.

"However," she continued, "there has been no direct effect on either the price or the availability of cocaine on our streets." That is hardly a sign of a successful policy. And of course, while crime rates have fallen in the past few years, today's crime rates look good only by the standards of the recent past; they remain much higher than the levels of the 1950s.

As for discouraging young people from using drugs, the massive federal effort has largely been a dud. Despite the soaring expenditures on antidrug efforts, about half the students in the United States in 1995 tried an illegal drug before they graduated from high school. According to the 1997 National Household Survey on Drug Abuse, 54.1 percent of high school seniors reported some use of an illegal drug at least once during their lifetime, although it should be noted that only 6.4 percent reported use in the month before the survey was conducted. Every year from 1975 to 1995, at least 82 percent of high school seniors have said they find marijuana "fairly easy" or "very easy" to obtain. During that same period, according to federal statistics of dubious reliability, teenage marijuana use fell dramatically and then rose significantly, suggesting that cultural factors have more effect than "the war on drugs."

The manifest failure of drug prohibition explains why more and more people — from Baltimore mayor Kurt Schmoke to Nobel laureate Milton Friedman, conservative columnist William F. Buckley Jr., and former secretary of state George Shultz — have argued that drug prohibition actually causes more crime and other harms than it prevents.

THE FAILURES OF PROHIBITION

Congress should recognize the failure of prohibition and end the federal government's war on drugs. First and foremost, the federal drug laws are constitutionally dubious. As previously noted, the federal government can only exercise the powers that have been delegated to it. The Tenth Amendment reserves all other powers to the states or to the people. However misguided the alcohol prohibitionists turned out to be, they deserve credit for honoring our constitutional system by seeking a constitutional amendment that would explicitly authorize a national policy on the sale of alcohol. Congress never asked the American people for additional constitutional powers to declare a war on drug consumers.

Second, drug prohibition creates high levels of crime. Addicts are forced to commit crimes to pay for a habit that would be easily affordable if it were legal. Police sources have estimated that as much as half the property crime in some major cities is committed by drug users. More dramatically, because drugs are illegal, participants in the drug trade cannot go to court to settle disputes, whether between buyer and seller or between rival sellers. When black-market contracts are breached, the result is often some form of violent sanction, which usually leads to retaliation and then open warfare in the streets.

Our capital city, Washington, D.C., has become known as the "murder capital" even though it is the most heavily policed city in the United States. Make no mistake about it, the annual carnage that stands behind America's still outrageously high murder rates has nothing to do with the mind-altering effects of a marijuana cigarette or a crack pipe. It is instead one of the grim and bitter consequences of an ideological crusade whose proponents will not yet admit defeat.

Third, drug prohibition channels over $40 billion a year into the criminal underworld. Alcohol prohibition drove reputable companies into other industries or out of business altogether, which paved the way for mobsters to make millions through the black market. If drugs were legal, organized crime would stand to lose billions of dollars, and drugs would be sold by legitimate businesses in an open marketplace.

Fourth, drug prohibition is a classic example of throwing money at a problem. The federal government spends some $16 billion to enforce the drug laws every year — all to no avail. For years drug war bureaucrats have been tailoring their budget requests to the latest news reports. When drug use goes up, taxpayers are told the government needs more money so that it can redouble its efforts against a rising drug scourge. When drug use goes down, taxpayers are told that it would be a big mistake to curtail spending just when progress is being made. Good news or bad, spending levels must be maintained or increased.

Fifth, the drug laws are responsible for widespread social upheaval. "Law and order" advocates too often fail to recognize that some laws can actually cause societal disorder. A simple example will illustrate that phenomenon. Right now our college campuses are relatively calm and peaceful, but imagine what would happen if Congress were to institute military conscription in order to wage a war in Kosovo, Korea, or the Middle East. Campuses across the country would likely erupt in protest — even though Congress obviously did not desire that result. The drug laws happen to have different "disordering" effects. Perhaps the most obvious has been turning our cities into battlefields and upending the normal social order.

Drug prohibition has created a criminal subculture in our inner cities. The immense profits involved in a black-market business make drug dealing the most lucrative endeavor for many people, especially those who care least about getting on the wrong side of the law.

Drug dealers become the most visibly successful people in inner-city communities, the ones with money, and clothes, and cars. Social order is turned upside down when the most successful people in a community are criminals. The drug war makes peace and prosperity virtually impossible in inner cities.

Sixth, the drug laws break up families. Too many parents have been separated from their children because they were convicted of marijuana possession, small-scale sale of drugs, or some other non-violent offense. Will Foster used marijuana to control the pain and swelling associated with his crippling rheumatoid arthritis. He was arrested, convicted of marijuana cultivation, and sentenced to 93 years in prison, later reduced to 20 years. Are his three children better off with a father who uses marijuana medicinally, or a father in jail for 20 years?

And going to jail for drug offenses isn't just for men any more. In 1996, 188,880 women were arrested for violating drug laws. Most of them did not go to jail, of course, but more than two-thirds of the 146,000 women behind bars have children. One of them is Brenda Pearson, a heroin addict who managed to maintain a job at a securities firm in New York. She supplied heroin to an addict friend, and a Michigan prosecutor had her extradited, prosecuted, and sentenced to 50 to 200 years. We can only hope that her two children will remember her when she gets out.

Seventh, drug prohibition leads to civil liberties abuses. The demand to win this unwinnable war has led to wiretapping, entrapment, property seizures, and other abuses of Americans' traditional liberties. The saddest cases result in the deaths of innocent people: people like Donald Scott, whose home was raided at dawn on the pretext of cultivating marijuana, and who was shot and killed when he rushed into the living room carrying a gun; or people like the Rev. Accelyne Williams, a 75-year-old minister who died of a heart attack when police burst into his Boston apartment looking for drugs — the wrong apartment, as it turned out; or people like Esequiel Hernandez, who was out tending his family's goats near the Rio Grande just six days after his 18th birthday when he was shot by a Marine patrol looking for drug smugglers. As we deliberate the costs and benefits of drug policy, we should keep those people in mind.

Students of American history will someday ponder the question of how today's elected officials could readily admit to the mistaken policy of alcohol prohibition in the 1920s but continue the policy of drug prohibition. Indeed, the only historical lesson that recent presidents and Congresses seem to have drawn from the period of alcohol prohibition is that government should not try to outlaw the sale of alcohol. One of the broader lessons that they should have learned is this: prohibition laws should be judged according to their real-world effects, not their promised benefits.

Intellectual history teaches us that people have a strong incentive to maintain their faith in old paradigms even as the facts become increasingly difficult to explain within that paradigm. But when a paradigm has manifestly failed, we need to think creatively and develop a new paradigm. The paradigm of prohibition has failed. I urge members of Congress and all Americans to have the courage to let go of the old paradigm, to think outside the box, and to develop a new model for dealing with the very real risks of drug and alcohol abuse. If the 106th Congress will subject the federal drug laws to that kind of new thinking, it will recognize that the drug war is not the answer to problems associated with drug use.

RESPECT STATE INITIATIVES

In addition to the general critique above, I would like to touch on a few more specific issues. A particularly tragic consequence of the stepped-up war on drugs is the refusal to allow sick people to use marijuana as medicine. Prohibitionists insist that marijuana is not good medicine, or at least that there are legal alternatives to marijuana that are equally good. Those who believe that individuals should make their own decisions, not have their decisions made for them by Washington bureaucracies, would simply say that that's a decision for patients and their doctors to make. But in fact there is good medical evidence about the therapeutic value of marijuana — despite the difficulty of doing adequate research on an illegal drug. A recent National Institutes of Health panel concluded that smoking marijuana may help treat a number of conditions, including nausea and pain. It can be particularly effective in improving the appetite of AIDS and cancer patients. The drug could also assist people who fail to respond to traditional remedies.

More than 70 percent of U.S. cancer specialists in one survey said they would prescribe marijuana if it was legal; nearly half said they had urged their patients to break the law to acquire the drug. The British Medical Association reports that nearly 70 percent of its members believe marijuana should be available for therapeutic use. Even President George [H. W.] Bush's Office of Drug Control Policy criticized the Department of Health and Human Services for closing its special medical marijuana program.

Whatever the actual value of medical marijuana, the relevant fact for federal policymakers is that in 1996 the voters of California and Arizona authorized physicians licensed in the state to recommend the use of medical marijuana to seriously ill and terminally ill patients residing in the state without being subject to civil and criminal penalties.

In response to those referenda, however, the Clinton administration announced, without any intervening authorization from Congress, that any physician recommending or prescribing medicinal marijuana under state law would be prosecuted. In the February 11, 1997, Federal Register the Office of National Drug Control Policy announced that federal policy would be as follows: (1) physicians who recommend and prescribe medicinal marijuana to patients in conformity with state law and patients who use such marijuana will be prosecuted; (2) physicians who recommend and prescribe medicinal marijuana to patients in conformity with state law will be excluded from Medicare and Medicaid; and (3) physicians who recommend and prescribe medicinal marijuana to patients in conformity with state law will have their scheduled-drug DEA [Drug Enforcement Administration] registrations revoked.

The announced federal policy also encourages state and local enforcement officials to arrest and prosecute physicians suspected of prescribing or recommending medicinal marijuana and to arrest and prosecute patients who use such marijuana. And adding insult to injury, the policy also encourages the IRS [Internal Revenue Service] to issue a revenue ruling disallowing any medical deduction for medical marijuana lawfully obtained under state law.

Clearly, this is a blatant effort by the federal government to impose a national policy on the people in the states in question, people who have already elected a contrary policy. Federal officials do not agree with the policy the people have elected; they mean to override it, local rule notwithstanding — just as the Clinton administration has tried to do in other cases, such as the California initiatives dealing with racial preferences and state benefits for immigrants.

Congress and the administration should respect the decisions of the voters in Arizona and California; and in Alaska, Nevada, Oregon, and Washington, where voters passed medical marijuana initiatives in 1998; and in other states where such initiatives may be proposed, debated, and passed. One of the benefits of a federal republic is that different policies may be tried in different states. One of the benefits of our Constitution is that it limits the power of the federal government to impose one policy on the several states.

REPEAL MANDATORY MINIMUMS

The common law in England and America has always relied on judges and juries to decide cases and set punishments. Under our modern system, of course, many crimes are defined by the legislature, and appropriate penalties are defined by statute. However, mandatory minimum sentences and rigid sentencing guidelines shift too much power to legislators and regulators who are not involved in particular cases. They turn judges into clerks and prevent judges from weighing all the facts and circumstances in setting appropriate sentences. In addition, mandatory minimums for nonviolent first-time drug offenders result in sentences grotesquely disproportionate to the gravity of the offense. Absurdly, Congress has mandated minimums for drug offenses but not for murder and other violent crimes, so that a judge has more discretion in sentencing a murder than a first-time drug offender.

Rather than extend mandatory minimum sentences to further crimes, Congress should repeal mandatory minimums and let judges perform their traditional function of weighing the facts and setting appropriate sentences.

CONCLUSION

Drug abuse is a problem, for those involved in it and for their family and friends. But it is better dealt with as a moral and medical than as a criminal problem — "a problem for the surgeon general, not the attorney general," as Mayor Schmoke puts it.

The United States is a federal republic, and Congress should deal with drug prohibition the way it dealt with alcohol Prohibition. The Twenty-First Amendment did not actually legalize the sale of alcohol; it simply repealed the federal prohibition and returned to the several states the authority to set alcohol policy. States took the opportunity to design diverse liquor policies that were in tune with the preferences of their citizens. After 1933, three states and hundreds of counties continued to practice prohibition. Other states chose various forms of alcohol legalization.

Congress should withdraw from the war on drugs and let the states set their own policies with regard to currently illegal drugs. The states would be well advised to treat marijuana, cocaine, and heroin the way most states now treat alcohol: It should be legal for licensed stores to sell such drugs to adults. Drug sales to children, like alcohol sales to children, should remain illegal. Driving under the influence of drugs should be illegal.

With such a policy, Congress would acknowledge that our current drug policies have failed. It would restore authority to the states, as the Founders envisioned. It would save taxpayers' money. And it would give the states the power to experiment with drug policies and perhaps devise more successful rules.

Repeal of prohibition would take the astronomical profits out of the drug business and destroy the drug kingpins that terrorize parts of our cities. It would reduce crime even more dramatically than did the repeal of alcohol prohibition. Not only would there be less crime; reform would also free police to concentrate on robbery, burglary, and violent crime.

The War on Drugs has lasted longer than Prohibition, longer than the War in Vietnam. But there is no light at the end of this tunnel. Prohibition has failed, again, and should be repealed, again.

☑ *NO*

Should the Federal Government's Prohibition of Drugs Be Ended?

DONNIE MARSHALL

Drug Legalization Would Be a Disaster

I am not a scientist, a doctor, a lawyer, or an economist. So I'll do my best to leave the scientific, the medical, the legal and the economic issues to others. At the Drug Enforcement Administration, our mission is not to enact laws, but to enforce them. Based on our experience in enforcing drug laws, I can provide you with information and with our best judgment about policy outcomes that may help put into context the various arguments in this debate.

I would like to discuss what I believe would happen if drugs were legalized. I realize that much of the current debate has been over the legalization of so-called medical marijuana. But I suspect that medical marijuana is merely the first tactical maneuver in an overall strategy that some hope will lead to the eventual legalization of all drugs.

Whether all drugs are eventually legalized or not, the practical outcome of legalizing even one, like marijuana, is to increase the amount of usage among all drugs. It's been said that you can't put the genie back in the bottle or the toothpaste back in the tube. I think those are apt metaphors for what will happen if America goes down the path of legalization. Once America gives into a drug culture, and all the social decay that comes with such a culture, it would be very hard to restore a decent civic culture without a cost to America's civil liberties that would be prohibitively high.

There is a huge amount of research about drugs and their effect on society, here and abroad. I'll let others better acquainted with all of the scholarly literature discuss that research. What I will do is suggest four probable outcomes of legalization and then make a case why a policy of drug enforcement works.

LEGALIZATION WOULD BOOST DRUG USE

The first outcome of legalization would be to have a lot more drugs around, and, in turn, a lot more drug abuse. I can't imagine anyone arguing that legalizing drugs would reduce the amount of drug abuse we already have. Although drug use is down from its high mark in the late 1970s, America still has entirely too many people who are on drugs.

In 1962, for example, only four million Americans had ever tried a drug in their entire lifetime. In 1997, the latest year for which we have figures, 77 million

Americans had tried drugs. Roughly half of all high school seniors have tried drugs by the time they graduate.

The result of having a lot of drugs around and available is more and more consumption. To put it another way, supply to some degree drives demand. That is an outcome that has been apparent from the early days of drug enforcement.

What legalization could mean for drug consumption in the United States can be seen in the drug liberalization experiment in Holland. In 1976, Holland decided to liberalize its laws regarding marijuana. Since then, Holland has acquired a reputation as the drug capital of Europe. For example, a majority of the synthetic drugs, such as Ecstasy (MDMA) and methamphetamine, now used in the United Kingdom are produced in Holland.

The effect of supply on demand can also be seen even in countries that take a tougher line on drug abuse. An example is the recent surge in heroin use in the United States. In the early 1990s, cocaine traffickers from Colombia discovered that there was a lot more profit with a lot less work in selling heroin. Several years ago, they began to send heroin from South America to the United States.

To make as much money as possible, they realized they needed not only to respond to a market, but also to create a market. They devised an aggressive marketing campaign which included the use of brand names and the distribution of free samples of heroin to users who bought their cocaine. In many cases, they induced distributors to move quantities of heroin to stimulate market growth. The traffickers greatly increased purity levels, allowing many potential addicts who might be squeamish about using needles to inhale the heroin rather than injecting it. The result has been a huge increase in the number of people trying heroin for the first time, five times as many in 1997 as just four years before.

I don't mean to imply that demand is not a critical factor in the equation. But any informed drug policy should take into consideration that supply has a great influence on demand. In 1997, American companies spent $73 billion advertising their products and services. These advertisers certainly must have a well-documented reason to believe that consumers are susceptible to the power of suggestion, or they wouldn't be spending all that money. The market for drugs is no different. International drug traffickers are spending enormous amounts of money to make sure that drugs are available to every American kid in a school yard.

Dr. Herbert Kleber, a professor of psychiatry at Columbia University College of Physicians and Surgeons, and one of the nation's leading authorities on addiction, stated in a 1994 article in the *New England Journal of Medicine* that clinical data support the premise that drug use would increase with legalization. He said:

> There are over 50 million nicotine addicts, 18 million alcoholics or problem drinkers, and fewer than 2 million cocaine addicts in the United States. Cocaine is a much more addictive drug than alcohol. If cocaine were legally available, as alcohol and nicotine are now, the number of cocaine abusers would probably rise to a point somewhere between the number of users of the other two agents, perhaps 20 to 25 million . . . the number of compulsive users might be nine times higher than the current number. When drugs have

been widely available — as . . . cocaine was at the turn of the century — both use and addiction have risen.

I can't imagine the impact on this society if that many people were abusers of cocaine. From what we know about the connection between drugs and crime, America would certainly have to devote an enormous amount of its financial resources to law enforcement.

LEGALIZATION WOULD CONTRIBUTE TO A RISE IN CRIME

The second outcome of legalization would be more crime, especially more violent crime. There's a close relationship between drugs and crime. This relationship is borne out by the statistics. Every year, the Justice Department compiles a survey of people arrested in a number of American cities to determine how many of them tested positive for drugs at the time of their arrest. In 1998, the survey found, for example, that 74 percent of those arrested in Atlanta for a violent crime tested positive for drugs. In Miami, 49 percent; in Oklahoma City, 60 percent.

There's a misconception that most drug-related crimes involve people who are looking for money to buy drugs. The fact is that the most drug-related crimes are committed by people under the influence of mind-altering drugs. A 1994 study by the Bureau of Justice Statistics compared Federal and state prison inmates in 1991. It found that 18 percent of the Federal inmates incarcerated for homicide had committed homicide under the influence of drugs, whereas 2.7 percent of these individuals had committed the offense to obtain money to buy drugs. The same disparities showed up for state inmates: almost 28 percent committed homicide under the influence versus 5.3 percent to obtain the money to buy drugs.

Those who propose legalization argue that it would cut down on the number of drug-related crimes because addicts would no longer need to rob people to buy their drugs from illicit sources. But even supposing that argument is true, which I don't think that it is, the fact is that so many more people would be abusing drugs, and committing crimes under the influence of drugs, that the crime rate would surely go up rather than down.

It's clear that drugs often cause people to do things they wouldn't do if they were drug-free. Too many drug users lose the kind of self-control and common sense that keeps them in bounds. In 1998, in the small community of Albion, Illinois, two young men went on a widely reported, one-week, non-stop binge on methamphetamine. At the end of it, they started a killing rampage that left five people dead. One was a Mennonite farmer. They shot him as he was working in his fields. Another was a mother of four. They hijacked her car and killed her.

The crime resulting from drug abuse has had an intolerable effect on American society. To me, the situation is well illustrated by what has happened in Baltimore during the last 50 years. In 1950, Baltimore had just under a million residents. Yet there were only 300 heroin addicts in the entire city. That's fewer than one out of every 3,000 residents. For those 300 people and their families, heroin was a big problem. But it had little effect on the day-to-day pattern of life for the vast majority of the residents of Baltimore.

Today, Baltimore has 675,000 residents, roughly 70 percent of the population it had in 1950. But it has 130 times the number of heroin addicts. One out of every 17 people in Baltimore is a heroin addict. Almost 39,000 people. For the rest of the city's residents, it's virtually impossible to avoid being affected in some way by the misery, the crime and the violence that drug abuse has brought to Baltimore.

People who once might have sat out on their front stoops on a hot summer night are now reluctant to venture outdoors for fear of drug-related violence. Drug abuse has made it a matter of considerable risk to walk down the block to the corner grocery store, to attend evening services at church, or to gather in the school playground.

New York City offers a dramatic example of what effective law enforcement can do to stem violent crime. City leaders increased the police department by 30 percent, adding 8,000 officers. Arrests for all crimes, including drug dealing, drug gang activity and quality of life violations which had been tolerated for many years, increased by 50 percent. The capacity of New York prisons was also increased.

The results of these actions were dramatic. In 1990, there were 2,262 homicides in New York City. By 1998, the number of homicides had dropped to 663. That's a 70 percent reduction in just eight years. Had the murder rate stayed the same in 1998 as it was in 1990, 1,629 more people would have been killed in New York City. I believe it is fair to say that those 1,629 human beings owe their lives to this effective response by law enforcement.

LEGALIZATION WOULD HAVE CONSEQUENCES FOR SOCIETY

The third outcome of legalization would be a far different social environment. The social cost of drug abuse is not found solely in the amount of crime it causes. Drugs cause an enormous amount of accidents, domestic violence, illness, and lost opportunities for many who might have led happy, productive lives.

Drug abuse takes a terrible toll on the health and welfare of a lot of American families. In 1996, for example, there were almost 15,000 drug-induced deaths in the United States, and a half-million emergency room episodes related to drugs. The Centers for Disease Control and Prevention has estimated that 36 percent of new HIV cases are directly or indirectly linked to injecting drug users.

Increasing drug use has had a major impact on the workplace. According to estimates in the 1997 National Household Survey, a study conducted by the Substance Abuse and Mental Health Services Administration (SAMHSA), 6.7 million full-time workers and 1.6 million part-time workers are current users of illegal drugs.

Employees who test positive for drug use consume almost twice the medical benefits as nonusers, are absent from work 50 percent more often, and make more than twice as many workers' compensation claims. Drug use also presents an enormous safety problem in the workplace.

This is particularly true in the transportation sector. Marijuana, for example, impairs the ability of drivers to maintain concentration and show good judgment on the road. A study released by the National Institute on Drug Abuse surveyed 6,000 teenage drivers. It studied those who drove more than six times a month after using marijuana. The study found that they were about two-and-a-half times more likely to be involved in a traffic accident than those who didn't smoke marijuana before driving.

The problem is compounded when drivers have the additional responsibility for the safety of many lives. In Illinois, for example, drug tests were administered to current and prospective school bus drivers between 1995 and 1996. Two hundred tested positive for marijuana, cocaine and other drugs. In January 1987, a Conrail engineer drove his locomotive in front of an Amtrak passenger train, killing 16 people and injuring 170. It was later determined that just 18 minutes before the crash, both he and his brakeman had been smoking marijuana.

In addition to these public safety risks and the human misery costs to drug users and their families associated with drug abuse, the Office of National Drug Control Policy has put a financial price tag on this social ill. According to the 1999 National Drug Control Strategy, illegal drugs cost society about $110 billion every year.

Proponents of legalization point to several liberalization experiments in Europe — for example, the one in Holland that I have already mentioned. The experiment in Holland is now 23 years old, so it provides a good illustration of what liberalizing our drug laws portends.

The head of Holland's best known drug abuse rehabilitation center has described what the new drug culture has created. The strong form of marijuana that most of the young people smoke, he says, produces "a chronically passive individual . . . someone who is lazy, who doesn't want to take initiatives, doesn't want to be active — the kid who'd prefer to lie in bed with a joint in the morning rather than getting up and doing something."

England's experience with widely available heroin shows that use and addiction increase. In a policy far more liberal than America's, Great Britain allowed doctors to prescribe heroin to addicts. There was an explosion of heroin use. According to James Q. Wilson, in 1960, there were 68 heroin addicts registered with the British Government. Today, there are roughly 31,000.

Liberalization in Switzerland has had much the same results. This small nation became a magnet for drug users the world over. In 1987, Zurich permitted drug use and sales in a part of the city called Platzspitz, dubbed "Needle Park." By 1992, the number of regular drug users at the park had reportedly swelled from a few hundred in 1982 to 20,000 by 1992. The experiment has since been terminated.

In April, 1994, a number of European cities signed a resolution titled "European Cities Against Drugs," commonly known as the Stockholm resolution. Currently the signatories include 184 cities or municipalities in 30 different countries in Europe. As the resolution stated: ". . . the answer does not lie in making harmful drugs more accessible, cheaper and socially acceptable. Attempts to do this have not proved successful. We believe that legalizing drugs will, in the long term, increase our problems. By making them legal, society will signal that it has resigned to the acceptance of drug abuse." I couldn't say it any better than that. After seeing the results of liberalization up close, these European cities clearly believe that liberalization is a bad idea.

You do not have to visit Amsterdam or Zurich or London to witness the effects of drug abuse. If you really want to discover what legalization might mean for society, talk to a local clergyman or an eighth grade teacher, or a high school coach, or a scout leader or a parent. How many teachers do you know who come and visit your offices and say, Congressman, the thing that our kids need more than anything else is greater availability to drugs. How many parents have you ever known to say, "I sure wish my child could find illegal drugs more easily than he can now."

Or talk to a local cop on the beat. Night after night, they deal with drug-induced domestic violence situations. They respond to a 911 call and there is a fight, and the people are high on pot or speed, or the husband or father is a heroin addict, and you can't wake him up or he's overdosed in the family bedroom. That's where you see the real effects of drugs.

Anyone who has ever worked undercover in drug enforcement has witnessed young children, 12- and 14-year old girls, putting needles into their arms, shooting up heroin or speed. To feed their habit, the kids start stealing from their parents and their brothers and sisters, stealing and pawning the watch that's been handed down from their grandmother to buy a bag of dope. Drug addiction is a family affair. It's a tragedy for everyone involved. And it wouldn't matter a bit to these families if the drugs were legal. The human misery would be the same. There would just be more of it.

LEGALIZATION WOULD PRESENT A LAW ENFORCEMENT NIGHTMARE

The fourth outcome of legalization would be a law enforcement nightmare. I suspect few people would want to make drugs available to 12-year old children. That reluctance points to a major flaw in the legalization proposal. Drugs will always be denied to some sector of the population, so there will always be some form of black market and a need for drug enforcement.

Consider some of the questions that legalization raises: What drugs will be legalized? Will it be limited to marijuana? What is a safe dosage of methamphetamine or of crack cocaine? If the principle is advanced that drug abuse is a victimless crime, why limit drug use to marijuana?

I know that there are those who will make the case that drug addiction hurts no one but the user. If that becomes falsely part of the conventional wisdom, there will certainly be pressure to legalize all drug use. Only when people come to realize how profoundly all of us are affected by widespread drug abuse will there be pressure to put the genie back in the bottle. By then, it may be too late.

But deciding what drugs to legalize will only be part of the problem. Who will be able to buy drugs legally? Only those over 18 or 21? If so, you can bet that many young people who have reached the legal age will divert their supplies to younger friends. Of course, these young pushers will be in competition with many of the same people who are now pushing drugs in school yards and neighborhood streets.

Any attempt to limit drug use to any age group at all will create a black market, with all of the attendant crime and violence, thereby defeating one of the goals purported of legalization. That's also true if legalization is limited to marijuana. Cocaine, heroin and methamphetamine will be far more profitable products for the drug lords. Legalization of marijuana alone would do little to stem illegal trafficking.

Will airline pilots be able to use drugs? Heart surgeons? People in law enforcement or the military? Teachers? Pregnant women? Truck drivers? Workers in potentially dangerous jobs like construction?

Drug use has been demonstrated to result in lower work-place productivity, and often ends in serious, life-threatening accidents. Many drug users are so debilitated by their habit that they can't hold jobs. Which raises the question, if drug users can't hold a job, where will they get the money to buy drugs? Will the right to use drugs imply a right to the access to drugs? If so, who will distribute free drugs? Government employees? The local supermarket? The college bookstore? If they can't hold a job, who will provide their food, clothing and shelter?

Virtually any form of legalization will create a patchwork quilt of drug laws and drug enforcement. The confusion would swamp our precinct houses and courtrooms. I don't think it would be possible to effectively enforce the remaining drug laws in that kind of environment.

DRUG ENFORCEMENT WORKS

This is no time to undermine America's effort to stem drug abuse. America's drug policies work. From 1979 to 1994, the number of drug users in America dropped by almost half. Two things significantly contributed to that outcome. First, a strong program of public education; second, a strict program of law enforcement.

If you look over the last four decades, you can see a pattern develop. An independent researcher, R. E. Peterson, has analyzed this period, using statistics from a wide variety of sources, including the Justice Department and the White House Office of National Drug Control Strategy. He broke these four decades down into two periods: the first, from 1960 to 1980, an era of permissive drug laws; the second, from 1980 to 1995, an era of tough drug laws.

During the permissive period, drug incarceration rates fell almost 80 percent. During the era of tough drug laws, drug incarceration rates rose almost 450 percent. Just as you might expect, these two policies regarding drug abuse had far different consequences. During the permissive period, drug use among teens climbed by more than 500 percent. During the tough era, drug use by high school students dropped by more than a third.

Is there an absolute one-to-one correlation between tougher drug enforcement and a declining rate of drug use? I wouldn't suggest that. But the contrasts of drug abuse rates between the two eras of drug enforcement are striking.

One historian of the drug movement has written about America's experience with the veterans of Vietnam. As you may recall from the early 1970s, there was a profound concern in the American government over the rates of heroin use by our military personnel in Vietnam. At the time, U.S. Army medical officers estimated that about 10–15 percent of the lower ranking enlisted men in Vietnam were heroin users.

Military authorities decided to take a tough stand on the problem. They mandated a drug test for every departing soldier. Those who failed were required to undergo drug treatment for 30 days. The theory was that many of the soldiers who were using heroin would give it up to avoid the added 30 days in Vietnam. It clearly worked. Six months after the tests began, the percentage of soldiers testing positive dropped from 10 percent to two percent.

There may be a whole host of reasons for this outcome. But it demonstrates that there is nothing inevitable about drug abuse. In fact, the history of America's experience with drugs has shown us that it was strong drug enforcement that effectively ended America's first drug epidemic, which lasted from the mid-1880s to the mid-1920s.

By 1923, about half of all prisoners at the Federal penitentiary in Leavenworth, Kansas, were violators of America's first drug legislation, the Harrison Act. If you are concerned by the high drug incarceration rates of the late 1990s, consider the parallels to the tough drug enforcement policies of the 1920s. It was those tough policies that did much to create America's virtually drug-free environment of the mid-20th Century.

Drug laws can work, if we have the national resolve to enforce them. As a father, as someone who's had a lot of involvement with the Boy Scouts and Little Leaguers, and as a 30-year civil servant in drug enforcement, I can tell you that there are a lot of young people out there looking for help. Sometimes helping them means saying "no," and having the courage to back it up.

Let me tell you a story about one of them. He was a young man who lived near Austin, Texas, in the early 1970's. He had a wife who was pregnant. To protect their identities, I'll call them John and Michelle. John was involved in drugs, and one night we arrested him and some of his friends on drug charges. He went on to serve a six-month sentence before being turned loose.

Sometime after he got out, he and his wife came to our office looking for me. They rang the doorbell out at the reception area, and my secretary came back and said they were here to see me. I had no idea what they wanted. I was kind of leery, thinking they might be looking for revenge. But I went out to the reception area anyway.

John and Michelle were standing there with a little toddler. They said they just wanted to come in so we could see their new baby. And then Michelle said there was a second reason they came by. When he got arrested, she said, that's the best thing that ever happened to them.

We had been very wholesome people, she said. John was involved in sports in high school. He was an all-American guy. Then he started smoking pot. His parents couldn't reach him. His teachers couldn't reach him. He got into other drugs. He dropped out of high school. The only thing that ever got his attention, she said, was when he got arrested.

Meanwhile, John was listening to all this and shaking his head in agreement. He said that his high school coach had tried to counsel him, but he wouldn't listen to him. He said his big mistake was dropping out of sports. He thought that if he had stayed in sports he wouldn't have taken the route he did. But mainly, he said he took this route because of the easy availability of drugs and their widespread usage by his peers.

When I arrested those kids that night I had no idea of the extent to which I would ultimately help them out of their problems and influence their lives in a positive way. In 30 years of dealing with young Americans, I believe that John is more typical than not. His human frailties were magnified by the easy availability of drugs and by peer pressure; and his life was brought near ruin.

America spends millions of dollars every year on researching the issue of drugs. We have crime statistics and opinion surveys and biochemical research. And all of that is important. But what it all comes down to is whether we can help young people like John — whether we can keep them from taking that first step into the world of drugs that will ruin their careers, destroy their marriages and leave them in a cycle of dependency on chemicals.

Whether in rural areas, in the suburbs, or in the inner cities, there are a lot of kids who could use a little help. Sometimes that help can take the form of education and counseling. Often it takes a stronger approach. And there are plenty of young people, and older people as well, who could use it.

If we as a society are unwilling to have the courage to say no to drug abuse, we will find that drugs will not only destroy the society we have built up over 200 years, but ruin millions of young people like John.

Drug abuse, and the crime and personal dissolution and social decay that go with it, are not inevitable. Too many people in America seem resigned to the growing rates of drug use. But America's experience with drugs shows that strong law enforcement policies can and do work.

At DEA, our mission is to fight drug trafficking in order to make drug abuse expensive, unpleasant, risky, and disreputable. If drug users aren't worried about their health, or the health and welfare of those who depend on them, they should at least worry about the likelihood of getting caught.

Questions for Discussion

1. What effect do drugs have on crime?
2. What effect would decriminalization of drugs have on solving the drug problem?

3. What relevance does U.S. experience with the prohibition of alcohol between 1920 and 1933 have on the issue of decriminalizing drugs today?
4. What is the best method to reduce the use of illegal drugs?
5. Is drug abuse a victimless crime? What are the reasons for your answer?

Suggested Resources

Web Sites

Drug Enforcement Administration
http://www.usdoj.gov/dea/

Drug Policy Alliance
http://www.drugpolicy.org

National Center on Addiction and Substance Abuse at Columbia University
http://www.casacolumbia.org

National Organization for the Reform of Marijuana Laws
http://www.norml.org

Publications

Barr, Bob, Eric Sterling, and Juan Williams. "The War on Drugs: Fighting Crime or Wasting Time?" *American Criminal Law Review* 38, no. 4 (Fall 2001): 1537–64.

Carpenter, Ted Galen. *Bad Neighbor Policy: Washington's Futile War on Drugs in Latin America.* New York: Palgrave, 2003.

Inciardi, James A. *The War on Drugs III: The Continuing Saga of the Mysteries and Miseries of Intoxication, Addiction, Crime, and Public Policy.* Boston: Allyn & Bacon, 2002.

Lamberton, Lance. "The Drug War's Assault on Liberty." *Ideas on Liberty* 50, no. 8 (August 2000): 46–50.

Levine, Herbert M. *The Drug Problem.* Austin, Tex.: Raintree/Steck-Vaughn, 1998.

MacCoun, Robert J., and Peter Reuter. *Drug War Heresies: Learning from Other Vices, Times, and Places.* New York: Cambridge University Press, 2001.

———, eds. "Cross-National Drug Policy." *Annals of the American Academy of Political and Social Science* 582 (July 2002): entire issue.

Orcutt, James D., and David R. Rudy, eds., *Drugs, Alcohol, and Social Problems.* Lanham, Md.: Rowman & Littlefield, 2003.

Streatfeild, Dominic. *Cocaine: An Unauthorized Biography.* New York: St. Martin's Press, 2002.

U.S. Cong., House of Representatives. *The Decriminalization of Illegal Drugs.* Hearing before the Subcommittee on Criminal Justice, Drug Policy, and Human Resources of the Committee on Government Reform, 106th Cong., 1st Sess., July 13, 1999.

————. *Is Drug Use Up or Down? What Are the Implications?* Hearing before the Subcommittee on Criminal Justice, Drug Policy, and Human Resources of the Committee on Government Reform, 106th Cong., 2d Sess., September 19, 2000.

————. *Pros and Cons of Drug Legalization, Decriminalization, and Harm Reduction.* Hearing before the Subcommittee on Criminal Justice, Drug Policy, and Human Resources of the Committee on Government Reform, 106th Cong., 1st Sess., June 16, 1999.

Walters, John P., "The Myth of 'Harmless' Marijuana." *Washington Post,* May 1, 2002, p. A25. See also, Keith Stroup and Paul Armentano. "The Problem Is Pot Prohibition." *Washington Post,* May 4, 2002, p. A19.

Wilson, James Q. "Against the Legalization of Drugs." *Commentary* 89, no. 2 (February 1990): 21–28.

Wisher, Ray. "The Powerful Link between Drugs and Crime." *American Enterprise* 12, no. 6 (September 2001): 43–45.

Will Gun Control
Reduce Violence?

Firearms take a heavy toll of life and limb in the United States. In 2000, of the 12,943 homicides reported, 66 percent (8,493) were committed with firearms. Of those committed with firearms, 79 percent (6,686) involved handguns.[1] Handguns are also responsible for suicides and accidental deaths, and they are used in a multitude of crimes, including theft, assault, and rape.

Young people live in a world of guns. Particularly in the inner cities, children of all ages hear gunshots on their streets; know people who have been threatened, wounded, or killed by guns; and even have guns of their own. Metal detectors have been installed in schools to prevent youngsters from carrying weapons into the classrooms.

National interest has focused on guns as responsible for much violent crime not only from personal experience but also because of incidents that have attracted national attention. To cite a few:

- In 1968, Robert Kennedy, a U.S. senator from New York, and brother of the slain president, was assassinated with a firearm.
- In 1981, John Hinckley used a handgun in attempting to assassinate President Ronald Reagan. He wounded the president and caused serious and permanent injury to James Brady, the president's press secretary.
- In January 1991, Patrick Purdy opened fire with a Kalashnikov-type semiautomatic rifle in a Stockton, California, schoolyard. He killed five children and wounded nearly thirty others.
- On December 7, 1993, Colin Furguson opened fire on a crowded Long Island Railroad commuter train. He declared war on "whites, Asians, and 'Uncle Tom' Negroes." He killed six people and wounded nineteen.
- On April 20, 1999, Eric Harris and Dylan Klebold, armed with guns, massacred thirteen people and wounded dozens of others before killing themselves at Columbine High School in Littleton, Colorado.

The high number of killings by firearms has led to calls for laws that would regulate their possession or use or even ban them. Already on the books is a 1934 statute, the National Firearms Act, which makes it difficult to obtain types of firearms perceived to be especially lethal or to be the chosen weapons of gangsters. Among these weapons are machine guns and sawed-off shotguns. The 1934 law also provides for a firearm registration system.

Passed in 1968, the Gun Control Act requires all persons dealing in firearms to be federally licensed. It also tightens federal licensing procedures, prohibits the interstate sale of handguns generally, prescribes categories of individuals to whom firearms and ammunition cannot be sold, prohibits the importation of nonsporting firearms or ammunition, requires that dealers maintain records of all commercial gun sales, and contains other regulatory provisions. In 1986, the McClure-Volkmer Amendments (named for Senator James A. McClure, a Republican from Idaho, and Representative Harold L. Volkmer, a Democrat from Missouri) to the Gun Control Act banned the further manufacture of machine guns. They also tightened enforcement of gun control laws at the same time that they modified or eliminated provisions of the existing law that were opposed by gun owners and the gun industry.

On November 30, 1993, President Bill Clinton signed into law the Brady Bill (named after James Brady). The law, which went into effect in 1994, requires a five-day waiting period during which local police are required to conduct a criminal background check of prospective handgun buyers. Some states and localities, moreover, have enacted laws that are more stringent than federal laws, including the banning of all handguns (except for law enforcement officers).

In 1994, President Clinton signed into law an anticrime bill. One of its provisions banned for ten years the manufacture, sale, and possession of nineteen types of assault weapons and "copycat" versions of those guns. Assault weapons are military-style or police-style weapons with large clips holding twenty to thirty bullets. The law also banned some guns with two or more features associated with assault weapons. But it specifically excluded 650 types of semiautomatic weapons.

In the past few years new laws on gun control have been enacted. The Federal Domestic Gun Ban (the Lautenberg Amendment in the Omnibus Appropriations Act for Fiscal Year 1997, P.L. 104–208) prohibits persons convicted of misdemeanor crimes of domestic violence from possessing firearms and ammunition. According to the Omnibus Consolidated and Emergency Appropriations Act, 1999, all federal firearm licensees must offer for sale gun storage and safety devices. The law also bans firearm transfers to, or possession by, nonimmigrants on temporary visas who have overextended their stay in the United States. The Treasury and General Government Appropriations Act, Fiscal Year 2000, requires background checks when people who sold their firearm to a pawnshop seek to get the weapon back.

The debate over gun control is a continuing one, involving such matters as social science research and legal issues. Advocates and opponents of gun control differ in their assessment of the facts, especially whether social science data prove that gun control deters violent crime. They also disagree in their interpretations of the Second Amendment to the Constitution, which reads: "A well regulated Militia, being necessary to the security of a free State, the right of the people to keep and bear Arms, shall not be infringed."

The Educational Fund to Stop Gun Violence, a nonprofit organization, argues for gun control. It contends:

1. Gun violence takes a heavy toll of life in the United States.
2. Women, children, and people of color are particularly vulnerable because of the easy availability of guns.
3. It is no wonder that the American people support gun control legislation.
4. The cost of gun violence to the American people is $100 billion a year.
5. The record for deaths by firearms in the United States is one of the worst in the industrialized world.
6. U.S. domestic firearm laws adversely affect neighboring countries to the north and south.
7. The Second Amendment to the Constitution does not guarantee an individual citizen the right to own and carry a gun.
8. More gun laws need to be enacted, and all gun laws need to be enforced.

Jim Babka, president of the American Liberty Foundation, takes issue with the advocates of gun control. In presenting a fantasy dialogue between himself and a gun control advocate, whom he calls "Bill," he makes his case. He contends:

1. Police are unable to provide security to everyone, so self-defense is the job of each individual.
2. Gun control does not keep guns out of the hands of criminals; rather, it keeps guns out of the hands of the victims of criminals.
3. Guns help provide safety. Women, in particular need guns for their safety.
4. The number of accidental deaths caused by guns has been exaggerated.
5. Gun control would not reduce crime.
6. Background checks, such as those required by the Brady Law, safety locks on guns, and laws against carrying concealed weapons, are really not effective in providing safety for innocent people.
7. Background checks are really unconstitutional since they are in conflict with the Second Amendment.
8. Citizens do have a right to bear arms, according to the Constitution.
9. Gun control is a policy of dictatorships, such as those instituted by Mao Zedong, Adolf Hitler, and Joseph Stalin, to keep their people under control.

NOTE

1. As cited in Congressional Research Service, "Gun Control Legislation in the 107th Congress," Issue Brief for Congress, August 27, 2002, p. CRS-3.

☑ *Y E S*

Will Gun Control Reduce Violence?

EDUCATIONAL FUND TO STOP GUN VIOLENCE
The Facts about Gun Violence

GUN VIOLENCE

Deaths from Gun Violence

Annually, about 30,000 people die of firearm injuries. In 1999, guns claimed 28,874 lives in the United States, the majority from suicides. Firearm deaths, 1999, by cause:

- Suicide — 16,599
- Homicide — 10,828
- Unintentional Shootings[1] — 1,447

Guns in the Home and the Myth of Self-Defense

Guns are rarely useful for self-defense. They only increase the risk of death and injury and create a false sense of security. A gun kept in the home is 4 times more likely to be involved in an unintentional shooting, 7 times more likely to be used in a criminal assault or homicide, and 11 times more likely to be used to commit or attempt suicide, than to be used in self-defense.[2]

Even police officers, who are trained in handling weapons, are at risk of having their guns used against them. A study published in the *American Journal of Public Health* found that 20 percent of police officers shot and killed in the last 15 years were killed with their own firearms. Research also shows that the use of a firearm to resist a violent assault actually increases the victim's risk of injury and death.

FIREARM OWNERSHIP

How many guns does each person own?

Most guns in America are concentrated within the hands of a small group of people.[3]

- 74 percent of gun owners own more than one firearm.
- 42 percent of individuals and 34 percent of households report owning 4 or more guns.

- This means that 9.7 million individuals own 105.5 million guns, with the remaining 34.4 million individuals owning just 86.6 million guns.

What types of guns do Americans own?

Of the approximately 200 million guns owned in America, approximately 65 million are handguns, 49 million are shotguns and 70 million are rifles.[4] Semi-automatics account for 40 percent of all shotguns and handguns.[5]

How much training have gun owners received?

Most gun owners have received some kind of training.[6]

- 58 percent of gun owners have received one or more types of formal training.
- 29 percent of gun owners have received at least informal training.
- 13 percent of gun owners have received no training of any kind.

How are guns commonly stored?

A notable amount of guns, particularly handguns, are not properly or safely stored.[7]

- Of all gun owners, 20 percent store their guns unlocked and loaded.
- Of all handguns, 57 percent are kept unlocked, while 55 percent are kept loaded.
- Handguns are kept unlocked *and* loaded by 30 percent of their owners.

How often are guns stolen?

Estimates of total firearm thefts range from 350,000 to 590,000 thefts a year.[8] Guns used in crime are often stolen.

- One survey found that, of incarcerated felons who had most recently used a handgun in crime, the gun was acquired through theft 32 percent of the time.[9] This points to the fact that guns in legal circulation often end up in the hands of criminals, thus increasing the threat society faces from the large amount of guns in circulation.

YOUTH AND GUN VIOLENCE

Too Many!

In 1999, 3,385 young people ages 1–19 were killed by a gun.[10] That's 9 young lives lost to gun violence every day.

- Teenagers are more likely to die of a gun injury than all other natural causes combined.[11]

Gun Violence Directly Affects Youth

Gun violence is often framed as a crime issue and described exclusively in terms of deaths attributed to gunfire, ignoring injuries and public health costs. The truth is, the issue runs much deeper, and young people often witness the problem first-hand.

- More than one-third of high school students knows someone who has been shot by a firearm.[12]
- One in three high school students personally know someone who has been threatened by a gun.
- Approximately 20 percent of high school students know someone who has carried a gun in school, or on the way to or from school.[13]

Youth Gun Violence, an American Phenomenon

Children in the United States are 12 times more likely to die from firearm-related death than are children in the other 25 industrial nations combined.[14] Cumulatively, compared to the 25 industrialized nations, a child in the United States is:

- 16 times more likely to be killed by a gun;
- 11 times more likely to commit suicide with a gun;
- 9 times more likely to die in a firearm-related accident.[15]

WOMEN AND GUN VIOLENCE

How many women and girls are killed by firearms?
In 1999, 4,174 women and girls died from firearms. Of these firearm-related deaths, 2,120 were suicides, 1,884 were homicides, 170 were accidental (117), undetermined (47), or a result of legal intervention (6).[16]

How does firearm violence differ between men and women?
Women are far less likely than men to be firearm homicide victims. In 1999, 8,944 men were murdered by a firearm compared to 1,884 women.[17]

But, women are far more likely to be shot by an intimate partner than men.[18] About twice as many women as men are shot by an intimate partner than are killed by strangers using firearms, knives, or any other means.[19]

Men are much more likely to commit homicide with a gun than are women. During the period from 1976 to 1987, men committed 96,923 homicides with guns compared to 14,916 committed by women.[20]

Can women protect themselves from victimization by owning a gun?
Women have traditionally had far lower rates of gun ownership than men. Recently, the gun industry has preyed on women's fears of victimization to attract potential female buyers and increase profits. Guns in general are not useful for self-defense.

- Studies show that in actuality, guns are more of a danger than a means of security. Victims of homicide are more likely than the general population to have had someone in their family purchase a handgun in the past.[21]

- A firearm(s) in the home raises a woman's risk of suicide by a factor of five, while her risk of homicide increases more than three times.[22]
- Individuals are five times more likely to use a gun against an intimate partner or a family member than against a stranger.[23]
- In 1992 for every time a woman used a handgun to justifiably kill a stranger, 239 women were murdered by a handgun.[24]

Do guns help women in situations of domestic violence?

Having a firearm in the home increases the likelihood that an abusive relationship will turn fatal.

- Family and intimate assaults that involved firearms are 12 times more likely to result in death than those that do not involve firearms.[25]
- Keeping a firearm in your home makes it three times more likely that you or a person you care about will be shot by another family member or intimate partner.[26]

GUN VIOLENCE—A CIVIL RIGHTS ISSUE

Key Facts on Race and Gun Deaths in America[27]

- Gun violence is a leading cause of death for people of color in America.
- Gun violence is the number one killer of African Americans ages 15–34.
- It is the second leading cause of death for Hispanic youth ages 15–24.
- Since 1981, more than 230,000 people of color have been killed by firearms in America.[28]
- Though people of color represent 29 percent of the U.S. population, they represent 54 percent of gun homicide victims.
- African Americans represent 13 percent of population but 51 percent of gun homicides.
- Hispanics represent 12 percent of population but 18 percent of gun homicides.
- African Americans have a gun homicide rate more than 4 times the national average.
- 72 percent of all homicide victims who are people of color in the U.S. are killed with guns.
  - Asian American and Pacific Islander—91 percent
  - African Americans—73 percent
  - Hispanics—70 percent
  - American Indians, Eskimos, and Aleutian—45 percent
- From 1990 to 1999 approximately 30,000 U.S. youth were murdered with a firearm—62 percent of the victims were youth of color.
- 95 percent of these were African American youth.

PUBLIC OPINION

National Polling Date

National polling reveals some interesting findings regarding how we talk about the gun issue with the public. When polled about gun control in general, support for it hovers in the 60 percent range. When polled on *specific gun law proposals,* however, support is significantly higher:

- 60 percent of Election 2000 voters support stronger gun laws (CNN exit polling, November 2000)
- 59 percent favor passing stricter national gun control laws (Lake, Snell, Perry, May 2001)
- 72 percent of Americans would vote to require licensing and registration on new handgun purchases (Gallup, October 2000)
- 85 percent of registered voters (73 percent of gun owners and 66 percent of self-described NRA [National Rifle Association] supporters) favor requiring a license before a handgun is purchased (Lake, Snell, Perry, May 2001)

THE COST OF GUN VIOLENCE

Many gunshot victims are uninsured, which means that their treatment is paid for by taxpayers. Stronger gun laws mean less gun violence — or in other words — stronger gun laws save taxpayers money.

The Cost of Treating the Victims of Gun Violence Is Far Higher Than the Cost of Treating Victims of Other Injuries

Firearm-related injuries make up 0.5 percent of all injuries, yet they represent 9 percent of total cost of injury over a lifetime. Almost 85–98 percent of all health-care expenses due to gunshot injuries and fatalities are *charged to taxpayers.*

Estimates of the Total Cost of Gun Violence Reach $100 Billion

- In their book *Gun Violence, The Real Costs,* Phillip Cook and Jens Ludwig look beyond the medical costs of gun violence and examine the *full cost* borne by Americans in a society where both gun violence and its ever-present threat mandate responses that touch every aspect of our lives. Their findings reveal that the annual cost of gun violence in America approaches $100 billion.

The Financial Costs of Gun Violence Place a Heavy Burden on Trauma Care Centers

- The cost of treating gunshot wounds can reach over $100 million a year at an average county hospital. Because many gunshot victims are uninsured, an estimated 85–96 percent of medical charges due to gunshots are paid by taxpayers through public health care and public debt.[29]
- A 1999 study revealed that for every firearm victim treated at a local trauma care center, an average of $8,664 was lost to uncompensated care.[30]
- Between 1986 and 1991, 92 of the 549 trauma care centers in the United States closed, primarily because of the cost of uncompensated care for injuries such as gun violence.[31]

U.S. GUN DEATHS — AN INTERNATIONAL COMPARISON

According to a 1997 study by the United Nations, the United States has weaker firearm regulations and higher numbers of deaths involving firearms than all other industrialized nations, and even most developing nations. The study surveyed 49 nations on their firearm legislation, manufacture, trade regulations, and rates of firearm crime and death.

Here are some facts from this study and others.

- The United States is one of only two countries — along with the Czech Republic — that does not have a firearm licensing system.[32]
- Thirty-five percent of households in the United States possess at least one firearm, over three times the average of other countries surveyed.[33]

Table 1. International Gun Death Rates

Country (Year of Statistic)	Firearm Deaths (Rate per 100,000)	Firearm Homicides (Rate per 100,000)	Firearm Suicides (Rate per 100,000)	Fatal Firearm Accidents (Rate per 100,000)
United States (1995)	13.7	6	7	0.5
Australia (1994)	3.05	0.56	2.38	0.11
Canada (1994)	4.08	0.6	3.35	0.013
Germany (1996)	1.47	0.21	1.23	0.03
Japan (1995)	0.07	0.03	0.04	0.01
Sweden (1992)	2.31	0.31	1.95	0.05
Spain (1994)	1.01	0.19	0.55	0.26
United Kingdom (1994)	0.57	0.13	0.33	0.02

Source: United Nations

- The United States is among only 22 percent of nations responding to the UN survey that do not have regulations regarding the storage of firearms.[34]
- While the United States rarely imports illegal firearms, it is one of only three countries that reported "frequent" instances of illegal exportation.[35]
- Of illegal handguns seized by the Japanese government from 1992–1996, 32.9 percent were manufactured in the United States, more than any other single country.[36]
- The total firearm death rate in the United States in 1995 was 13.7 per 100,000 people, three times the average rate among other responding countries, and the third highest, after Brazil and Jamaica.[37]
- In 1995, 1,225 people in the U.S. died from firearm accidents. This figure is over three times higher than the average rate of other responding countries.[38]
- The U.S. had the highest firearm suicide rate of all the countries surveyed, 7 per 100,000 people in 1995, nearly seven times greater than the average among other responding countries.[39]
- Children in the U.S. are 12 times more likely to die from firearm injury than are children in other industrialized nations.[40]
- In 1997, the United Kingdom joined Japan and Vietnam, banning the private ownership of all, or nearly all, handguns.
- Canada passed legislation in 1995 banning short-barreled handguns, as well as semi-automatic assault weapons.
- Australia followed in 1997 by banning semi-automatic rifles, adding to already tight restrictions on handguns.

INTERNATIONAL SMALL ARMS TRAFFICKING

Weak domestic firearm laws in the United States adversely affect neighboring countries to the north and south. The United States is Mexico's leading source of black market arms — despite Mexico's own strict gun control policy. Tight laws on gun sales in Canada are also circumvented by arms smugglers along the 3,000-plus mile U.S./Canada border.

- Unlike drugs, small arms are durable goods that can cross national borders and can be sold and resold many times.
- Most small arms start out in the legal market and find their way into the illicit market.
- Stocks of weapons in government warehouses can be stolen or diverted where they may be used in crimes, suicides, and homicides.

THE SECOND AMENDMENT

The Truth about the Second Amendment: Countering Gun Lobby Myths

Gun Lobby Myth #1:
The Second Amendment to the Constitution
Guarantees an Individual Citizen the Right to Own and Carry a Gun

FACT: While the gun lobby focuses its arguments on the second half of the Amendment, the right to keep and bear arms as stated in the Constitution is fundamentally based on states' need for a well-regulated militia.

The Second Amendment was adopted to ensure the right of states to maintain their own militia to protect themselves against foreign and federal encroachment. It does not guarantee the individual a right to own firearms for self-defense. The National Guard, created in 1903, is the contemporary equivalent of the organized state militia. The citizens in the National Guard are provided with arms when called to duty and are not required to privately own firearms for service.

No federal court, including the U.S. Supreme Court, has ever overturned a gun control law on the grounds of the Second Amendment.

The federal judiciary, including the Supreme Court, has been remarkably consistent in finding that the Second Amendment protects a state's right to keep a well-regulated militia, rather than an individual's right to bear arms. One definitive Supreme Court case, *United States v. Miller,* claimed that his Second Amendment rights were violated by a federal law that prohibits the possession of sawed-off shotguns. The Court ruled, "In the absence of any evidence tending to show that possession or use of a [shotgun] at this time has some reasonable relationship to the preservation or efficiency of a well-regulated militia, we cannot say that the Second Amendment guarantees the right to keep and bear such an instrument." The federal courts have always upheld gun control laws when they have been contested on Second Amendment grounds.

Gun Lobby Myth #2:
The Founding Fathers of This Nation
Intended to Give Every Individual the Right to Own Firearms.

FACT: The founding fathers never intended to provide individuals with the right to firearm ownership.

As the Bill of Rights was being drafted, the founders deliberately wrote the Second Amendment so that it binds firearm possession to the military needs of the state. Therefore, the gun lobby distorts the words of the founding fathers when it ignores the importance of state militia in the Second Amendment.

The Second Amendment was drafted by the founding fathers as a response to the fear that states would be oppressed by a tyrannical federal government.

The founding fathers drafted the Bill of Rights at a time when the people were fearful of a totalitarian, militaristic federal government that denied basic rights to its subjects. The states were demanding the right to keep their own armed militias to ensure that they could stop the new U.S. government from becoming a tyranni-cal force as the British government had been over the colonies. The Amendment was therefore meant to create a system of checks and balances between the state and federal governments.

While some people today still hold extremist fears of a tyrannical U.S. govern-ment, it is important to emphasize that the right to defense against the federal gov-ernment is a state right rather than an *individual* right.

A proposal by Thomas Jefferson to include in the Virginia Declaration of Rights a provision that "no freeman shall be debarred the use of arms" was rejected. Yet the NRA deliberately and incorrectly refers to this provision as an early U.S. law enabling citizens to keep their own arms.

Gun Lobby Myth #3:
The Solution to Oppression and Totalitarian Governments
Is for All Citizens to Own Guns.

FACT: Arming all citizens does not prevent or eliminate systems of oppression.

The gun lobby often cites the Holocaust, violence in Bosnia, hunger in Somalia, and racism in the U.S. as problems that would have been or could be overcome if only oppressed individuals were armed. Yet it is precisely the rampant prolifera-tion of guns that can make tragedies such as these possible. There are numerous countries which have extensive restrictions of firearms ownership that have not fallen into tyranny, such as Canada, Japan, and Australia. Clearly, democracy still thrives in nations with few firearms. Furthermore, in recent history, many oppres-sive governments, such as those in Eastern Europe and South Africa, have been overthrown by citizens working through activism and nonviolent protest, not by individuals taking up arms.

HANDGUNS

- Handguns pose a serious public health threat. Even though they account for only one-third of all firearms privately owned in the U.S., handguns cause over two-thirds of all firearm deaths and injuries.
- In 2000, handguns were used in 78.7 percent of all homicides involving a firearm, according to the FBI's [Federal Bureau of Investigation] Uniform Crime Report.
- Handguns are the most popular type of firearm used in suicide. One study found that 69 percent of those who commit suicide with a firearm use a handgun.[41]

Junk Guns

- Junk guns are handguns that do not meet the quality and safety tests required of imported handguns. In accordance with the Gun Control Act of 1968, the Bureau of Alcohol, Tobacco and Firearms (ATF) established a criteria for assessing the sporting utility of imported handguns based on size, safety, weight, quality of construction, and caliber. Handguns that would fail to meet basic safety standards are commonly referred to as junk guns or Saturday Night Specials.
- Junk guns are small, inexpensive, easily concealed, poorly made handguns that usually lack adequate safety devices. The combined length and height of a junk gun is typically less than 10 inches and it can be concealed in the palm of a hand. These guns are sold at retail prices as low as $69.[42] These are dangerous consumer products that lack minimum design and safety standards.
- In the Gun Control Act of 1968, Congress prohibited the *importation* of firearms not "generally recognized as particularly suitable for or readily adaptable to sporting purposes."[43] In determining sporting purpose, ATF considers the following characteristics: size, safety, weight, quality of construction, and caliber. Thus, the 1968 Act effectively banned *foreign* junk guns.
- In 1968, most junk guns were manufactured outside of the United States. Therefore, domestic manufacturers were not included in the restrictions. The result was the creation of a protected industry that produces and sells weapons in the U.S. that Congress found too dangerous to be imported. Consequently, by the mid-1970s, ATF estimated that over half of all handguns made in the U.S. for civilians could not be imported legally.[44]

NOTES

1. Includes causes: accidental, undetermined and legal intervention. Hoyert D. L., Arias E., Smith B. L., Murphy S. I., and Kochanek K. D. *Deaths: Final Data for 1999.* National vital statistics reports; vol. 49, no. 8. Hyattsville, Md.: National Center for Health Statistics. 2001, Table 17, p. 68.

2. Arthur L. Kellermann, MD, MPH, et al. "Injuries and Deaths Due to Firearms in the Home." *Journal of Trauma,* 1998, vol. 45, p. 263.

3. Cook, Philip J., and Ludwig, Jens. *Guns in America, Results of a Comprehensive National Survey on Firearms Ownership and Use, Summary Report.* Washington, D.C.: Police Foundation, 1996, p. 15.

4. Cook, Ludwig, pp. 13–14.

5. Cook, Ludwig, p. 13.

6. Cook, Ludwig, p. 22.

7. Cook, Ludwig, p. 22.

8. Philip J. Cook, Stephanie Molliconi, and Thomas B. Cole, "Regulating Gun Markets," *The Journal of Marketing Research,* 86, no. 1. 1995. pp. 59–92.

9. Cook, Ludwig, p. 29.

10. Hoyert D. L., Arias E., Smith B. L., Murphy S. I., and Kochanek K. D. *Deaths: Final Data for 1999*. National vital statistics reports; vol. 49, no. 8. Hyattsville, Md.: National Center for Health Statistics. 2001, p. 10, Table 17, p. 68.

11. American Academy of Pediatrics Task Force on Violence, "The Role of the Pediatrician in Youth Violence Prevention in Clinical Practice and at the Community Level," *Pediatrics*, vol. 103, no. 1, January 1999, p. 173.

12. Teenage Research Unlimited, "National Survey of Teens Attitudes towards Gun Violence." Uhlich Children's Home, Chicago, IL. June 2000.

13. Gilbert, Dennis, et al. "Hamilton College Youth and Guns Poll," August 2000.

14. Centers for Disease Control and Prevention, "Rates of Homicide, Suicide, and Firearms-Related Deaths among Children — 26 Industrialized Countries," *Morbidity and Mortality Weekly Report*, vol. 46, no. 5, February 7, 1997, p. 103.

15. Centers for Disease Control and Prevention.

16. Hoyert D. L., Arias E., Smith B. L., Murphy S. I., and Kochanek K. D. *Deaths: Final Data for 1999*. National vital statistics reports; vol. 49, no. 8. Hyattsville, Md.: National Center for Health Statistics. 2001, p. 10, Table 17, p. 68.

17. Hoyert D. L., Table 17, p. 68.

18. Arthur L. Kellermann, MD, MPH; and James A. Mercy, PhD; "Men, Women, and Murder: Gender-specific Differences in Rates of Fatal Violence and Victimization," *The Journal of Trauma*, vol. 33, no. 1, July, 1992, p. 2.

19. Kellermann and Mercy, p. 1.

20. Kellermann and Mercy, pp. 1–5.

21. Peter Cummings, MD, MPH; Thomas D. Koepsell, MD, MPH; David C. Grossman, MD, MPH; James Savarino, PhD, MS; and Robert S. Thompson, MD; "The Association between the Purchase of a Handgun and Homicide and Suicide," *American Journal of Public Health*, vol. 87, no. 6, June 1997, p. 976.

22. Glick, Susan, "Who Dies?" Violence Policy Center. Feb. 1999. p. 9.

23. Kellermann and Mercy. p. 1.

24. Federal Bureau of Investigation (FBI), Unpublished justifiable homicide statistics, 1992.

25. Linda E. Saltzman, PhD; James A. Mercy, PhD; Patrick W. O'Carroll, M.D, MPH; Mark L. Rosenberg, MD, MPP; and Philip H. Rhodes, MS, "Weapon Involvement and Injury Outcomes in Family and Intimate Assaults," *Journal of the American Medical Association*, vol. 267, no. 22, June 10, 1992, p. 3043.

26. Arthur Kellermann, MD, MPH; Frederick P. Rivara, MD, MPH; Norman B. Rushforth, PhD; Joyce G. Banton, MS; Donald T. Reay, MD; Jerry T. Francisco, MD; Ana B. Locci, PhD; Janice Prodzinski, BS; Bela B. Hackman, MD; and Grant Somes, PhD, "Gun Ownership as a Risk Factor for Homicide in the Home," *New England Journal of Medicine*, vol. 329. no. 15, October 7, 1993.

27. Unless otherwise noted, all statistics derived from the Centers for Disease Control's Web-based Injury Statistics Query and Reporting System (WISQARS), *http://www.cdc.gov/ncipc/wisqars/*

28. Centers for Disease Control's Web-based Injury Statistics Query and Reporting System (WISQARS), *http://www.cdc.gov/ncipc/wisqars/*, Centers for Disease Control's Web-based Injury Statistics Query (WONDER) *http://wonder.cdc.gov/mortICD10J.shtml*, Federal Bureau of Investigation's "Uniform Crime Reports," *http://www.fbi.gov/ucr/ucr.htm.*

29. Michael Martin, Thomas Hunt, and Stephen Hulley, "The Cost of Hospitalization for Firearm Injuries," *The Journal of the American Medical Association*, vol. 260. November 25, 1988, p. 3048. and G. J.

30Ordog, J. Wasserberger, and G. Ackroyd, "Hospital Costs of Firearm Injuries." Abstract. *Journal of Trauma*, February 1995, p. 1.

31. Fath, et al. "Urban Trauma Care Is Threatened by Inadequate Reimbursement." *The American Journal of Surgery*. 1999 p. 371, 4; "Congress Acts to Resuscitate Nation's Financially Ailing Trauma Care Systems," *The Journal of the American Medical Association*, vol. 267, June 10, 1992, p. 2996.

32. Cook, Philip J., and Ludwig, Jens. *Guns in America, Results of a Comprehensive National Survey on Firearms Ownership and Use, Summary Report.* Washington, D.C.: Police Foundation, 1996; United Nations, Crime Prevention and Criminal Justice Division, United Nations Office at Vienna, *International Study on Firearm Regulation.* 1997. p. 109.

33. Cook, Philip J.; United Nations.

34. United Nations.

35. United Nations.

36. Firearms Division, National Police Agency. Tokyo, Japan. 1997.

37. United Nations; Anderson, Kochanek, and Murphy, "Report of Final Mortality Statistics, 1995." *Monthly Vital Statistics Report.* Hyattsville, Md.: National Center for Health Statistics, vol. 45, no. 11. June 12, 1997 pp. 55–56.

38. United Nations; Anderson.

39. United Nations; Anderson.

40. Fingerhut, Cox, and Warner, "International Comparative Analysis of Injury Mortality." Centers for Disease Control and Prevention. National Center for Health Statistics. October 7, 1998.

41. Robert N. Anderson, PhD, et al., "Report of Final Mortality Statistics, 1995, ‰ Monthly Vital Statistics Report. National Center for Health Statistics, pp. 55–56.

42. Warner, Ken. *Gun Digest 1996.* DBI Books, Inc.

43. 18 U.P.S.C. Section 935(d).

44. Wintemute, G. J. *Ring of Fire: The Handgun Makers of Southern California,* Sacramento, Calif.: Violence Prevention Research Program, 1994.

☑ NO

Will Gun Control Reduce Violence?

JIM BABKA

Gun Control Only Seems Like a Good Idea!

Perhaps you've debated a gun control advocate before. Then a lot of the questions and statements below might seem familiar to you. This is a very well documented set of factual answers to those typical questions, demonstrating that the Second Amendment Saves Lives.

This page was originally designed as an FAQ but evolved into a fantasy dialogue between a gun control advocate and me. Every answer I give causes the gun control advocate, whom I'll call "Bill," to essentially say, "OK, I'm drawing a line here, this far but no further." And then after I answer Bill again, he retreats and says, "OK, but now I'm drawing the line here," just a few feet closer to my position — gun control is dangerous but private ownership of firearms is a desirable benefit (even for Bill). . . .

It's fun writing an argument where you win hands down. But my real hope is that you find this dialogue useful when you meet your next "Bill."

Bill: Won't the police protect my loved ones and me? Isn't it sensible that the police should be the only ones to own and utilize firearms?

Me: U.S. Courts have ruled over and over again that the police have no legal obligation to protect individuals from harm, only the public in general.[1] Consider *Warren v. D.C.* in which the court affirmed, " . . . when a municipality or other government entity undertakes to furnish police services, it assumes a duty only to the public at large and not to individual members of the community."[2]

And of course the Court was using common sense. Think about it. There are approximately 654,600 officers *employed* to provide law enforcement services to approximately 265 million of the nation's inhabitants, an average of only 2.5 officers for every 1,000 individuals.[3] This statistic, of course, does not reflect the average number of officers actively *deployed or on duty* during a particular shift. So face it — self-defense is your job!

Bill: Don't we need more gun control laws to keep guns out of the hands of criminals?

Me: Criminals by definition don't obey laws. Gun control only restricts law-abiding citizens from purchasing or owning a gun, increasing the odds that they too will be victims. People are much less likely to be victims if they are armed.

Bill: Guns are dangerous. I've heard that the safest response to an armed attacker is to simply do nothing.

Me: Perhaps in some situations that would be true. But criminologists have demonstrated that individuals use guns as often as 2.5 million times per year to protect themselves. In over 90 percent of these cases, the individual merely brandished their gun or fired a warning shot to scare off the attacker.[4]

For example, 3/5 of felons polled agreed that "a criminal is not going to mess around with a victim he knows is armed with a gun,"[5] and 74 percent of felons agreed that, "one reason burglars avoid houses when people are at home is that they fear being shot during the crime."

Women, in particular, need guns for safety. In 89.6 percent of violent crimes where women are the intended victims, the offender does not have a gun; and only 10 percent of rapists carry a gun.[6] So armed women have an advantage over their attackers.

Bill: It's not adult women that are in real danger — it's children. Guns in the home kill kids.

Me: Let's look at the statistics. Causes of death for children ages 0–14 in 1995, in order, were motor vehicle (3,059), drowning (1,060), fires and burns (833), mechanical suffocation (459), ingestion of food or object (213), and firearms (181).[7]

And accidental gun deaths among children declined by nearly 50 percent between 1970-1991, even though the population (and the gun supply) continued to expand.[8]

And notwithstanding the low quantity of firearm accidents among children (see above), most of these fatalities are not truly "accidents." According to Dr. Gary Kleck, many such accidents are misnamed — those "accidents" are probably from either suicides or extreme cases of child abuse.[9]

And it is a myth that one child (or more) is accidentally killed by a gun every day. To attain this number, anti-gun crusaders must include so-called "children" ages 18–24[10] or count minors who were "drive-by" shooting victims.

Bill: Ok, ok. Maybe I'd agree law-abiding citizens should be able to have guns in their homes, provided they keep a trigger lock on them.

Me: Holding handgun owners accountable for permitting a minor access to a loaded gun is reasonable. Dictating to them the kind of security gadget they are obligated to use is not.

A gun in the home is much more likely to save a life than to kill someone accidentally. Surveys indicate that guns are used for self-defense about 2 million times a year.[11]

However, a trigger lock makes a firearm less available in a crisis. Individuals owning guns need to consider a variety of issues, including neighborhood crime rates and the presence of young children, before determining how to store their weapons.

Bill: But if there were fewer guns, wouldn't there be less crime?

Me: That would fly in the face of the facts.

Between 1973 and 1992, the number of privately owned firearms in the United States increased 73 percent — from 122 million to nearly 222 million. The number of privately owned handguns increased by 110 percent, from 37 million to 78 million, and the rate of gun ownership increased by 45 percent. But during this same period, the national homicide rate *fell* by nearly 10 percent.

Moreover, areas with relatively high gun ownership rates tend to report relatively low violent crime rates, and vice versa.[12]

The most interesting example of this came in 1982 when Kennesaw, Georgia, enacted a law compelling each head of household to possess at least one firearm. The residential burglary rate dropped 89 percent in Kennesaw, while the state of Georgia dropped 10.4 percent as a whole.[13]

Bill: Don't get me wrong, I think people should be allowed to own firearms, but only if they pass a background check.

Me: Background checks don't work. A Justice Department study of felons showed that 93 percent of firearm criminals obtained their most recent guns "off-the-record."[14] News accounts have shown that a small number of criminals obtain their guns through retail outlets but they use easily acquired fake IDs or use substitute buyers, known as "straw purchasers," to buy their weapons.[15]

Bill: Sure some people get around background checks, but the issue is really safety. Overall, aren't people safer with background checks?

Me: Again, no. Background checks create waiting periods and waiting periods put innocent people in greater danger. Here are a couple examples:

- Bonnie Elmasri attempted to purchase a gun to defend herself from a husband who threatened to kill her on several occasions. However, when she went to buy a gun she was informed she'd have to wait two days to pick it up, because there was a mandatory 48 hour waiting period. The police were aware of her plight so Bonnie Elmasri crossed her fingers and hoped she'd be safe. The next day her husband killed her and her two sons.[16]

- A *USA Today* account of the Los Angeles riots noted people rushing to the stores to buy guns to protect themselves. According to the account, many of these people were "lifelong gun-control advocates, running to buy an item they thought they'd never need." Ironically, they were outraged to discover they had to wait 15 days to buy a gun for self-defense.[17]

Bill: Those are rather extreme examples but they both could've been solved with "Instant" background checks. Even the National Rifle Association agrees with that, right?

Me: There are two more problems with background checks, even the instant kind.

First, background checks are the first step to eventual gun registration. In the mid-1960s officials in New York City began registering long guns. They promised they would never use such lists to take away firearms from honest citizens. But in 1991, the city banned (and soon began confiscating) many of those very guns.[18]

But there's other modern evidence of this phenomenon as well. In two separate instances the Justice Department has attempted to register gun owners.

In 1994 they gave a grant to the city of Pittsburgh and Carnegie Mellon University to construct a complex gun database using data compiled from background check programs. Fortunately, this project was struck down in the courts.[19]

In 1996 the Justice Department distributed another computer program so that police officials could effortlessly (and unlawfully) build a registry of gun buyers. The program — called FIST [Firearms Inquiry Statistical Tracking] — kept detailed information about gun purchases and specifications.[20]

Then the FBI [Federal Bureau of Investigation], the principal investigative arm of the Justice Department, in the face of specific prohibitions in the Brady Law (which authorized these checks), announced in 1998 that it would begin keeping buyers' names on hand for six months. Originally they had planned on 18 months, but chose the shorter period in response to pressure from gun rights organizations.[21]

Background checks have turned into registration databases in California as well, without legislative authority to do so.[22] In fact, civil rights attorney and author David Kopel says that several states are doing exactly the same thing as the Justice Department and California have.[23]

By the way, the National Rifle Association doesn't speak for all gun rights advocates. You are correct in asserting that the NRA supports Instant Background Checks. They also are fond of saying, "We don't need any more gun control laws; instead we should enforce the 20,000 gun control laws on the books already." I'm not interested in enforcing 20,000 bad laws.

Bill: You've taken the extreme side of this issue; surely background check laws like Brady have done *some* good, haven't they?

Me: According to the federal government's General Accounting Office (GAO), the answer is a resounding, "No."

To start with, the Brady Law has denied firearms to thousands of individuals, with over 50 percent of the total denials coming as a result of administrative snafus, traffic violations, or reasons other than felony convictions.[24]

Also, during the first 18 months the Brady Law was implemented, there were only seven successful prosecutions for making false statements on Brady handgun purchase forms — and only three of those prosecuted were actually incarcerated.[25] Surely there are more than three violent criminals with handguns in the entire U.S.

Perhaps the reason there were only seven successful prosecutions is because criminals can easily evade the checks using straw purchasers — if they haven't already bought a gun off the street, or just stolen one.[26]

Bill: I suppose next you're going to say that federal background checks are unconstitutional, despite the fact that the Second Amendment was written 212 years ago when people needed single shot muskets to protect themselves from wild bears or to hunt for their dinner.

Me: You're right. Background checks are *not* constitutional! The Second Amendment protects an individual right.

As recently as 1982 a Senate Subcommittee on the Constitution confirmed this. "The conclusion is thus inescapable that the history, concept, and wording of the second amendment to the Constitution of the United States, as well as its interpretation by every major commentator and court in the first half-century after its ratification, indicates that what is protected is an individual right of a private citizen to own and carry firearms in a peaceful manner."[27]

But the Supreme Court also asserts that rights should be free from prior restraints. In *Near v. Minnesota* the Court established that government officials should punish the abuse of a right, but could not place prior restraints on the free exercise of that right.[28]

Simply put, government cannot restrict a constitutional right just because someone may abuse it. Doing so would be like prohibiting the use of automobiles because some people are reckless or irresponsible with them.

If you really believe the Second Amendment is inappropriate for today's America, you should work to repeal it. The Constitution has been amended 27 times to reflect changing attitudes toward it. The remedy for an out-of-date provision is to amend the Constitution, not to ignore it.

Bill: You said that the Second Amendment is an individual right. But it really says the right to bear arms was for militia purposes. Last time I checked the National Guard had all the munitions and guns it needed. Individuals should stop hiding behind the Second Amendment because it doesn't apply to them.

Me: According to the report by the U.S. Senate Subcommittee on the Constitution, "There can be little doubt from this that when the Congress and the people spoke of a 'militia,' they had reference to the traditional concept of the entire populace capable of bearing arms, and not to any formal groups such as what today is known as the National Guard."[29]

The Founding Fathers endorsed this view. George Mason said, "I ask, who are the militia? They consist now of the whole people, except a few public officers."[30] Richard Henry Lee said, "To preserve liberty, it is essential that the whole body of people always possess arms, and be taught alike, especially when young, how to use them. . . . The mind that aims at a select militia [like the National Guard] must be influenced by a truly anti-republican principle."[31]

Bill: You can quote the Founding Fathers all you want; we don't need the Second Amendment today. We need to get with the times and repeal it.

Me: There is ample evidence in recent history of the need for an armed population. Mao, Stalin, and Hitler — all needed disarmed populations and all kept them that way. Castro still keeps his population disarmed. Tyrants need to know that their subjects have little or no ability to defend themselves. The Second Amendment is the final protector of all our other rights.

Bill: I still think that the ideal situation is if no one had guns, like in England. After all, gun control has worked elsewhere.

Me: A 1998 study organized by a British professor and an American statistician established that, for the most part, crime is now worse in England than in the U.S. According to a *Reuters* report summarizing the study, "You are more likely to be mugged in England than in the United States. The rate of robbery is 1.4 times higher in England and Wales than in the United States, and the British burglary rate is nearly double America's."[32] According to that same study, "the difference between the [murder rates in the] two countries has narrowed over the past 16 years."[33]

And the data continues to roll in. An August 2001 story in *USA Today* reported that, "criminal use of handguns in Britain has increased by almost 40 percent in three years, according to a report by the Center for Defense Studies at King's College" and "armed robberies involving handguns have increased dramatically in recent years." The story went on to point out that, "Although the 'bobby' on the beat still patrols unarmed, specially trained armed response units of each police force are being called out more often. The number of incidents in which armed officers have responded has increased two-fold — from about 6,000 in 1994 to 12,000 in recent years."[34]

Hardly anyone mentions that other countries with much tougher gun bans (i.e., Brazil and Russia) have murder rates that are four times those of the U.S.[35] Australia, which banned almost all guns following the tragic multiple shooting in Tasmania (1996), has seen armed robberies increase by 73 percent, unarmed robberies increase by 28 percent, assaults by 17 percent, and kidnappings increase by 38 percent.[36]

Finally, a burglar is far less likely to break into your house when you're home if you live in an area where some civilians own firearms, because the burglar has no way of knowing which civilians have firearms. The percentage in Great Britain, Canada, and the Netherlands, of burglaries occurring with the homeowner present, is 45 percent (average of all three). But in the United States, it's 12.7 percent.[37]

Bill, you're safer when there are more guns around. And you're safer yet when "Concealed Carry" laws are passed, giving citizens the ability to carry firearms in public places.

Bill: If we allow people to carry concealed guns in public places, the United States will become like the chaotic days of the Wild West, with shootouts all over the place. Surely you aren't going to argue everyone should be able to carry a gun in public?

Me: Yale Law professor John Lott has compiled the most extensive research on this subject to date. He published his findings in a well-documented book called, *More Guns, Less Crime.* No book on either side of the issue is as thorough in its documentation.

According to Lott, if states that didn't have concealed-carry laws had actually had them in 1992, there would have been at least 1,140 fewer murders, 3,700 fewer rapes, 60,400 fewer aggravated assaults, and 10,990 fewer robberies — all based on state and county government crime reports.[38]

Bill: All the points you make are really good, but you have to admit it's a good thing the government has banned semi-automatic "assault weapons."

Me: What is an assault weapon? Semi-automatic assault rifles are virtually identical to the semi-automatic hunting rifles, many of which have been on the market since World War II. Basically, the difference is one looks more "military." And the expression "assault weapon" is a misnomer anyway because a true assault weapon is capable of flipping back and forth between semi-automatic and automatic with the flick of a switch. Also 10, 20, and 30 round magazines have existed for hunting rifles for decades.[39]

The rifles in question didn't appear to be posing any real threat when they were banned. In 1993 the Bureau of Justice Statistics reported that violent criminals use a "military-type gun" only in about 1 percent of crimes nationally.[40] In Chicago, crime statistics indicated that someone was 67 times more likely to be stabbed or beaten to death than to be shot by an assault weapon.[41]

But assault rifles are excellent for self-defense. Korean merchants protected themselves during the Los Angeles riots with guns that are now banned as assault weapons. Their stores were left standing while others were burned to the ground.[42] Certainly there are situations where more than six bullets are necessary to protect and defend oneself.

A report by the U.S. Senate Subcommittee on the Constitution goes further. It says, "In the Militia Act of 1792, the second Congress defined 'militia of the United States' to include almost every adult male in the United States. These persons were obligated by law to possess a [military style] firearm and a minimum supply of ammunition and military equipment."[43] I think that speaks for itself.

Bill: You really know your stuff. I'm going to have to re-think my position.

NOTES

1. John D. Brophy, "Public Safety: Fact or Fiction," *members.aol.com/copcrimes/ brophy.html.*

2. *Warren v. District of Columbia,* D.C. App., 444 A. 2d 1 (1981).

3. Federal Bureau of Investigation, *Crime in the United States (1998),* p. 291.

4. Gary Kleck and Marc Gertz, "Armed Resistance to Crime: The Prevalence and Nature of Self-Defense With a Gun," *The Journal of Criminal Law and Criminology,* Northwestern University School of Law (Fall 1995), vol. 1, pp. 173, 185. (Specific issue is not online.)

5. U.S. Department of Justice, National Institute of Justice, "The Armed Criminal in America: A Survey of Incarcerated Felons," *Research Report* (July 1985), p. 27. See also *DaveKopel.org/2A/LawRev/LawyersGunsBurglars.htm.*

6. Don B. Kates Jr., *Guns, Murders, and the Constitution: A Realistic Assessment of Gun Control* (1990), p. 29, citing U.S. Bureau of Justice Statistics.

7. National Safety Council, *Accident Facts: 1998 Edition,* pp. 10–11, 18.

8. David B. Kopel (ed.), *Guns: Who Should Have Them?* (1995), p. 311.

9. Gary Kleck, *Point Blank: Guns and Violence in America* (1991), pp. 271, 276.

10. Gary Kleck, *Point Blank: Guns and Violence in America* (1991), pp. 276–277.

11. American Liberty Foundation, *Supporting the Claim of the "Intruder" Ad.*

12. Daniel D. Polsby and Dennis Brennen, "Taking Aim at Gun Control," Heartland Executive Summary (1995), *Heartland.org/studies/polsby-sum.htm.*

13. Gary Kleck, "Crime Control Through the Private Use of Armed Force," *Social Problems* (February 1988), vol. 35, p. 15. See also *www.FBI.gov/ucr/cius_00/00crime6.pdf* (350k PDF file).

14. Department of Justice, "Survey of Incarcerated Felons," p. 36.

15. Pierre Thomas, "In the Line of Fire: The Straw Purchase Scam," *The Washington Post,* August 18, 1991. See also Pierre Thomas, "Va. Driver's License Is Loophole for Guns: Fake Addresses Used in No-Wait Sales," *The Washington Post,* January 20, 1992. See also *"Straw Guns Linked to Crime"* (OregonLive.com/news/00/01/st011601.html) and *ATF Crime Gun Trace* (ATF.treas.gov/firearms/ycgii/1999html/ycgii/index.htm).

16. *Congressional Record,* May 8, 1991, pp. H2859, H2862.

17. Jonathan T. Lovitt, "Survival for the Armed," *USA Today,* May 4, 1992. (Not online; may be purchased from *USA Today.*)

18. *Local Law 78 of 1991,* signed by Mayor David Dinkins on August 16, 1991.

19. Bureau of Justice Assistance, Grant Manager's Memorandum, Pt. 1, Project Summary, September 30, 1994, Project Number: 94-DD-CX-0166.

20. Copy of "FIST" (Firearms Inquiry Statistical Tracking) software at GOA headquarters, Springfield, Virginia. See also *Pennsylvania Sportsman's News,* (October/November 1996). The default on the "FIST" computer software is for police officials to indefinitely retain the information on gun owners — despite the fact that the Brady law only allows officials to retain the data for 20 days. One wonders who will ensure that this information will be deleted after the twentieth day.

21. National Instant Criminal Background Check System Regulation, *Federal Register,* vol. 63, no. 210, p. 58311 (October 30, 1998).

22. David Kopel, *Policy Review* 36 (Winter 1993), p. 36.

23. David Kopel (ed.), *Guns: Who Should Have Them?* (1995), p. 88.

24. General Accounting Office, "Gun Control: Implementation of the Brady Handgun Violence Prevention Act," January 1996, pp. 39–40, 64–65. (Report is unavailable online but may be ordered from the GAO.) See also *"The Brady Scam"* (CivilLiberty.about.com/library/ weekly/aa062998.htm?terms=Brady).

25. General Accounting Office, "Gun Control: Implementation of the Brady Handgun Violence Prevention Act," January 1996, p. 8. (Report is unavailable online but may be ordered from the GAO.)

26. General Accounting Office, "Gun Control: Implementation of the Brady Handgun Violence Prevention Act," January 1996, p. 4. (Report is unavailable online but may be ordered from the GAO.)

27. U.S. Senate, *The Right to Keep and Bear Arms*, Report on the Subcommittee on the Constitution of the Committee on the Judiciary (1982), p. 12. See also *AmericanSelfDefense.com/gunfacts3.0.pdf* (423k PDF file).

28. *Near v. Minnesota*, 283 U.S. 697, 51 S. Ct. 625, 75 L. Ed. 1357 (1931).

29. U.S. Senate, *The Right to Keep and Bear Arms*, Report on the Subcommittee on the Constitution of the Committee on the Judiciary (1982), p. 7.

30. Johnathan Elliot (ed.), *The Debates in the Several State Conventions on the Adoption of the Federal Constitution*, vol. 3, p. 425.

31. Richard H. Lee (?), "Letter from the Federal Farmer," *Poughkeepsie Country Journal, Letter XVIII, January 25, 1788.*

32. "Most Crime Worse in England Than US, Study Says," Reuters, October 11, 1998. See also Bureau of Justice Statistics, *Crime and Justice in the United States and in England and Wales, 1981–96*, (October 1998).

33. Bureau of Justice Statistics, *Crime and Justice in the United States and in England and Wales, 1981–96*, (October 1998) p. 116:iii.

34. Ellen Hale, "British Fear Rise of 'Gun Culture'," *USA Today*, August 7, 2001.

35. John Lott, *More Guns, Less Crime: Understanding Crime and Gun Control* (2000; second edition), p. 241.

36. Australia Bureau of Statistics, as cited in *More Guns, Less Crime.*

37. Gary Kleck, *Point Blank: Guns and Violence in America* (1991), p. 140.

38. Gary Kleck, *Point Blank: Guns and Violence in America* (1991), p. 54.

39. Officer William R. McGrath, "An Open Letter to American Politicians," *The Police Marksman*, (May/June 1989), p. 19.

40. U.S. Department of Justice, Bureau of Justice Statistics, *Survey of State Prison Inmates, 1991*, (March 1993), p. 18.

41. Matt L. Rodriguez, Superintendent of Police for the City of Chicago, *1993 Murder Analysis*, p. 12–13.

42. "Koreans Make Armed Stand to Protect Shops from Looters," *Roanoke Times and World News.*

43. U.S. Senate, *The Right to Keep and Bear Arms*, Report on the Subcommittee on the Constitution of the Committee on the Judiciary (1982), p. 7.

Questions for Discussion

1. What would be the consequences of a law banning the possession of handguns to (a) criminal violence, (b) accidental injury, and (c) self-defense?
2. How would a ban on handguns be enforced?
3. Would a ban on handguns be more or less effective than the ban on illegal drugs? What are the reasons for your answer?
4. Have gun control laws been effective in reducing violence? What are the reasons for your answer?
5. Does the large number of guns available to Americans cause violence, or does violence cause the possession of large numbers of guns? What are the reasons for your answer?

Suggested Resources

Web Sites

Brady Campaign to Prevent Gun Violence
http://www.bradycampaign.org/

Citizens Committee for the Right to Keep and Bear Arms
http://www.ccrkba.org

Coalition to Stop Gun Violence
http://gunfree.org

National Rifle Association
http://www.nra.org

Publications

Bellesiles, Michael A. *Arming America: The Origins of a National Gun Culture.* New York: Knopf, 2000.

Brady, Sarah, with Merrill McLoughlin. *A Good Fight.* New York: Public Affairs, 2002.

Brown, Peter H., and Daniel G. Abel. *Outgunned: Up Against the NRA: The First Complete Insider Account of the Battle over Gun Control.* New York: Free Press, 2003.

Jacobs, James B. *Can Gun Control Work?* New York: Oxford University Press, 2002.

Kleck, Gary, and Don B. Kates. *Armed: New Perspectives on Gun Control.* Amherst, N.Y.: Prometheus Books, 2001.

LaPierre, Wayne R., and James J. Baker. *Shooting Straight: Telling the Truth about Guns in America.* Washington, D.C.: Regnery, 2002.

Levine, Herbert M. *Gun Control.* Austin, Tex.: Raintree Steck-Vaughn, 1998.

Lott, John R., Jr. *More Guns, Less Crime: Understanding Gun Control Laws,* 2d ed. Chicago: University of Chicago Press, 2000.

Ludwig, Jens, and Philip J. Cook, eds. *Evaluating Gun Policy: Effects on Crime and Violence.* Washington, D.C.: Brookings Institution Press, 2003.

Malcolm, Joyce Lee. *To Keep and Bear Arms: The Origins of an Anglo-American Right.* Cambridge, Mass.: Harvard University Press, 1994.

McClurg, Andrew, David Kopel, and Brannon Denning, eds. *Gun Control and Gun Rights: A Reader and Guide.* New York: New York University Press, 2002.

Spitzer, Robert J. *The Politics of Gun Control,* 3d ed. New York: Chatham House, 2002.

Sugarmann, Josh. *Every Handgun Is Aimed at You: The Case for Banning Handguns.* New York: New Press, 2001.

U.S. Cong., Senate. *Whose Right to Keep and Bear Arms?* Hearing before the Subcommittee on the Constitution, Federalism and Property Rights of the Committee on the Judiciary, 105th Cong., 2d Sess., 1998.

Is "Smart Growth" a Smart Idea to Control Suburban Sprawl?

In many metropolitan areas, driving to work has become a major problem. With traffic congestion comes long delays and wasted time for individuals in their cars. And gas fumes and pollutants emitted from the cars cause environmental problems that can have a harmful effect on the health of the community.

To a large extent congestion is a reflection of population growth. Between 1990 and 2000, the 2,586 suburbs in the 35 largest metropolitan areas experienced population growth on average by 14 percent. To be sure, not all of the suburbs grew in population, but most of them did. The median growth rate for cities during the 1990s more than doubled from that of the 1980s.[1]

In addition to problems of congestion and air pollution, metropolitan areas have to deal with concerns that are in part a reflection of the rising population. Among these concerns are: constructing new housing, expanding public transportation, creating jobs, and building new roads and schools. As a consequence, construction projects are undertaken in areas that were previously used as farms.

"Urban sprawl" became the term used to describe this transformation, which had its advocates and its critics. Some people were delighted to live in the suburbs. They had decided that compared to city life, housing was cheaper, and overall, the quality of their lives was much superior.

But other people felt that sprawl was an undesirable feature not only for the suburbs but for the neighboring city itself. Many of them used the term "smart growth" to describe the development that they preferred for the metropolitan area. To be sure, there is no universally accepted definition of the term, "smart growth," but the term was quite pleasing to its advocates.

To those horrified by sprawl, smart growth meant an acceptance of growth in a manner that would prevent or minimize the problems that metropolitan areas were experiencing for unplanned growth. They favored development that would reduce the necessity to use an automobile, expand public transportation, increase the density of population in the city so as to encourage people not to move to the suburbs, create areas for mixing land uses — commercial, residential, recreational, educational, and others — rather than a single purpose, provide open spaces, preserve wildlife, and protect the environment. They sought to use both the private sector and government to achieve these goals. Private development would be welcome, and government would encourage practices consistent with the smart growth approach.

Patrick Gallagher, senior attorney for the Sierra Club Environmental Law Program in San Francisco, supports smart growth. He contends:

1. Sprawl damages air quality by creating a car-intensive culture, which enlarges cancer risk, contributes to global warming, and raises energy consumption.
2. Sprawl results in adverse water-related damage in that it increases water consumption through overuse of surface and ground water, interferes with ground water recharge, pollutes waterways, puts strains on sewer and storm water conveyance systems, damages wetlands, and escalates the risk of flooding.
3. Sprawl development poses a serious risk to wildlife, largely through the destruction of natural habitat, and it also hurts human communities.
4. Sprawl consumes open spaces and natural habitats.
5. It draws resources from cities, towns, and villages, which can disproportionately impact low-income and minority communities.
6. It burdens new communities with often unanticipated economic costs and inefficiencies.
7. It deprives people of a "sense of place."

Economist Thomas J. DiLorenzo takes issue with the critics of sprawl. He contends:

1. The problems of sprawl cited by the critics have either been greatly exaggerated or simply fabricated.

2. The proposed solution to these problems — centralized governmental planning of where people live and work and how they commute — is bound to be economically inefficient, harmful to growth, and inherently inequitable.

3. Suburban development is not destroying America's farmland since nonagriculture uses of land in the United States amount to just 3.6 percent of the total land, and cropland has remained virtually constant at 24 percent of the U.S. land mass, since 1945.

4. The types of policies that smart growth advocates favor would increase traffic congestion and exacerbate air pollution.

5. Smart growth policies would slash the supply of housing in the suburbs, thereby making it more expensive there, while increasing the demand (and price) for urban housing.

6. Though proposed in the name of efficiency, increased government subsidies for mass transit are among the most inefficient of all uses of taxpayer dollars.

7. Smart growth policies are inherently undemocratic.

NOTE

1. William H. Lucy, and David I. Phillips, "Suburbs and the Census: Patterns of Growth and Decline," *The Bookings Institution Survey Series*, December 2001.

 ☑ Y E S

Is "Smart Growth" a Smart Idea to Control Suburban Sprawl?

PATRICK GALLAGHER

The Environmental, Social, and Cultural Impacts of Sprawl

In Edward Abbey's novel, *The Fool's Progress* (Henry Holt and Company, Inc., 1988), the protagonist Henry Lightcap makes a pilgrimage of sorts from Tucson, Arizona, to his childhood home in West Virginia. As he approaches the border between Kansas and Missouri, he describes the landscape:

> I latch on to the tail draft of a forty-ton Mayflower moving van and let it suck me like a bug through the near-continuous development—gas stations, boxfood joints, suburban box homes, condominiums, truck stops, shopping centers, redlight greenlight intersections, office buildings of pink cement and dark glass, assembly plants with walls of slump block and no windows at all, block-long warehouses and storage depots of bolted-together sheet metal— that walls in the four-lane superhighway from Emporia to Kansas City.

What Henry Lightcap described, we have come to know as sprawl. But beyond "boxfood joints" and "suburban box homes," what is sprawl and what are its effects?

Urban or suburban sprawl is uncontrolled development that expands outward from city centers and consumes otherwise undeveloped land. Like the vivid picture painted by Edward Abbey in *The Fool's Progress,* sprawl can be visually offensive, but more importantly, it exacerbates air pollution, diminishes water supply, degrades water quality, and consumes open spaces and natural habitats. Sprawl development also drains resources from cities, towns and villages, which can disproportionately impact low-income and minority communities. It burdens new communities with often unanticipated economic costs and inefficiencies, such as traffic gridlock, school overcrowding, and flooding. Over time, sprawl takes a social, cultural, and psychological toll on citizens by depriving them of a "sense of place."

As a citizenry, we deplore sprawl and its effects. In fact, opinion polls rank sprawl right along with crime as a top public concern. In 1998, voters passed 70 percent of a record 240 ballot initiatives relating to sprawl control. In 1999, an "off" year politically, voters passed twenty-eight of thirty-four ballot initiatives (82 percent). A July 1999 American Institute of Architects study reported that, of 351 state and local decision makers, four out of five identified livable communities as one of the most important issues facing them. Additionally, more than two-thirds of the officials believed that concern over livable communities is growing. In January 2000, at least thirty governors mentioned smart growth and/or sprawl in their state of the state addresses. In January 2001, President [George W.] Bush's nomination announcement of Christine Whitman as EPA [Environmental Protection Agency] Administrator included statements about the need to stop sprawl.

Ironically, much of what causes sprawl derives from the demands of the citizenry for convenience, personal space, backyards and barbecues, and many other goods and services, both public and private, that together generate extensive and often uncontrolled development. Responding to these demands, communities often embrace measures to encourage development like tax incentives and subsidized infrastructure. The result — urban and suburban sprawl. Solving the problems discussed below will require, among other things, a reconciliation of the public's distaste for sprawl with its competing demands for what we might call "the sprawl lifestyle."

This article identifies and discusses many of the environmental, social, and cultural effects of sprawl. . . .

AIR QUALITY IMPACTS

One of sprawl's most harmful effects is on air quality. Sprawl creates a car-intensive culture: lots of new roads, long-distance commutes, and the need to get in the car for just about everything. Automobile emissions of volatile organic compounds (VOCs) and nitrogen oxides (NO_x) combine to form ground-level ozone, also known as smog. Ground-level ozone is a danger to those with respiratory problems and can impair lung function in healthy adults. Recently, in Houston, members of a high school football team were hospitalized after practicing in severe ozone conditions. An increasing body of evidence now attributes a near epidemic of asthma to high levels of ozone.

To many, Los Angeles is synonymous with smog, but most large, urban regions, like Phoenix, Atlanta, Houston, and Denver, also suffer from the problem. None of these areas are in compliance with Clean Air Act standards for ground-level ozone. In fact, Houston recently moved into first place (or last place, depending upon how you view it) among U.S. cities with the worst air quality. A recent *New York Times* article reported that Houston's poor air quality results in part from the fact that the city has "perhaps the worst sprawl in the nation."[1]

Ozone is not the only air quality concern associated with sprawl. Two major studies released in early 2000 document a connection between vehicle emissions and cancer, particularly among children, in communities near highways. In March 2000, the South Coast Air Quality Management District (SCAQMD) finalized a study entitled *The Multiple Air Toxics Exposure Study* (MATES-II Study). SCAQMD is the public agency that regulates air quality in the Los Angeles area. The MATES-II Study is a landmark study of the cancer risk associated with toxic air contaminants.

The MATES-II Study concluded that the risk of cancer in the Los Angeles–area air basin is 1,400 cases per million population, and 90 percent of this cancer incidence is associated with mobile sources. Further, the modeling results for this study showed that higher risk levels occurred near freeways. The MATES-II Study presents disturbing evidence that vehicle emissions pose a significant risk to public health. Worse yet, evidence from another recent study indicates that children are at the greatest risk.

In February 2000, the Air and Waste Management Association published a study by the Electric Power Research Institute entitled *Distance Weighted Traffic Density in Proximity to a Home Is a Risk Factor for Leukemia and Other Childhood Cancers.* This case-control study evaluated childhood cancer rates in proximity to Denver-area highways. It represents a significant development in the scientific literature and reports a strong association between childhood cancer and vehicle emissions in major highway corridors.

Sprawl also contributes significantly to global warming. Carbon dioxide (CO_2) emissions from vehicles and other fossil fuel combustion sources create the so-called greenhouse effect. The average car on the road today will emit 50 tons of CO_2 during its useful life. Every day, the number of vehicle miles traveled translates directly into pounds of CO_2 emitted.

Also, sprawl increases energy consumption and resulting CO_2 emissions from energy generation. Recent research shows that deforested, paved areas become "urban heat islands" where temperatures may increase 10 degrees to 15 degrees above normal. Higher temperatures lead to increased utility use and higher power demand, which in turn leans to more fuel combustion, more CO_2 emissions, and ultimately, to accelerated global warming.

Deforestation associated with sprawl also exacerbates global warming by destroying the natural carbon sink. Trees absorb carbon dioxide and lock it up in their biomass. When trees are cut for development, they no longer serve as a carbon sink, and their carbon eventually is released back into the atmosphere. Approximately 50 acres of tree cover *per day* are lost to sprawl development in the Atlanta region alone.

These air quality and related human-health effects would be reason enough to address the sprawl problem, but air pollution is by no means the only significant environmental effect of sprawl. It also presents significant water supply and water quality issues.

WATER-RELATED IMPACTS

Sprawl results in increased water consumption. The sprawl lifestyle, which often includes lawns, car washes, and swimming pools, contributes to overdraft of water resources across the country. For example, the expansion of urban areas in south-western Sunbelt states is taking a toll on the once mighty Colorado River. Additionally, the "mining" of ground water, as it is known in Arizona, represents a serious threat to long-term aquifer productivity in many regions. Sprawl's impact on water supply, however, arises not just by overuse of surface and ground water, but also by interference with ground water recharge: sprawl means pavement, and a paved area will prevent ground water recharge.

Sprawl's disruption of natural hydrologic cycles also contributes to pollution of waterways. Paved areas cannot absorb and filter precipitation. Storm events, which once nourished natural communities and recharged ground water, now traverse parking lots and streets as sheet flow, carrying sediment, chemicals and litter into surface waters. A 1999 study by the Natural Resources Defense Council [NRDC], *Stormwater Strategies,* reports that ecological stress becomes apparent when 10 percent to 20 percent of a watershed consists of impervious material. By comparison, the NRDC study reports that the impervious surface area of an average medium-density subdivision ranges from 25 percent to 60 percent, whereas a strip mall may be 100 percent impervious.

Sprawl also places excessive strains on existing sewer and storm water conveyance systems, creating two notorious sources of water pollution — the combined sewer overflow (CSO) and the sanitary sewer overflow (SSO). CSOs occur when systems designed to receive and treat combined storm water and sewage become overwhelmed in storm events and sewage overflows directly into waterways. The U.S. Environmental Protection Agency (EPA) has identified CSOs as one of the most serious threats to water quality in the nation.

SSOs occur when the capacity of a separate sanitary sewer is overwhelmed because of high volume or structural problems, leading to discharges from the sewer system into the environment. The experience in Little Rock, Arkansas, shows how sprawl can lead to this problem. Little Rock has grown rapidly along its western boundary, with local officials approving piecemeal annexations and development projects. The main sewer trunk lines leading from the western area of the city to wastewater treatment plants on the city's eastern boundary have experienced chronic discharges of untreated sewage, attributed to the inability of the older sewer system to handle the increased waste from the new development.

Wetlands also are a victim of sprawl. Almost half of all annual wetland losses are caused by sprawl development, attributable in part to increased development in coastal areas. A study reported in the *Philadelphia Chronicle* this past summer traced a surge in sprawl along coastal areas of the eastern seaboard. The study attributed this trend in part to the "new economy" in which employers and employees are no longer bound to the industrial urban areas. Many of these untethered workers now want to make their homes in what were formerly summer resort areas. For example, in years past, the pace of life in Cape Cod slowed to a crawl during the off-season. Now it is becoming an exurb of Boston and other cities, and the once rural landscape is increasingly suburbanized.

Historically, the U.S. Army Corps of Engineers' implementation of the Clean Water Act allowed many development projects to proceed under Nationwide Permit 26, a general permit that required little in the way of mitigation or public involvement in wetland decisions. This practice contributed to significant wetland losses. Recent legal reforms in this area may require closer scrutiny of more projects, but many believe incentives still exist for developers to fill wetlands first and ask questions later. For example, the so-called Tulloch Rule exemption, which was intended to exempt the "incidental" discharge of fill material into wetlands, has been exploited in some cases to fill areas slated for development.

Development of floodplains also causes a whole suite of problems. Floodplains are not regulated like wetlands, so the area of floodplains developed every year greatly exceeds wetland loss. Floodplains provide a crucial "ecological service" by acting as natural diversion and retention structures for flood waters. As the number of frequency of severe storm events appears to be on the rise, floodplain services will play an increasingly important role in preserving public health and the environment.

By developing floodplains, sprawl increases the risk and severity of flooding. Between 1990 and 1998, floods killed more than 850 people in the United States and caused $89 billion in property damage. Much of this flooding occurred in places where weak zoning laws allowed development in floodplains. A recent study conducted by the Sierra Club in Wisconsin found that local communities suffered about twenty-five times more flood damage in the 1990s than the 1980s, largely as a result of poorly planned construction in floodplains. The Federal Emergency Management Agency has begun to recognize this problem and has instituted programs to buy out properties in floodplains; however, the ultimate responsibility for this problem lies with state and local planning agencies.

WILDLIFE HABITAT IMPACTS

Sprawl development also poses a serious risk to wildlife, largely through destruction of natural habitat. The rate of habitat destruction is staggering. For example, sprawl in the Phoenix region consumes desert habitat at the rate of approximately *one acre per hour*. These sprawl-related risks are, of course, most urgent with respect to threatened and endangered species, most of which rely heavily on private land for critical habitat needs. The relentless conversion of this land by new development pushes these species ever closer to extinction. In many areas, the only thing standing between endangered species and sprawl-induced extinction is the Endangered Species Act (ESA). In *Babbit v. Sweet Home Chapter of Communities for a Great Oregon*, 515 U.S. 687, 115 S. Ct. 2407 (1995), the U.S. Supreme Court held that habitat destruction may be defined as a "take" and therefore is prohibited under the ESA. For the moment, this decision has put conservation of endangered species in the path of sprawl.

In the wake of the *Sweet Home* decision, however, increasing numbers of developers now pursue approval of habitat conservation plans (HCPs) to satisfy their ESA obligations. HCPs ostensibly provide assurances that land development will not harm the viability of a species, notwithstanding the "incidental" take of some number of animals. However, many view the HCP process as a pretext for habitat destruction.

The HCP track record often corroborates this suspicion. A coalition of environmental groups, including the Mountain Lion Foundation, recently won a judgment against the proponents of an HCP for the Natomas Basin outside Sacramento, California. This case was based on, among other things, evidence that an endangered hawk nesting site was destroyed almost as soon as the HCP was issued. As in this case, the adequacy and oversight of mitigation measures in many HCPs leave much to be desired and hold little promise for conserving species.

Even where sprawl does not destroy habitat, it often fragments habitat into haphazard, often isolated, areas, reducing its ecological value and sustainability. Fragmented habitat disrupts the natural migration needs of mammals and birds. Species like the mountain lion, marten, bobcat and many forms of raptors and songbirds require large home ranges to survive. For example, the mountain lion requires a habitat patch of 1,000 hectares or larger. Their young must disperse to new home ranges when they come of age. Isolated habitat leads to interbreeding and genetic deformity. Many animals, such as the Florida panther, suffer the effect of gene pool isolation as their breeding populations gradually diminish in "islands" of suitable habitat.

Another problem with habitat fragmentation is the "edge effect." The "edge" is the boundary between natural habitat and the developed area. Noxious and pest species tend to thrive in edge areas, while native species suffer. Songbirds are particularly susceptible to damage from pest species. Brown-headed cowbirds steal their eggs, and raccoons, crows, and feral cats hunt them as prey. A 1995 study of wood thrushes concluded that in forests with less than 55 percent cover, nest parasitism by brown-headed cowbirds was common, while parasitism almost never occurred in denser canopy forest.

Sprawl encroachment into wildlife habitat also leads to conflict between humans and wildlife. Such conflicts in the Lake Tahoe region are in the news almost weekly in California as conservationists try to save the region's bears from being shot as pests because of their attraction to exposed garbage left by homeowners. In the Santa Ana Mountains of southern California, roadkill on a new toll road in mountain lion territory is eliminating 10 percent of the local lion population annually. In Florida, almost half of all known panther deaths are from roadkill. In response to the latest lion roadkill in southern California (particularly tragic because the female victim was entering her breeding prime), a spokeswoman for the U.S. Fish and Wildlife office was quoted as saying: "When you have housing developments crawling right up into the hills in areas that used to be remote, the wildlife keeps getting bounced out. And they have to go to less desirable habitats along these urban interfaces."[2]

In addition to roadkill and habitat destruction, roads damage ecosystems in other ways. Many animals refuse instinctively to cross roads and so their natural migration patterns are disrupted. Creeks, marshes, and rivers are often channeled or rerouted, substantially reducing their ecological value. And, another disturbing line of research indicates that traffic noise can disrupt songbird breeding by interfering with communications between birds. For all these reasons, sprawl represents a serious threat to wildlife and ecosystems.

While the justifiable tendency is to worry over sprawl's impacts to "birds and bunnies," there also are profound sprawl-related effects to human communities beyond the wildlife and air and water quality issues discussed above. A good example is farmland destruction. The U.S. Department of Agriculture recently issued a report documenting an alarming trend — the rate of farmland and forest conversion has increased rapidly in the last decade. The development of farmland, forests and other open space doubled during this decade to more than 3 million acres per year. Nearly 16 million acres were converted to development between 1992 and 1997, according to the USDA study. By comparison, the development rate was 1.4 million acres a year between 1982 and 1992. According to the American Farmland Trust, 70 percent of this country's prime farmland lies in the path of sprawl development. Sprawl is literally consuming the heart of the country.

But perhaps the most profound impacts of sprawl on the human community are social, cultural, and psychological. Many believe and have documented that sprawl leads to community disintegration and disinvestment. The classic sprawl pattern sees construction, jobs, and population explode haphazardly in rural areas, while city and town centers decline. Social troubles are sure to follow.

A 1996 Sierra Club report, *The Dark Side of the American Dream,* profiled several U.S. cities, including St. Louis and Minneapolis, where explosive growth in outlying areas was accompanied by severe urban decline. For example, between 1990 and 1996, several outlying counties in the St. Louis area grew by 20 percent or more, while the city's population declined by 11 percent and employment declined by one-third. A January 2000 case study in the Minneapolis–St. Paul region documents in detail how the flight of employers from the urban core to a heavily subsidized, suburban business park handicaps the urban communities left behind.

Often, this flight from the city center causes disparate harm to low-income and minority communities. A recent, comprehensive study of sprawl in Atlanta, *Sprawl City,* documents this effect. While the affluent north side of Atlanta grows, the poorer south side declines. New development in the region often excludes moderate and low-cost housing. Wealth barriers prevent the poor from living in the suburbs and accessing jobs and services that have relocated out of the city center.

Along these lines, the Minneapolis–St. Paul case study referenced above concluded that relocation of jobs outside the urban core made them inaccessible to public transit and further removed from the region's poor and people of color. Similarly, a profile of Chicago reported in the Natural Resources Defense Council's 1999 publication *Once There Were Greenfields* notes that the inner-suburbs of Chicago left in sprawl's wake have been likened to a struggling third-world community.

Adding insult to injury, the infrastructure projects required to support suburban sprawl development often directly harm the urban dwellers left behind. A case in point is the U.S. 95 freeway project in Las Vegas that the Sierra Club is challenging. Las Vegas has sprawled faster than any region in the country in the last decade. Predictably, the area's highways have experienced gridlock as a result.

Enter the U.S. 95 expansion project. As U.S. 95 no longer can squeeze through the hundreds of thousands of vehicle trips generated by the region's growth, the state Department of Transportation and the Federal Highway Administration plan to widen the road from six to ten lanes. To do so, they must condemn and demolish hundreds of residences and businesses in the older sections of northwest Las Vegas. Not surprisingly, many of the older residents are frustrated and angry. This story repeats itself throughout the country.

Often ignored in this process is the reality that new roads encourage increased auto use and sprawl and so perpetuate the vicious cycle. Even when the avowed purpose of new highways is to decrease traffic, the strategy frequently backfires. Scientific research increasingly documents this feedback phenomenon known as "induced travel." New highways facilitate the sprawl lifestyle by making it faster and more convenient to drive long distances to work and other pursuits. The National Academy of Sciences/National Research Council report, *Expanding Metropolitan Highways: Implications for Air Quality and Energy Use* (1995), acknowledges the problem of induced travel literature for its Science Advisory Board and concluded that this research makes a strong case for the existence of induced travel and suggests that a large fraction of growth in vehicle miles traveled is directly attributed to increases in road capacity.

Las Vegas presents a good example of the phenomenon. Recently, after years of local frustration with increasing gridlock, the so-called Spaghetti Bowl interchange was widened. Transportation planners projected that the expansion would provide congestion relief for several years. The increased volume of cars and trucks using the newly expanded interchange, however, has surprised local planners, who now admit that the road will be filled to capacity much sooner than they expected. Soon, the calls will go out again for more roadway capacity.

The human toll of sprawl afflicts not just the abandoned urban areas or freeway rights-of-way. Even those who embrace the suburban lifestyle cannot escape its effects. A 1999 report by the American Planning Association, *Planning Communities for the 21st Century,* observes that sprawl creates a void in the human psyche:

> Something is missing. Apart from the absence of a swift, uninterrupted journey to work or the store, there is a sense that we have lost something perhaps less tangible in the process of growth and change. A frequent observation is that American communities, particularly the newer ones, no longer provide a "sense of place."

That something missing is sustainable and enriching culture. Sprawl development typically generates little in the way of culture other than consumption and convenience and fails to facilitate sound interaction among people.

One might reasonably ask how it is that a phenomenon that inflicts so much environmental and social damage continues at such a break-neck pace. The exploitation of rural and natural resources, at the expense of city and town culture, continues in large part because of distorted economic policies. Federal, state, and local governments have for decades pursued a model of economic growth that leads to environmental and social degradation. The growth patterns that pit suburbs against cities and towns initially grew out of the post–World War II boom, but governments persist in subsidizing growth heavily to this day.

A 1999 Sierra Club report, *Sprawl Costs Us All,* chronicles the sprawl subsidies that federal, state, and local governments continue. The most unabashed incentives for sprawl are tax breaks and other direct monetary subsidies. The growth in Minneapolis referenced above resulted from a free land subsidy that enticed businesses to relocate outside the urban area. The 1999 Sierra Club report identifies other examples of this sort of subsidy as well. For example, New Jersey's Hopewell Township promised Merrill Lynch about $200 million in subsidies to install a commercial park on rural land far removed from any housing, public transportation, or stores. The site consisted predominantly of farmland, forest, and wetlands. The siting of the commercial park in this rural setting all but guarantees that it will become a catalyst for further sprawl in the region.

Some of the biggest sprawl subsidies relate to highway construction. This country spends billions of local tax dollars and federal transportation funds on new freeways that encourage the destruction of rural areas and the decline of urban centers. A case in point is the "Grand Parkway" in the greater Houston area. Houston already has several beltway freeways ringing the city. The Grand Parkway would add yet another, this time intruding into some of the last pristine wetlands and agricultural lands in southern Texas. The Environmental Impact Statement for one segment of this project, rationalizing the need for a new beltway, reads like a recipe for sprawl:

> Residential and commercial development has kept pace with the growth in population, as evidenced by several residential subdivisions located in the study area. There is a great demand for office space and manufacturing facilities in Fort Bend County. Consequently, a number of developers have announced and begun construction of new office buildings and new speculative manufacturing and warehouse facilities in Fort Bend County. . . . A 700,000 square foot destination mall, Katy Mills, opened in October 1999.

As in this EIS, the rationale for sprawl often appears to be growth for growth's sake. No one seems to question whether a 700,000 square foot mall on the rural fringe of the city is wise land use or what it portends for the future.

Communities also spend local tax dollars providing infrastructure for sprawl — schools, sewers, water, fire and police — and end up draining public resources. Even from a purely fiscal standpoint, the costs of sprawl often far outweigh the benefits. For example, the *Sprawl Costs Us All* report describes a recent study of "wildcat subdivisions" in Pima County, Arizona. A local investigation there found that each home in a wildcat subdivision cost the county $23,000, while contributing only $1,700 in tax revenues. A similar study by the American Farmland Trust found that the average revenue-to-cost ratio for residential development is $1.00 to $1.15.

In *The Fool's Progress,* Abbey's character Henry Lightcap becomes increasingly morose as he ventures eastward across Missouri toward West Virginia. After passing endless franchise strips and pizza joints, Lightcap bemoaned the fate of the land:

> Everything that's beautiful decays from neglect; the cheap false synthetic transitory structures inspired by greed spread along the highway like mustard weed, like poison ivy, like the creeping kudzu vine. . . . Ill fares the land.

Abbey's book was published in 1988. He foresaw the increasing public sentiment against sprawl. Now that we appear to have the sentiment, maybe, just maybe, we will do something about the problem.

NOTES

1. Jim Yardley, "Houston, Smarting Economically from Smog, Searches for Remedies." *New York Times,* September 24, 2000.
2. *Los Angeles Times,* September 3, 2000.

 NO

Is "Smart Growth" a Smart Idea to Control Suburban Sprawl?

THOMAS J. DiLORENZO
The Myth of Suburban Sprawl

To millions of Americans, a house in the suburbs with a nice yard, garden, and a little open space is the American Dream. To environmentalists and urban planners, though, it is a nightmare. The invectives they use to describe suburbia reveal a visceral hatred of it:

- Urban affairs writer Neal Pierce has referred to "suburban sprawl" as "a virus eating us from the inside out."
- The *Arizona Republic* has called the suburbs "insane," "destructive," and "nightmarish."
- The Sierra Club views suburban development as a "menace" and a threat to Americans' "rural legacy" that must be eliminated.
- Urban planner Andres Duany believes suburban sprawl is "a cancerous growth" on society.
- Suburban living is "something to be opposed instead of welcomed," according to Vice Pres. Al Gore.
- New Jersey Gov. Christine Todd Whitman compares the war against suburban sprawl to the struggle against communism: "This time the enemy isn't the Soviets, but sprawl."

Its critics have compiled a list of alleged disasters caused by suburban living that verges on the hysterical. They claim that it is responsible for profound environmental stress, intractable traffic congestion, expensive housing, loss of open space, the virtual destruction of U.S. cities, isolated lives, racial segregation, ugliness, destruction of wetlands and recreational areas, higher taxes, asthma among children, vehicular accidents, unemployment and poverty, destruction of the family farm, demise of the public schools, and, according to Sprawl Watch Clearinghouse, even the menacing spectacle of "neo-Nazi young people." Vice Pres. Gore has even stated that, in contrast to the calm serenity of, say, Manhattan traffic, driving in the suburbs is the root cause of "road rage."

Many of the problems the critics of suburbia are concerned with have been either greatly exaggerated or simply fabricated. Moreover, the proposed "solution" to these problems — centralized governmental planning of where people live and work and how they commute (*i.e.*, regulatory sprawl) is bound to be economically inefficient, harmful to growth, and inherently inequitable.

Smart growth is the environmental movement's chosen euphemism for centralized governmental planning. The essential idea is that the free choices and careful lifestyle planning done by individual families in cooperation with the housing industry and local public officials are inherently "stupid" and socially destructive, whereas the coercive planning schemes favored by environmentalists and urban planners are "smart" and socially enlightened.

The "Smart Growth Network" is a coalition of environmental organizations, urban planners, and city politicians. The ultimate aim of the latter group is apparently to force people to move back into the metropolises where they can pay city, rather than suburban, taxes. It is a "bootleggers and Baptists" kind of coalition, to borrow economist Bruce Yandle's phrase that he used to describe the coalition in favor of alcohol prohibition in the 1920s. The Baptists favored prohibition for moral reasons, while the bootleggers wanted it for purely economic motives — it eliminated their competition. Similarly, the attack on suburbia is an important element of the secular "religion" of environmentalism, whereas urban politicians are in it for the (tax) money.

In order to correct all of the supposed inefficiencies of suburban development, smart growth proponents have proposed an ever-growing list of regulations, taxes, and myriad other governmental interventions. The charge that suburban development is economically inefficient ignores the most elementary of economic principles. Allocative efficiency means that, in competitive markets, resources tend to be used by those who value them most highly. Those people who value a particular parcel of land more than the current owners do, for example, will offer the owners a price they find too attractive to refuse. It is in this way that resources tend to be allocated to the most highly valued uses.

Smart growth advocates are using a bogus definition of "efficiency" that ignores the preferences of market participants (buyers and sellers), and simply reflects their personal preferences. Suburban residents who have moved out of the city clearly have decided that they are willing to endure more time spent in an automobile in exchange for a larger house with more open space. It is a tradeoff they are willing to make. Smart growth advocates are expressing their disapproval of those choices and believe that their preferences are more important than those of the more than 100,000,000 Americans who live in the suburbs.

All the talk of "unplanned" suburban development is misleading. It is not a matter of planned vs. unplanned suburban development, but *who is to do the planning.* People who build or purchase homes in the suburbs do so as part of their work, lifestyle, and family planning. Developers who build houses and towns and shopping centers for them do so because that is what the people want. Thus, the profit motive provides powerful incentives for developers to cater to the preferences of consumers. Those who do the best job will prosper, while those who don't will fail. This is the very essence of economic efficiency and involves a great deal more planning (and more efficient planning, at that) than can be accomplished by any governmental planning board.

Some governmental policy actually fosters "sprawl." Examples include tax incentives that encourage businesses to locate in one place rather than another; minimum-lot zoning that artificially reduces land density; and governmental pricing of such services as water and electricity at average, rather than marginal, cost, artificially enhancing dispersed development. The latter can create nuisances, such as congestion, crowding, or environmental degradation, but these are inefficiencies that can be altered through privatization, tax and regulatory reform, or common-law remedies, without effectively eliminating the private suburban real estate market and replacing it with a bureaucratic, command-and-control, central planning scheme.

When smart growth advocates argue that suburban development imposes costs on cities by allegedly creating poverty and unemployment and harming public schools, they have their causation backwards. It is the destructive policies of the past generation of urban planners that have led to escalating crime, unemployment, and poverty in the cities as well as the decline of the public schools. The handiwork of urban planners over the past 30 years — and the heavy tax burdens that have accumulated to pay for all their schemes — has encouraged millions of Americans to leave the cities for the suburbs.

In his landmark book, *The Federal Bulldozer,* Martin Anderson documented in great detail how, as early as 1962, Federal urban renewal programs (in force since 1949) had been "a thundering failure." They forcibly displaced millions of Americans, seizing homes, businesses, and property — sometimes with no compensation. The process destroyed thousands of low-rent homes and squandered billions of tax dollars.

By 1963, more than 50,000 lower-income families had been evicted by Federal urban planners. Most were forced to find more expensive housing or live in government-subsidized housing projects that quickly turned into dilapidated, crime-ridden slums. Only half of these families received any kind of compensation for their property losses. Four times more housing units were destroyed by urban planners than were replaced, causing a housing crisis for the poor. Approximately 26,000 small businesses had their property "acquired" by the state. About one-fourth of them ended up going out of business altogether.

A case can be made that no city in the U.S. has been subjected to more urban planning over the past 35 years than Washington, D.C. The results have been disastrous and are undoubtedly the reason why thousands of former residents have migrated from the nation's capital to the nearby suburbs. This model of urban planning and social engineering now has the highest tax burden of any local government jurisdiction and, arguably, the worst public services.

REFUTING REGULATORY RATIONALES

Disappearing Farms

One frequently cited rationale for smart growth regulation is that suburban development allegedly is eating up America's farmland, threatening the agriculture industry and even our ability to feed ourselves in the future. This purported market failure must be remedied by regulatory restrictions on suburban development.

The facts are that non-agriculture uses of land in the U.S. — cities, highways, railroads, airports — amount to just 3.6 percent (82,000,000 acres) of the total land, and cropland has remained virtually constant, at 24 percent of the U.S. land mass, since 1945. Over three-fourths of the states have more than 90 percent of their land in rural uses — including forests, cropland, pastures, wildlife reserves, and parks — and just 4.8 percent of the total land area of the U.S. is developed.

It is somewhat surprising that so much land remains devoted to agriculture, given the vast improvements in U.S. agricultural productivity during the last half-century. Today, the agricultural sector is approximately one and a half times more productive than it was 50 years ago. Thus, it is capable of producing more food on less land.

Though total agricultural land (not just that which is used to grow crops) is 20 percent less than it was in 1950, this is primarily a result of increased agricultural productivity, not sprawling suburbs. Moreover, the rate of loss of total agricultural land has significantly *slowed* in recent years, from a rate of 6.2 percent during the 1960s to 5.8 percent in the 1970s, 5 percent in the 1980s, and 2.7 percent in the 1990s. The U.S. Department of Agriculture's Economic Research Service concluded in 1997 that "losing farmland to urban uses does not threaten total cropland or the level of agricultural production which should be sufficient to meet food and fiber demand into the next century."

The main reason why even more agricultural land hasn't been disinvested is the massive governmental subsidies to agriculture, primarily in the form of Federal low-interest loans and grants, price supports, and quotas and tariffs on imported agricultural products. Because of these subsidies, there are many farm businesses that are inefficiently operated and that would not (and should not) survive were it not for the subsidies. There are too many farms and too many farmers if economic efficiency is the criterion to be applied.

The notion that the conversion of farmland to suburban development is necessarily harmful to nature and the environment is questionable. Geologist James R.

Dunn has rejected the Sierra Club's assertion that suburbanization is "the biggest threat to America's wildlife heritage." He notes that, in many areas, abandoned farmland reforests naturally, and, when people move to the suburbs, they tend to plant abundant amounts of trees and vegetation, which often make better animal habitat than what was provided by farmland.

Traffic Congestion

Politicians promoting smart growth usually claim to sympathize with suburban commuters who are annoyed by too much traffic congestion and propose to do something about it. However, the types of policies they advocate would increase traffic congestion and exacerbate air pollution.

Smart growth advocates do not want to build any more highways — in the cities *or* the suburbs. Their goal is to pack the population into the cities or more densely populated suburban areas. This may lead to a slight reduction in driving time, but, combined with a large percentage increase in population, the inevitable result is *more* traffic congestion, not less. In fact, urban planners in Portland, Ore., have openly stated that their objective is to increase traffic congestion so much and make life so miserable for that city's commuters that they will abandon their vehicles. "Congestion signals positive urban development," they announced in 1999.

In contrast, the U.S. Department of Transportation's Nationwide Transportation Survey shows that, as people and jobs have moved to the suburbs, commuting times *decreased* from an average of 22 minutes per commute in 1969 to 20.7 in 1995. Contrary to the impression most Americans have of the Los Angeles "commuting nightmare," the typical resident has just a 20-minute commute to one of myriad suburban employment locations.

Air pollution has also declined as America has suburbanized. Conversely, according to the Federal government's Roadway Congestion Index, urban areas with higher population densities have higher levels of traffic congestion and air pollution, contrary to what smart growth proponents would have us believe.

Soaring Housing Prices

The principal objective of smart growth advocates is to reduce significantly the supply of housing in the suburbs and to use the tax and regulatory powers of the state to force a segment of the population back into the cities. The effect of such a scheme on housing markets would be to slash the supply of housing in the suburbs, thereby making it more expensive there, while increasing the demand (and price) for urban housing. In addition, the myriad building code and other regulations that are proposed for urban areas would raise the cost of housing. The end result would be higher-priced housing in urban areas as well as in suburbia. Higher housing prices triggered by smart growth would effectively constitute a regressive tax on lower-income families, who can least afford the higher housing costs.

A variety of techniques are promoted ostensibly to control growth. States provide subsidies to local governments that grant property tax abatements to the owners of farms or purchase land and place it off-limits to development. Agricultural zoning that prohibits development altogether and minimum-lot zoning, including "super-zoning" such as exists in parts of Marin County, Calif., where 60-acre lots are required, are also advocated. Moratoria on new connections to public utility systems and higher development charges, whereby developers are assessed hefty fees to subsidize local governmental budgets are other tools in the tinkers' toolboxes. Ecological hurdles such as environmental impact statements and lawsuits to protect "endangered" species such as the spotted owl or the kangaroo rat can be used to block development.

Mass Transit

Another key element of the smart growth agenda is increased government subsidies for mass transit, particularly buses and light rail systems (i.e., streetcars). Though proposed in the name of economic efficiency, mass transit subsidies are among the most inefficient of all uses of taxpayer dollars.

Public transit ridership peaked during the World War II years and has declined by about two-thirds (from 23,000,000,000 trips annually to about 8,000,000,000) since that time, despite the tens of billions of dollars in government subsidies. Public transit's share of urban passenger miles has fallen from more than 30 percent in 1945 to barely 2 percent today. The free market worked quite efficiently as consumers chose to travel more by automobile and the auto industry accommodated them with better cars.

Smart growth advocates complain that automobile travel has been subsidized by the government and that their proposals seek to correct this government-induced distortion. While it is true that building the interstate highway system subsidized automobile travel, it is not at all clear that government policy has artificially stimulated automobile travel above what it would otherwise have been. Drivers have been paying heavy Federal and state gasoline taxes for decades, which tend to reduce the number of miles driven. Other governmental policies such as environmental and safety regulations have increased the price of cars and, thus, the cost of auto travel. It is impossible to know what kinds of roads might have been built had private entrepreneurs been given more leeway in building interstate highways, much as financier James J. Hill built a transcontinental railroad in the 19th century without a dime of government subsidy, not even land grants.

Government subsidies to public transit have been a futile, wasteful, and sometimes corrupt attempt to foil the efficiency of the marketplace by subsidizing less-efficient means of transportation, amounting to more than $155,000,000,000 since 1964. Despite this influx of funding, every U.S. public transit system with a rail element operates at a loss, according to the American Public Transit Association. In no city do riders pay even half the cost of their own transportation.

Mass transit not only costs more than automobile travel, it is slower. The average time spent commuting to work by car is 21 minutes, compared to an average 38-minute bus trip or 45 minutes by rail or subway. Public transit systems with a rail component even consume 22 percent more BTUs per person-mile than automobiles.

MONOPOLY GOVERNMENT

Smart growth policies are inherently undemocratic, because a key component of the overall strategy is the creation of governmental authorities in metropolitan areas vested with more-or-less-authoritarian land-use powers over entire regions. These governmental bodies are not referred to by smart growth advocates as monopolistic, of course. Euphemisms such as "consolidated," "metropolitan," or "regional" government are used instead.

Since 1925, the idea of monopoly government for metropolitan areas has been known by political scientists as the urban "reform tradition." The key elements, first championed by Pres. Woodrow Wilson, are a single government in every urban area, few elected officials in governments run mostly by unelected bureaucrats, no separation of powers within the government, and an exceptionally powerful chief executive.

The idea is to substitute the rule of experts for individual choice. Yet, in a metropolitan area with several competing governmental jurisdictions, if one imposes land-use or other policies that are not to the liking of a majority of the voting population, the result will be out-migration of population, industry, and the tax base to more favorable jurisdictions. Citizens' ability to "vote with their feet" imposes a degree of discipline on government. If one's objective is to have a government that is the servant, rather than master, of the people, decentralized metropolitan government is much more conducive to that end than is one large, monopolistic government that is mainly detached from electoral pressures.

There is much empirical support for this proposition in the economics literature. Writing in the *National Tax Journal,* for instance, David L. Sjoquist reported the results of an econometric study that concluded that "expenditures per capita in the central city fall as the number of jurisdictions in a metropolitan area increases."

Smart growth advocates persistently push for annexation, consolidation, and regional "tax-base sharing" that deprives citizens of the benefits of greater autonomy and creates an inherently inefficient and uncontrollable (by taxpayers) governmental system. Then again, that is apparently the idea for smart growth proponents, who want as little citizen interference with their plans as possible.

Questions for Discussion

1. What causes urban sprawl?
2. What would have to happen for urban sprawl to be stopped?
3. Is urban planning undemocratic? What are the reasons for your answer?
4. What impact has sprawl had on cities?
5. Can smart growth succeed in its objectives? What are the reasons for your answer?
6. What is the future of urban sprawl?

Suggested Resources

Web Sites

Center for Free Market Environmentalism
http://www.perc.org

Congress for the New Urbanism
http://www.cnu.org/

Natural Resources Defense Council
http://www.nrdc.org

Sierra Club
http://www.sierraclub.org/

Smart Growth Online
http://www.smartgrowth.org

Publications

Benfield, F. Kaid, Matthew D. Raimi, and Donald D.T. Chen. *Once There Were Greenfields: How Urban Sprawl Is Undermining America's Environment, Economy and Social Fabric.* New York: Natural Resources Defense Council, 1999.

Benfield, F. Kaid, Jutka Terris, and Nancy Vorsanger. *Solving Sprawl: Models of Smart Growth in Communities across America.* New York: Natural Resources Defense Council, 2001.

Burchell, Robert W., et al. *The Costs of Sprawl — Revisited.* Washington, D.C.: National Academy Press, 1998.

DiLorenzo, Thomas J. "Suburban Legends." *Society* 38. no. 1 (November/December 2000): 11–18.

Freilich, Robert H. *From Sprawl to Smart Growth.* Chicago: Section of State and Local Government Law, American Bar Association, 1999.

Gordon, Peter, and Harry R. Richardson. "The Sprawl Debate: Let Markets Plan." *Publius* 31, no. 3 (Summer 2001): 131–49.

Herson, Lawrence J. R., and John M. Bolland. *The Urban Web: Politics, Policy, and Theory,* 2d ed. Chicago: Nelson-Hall, 1998.

Huber, Peter. *Hard Green — Saving the Environment from the Environmentalists: A Conservative Manifesto.* New York: Basic Books, 1999.

Nivola, Pietro S. *Laws of the Landscape: How Policies Shape Cities in Europe and America.* Washington, D.C.: Brookings Institution Press, 1999.

O'Toole, Randal. "The Folly of 'Smart Growth.'" *Regulation* 24, no. 3 (Fall 2001): 20–25.

Pack, Janet Rothenberg. *Growth and Consequences in Metropolitan America.* Washington, D.C.: Brookings Institution Press, 1999.

Shaw, Jane S., and Ronald D. Utt, eds. *A Guide to Smart Growth: Shattering Myths, Providing Solutions.* Washington, D.C.: Heritage Foundation; Bozeman, Mont.: PERC, 2000.

Squires, Gregory D., ed. *Urban Sprawl: Causes, Consequences, and Policy Responses.* Washington, D.C.: Urban Institute Press, 2002.

Szold, Terry S., and Armando Carbonell, eds. *Smart Growth: Form and Consequences.* Cambridge, Mass.: Lincoln Institute of Land Policy, 2002.

Williams, Donald C. *Urban Sprawl: A Reference Handbook.* Santa Barbara, Calif.: ABC-CLIO, 2000.

Whoriskey, Peter. "Density Limits Only Add to Sprawl." *Washington Post,* March 9, 2003, pp. A1, A14–A15.

Should the United States Resist Globalization?

- A person in Great Britain calls an airline office in London for information, and an airline representative in India answers the phone and provides the information that the caller needs.
- A man buys a t-shirt with a patriotic USA message, and the shirt label indicates "Made in China."
- A Japanese woman uses her Japanese credit card to pay for a meal in a restaurant in Italy.
- An American tourist on her first trip to France is astonished to find many familiar American features in that country, including McDonald's, Holiday Inn, and Kentucky Fried Chicken.

These are everyday occurrences in our contemporary world, and examples of the impact of foreign trade, modern communications, and travel that in recent years have been described as *globalization*. Foreign trade is not a new development; it has been going on for centuries. But the level of financial transactions and trade across national boundaries today is greater than it has been in the past.

International trade is accompanied by the growth of multinational corporations in finance and industry. Companies in the United States and in other developed countries that used to manufacture their own products at home now go to countries where labor costs are cheaper and make the same products there for markets not only in their home countries but also in other countries. Many of the top multinational corporations have higher annual revenues than the gross national product of most developing nations and even of some developed nations.

"Globalization" has become the buzz word for much controversy and street protest, such as demonstrations in Seattle and Washington, D.C., within the past few years. Too often, however, media accounts of these demonstrations stress the disorderly conduct and undermine the seriousness of the issues involved with globalization. Among these issues are: the necessity and value of globalization; the power of multinational corporations; the role of international economic institutions, such as the International Monetary Fund (IMF), the World Bank, and the World Trade Organization (WTO); income disparity between the rich and poor in both the developed and developing nations; and debt and inflation in developing nations. The prospect of globalization raises other issues, including the impact of globalization on the environment, culture, democracy, and human rights.

The debate below considers many of these issues. The Alternatives Committee of the International Forum on Globalization is critical of globalization and calls for alternatives. It contends:

1. The corporations that promote globalization are increasing inequality, eroding trust, and promoting the failure of planetary life support systems.
2. The corporations are undemocratic and are shielded from accountability. Popular movements that fight globalization reflect the democratic challenge to these selfish corporations. These movements favor democracy and environmental protection.
3. The World Bank, IMF, and WTO serve the interests of the corporations at the expense of the people.
4. Alternatives to globalization would promote economic equality, save the environment from corporate predators, improve the standard of living of the masses of people, contribute to a healthier society, protect jobs, defend local resource management systems that work, and achieve other noble purposes.

Murray Weidenbaum, chair of the Center for the Study of American Business at Washington University in St. Louis, is critical of the antiglobal activists. Among his comments are:

1. The corporations are not trying to "homogenize" the whole world so that every country is a carbon copy of other countries.
2. Corporations respect economic diversity.
3. International organizations, such as the IMF and the WTO, are not as powerful as critics claim but rather are held to account by the sovereign nations that join them.
4. Business corporations are the most effective source of economic development in the poorer nations in which they invest and provide new technology.
5. Public health in the world is better than it was in the past as a result of the application of technology to agriculture.
6. In nearly all measures of environmental health, we are improving.
7. If the antiglobalist agenda were adopted, the immediate effect for the United States and other industrialized countries would be to become isolationist.
8. The multinational corporations have been in the vanguard of improving living standards and working conditions at home and abroad.

☑ *YES*

Should the United States Resist Globalization?

ALTERNATIVES COMMITTEE OF THE
INTERNATIONAL FORUM ON GLOBALIZATION
A Better World Is Possible! Alternatives to Economic Globalization

INTRODUCTION

Global Resistance

Society is at a crucial crossroads. A peaceful, equitable and sustainable future depends on the outcome of escalating conflicts between two competing visions: one corporate, one democratic. The schism has been caught by media images and stories accompanying recent meetings of global bureaucracies like the World Trade Organization (WTO), the International Monetary Fund (IMF), the World Bank, the Free Trade Area of the Americas (FTAA), and numerous other gatherings of corporate and economic elites, such as the World Economic Forum at Davos, Switzerland. . . .

Over the past five to ten years, millions of people have taken to the streets in India, the Philippines, Indonesia, Brazil, Bolivia, the United States, Canada, Mexico, Argentina, Venezuela, France, Germany, Italy, the Czech Republic, Spain, Sweden, England, New Zealand, Australia, Kenya, South Africa, Thailand, Malaysia, and elsewhere in massive demonstrations against the institutions and policies of corporate globalization. All too often the corporate media have done more to mislead than to inform the public on the issues behind the protests. Thomas Friedman, *The New York Times* foreign affairs columnist, is typical of journalists who characterize the demonstrators as "ignorant protectionists" who offer no alternatives and are unworthy of serious attention.

The claim that the protesters have no alternatives is as false as the claims that they are anti-poor, xenophobic, anti-trade, and have no analysis. In addition to countless books, periodicals, conferences, and individual articles and presentations setting forth alternatives, numerous consensus statements have been carefully crafted by civil society groups over the past two decades that set forth a wealth of alternatives with a striking convergence in their beliefs about the underlying values human societies can and should serve. Such consensus statements include a collection of citizen treaties drafted in Rio de Janeiro in 1992 by the 18,000 representatives of global civil society who met in parallel to the official meetings of the United Nations Conference on Environment and Development (UNCED). A subsequent initiative produced The Earth Charter, scheduled for ratification by the UN General Assembly in 2002 — the product of a global process that involved thousands of people. In 2001 and 2002, tens of thousands more gathered in Porto Alegre, Brazil, for the first annual World Social Forum on the theme "Another World Is Possible" to carry forward this process of popular consensus building toward a world that works for all.

Different Worlds

The corporate globalists who meet in posh gatherings to chart the course of corporate globalization in the name of private profits, and the citizen movements who organize to thwart them in the name of democracy and diversity are separated by deep differences in values, world view, and definitions of progress. At times it seems they must be living in wholly different worlds — which in many respects they are.

Corporate globalists inhabit a world of power and privilege. They see progress everywhere because from their vantage point the drive to privatize public assets and free the market from governmental interference appears to be spreading freedom and prosperity throughout the world, improving the lives of people everywhere, and creating the financial and material wealth necessary to end poverty and protect the environment. They see themselves as champions of an inexorable and beneficial historical process toward erasing the economic and political borders that hinder corporate expansion, eliminating the tyranny of inefficient and meddlesome public bureaucracies, and unleashing the enormous innovation and wealth-creating power of competition and private enterprise.

Citizen movements see a starkly different reality. Focused on people and the environment, they see a world in deepening crisis of such magnitude as to threaten the fabric of civilization and the survival of the species — a world of rapidly growing inequality, erosion of relationships of trust, and failing planetary life support systems. Where corporate globalists see the spread of democracy and vibrant market economies, citizen movements see the power to govern shifting away from people and communities to financial speculators and global corporations dedicated to the pursuit of short-term profit. They see corporations replacing democracies of people with democracies of money, self-organizing markets with centrally planned corporate economies, and diverse cultures with cultures of greed and materialism.

Transformational Imperative

In a world in which a few enjoy unimaginable wealth, 200 million children under five are underweight due to a lack of food. Fourteen million children die each year from hunger-related disease. A hundred million children are living or working on the streets. Three hundred thousand children were conscripted as soldiers during the 1990s and six million were injured in armed conflicts. Eight hundred million people go to bed hungry each night. Human activity — most particularly fossil fuel combustion — is estimated to have increased atmospheric concentrations of carbon dioxide to their highest levels in 20 million years. According to the World-Watch Institute, natural disasters — including weather related disasters such as storms, floods, and fires — affected more than two billion people and caused in excess of $608 billion in economic losses worldwide during the decade of the 1990s — more than the previous four decades combined.

Economic Democracy

Humanity has reached the limits of an era of centralized institutional power and control. The global corporation, the WTO, the IMF, and the World Bank are structured to concentrate power in the hands of ruling elites shielded from public accountability. They represent an outmoded, undemocratic, inefficient and ultimately destructive way of organizing human affairs that is as out of step with the needs and values of healthy, sustainable and democratic societies as the institution of monarchy. The current and future well-being of humanity depends on transforming the relationships of power within and between human societies toward more democratic and mutually accountable modes of managing human affairs that are self-organizing, power-sharing, and minimize the need for coercive central authority.

Global Governance

The concern for local self-reliance and self-determination have important implications for global governance. For example, in a self-reliant and localized system the primary authority to set and enforce rules must rest with the national and local governments of the jurisdictions to which they apply. The proper role of global institutions is to facilitate the cooperative coordination of national policies on matters where the interests are inherently intertwined — as with action on global warming.

Building Momentum

Growing public consciousness of the pervasive abuse of corporate power has fueled the growth of a powerful opposition movement with an increasingly impressive list of achievements. Unified by a deep commitment to universal values of democracy, justice, and respect for life this alliance functions with growing effectiveness without a central organization, charismatic leader, or defining ideology — taking different forms in different settings.

In India, popular movements seek to empower local people through the democratic community control of resources under the banner of a million strong Living Democracy Movement (*Jaiv Panchayat*). In Canada, hundreds of organizations have joined in alliance to articulate a Citizens' Agenda that seeks to wrest control of governmental institutions back away from corporations. In Chile, coalitions of environmental groups have created a powerful Sustainable Chile (*Sustainable Chile*) movement that seeks to reverse Chile's drift toward neoliberalism and reassert popular democratic control over national priorities and resources. The focus in Brazil is on the rights of the poor and landless. In Bolivia it takes the form of a mass movement of peasants and workers who have successfully blocked the privatization of water. In Mexico, the Mayan people have revived the spirit of Zapata in a movement to confirm the rights of indigenous people to land and resources. Farmers in France have risen up in revolt against trade rules that threaten to destroy small farms. The construction of new highways in England has brought out hundreds of thousands of people who oppose this desecration of the countryside in response to globalization's relentless demand for ever more high speed transport.

These are only a few examples of the popular initiatives and actions in defense of democratic rights that are emerging all around the world. Together these many initiatives are unleashing ever more of the creative energy of humanity toward building cooperative systems of sustainable societies that work for all.

CRITIQUE OF ECONOMIC GLOBALIZATION

The alternatives offered in this report grow from the widespread damage inflicted by economic globalization over the past five centuries as it passed from colonialism and imperialism through post-colonial, export-led development models. The driving force of economic globalization since World War II has been several hundred large private corporations and banks that have increasingly woven webs of production, consumption, finance, and culture across borders. Indeed, today most of what we eat, drink, wear, drive, and entertain ourselves with is the product of globe-girdling corporations.

Key Ingredients and General Effects

Economic globalization (sometimes referred to as corporate-led globalization), features several key ingredients:

- Corporate deregulation and the unrestricted movement of capital;
- Privatization and commodification of public services, and remaining aspects of the global and community commons, such as bulk water and genetic resources;
- Integration and conversion of national economies (including some that were largely self-reliant) to environmentally and socially harmful export-oriented production;
- Promotion of hyper-growth and unrestricted exploitation of the planet's resources to fuel the growth;
- Dramatically increased corporate concentration;
- Undermining of national social, health and environmental programs;
- Erosion of traditional powers and policies of democratic nation-states and local communities by global corporate bureaucracies;
- Global cultural homogenization, and the intensive promotion of unbridled consumerism.

Pillars of Globalization

The first tenet of economic globalization, as now designed, is the need to integrate and merge all economic activity of all countries within a single, homogenized model of development; a single centralized system. A second tenet of the globalization design is that primary importance is given to the achievement of ever more rapid, and never ending corporate economic growth—hyper growth—fueled by the constant search for access to natural resources, new and cheaper labor sources, and new markets. A third tenet concerns privatization and commodification of as many traditionally non-commodified nooks and crannies of existence as possible — seeds and genes for example. A fourth important tenet of economic globalization is its strong emphasis on a global conversion to export-oriented production and trade as an economic and social nirvana.

Beneficiaries of Globalization

The actual beneficiaries of this model have become all too obvious. In the United States, for example, we know that during the period of the most rapid globalization, top corporate executives of the largest global companies have been making salaries and options in the many millions of dollars, often in the hundreds of millions, while real wages of ordinary workers have been declining. The Institute for Policy Studies reports that American CEOs are now paid, on average, 517 times more than production workers, with that rate increasing yearly. The Economic Policy Institute's 1999 report says that median hourly wages are actually down by 10 percent in real wages over the last 25 years. As for lifting the global poor, the U.N. Development Program's 1999 *Human Development Report* indicated that the gap between the wealthy and the poor within and among countries of the world is getting steadily larger, and it named inequities in the global trade system as being one of the key factors.

Bureaucratic Expressions of Globalization

Creating a world that works for all must begin with an effort to undo the enormous damage inflicted by the corporate globalization policies that so badly distort economic relationships among people and countries. The thrust of those policies is perhaps most dramatically revealed in the structural adjustment programs imposed on low and intermediate income countries by the IMF and the World Bank — two institutions that bear responsibility for enormous social and environmental devastation and human suffering. Structural adjustment requires governments to:

- Cut government spending on education, healthcare, the environment, and price subsidies for basic necessities such as food grains, and cooking oils in favor of servicing foreign debt.
- Devalue the national currency and increase exports by accelerating the plunder of natural resources, reducing real wages, and subsidizing export-oriented foreign investments.
- Liberalize financial markets to attract speculative short-term portfolio investments that create enormous financial instability and foreign liabilities while serving little, if any, useful purpose.
- Increase interest rates to attract foreign speculative capital, thereby increasing bankruptcies of domestic businesses and imposing new hardships on indebted individuals.
- Eliminate tariffs, quotas and other controls on imports, thereby increasing the import of consumer goods purchased with borrowed foreign

exchange, undermining local industry and agricultural producers unable to compete with cheap imports, which increases the strain on foreign exchange accounts, and deepening external indebtedness.

The World Bank and the IMF, along with the General Agreement on Tariffs and Trade/World Trade Organization (GATT/WTO) are together known as the Bretton Woods institutions — the collective product of agreements reached at an international gathering held in Bretton Woods, New Hampshire, in July, 1944, to create an institutional framework for the post–World War II global economy.

Conclusions

The Bretton Woods institutions have a wholly distorted view of economic progress and relationships. Their embrace of unlimited expansion of trade and foreign investment as measures of economic progress suggests that they consider the most advanced state of development to be one in which all productive assets are owned by foreign corporations producing for export; the currency that facilitates day-to-day transactions is borrowed from foreign banks; education and health services are operated by global corporations on a for-profit, fee-for-service basis; and most that people consume is imported. When placed in such stark terms, the absurdity of the "neoliberal" ideology of the Bretton Woods institutions becomes obvious. It also becomes clear who such policies serve. Rather than enhance the life of people and planet, they consolidate and secure the wealth and power of a small corporate elite, the only evident beneficiaries, at the expense of humanity and nature. In the following section, we outline the principles of alternative systems that posit democracy and rights as the means toward sustainable communities, dignified work, and a healthy environment.

TEN PRINCIPLES FOR DEMOCRATIC AND SUSTAINABLE SOCIETIES

The current organizing principles of the institutions that govern the global economy are narrow and serve the few at the expense of the many and the environment. Yet, it is within our collective ability to create healthy, sustainable societies that work for all. The time has come to make that possibility a reality. Sustainable societies are rooted in certain core principles. The following ten core principles have been put forward in various combinations in citizen programs that are emerging around the world.

New Democracy

The rallying cry of the amazing diversity of civil society that converged in Seattle in late 1999 was the simple word "democracy." Democracy flourishes when people organize to protect their communities and rights and hold their elected officials accountable. For the past two decades, global corporations and global bureaucracies have grabbed much of the power once held by governments. We advocate a shift from governments serving corporations to governments serving people and communities, a process that is easier at the local level but vital at all levels of government.

Subsidiarity

Economic globalization results first, and foremost, in de-localization and disempowerment of communities and local economies. It is therefore necessary to reverse direction and create new rules and structures that consciously favor the local, and follow the principle of subsidiary, i.e., whatever decisions and activities can be undertaken locally should be. Whatever power can reside at the local level should reside there. Only when additional activity is required that cannot be satisfied locally, should power and activity move to the next higher level: region, nation, and finally the world.

Ecological Sustainability

Economic activity needs to be ecologically sustainable. It should enable us to meet humans' genuine needs in the present without compromising the ability of future generations to meet theirs, and without diminishing the natural diversity of life on Earth or the viability of the planet's natural life-support systems.

Common Heritage

There exists common heritage resources that should constitute a collective birthright of the whole species to be shared equitably among all. We assert that there are three categories of such resources. The first consists of the shared natural heritage of the water, land, air, forests, and fisheries on which our lives depend. These physical resources are in finite supply, essential to life, and existed long before any human. A second category includes the heritage of culture and knowledge that is the collective creation of our species. Finally, basic public services relating to health, education, public safety, and social security are "modern" common heritage resources representing the collective efforts of whole societies. They are also as essential to life in modern societies as are air and water. Justice therefore demands that they be readily available to all who need them. Any attempt by persons or corporations to monopolize ownership control of an essential common heritage resource for exclusive private gain to the exclusion of the needs of others is morally unconscionable and politically unacceptable.

Human Rights

In 1948, governments of the world came together to adopt the United Nations Universal Declaration on Human Rights, which established certain core rights, such as "a standard for living adequate for ... health and well-being ..., including food, clothing, housing and medical care, and necessary social services, and the right to security in the event of unemployment." Traditionally, most of the human rights debate in the United States and other rich nations has focused on civil and political rights as paramount. We believe that it is the duty of governments to ensure these rights, but also to guarantee the economic, social and cultural rights of all people.

Jobs/Livelihood/Employment

A livelihood is a means of living. The right to a means of livelihood is therefore the most basic of all human rights. Sustainable societies must both protect the rights of workers in the formal sector and address the livelihood needs of the larger share of people who subsist in what has become known as the non-material, or "informal sector" (including small-scale, indigenous, and artisanal activities) as well as those who have no work or are seriously underemployed. Empowering workers to organize for basic rights and fair wages is vital to curb footloose corporations that pit workers against each other in a lose-lose race to the bottom. And, the reversal of globalization policies that displace small farmers from their land and fisherfolk from their coastal ecosystems are central to the goal of a world where all can live and work in dignity.

Food Security and Food Safety

Communities and nations are stable and secure when people have enough food, particularly when nations can produce their own food. People also want safe food, a commodity that is increasingly scarce as global agribusiness firms spread chemical- and biotech-intensive agriculture around the world.

Equity

Economic globalization, under the current rules, has widened the gap between rich and poor countries and between rich and poor within most countries. The resulting social dislocation and tension are among the greatest threats to peace and security the world over. Greater equity both among nations and within them would reinforce both democracy and sustainable communities. Reducing the growing gap between rich and poor nations requires first and foremost the cancellation of the illegitimate debts of poor countries. And, it requires the replacement of the current institutions of global governance with new ones that include global fairness among their operating principles.

Diversity

A few decades ago, it was still possible to leave home and go somewhere else where the architecture was different, the landscape was different, the language, lifestyle, food, dress, and values were different. Today, farmers and filmmakers in France and India, indigenous communities worldwide, and millions of people elsewhere, are protesting to maintain that diversity. Tens of thousands of communities around the world have perfected local resource management systems that work, but they are now being undermined by corporate-led globalization. Cultural, biological, social, and economic diversity are central to a viable, dignified, and healthy life.

Precautionary Principle

All activity should abide by the precautionary principle. When a practice or product raises potentially significant threats of harm to human health or the environment, precautionary action should be taken to restrict or ban it even if scientific uncertainty remains about whether or how it is actually causing that harm. Because it can take years for scientific proof of harm to be established — during which time undesirable or irreversible effects may continue to be inflicted — the proponents of a practice or product should bear the burden of proving that it is safe, before it is implemented.

☑ *N O*

Should the United States Resist Globalization?

MURRAY WEIDENBAUM
A Response to the Assault on the Global Economy

One of the great ironies of our time is that globalization has been a great success both in terms of generating prosperity at home and raising living standards abroad. Nevertheless, the supporters of globalization are on the defensive. The global marketplace is under assault by a strange alliance of radical groups and environmental organizations.

Those of us who support an open economy have been rather quiet, but we should not remain silent. The organizations from the far left, such as the Institute for Policy Studies, are long-term opponents of the capitalist system, so their opposition to trade between nations is neither new nor newsworthy.

It is surprising, however, that the Sierra Club and the Friends of the Earth have let their names be associated with this effort to oppose the modern economy. Therefore, those views need a response, especially since they are being circulated via expensive full-page advertisements in national media under the heading "Economic Globalization." Here are their major arguments and my personal responses:

1. "The goal of the global economy is that all countries should be homogenized."

One of the ads states that, "a few decades ago, it was still possible to leave home and go somewhere else: the landscape was different, the language, lifestyle, dress, and values were different." I haven't been able to find any evidence to support the charge that homogenization is the goal of any company, industry, or business association involved in the global marketplace. Nor does it make any sense for such a goal to be adopted.

There is no economic logic for each country becoming a carbon copy of every other nation. It runs counter to the division of labor that is so basic to the success of the global economy. By the way, it is commonplace for managers in the international economy to urge their employees to "Think global, but act local."

Of course, it makes good sense for people — be they business and government decisionmakers or individual investors and consumers — to take account of the important trends occurring outside of their community or nation. Nevertheless, every business that has operated successfully in more than one country has learned, often the hard way, that people's tastes are hardly uniform. Despite the rise of the European Union, the French are not stampeding for German wines and the British are still driving on the wrong side of the road.

Consider these pairs of nations: France and China, Poland and New Zealand, and Denmark and Thailand. Anyone who has visited them knows that they are vastly different in landscape, language, lifestyle, dress, and — especially — values. The kindest response is that the organizations that have lent their names to these wild statements either did not read the ads very carefully or spend any length of time in those countries. Indeed, there is little evidence from the world around us to support the contention that "Every place is becoming every place else."

I still recall an incident at the Hotel Crillon, one of the more fashionable Parisian establishments. Several of us were staying there in connection with the Organization for Economic Cooperation and Development meetings. A colleague of mine got on the elevator and said "Two" to the operator, while I, in my broken French, requested *"troisiene, s'il vous plait."* The operator took the French-speakers to the third floor first and then proceeded to drop off the other passenger on the second floor. This happened more than once. We may think that English is the Latin of our time, but it does not always suffice in the global economy.

2. "Diversity is an enemy because it requires differentiated sales appeal."

This statement — which appears in one of those full-page ads — betrays ignorance of the actual operation of the private enterprise system. In recent years, diversity in all its dimensions has become a watchword in the modern corporation. Moreover, it is those differences that provide "niches" individual corporations love to focus on in their constant efforts to achieve product differentiation and greater competitiveness.

3. "... the ultra-secretive World Trade Organization (WTO) ... now rivals the International Monetary Fund (IMF) as the most powerful, yet undemocratic body in the world."

Such blatant exaggerations feed on the public's unawareness of what these organizations are and how they operate. Neither the WTO nor the IMF has its own financing or military forces, the two key elements of international power. Both depend on the sovereign nations that join them, and each of those members has full voting rights. It is ironic that these organizations, whose own deliberations continue to be so secretive, have the temerity to raise such charges.

4. "Every country loses while global corporations win."

I am reminded of the advice given to a young diplomat by the great French states-man Charles-Maurice Talleyrand, *"Pas de zèle!"* ("Not so zealous!"). (In today's English, he'd probably say, "Cool it, man.") The truth is that the business enter-prises operating in the international economy typically are the most effective source of economic development in the poorer nations in which they invest and provide new technology. These enterprises also are among the most productive companies at home and typically pay well above average wages and benefits.

The acid test, as was made clear in the Seattle discussions in December, 1999, is that the developing nations welcome foreign investment by multinational cor-porations. As was true in the U.S. in the first half of the 19th century, a developing country needs to import foreign capital and benefits from doing so.

5. "Millions . . . have protested against the invasion and promotion of genetically engineered foods which are destroying local livelihoods and threatening public health."

It is a fact that millions of people have been scared — needlessly — by the spon-sors of the assault on the global economy. However, there is no evidence of any public health danger from genetically engineered foods or of livelihoods being threatened.

Moreover, such applications of advanced technology to agriculture are the most effective way of increasing the world's food supply and simultaneously reducing the use of the pesticides and insecticides the same critics oppose — and for good reason. Calling genetically modified foods "Frankenfoods," as one ad does, is the modern equivalent of the discredited superstitions of the Dark Ages.

6. ". . . the European Union (EU) was told [by the WTO] it could not forbid imports of beef from animals fed potentially carcinogenic hormones."

The WTO never made such a ruling. Moreover, there is no credible evidence of potential carcinogenicity of those products. By the way, that is U.S.-produced beef they are referring to.

7. "Under globalized free trade, countries as diverse as Sweden and India, Canada and Thailand, Bolivia and Russia are meant to merge their economies . . ."

It is hard to believe that the organizations sponsoring these ads really think that there is any effort — under way or even contemplated — to merge such diverse and independent nations.

The kindest interpretation I can suggest is that perhaps the sponsors of the ads merely mean to refer to the increased opportunities free trade provides citizens of one country to interact with another. Of course, when you put it that far more accurate way, the global marketplace does not sound so sinister.

8. "... we are on the brink of a global environmental collapse."

That is not what the U.S. Environmental Protection Agency [EPA] has been saying. EPA regularly reports on the substantial improvements that have been achieved in the quality of the air we breathe and the water we drink and in just about every other measure of environmental health.

9. "Any nation's people are most secure when they can produce their own food..."

History surely does not demonstrate that a country is secure, much less "most secure," when it has attained agricultural autarchy — that is, when it has totally eliminated dependence on imports.

The security of a society is strongly influenced by such key factors as the strength of its armed forces and the support of its people. In fact, the success of the economy — which undergirds both of these key factors — would be denigrated if any country tried to produce all of its own food. Economic strength is a very positive determinant of a nation's independence.

The critics' position was exemplified by a sign carried by a protester in Seattle: "Food is for people, not for export." Frankly, I don't know how to reason with those who hold that viewpoint. They seem oblivious to the role of American agriculture in preventing hunger in so many parts of the world. At home, think of all the farms that would go broke if they lost the income from exports.

By the way, I've gotten some rejoinders to my response on this score. One person wrote, "yes, but companies export to make a profit." The implication is that altruism is the only acceptable motivation for economic activity. Funny how the greedy capitalist nations wind up feeding the poor hungry totalitarian nations. Clearly, we have a job of economic education to perform.

10. "Anyway, industrial food is less healthy; heavy with chemicals that pollute soil and water and cause public health problems."

Along with "Frankenfoods," apparently we now also have "industrial foods" to attack. It seems that there is no limit to the length that the foes of globalization will go to scare people.

We can only guess what "industrial foods" are. If not food grown in factories, perhaps it is food sold by large enterprises. Of course, the chemicals are still in use, whatever the size of the producer, because of the same groups' widespread opposition to the more benign substitution of genetic modification!

I have tried to present a small, but representative, sample of the wild charges carelessly tossed out by the opponents of "economic globalization." If the full policy agenda of the antiglobal activists were adopted, the immediate effect would be for the U.S. and other industrialized nations to become isolationist. In the longer run, each of them would lose the benefits of the international specialization of labor and suffer severe declines in standards of living.

It is ironic that the economic costs would soon be translated into environmental costs. This unexpected negative result would be caused by the strong connection between economic growth and environmental improvement. Wealthier countries can afford to devote more resources to achieving a cleaner and healthier environment, and history shows that they do so. Thus, it is wrong to justify reversing economic progress because of environmental considerations. Poorer countries can and do far less to clean up the environment. The opponents of free trade and economic growth have ignored that fact.

UNION CRITICISM

It is useful to remind ourselves that the often-maligned multinational corporation has been in the vanguard in terms of delivering rising living standards and improved working conditions, at home and abroad. American companies operating overseas have frequently been the leaders in offering higher wages and setting more enlightened business standards. That is certainly the case in the parts of China that I have visited.

However, this brings up a related line of criticism of the global economy — the new concern on the part of labor unions about overseas working conditions. Some cynics might dismiss this as disguised self-interest. After all, business firms don't exactly welcome lower-cost competitors, be they domestic or foreign. Why should we be surprised if unions take a similar position?

In any event, the large and growing trade deficits experienced by the U.S. in recent years have energized important elements of the labor movement to take a very suspicious, if not antagonistic, attitude toward free trade. Economists may readily see the overall benefit of open international markets — in terms of greater product variety, lower prices, and a powerful impetus to enhance American productivity and competitiveness.

The data show that large trade deficits are associated with *good* times in the U.S., not bad. Anyone with the slightest acquaintance with American economic history knows that trade deficits rise in times of prosperity and decline when the economy slows down or goes into recession. When you stop to think about it, that's not very surprising.

Today [2000], the U.S. is closer to full employment than it has been in a quarter of a century. Under these circumstances, imports provide a safety valve, keeping inflation down and postponing the time of monetary austerity in order to maintain price stability. However, the people who are hurt by imports — or even those who think they are adversely affected — can be expected to take a less generous view of the global marketplace.

The truth of the matter is that any significant economic change, whether it arises from domestic or overseas sources, is going to generate winners as well as losers.

We cannot simply dismiss this concern just because there are more winners than losers from trade. The challenge is not to redistribute the pain of those who are hurt by change. Rather, we need to help them without doing far greater harm to those who benefit from it. The constructive approach in this case is to enhance the competitiveness of American business and labor.

There is an important role here for education and training. In recent decades, we have seen the increased benefits that accompany more education. It is sad, therefore, to note that the new union assault on globalization takes a very backward position on this important subject.

In an article in *Foreign Affairs,* the chairman of the AFL-CIO International Affairs Committee lists examples of actions by other nations "that did not play by the rules." One of the charges the AFL-CIO makes is that these countries "invested in education" — and, furthermore, that Washington "winked" at this practice during the Cold War. It boggles the mind to think that investing in education is considered unfair by the AFL-CIO.

As I stated earlier, we have a big job of economic education ahead of us. There is no need to guess what impact the new isolationist pressures could generate if they succeed. China provides a cogent example. During the 1500s, China was by far the most economically progressive and culturally advanced nation on the face of the globe. It was the Chinese who invented clocks, the magnetic compass, paper, the wheelbarrow, moveable type, the rear rudder, and cast iron.

That abruptly ended when one Chinese emperor arbitrarily decided to cut off international trade with foreigners. He literally pulled up the drawbridge and stopped the flow of people, goods, and ideas between China and the rest of the world. China quickly shifted from being a world leader to being a poor backwater among nations. To this day, China has not recovered from the misguided isolationist policies of that 16th-century emperor.

Today, it is more than futile to adopt the isolationist position, "Stop the world, I want to get off." It would be one of the most dangerous things that America could do.

Questions for Discussion

1. What is the impact of free trade on the economies of developing nations?
2. In the United States who would benefit and who would be hurt if the United States adopted the antiglobalist view toward free trade?
3. What impact does globalization have on the quality of health among the trading partners?
4. What impact does free trade have on human rights?
5. What impact does free trade have on the culture of a developing nation? Is that impact good or bad? What are the reasons for your answer?

Suggested Resources

Web Sites

Citizens Trade Campaign
  http://www.citizenstrade.org

Economic Policy Institute
  http://www.gpn.org

International Monetary Fund
  http://www.imf.org

Public Citizen: Global Trade Watch
  http://www.citizen.org/trade

World Trade Organization
  http://www.wto.org

Publications

Barber, Benjamin. *Jihad vs. McWorld.* New York: Ballantine Books, 1996.

Barfield, Claude E. *Free Trade, Sovereignty, Democracy: The Future of the World Trade Organization.* Washington, D.C.: AEI Press, 2001.

Bhagwati, Jagdish. "Coping with Antiglobalization: A Trilogy of Discontents." *Foreign Affairs* 81, no. 1 (January/February 2002): 2–7.

Chua, Amy. *World on Fire: How Exporting Free Market Democracy Breeds Ethnic Hatred and Global Instability.* New York: Doubleday, 2003.

Danaher, Kevin, and Roger Burbach, eds. *Globalize This! The Battle against the World Trade Organization and Corporate Rule.* Monroe, Me.: Common Courage Press, 2000.

French, Hilary. *Vanishing Borders: Protecting the Planet in the Age of Globalization.* New York: W. W. Norton, 2000.

Friedman, Thomas L. *The Lexus and the Olive Tree,* rev. ed. New York: Farrar, Straus and Giroux, 2000.

Galbraith, James K. "A Perfect Crime: Inequality in the Age of Globalization." *Daedalus* 131, no. 1 (Winter 2002): 11–25.

Hansen, Brian. "Globalization Backlash." *CQ Researcher* 11, no. 33 (September 28, 2001): 761–84.

Larsson, Tomas. *The Race to the Top: The Real Story of Globalization.* Washington, D.C.: Cato Institute, 2001.

Munck, Ronaldo, and Barry K. Gills, eds. "Globalization and Democracy." *Annals of the American Academy of Political and Social Science* 581 (May 2002): entire issue.

Nye, Joseph S., Jr., "The Dependent Colossus: Although Globalization Today Reinforces American Power, Over Time It Promises to Have the Opposite Effect." *Foreign Policy* no. 129 (March 2002): 74–76.

Sandbrook, Richard, ed. *Civilizing Globalization: A Survival Guide.* Albany: State University of New York Press, 2003.

Saunders, Paul J. "Why 'Globalization' Didn't Rescue Russia." *Policy Review* no. 105 (February/March 2001): 27–39.

Stiglitz, Joseph E. *Globalization and Its Discontents.* New York: W. W. Norton, 2002.

Tabb, William K. *Unequal Partners: A Primer on Globalization.* New York: New Press, 2002.

Taylor, Timothy. "The Truth about Globalization." *Public Interest* no. 147 (Spring 2002): 24–44.

U.S. Cong., Senate. *Globalization and American Trade Policy.* Hearing before the Finance Committee, 107th Cong., 1st Sess., February 27, 2001.

Weidenbaum, Murray. "Globalization: Wonder Land or Waste Land?" *Vital Speeches of the Day* 68, no. 9 (February 15, 2002): 273–77.

Yergin, Daniel. "Globalization: The Inside Story of Our New Interconnected World." *Social Education* 66, no. 2 (March 2002): 111–14, 116.

Acknowledgments

Chapter 1

Thurgood Marshall, "The Constitution: Past and Present," speech at the Annual Seminar of the San Francisco Patent and Trademark Law Association, Maui, Hawaii, May 6, 1987. Notes have been omitted.

William Bradford Reynolds, "The Wisdom of the Framers," speech at the Vanderbilt University Reunion 1987 Celebration Luncheon, University Club, Nashville, Tennessee, May 23, 1987.

Chapter 2

Kirk Cox, prepared statement for U.S. Cong., House of Representatives, *The Perspective of State and Local Governments and the Impact of Federal Regulation.* Hearing before the Committee on the Budget, 104th Cong., 1st Sess., 1995, pp. 87–89.

John G. Kester, "Forever Federal," *Washingtonian* 31, no. 3 (December 1995): 47–48, 51. Reprinted by permission of the author.

Chapter 3

John Ashcroft, testimony of Attorney General John Ashcroft before the Senate Committee on the Judiciary, *DOJ Oversight: Preserving Our Freedoms while Defending against Terrorism,* 107th Cong., 1st Sess., December 6, 2001.

Michael Ratner, "Moving Toward a Police State or Have We Arrived? Secret Military Tribunals, Mass Arrests and Disappearances, Wiretapping and Torture," from Michael Ratner's Web site at www.humanrightsnow.org. Reprinted by permission.

Chapter 4

Amitai Etzioni, "You'll Love Those National ID Cards." Reprinted with permission of the author. This article first appeared in the *Christian Science Monitor,* January 14, 2002, p. 11 (www.csmonitor.com).

Katie Corrigan, testimony before the Subcommittee on Government Efficiency, Financial Management and Intergovernmental Relations of the House Committee on Government Reform on the Establishment of a National ID Card System, 107th Cong., 1st Sess., November 16, 2001.

Chapter 5

Walter E. Williams, "Racial Profiling," *Ideas on Liberty* 51, no. 14 (April 2001): 63–64. Copyright © 2001 by The Foundation for Economic Freedom.

David A. Harris, prepared statement for U.S. Cong., Senate, *Racial Profiling within Law Enforcement Agencies,* Hearing before the Subcommittee on the Constitution of the Committee on Judiciary, 106th Cong., 2d Sess., March 20, 2000, pp. 34–41.

Chapter 6

Senator Russ Feingold, "A New Millennium: Time to Stop Tinkering with the Machinery of Death," remarks at Columbia University School of Law, April 10, 2000.

Matthew T. Mangino, "Death Penalty Moratorium," *York* [Pennsylvania] *Sunday News,* June 9, 2002. Reprinted by permission of Matthew T. Mangino, Lawrence County (Pennsylvania) District Attorney.

Chapter 7

Roy S. Moore, "Putting God Back in the Public Square," *USA Today* magazine (September 2000). This article is based on a lecture at Hillsdale (Michigan) College. Reprinted by permission of the Society for the Advancement of Education.

Roger Bertschausen, "Rethinking the Separation Between Church and State," from Web site www.fvuuf.org, March 2–3, 2002. Reprinted by permission.

Chapter 8

Stanley Fish, "Affirming Affirmative Action," *Howard Law Journal* 39, no. 3 (Spring 1996): 731–35. Copyright © 1996 by the Howard University School of Law. Reprinted by permission.

Roger Clegg, testimony before the United States Commission on Civil Rights regarding Racial and Ethnic Preferences in Higher Education, May 14, 1999.

Chapter 9

Ruth Conniff, "The Progressive Interview: Richard Grossman," *The Progressive* 66, no. 3 (March 2002): 32–36. Reprinted by permission.

James Rolph Edwards, "Do Big Corporations Control America?" *Ideas on Liberty* 52, no. 3 (March 2002): 42–45. Copyright © 2002 by The Foundation for Economic Freedom.

Chapter 10

Michael Lerner, "Don't Vote Lesser Evil Politics!" *Tikkun* 15, no. 5 (September 2000): 31–35. Reprinted by permission.

Barney Frank, "Response to Lerner on Lesser Evil Politics," *Tikkun* 15, no. 5 (September 2000): 37–38. Reprinted by permission.

Chapter 11

Joseph I. Lieberman, *Congressional Record*, Senate, March 19, 2001, *Cong. Rec.* S. 2530–31.

Bradley A. Smith, "Campaign Finance Reform: Faulty Assumptions and Undemocratic Consequences." *USA Today* magazine 126, no. 2632 (January 1998): 10–13. Reprinted by permission of the Society for the Advancement of Education.

Chapter 12

Richard J. Durbin, *Congressional Record*, Senate, December 6, 2000, 146 *Cong. Rec.* S. 11618.

Judith A. Best, testimony, *Proposals for Electoral College Reform: H. J. Res. 28 and H. J. Res. 43*, Hearing before the U.S. Cong., House of Representatives, Committee on the Judiciary, Subcommittee on the Constitution, 105th Cong., 1st Sess., September 4, 1997.

Chapter 13

Jeff Jacoby, "U.S. Media Retain Their Liberal Bias," *Boston Globe*, December 15, 2002. Reprinted by permission.

Bernie Sanders, "Corporations Have Chokehold on U.S. Media," available at *http://bernie.house.gov/documents/opeds/20020612104617.asp.*

Chapter 14

Herbert M. Levine, *Political Issues Debated.* © Reprinted by permission of Pearson Education, Inc., Upper Saddle River, N.J.

Chapter 15

John Yoo, testimony, *Applying the War Powers Resolution in the War on Terrorism*, Hearing before the U.S. Senate Committee on the Judiciary, 107th Cong., 2d Sess., April 17, 2002.

Louis Fisher, testimony, *Applying the War Powers Resolution in the War on Terrorism*, Hearing before the U.S. Senate Committee on the Judiciary, 107th Cong., 2d Sess., April 17, 2002.

Chapter 16

Laurence H. Tribe, prepared statement for *Should Ideology Matter? Judicial Nominations 2001*, Hearing before the Senate Judiciary Committee, Subcommittee on Administrative Oversight and the Courts, 107th Cong., 2d Sess., June 26, 2001.

Douglas W. Kmiec, prepared statement for *Should Ideology Matter? Judicial Nominations 2001*, Hearing before the Senate Judiciary Committee, Subcommittee on Administrative Oversight and the Courts, 107th Cong., 1st Sess., September 4, 2001.

Chapter 17

Jacob G. Hornberger, "The Preservation of the Bureaucracy," *Freedom Daily*," a publication of The Future of Freedom Foundation Web site at www.fff.org. Copyright © The Future of Freedom Foundation. All rights reserved.

Ellsworth Barnard, "In Defense of Government," *Virginia Quarterly Review* 77, no. 3 (Autumn 2001): 615–24. Copyright © 2001 Virginia Quarterly Review, The University of Virginia. Reprinted by permission.

Chapter 18

Jeffrey M. Shaman and J. Clifford Wallace, "Interpreting the Constitution," *Judicature: Journal of the American Judicature Society* 71, no. 2 (August/September 1987): 80–87, 122. Reprinted by permission of the authors.

Chapter 19

David Boaz, testimony, *Pros and Cons of Drug Legalization, Decriminalization, and Harm Reduction*, Hearing before the Subcommittee on Criminal Justice of the Committee on Government Reform. U.S. Cong., House of Representatives, 106th Cong., 1st Sess., June 16, 1999, pp. 223–37.

Donnie Marshall, testimony, *Pros and Cons of Drug Legalization, Decriminalization, and Harm Reduction*, Hearing before the Subcommittee on Criminal Justice of the Committee on Government Reform. U.S. Cong., House of Representatives, 106th Cong., 1st Sess., June 16, 1999, pp. 120–39.

Chapter 20

Adapted from the Educational Fund to Stop Gun Violence, *The Citizens' Conference Briefing Book*. Copyright © 2002 by the Educational Fund to Stop Gun Violence. Reprinted by permission.

Adapted from Jim Babka, "Gun Control Only Seems Like a Good Idea" on American Liberty Foundation Debate Center Web site on August 23, 2002. Reprinted by permission.

Chapter 21

Patrick Gallagher, "The Environmental, Social, and Cultural Impacts of Sprawl," *Natural Resources and Environment* 15, no. 4 (Spring 2001): 219–23, 267. Reprinted by permission of the American Bar Association.

Thomas J. DiLorenzo, "The Myth of Suburban Sprawl," *USA Today* magazine (May 2000). Reprinted by permission of the Society for the Advancement of Education.

Chapter 22

Alternatives Committee of the International Forum on Globalization, "Report Summary: A Better World Is Possible!" *Alternatives to Economic Globalization* (San Francisco, Calif.: International Forum on Globalization, Spring 2002), pp. 4–10. Reprinted by permission.

Murray Weidenbaum, "A Response to the Assault on the Global Economy," *USA Today* magazine (November 2000). Reprinted by permission of the Society for the Advancement of Education.

Contributors

HERBERT M. LEVINE *taught political science at the University of Southwestern Louisiana (now the University of Louisiana at Lafayette) for twenty years. He has written and edited several political science textbooks. He is the author of* Chemical and Biological Weapons in Our Times *(Franklin Watts) and four books in the American Issues Debated Series published by Raintree Steck-Vaughn. He is currently a writer who lives in Chevy Chase, Maryland.*

ALTERNATIVES COMMITTEE OF THE INTERNATIONAL FORUM ON GLOBALIZATION (IFG) is a group made up of nineteen members of the board of directors of that organization and several other contributors. The IFG was formed to deal with issues of globalization.

JOHN ASHCROFT serves as the attorney general of the United States in the administration of President George W. Bush.

JIM BABKA is the president of the American Liberty Foundation, which is a nonprofit, nonpartisan educational foundation.

ELLSWORTH BARNARD is a retired professor of English at the University of Massachusetts at Amherst. He is the author of *Shelley's Religion; Edward Arlington Robinson: A Critical Study;* and *Wendell Willkie: Fighter for Freedom.*

ROGER BERTSCHAUSEN is minister of the Fox Valley Unitarian Universalist Fellowship in Appleton, Wisconsin.

JUDITH A. BEST is Distinguished Teaching Professor of Political Science at the State University of New York at Cortland.

DAVID BOAZ is executive vice president of the Cato Institute.

ROGER CLEGG is vice president and general counsel of the Center for Equal Opportunity.

RUTH CONNIFF is political editor of *The Progressive* magazine.

KATIE CORRIGAN is the legislative counsel on privacy at the American Civil Liberties Union.

KIRK COX is a member of the House of Delegates, Commonwealth of Virginia.

THOMAS J. DiLORENZO is a professor of economics in the Sellinger School of Business and Management at Loyola College in Baltimore, Maryland.

RICHARD J. DURBIN is a U.S. senator from Illinois.

EDUCATIONAL FUND TO STOP GUN VIOLENCE, a sister organization to the Coalition to Stop Gun Violence, is an educational nonprofit association dedicated to stopping gun violence by fostering effective community and national action.

JAMES ROLPH EDWARDS is an associate professor of economics at Montana State University–Northern in Havre, Montana.

AMITAI ETZIONI, the first University Professor of the George Washington University, is the author of *The Limits of Privacy* (Basic Books, 1999).

RUSS FEINGOLD is a U.S. senator from Wisconsin.

STANLEY FISH is dean of the College of Liberal Arts and Sciences at the University of Illinois at Chicago.

LOUIS FISHER is senior specialist in separation of powers at the Congressional Research Service at the Library of Congress.

BARNEY FRANK is a U.S. representative from Massachusetts.

PATRICK GALLAGHER is a senior attorney for the Sierra Club Environmental Law Program in San Francisco.

RICHARD GROSSMAN is cofounder and codirector of the Program on Corporations, Law, and Democracy.

DAVID A. HARRIS is Balk Professor of Law and Values, University of Toledo College of Law, Toledo, Ohio, and Soros Senior Justice Fellow at the Center for Crime, Communities and Culture in New York.

JACOB G. HORNBERGER is founder and president of the Future of Freedom Foundation in Fairfax, Virginia.

JEFF JACOBY is a columnist for the *Boston Globe.*

JOHN G. KESTER is an attorney with Williams & Connolly in Washington, D.C. He was once a law clerk to Justice Hugo Black.

DOUGLAS W. KMIEC is dean and St. Thomas More Professor of Law at the Catholic University of America School of Law, Washington, D.C.

MICHAEL LERNER is editor of *Tikkun* magazine and author of *Jewish Renewal: A Path to Healing and Transformation* (Putnam).

JOSEPH I. LIEBERMAN is a U.S. senator from Connecticut. He was the Democratic Party's candidate for vice president in 2000.

MATTHEW T. MANGINO is district attorney of Lawrence County, Pennsylvania.

DONNIE MARSHALL is a former administrator of the Drug Enforcement Administration.

THURGOOD MARSHALL (1908–1993) served as associate justice of the U.S. Supreme Court from 1967 to 1991. As chief counsel for the National Association for the Advancement of Colored People Legal Defense and Educational Fund, he argued and won the 1954 landmark school desegregation case, *Brown v. Board of Education of Topeka, Kansas.*

ROY S. MOORE is chief justice of the Supreme Court of Alabama.

MICHAEL RATNER is a human rights attorney and president of the Center for Constitutional Rights.

WILLIAM BRADFORD REYNOLDS served as counselor to the attorney general and assistant attorney general in the Civil Rights Division of the Justice Department in the Reagan administration. He is an attorney in the law firm of Howrey Simon Arnold & White in Washington, D.C.

BERNIE SANDERS is an Independent from Vermont in the U.S. House of Representatives.

JEFFREY M. SHAMAN is Wicklander Professor of Law, De Paul College of Law in Chicago.

BRADLEY A. SMITH has been a commissioner on the Federal Election Commission since 2000. Prior to his appointment, he was professor of law at Capital University Law School in Columbus, Ohio.

LAURENCE H. TRIBE is the Tyler Professor of Constitutional Law at Harvard Law School, Cambridge, Massachusetts.

J. CLIFFORD WALLACE is a judge, U.S. Court of Appeals for the Ninth Circuit.

MURRAY WEIDENBAUM is chair of the Center for the Study of American Business, Washington University, St. Louis.

WALTER E. WILLIAMS is the John M. Olin Distinguished Professor of Economics at George Mason University in Fairfax, Virginia. From 1995 to 2001, he served as chairman of the Economics Department at George Mason.

JOHN YOO is deputy assistant attorney general, Office of Legal Counsel, U.S. Department of Justice.